The Digital Paper Trail

in Real Estate Transactions
Revised Edition

Forms, Letters, Clauses and E-mails

Oliver E. Frascona, Esq., GRI
Katherine E. Reece, CRS, GRI

oliver@frascona.com
kathy@frascona.com

ISBN 0-941937-04-6 (hardback)
ISBN 0-941937-05-4 (hardback and compact disk)
Library of Congress Control Number: 2003096350

Back Cover Photos of Authors by Marc Bernardi, Photographer
www.aquatic-encounters.com

Back Cover Design by Alexander Frascona
www.toucanland.com

Real Estate Law Series
from
Real Law Books, Inc.
Post Office Box 3113
Boulder, Colorado 80307-3113
U.S.A.
Telephone 303-494-6661
Printed in the United States of America

Dedication

This book is dedicated to professional real estate people who assist us all in the search, acquisition, financing and sale of real estate, one of the most precious commodities in our free society. Acknowledgment is also made to the National Association of REALTORS®, which works tirelessly through the never-ending efforts of its members to preserve the rights of each of us to buy, own, use, and sell real estate. The authors greatly appreciate the efforts of the National Association of REALTORS® for its continuing commitment to educate REALTORS®, the public, and national, state and local governments about the ever-changing aspects of private property ownership. **If you are not a REALTOR®, join now.**

It is appropriate to pause to thank the real estate professionals, brokers and salespeople, executive officers, clients and friends, in and out of the real estate profession, who have encouraged this effort. It is through the unconditional support and help given by these friends and family that we have been able to complete what we feel is a comprehensive manual for the real estate professional, whether just entering the profession or having been in practice for a number of years.

To those who recognize some of the facts and wording, thank you for your prior written permission that allowed us to use your real-life experiences. Any names that you may recognize were used with permission.

A special thank you to Monica Frascona and Alexander Frascona. Once again they allowed us to work on this project rather than spend time with them. We love you both so much. Katherine, you were the breath of fresh air, the connection with someone who actually sold real estate every day, that helped to make this book all that I have dreamed it might be.

To all my special friends who have given me their unconditional support and encouragement to accept the challenges and rewards of new dimensions in my life, I thank you. The book is dedicated to the memory of my parents, Thomas J. Reece and Alma Kathleen Reece, whose guidance over the years instilled in me both a sense of survival and the knowledge that all things are possible if you just believe in your ability to accomplish any dream. Oliver, you are the source of inspiration that propelled me to reach for the dream.

Real Help for **Real** People in **Real** Estate®

Preface

Selling real estate was once a relatively simple pastime. It is now one of the most complex and litigious professions in America. The money that the average person invests in a home represents a substantial portion of the individual's net worth. Purchasing a home is one of the most important decisions that any family will make. Whereas people once bought a home and lived there for a long period, they now move around the country and the world as easily as walking to the store for a soda. The state and federal laws that govern the buying, selling and financing of real estate are voluminous and constantly changing. The public can not possibly be familiar with all aspects of even the average real estate transaction. They just want to buy or sell real estate.

Disclosure requirements, fair housing guidelines, environmental hazards, property inspections, and multiple forms of third party and seller financing are just a few of the many hurdles that a "normal" transaction must overcome. Enter the real estate broker and salesperson. As if just trying to keep abreast of the rules and regulations that affect their industry were not overwhelming enough, real estate professionals, like so many other professionals, must also protect themselves against the very public they strive to serve. The rationale of the thinking of many buyers and sellers is that they are not responsible for anything, much less their own decisions! If a problem arises from the transaction, it must be the fault of someone else, i.e., the real estate professional.

As a matter of course, in an ever increasing number of states, the real estate broker has become the drafter of a multiplicity of clauses that are required to tailor a transaction to the individual desires of the buyer and seller. The broker and salesperson need a guide where they can find the information they require to assist them. The employing broker needs a reference book where the salespeople, associate brokers, personal assistants and managing brokers can obtain instruction, standard forms, clauses and similar information, so that they can properly assist the public with its real estate needs. The licensee needs a quick reference, a place to start, a form to review, or a format that is almost what is needed, if not exactly what is required. Finally, the "personal assistant," who is assigned an ever increasing number of projects, needs a reference on a daily basis for "wording" and guidance. We hope that this book fulfills those needs. In the numerous offices across the nation where this book is standard issue to every agent each individual has the same reference as a base line.

This book is an attempt to give the real estate professional an observation point from which to map descriptive correspondence, draft clauses, design and complete standard forms, or draft a contract, addendum, form, cover letter or e-mail. We hope that real estate professionals will use this book to achieve the high ground of excellence and reap many more successful real estate transactions. We hope that it will help eliminate or reduce the ever-pressing sensation of needing to look backwards over one's shoulder for potential disputes, confrontations, and litigation. Instead, look forward to strengthening your own internal personal and office standard of practice and communication. It is the strength of your own standard as an example, properly imparted to those with whom you transact business, which will ultimately determine your success in dealing with people.

Creating a traditional "paper trail" or a "digital paper trail" will ensure that others are fully informed of the alternatives presented, contract preparation is tightened, decision-making skills are improved, and liability is reduced. Success there, in turn, will arise from an increased ease and efficiency in stating clearly to everyone – clients and customers, lenders, the public, suppliers, and others on whom we all rely for support and business – the pertinent facts of any transaction, the limits of liability, and the necessary notifications and confirmations.

Although we have used the names of friends and associates, that should not be interpreted as an endorsement or disparagement. Cases in point are just that, actual cases. The names have been changed in some cases to protect us all.

The Authors

Oliver E. Frascona, Esq., GRI, is a Colorado native, born and raised in Boulder, Colorado. He did his undergraduate work at the University of Colorado, graduating with a Bachelor of Science in Business with an emphasis in Finance and Real Estate.

After serving as an officer in the United States Naval Reserve, Oliver returned to Colorado where he became a licensed real estate salesperson in 1972, a REALTOR®, and subsequently a licensed Colorado real estate broker. He has listed and sold residential real estate. He attended law school at night, while working as a residential real estate salesman during the day, and graduated with a Doctor of Jurisprudence degree from the University of Denver School of Law in 1974. He began his legal career as an extension of his real estate career by practicing real estate and business law. He continues to develop residential and commercial subdivisions and construct single family and commercial buildings.

A shareholder in the law firm of Frascona, Joiner, Goodman and Greenstein, P.C., Mr. Frascona limits his personal practice to real estate, business and association law. He currently is: a Certified Advanced Law (I, II, III and IV), Contracts, Advanced Contracts, Agency and Risk Reduction Instructor for the Colorado Association of REALTORS®, of which he is a REALTOR® member; the attorney for twenty local boards/associations of REALTORS®; a member of Certified Closers; the attorney for many real estate companies, large and small; and the author of Ethics Update Courses dealing with N.A.R. quadrennial update requirements.

Oliver's wide experience and insight have given him the opportunity to lecture frequently to the national and state associations of REALTORS®, the memberships of large and small brokerage concerns, and various other groups on topics relating to real estate, motivation and other timely matters of business and association law throughout the United States.

As an active investor for his personal account, Mr. Frascona has the opportunity to, and regularly does, utilize the services of REALTORS® to assist him with the purchase, sale, and management of real estate on behalf of his clients and himself. He lists with professional REALTORS®, pays a full fee and appreciates the efforts of those that represent and assist him as a buyer or seller.   He is the author of other manuals for the real estate professional and considers his mission as a lawyer to be that of a deal maker, rather than a deal breaker. He is dedicated to organized real estate and those that practice it every day.

Katherine E. Reece, CRS, GRI, is a native of Georgia who has lived in Germany, Florida, Texas, Washington, Hawaii and now Colorado. She began her real estate career as a sales associate when she moved to Oahu, Hawaii, in 1985. Katherine consistently maintained a multi-million production and was recognized in both the state and nation for her outstanding production. One such honor ranked her tenth among thirty-five thousand agents in a national franchise. Her ongoing commitment to provide professional services to relocating families earned her a recognition as a national relocation specialist.

Katherine obtained her Broker's license in 1988, earned her Graduate REALTOR® Institute designation in 1989 and completed all requirements for accreditation as a

Certified Residential Specialist in 1991. In 1992 Katherine was co-founder and President of her own real estate company. Katherine obtained her Colorado Broker's License in 1995.

As a real estate professional, Katherine has been proud to be a member of the National Association of REALTORS®. Her involvement with both the Hawaii Association of REALTORS® and the Honolulu Board of REALTORS® placed her as a director on both boards, as well as a participant for membership, legislative, convention, and standard forms committees. She often testified before city, county and state governments on important housing issues.

Caveat – Disclaimer

Yes, there must be one. This book would not work if we did not have one. This material is designed to give the reader as many "places to start" as possible. Although great care has been taken to ensure that the information contained is accurate, pertinent, and to the point, each situation and each intended use is different. All clauses, forms, and letters should be the work product of the reader as an individual author. While written for general use throughout the United States, the reader should seek competent local legal advice before using any of the material contained herein. The real estate business is conducted differently in each city, township, county and state. Further compound the issue by crossing international lines, factor in the differences in residential, commercial, or investment real estate, and you can recognize the futility of trying to incorporate all the variables in any one book.

To our Canadian and Australian readers, we remind you that while the United States, Australia and Canada have very similar housing markets, there are different rules for the use of the information contained in this book. Remember to seek "competent" legal counsel and understand that while this book is used throughout Canada and in Australia, it is not written and edited by Canadian or Australian authorities.

Finally, to the ever increasing number of people from outside the U.S., Canada and Australia that purchase this book, we thank you. A substantial amount of the material will be of great help to you. Again, we recommend that you seek such localized "competent" counsel as is appropriate. It is always best to use a "real estate" attorney.

This publication is sold with the understanding that neither the authors nor the real estate or law firms of which they are members are giving legal or other professional advice, nor are they recommending the use of these letters or other material in the form in which they appear in this book. This publication is not intended to be, and should not be used as, a substitute for legal advice.

We are also concerned that there may be a typographical error or that a particular local law or custom may contradict the contents of the material presented. Therefore, we must indicate that we make no representations as to the accuracy of the information contained herein and are not liable to anyone for its use or misuse.

We want to encourage everyone to have a personal copy that can contain his or her own notes and modifications accordingly. Use this publication and the material contained herein at your own risk. THERE ARE NO WARRANTIES, EXPRESS OR IMPLIED, INCLUDING FITNESS FOR A PARTICULAR PURPOSE, MADE WITH RESPECT TO THIS MATERIAL.

All companies are fictitious and are not in any way associated with real existing real estate companies. Any resemblance to real companies is in the eyes of the reader, not the authors. The offices, characters and names indicated in some of the letters are either real people who have given consent to the use of their name or they are fictitious. The authors are not engaged in the real estate business under any of the entity names used in this book

We welcome your input and requests for new forms, e-mails and disclosures. Please keep those cards and letters coming. Remember to tell us where you are from, how long you have been in the business, what type of real estate you practice and the intended use of the material that you submit.

The Copyright

This book is intended for the private use of the individual owner of the book. Likewise, the CD is also protected by copyright and intended for the exclusive use of the individual owner of the CD. What may you do with the clauses, forms, letters, e-mails and information that are in this book or on the disk? Yes, it is copyrighted material. That means that nothing in this book may be photocopied or reproduced in any manner for *resale to others* without the prior written consent of the authors. However, you may copy the material in the book and on the CD and edit it for your *own personal* use in *your* documents and e-mails as you desire. We wrote this book, so that you could use the information in your daily practice.

Computer Disk "CD"

The "forms" are instantly available through the CD which includes the entire book in **Microsoft® Word** (.doc) and **Corel WordPerfect®** (.wpd) word processor formats, as well as **Adobe Acrobat®** (.pdf) format. We intentionally eliminated the page numbers on forms' pages to ease instant printing on your selected printer.

Word or WordPerfect formats will appear in 14.5 point fonts (Times Roman and Arial) with small margins. This was done so that the final product could be sent to Adobe and then reduced by the printers to the final book format. These word processor formats are best used by opening the respective word processor program and then opening the entire document. As part of your editing procedure, modify the fonts and margins, left, right, top and bottom to suit your printer and your desired final output format. Once in the document, we recommend that you select those pages that you wish to use or revise and use and save them under a separate file name using the page number in the book as an identifier. For example, make a directory called The Digital Paper Trail or TDPT. Then, name your documents: "TDPT Page 221 [Name of Document] Version A1.doc." Your TDPT Forms will all appear in page number sequence and you will easily be able to see the name of the form and the applicable revision. **Do not** "save" or "save-as" the entire book as it will take up too much space on your disk. Just save the form you are using.

Adobe Acrobat® files (.pdf) can be read with Adobe Reader, which is available for free downloading at www.adobe.com. There is an index in Adobe that will allow you to link directly to the section you desire from the index. Adobe files will print each page perfectly exactly as you see them on your screen directly to your printer. That is the beauty of Adobe Acrobat. If in fact, you have the capability to print from your word processor into Adobe as the selected printer using the encoding (full version of Adobe Acrobat). Once so saved, these edited Adobe files with the .pdf extension can be opened in Adobe Reader for all to use without modification. This is a great way to establish a perfect unmodifiable master set of office forms that will print over and over exactly as you edited them.

Introduction

In order to be helpful, the book had to have a structure. We have chosen the pattern of events in the "normal" real estate transaction, if there still is such a thing! We hope that the information and ideas contained in this book will spark your thought process and give you an idea base from which to work. From that base, you can always create a polite and clear note or letter which meets your need to disclose information to your clients and customers, disclaim liability for actions that were never yours from the start, and answer questions for the record. It is simple. It is a good habit. You will see how the use of professional correspondence not only protects you and your broker, but also consistently helps you sell real estate.

As a modern real estate professional, you must work with, and literally depend upon, information from many different members of the public at large. You say many things to various clients, customers, subagents, agents for other parties, lenders, title companies, inspectors, appraisers, investors and other people. You often make these statements intending to encourage or induce someone to take a particular action – to purchase, sell, finance, lease, appraise or otherwise deal with real property. In addition, as a cautious professional, you are becoming more and more aware of the duty being imposed upon real estate professionals by brokers, lenders, other agents, regulatory authorities, boards, legislatures, and courts to disclose ever-increasing amounts of information. Often, the standard by which you might be judged is not even available for inspection until the authority actually decides the case.

Even clear, concise, consistent speech has always been susceptible to various interpretations at the time it is uttered. Later, the memory tends to remember what one wants it to remember. The golden rule of "the test of the meaning of a communication is what a person in the position of the addressee can reasonably understand it to mean" is being stretched to the limit. In an effort to protect us all from even ourselves, the court system, the regulators and the legislatures, at all levels, are increasing the amount of regulation to be imposed on the business of providing access to shelter, the most basic of all brokerage businesses.

Carefully drafted contracts now potentially require many different clauses. Some clauses are used and others are considered and discarded in the process of selection and refinement of the modern real estate contract. The use of a "forms" or "clauses" collection is a must. To draft from scratch is too time consuming and leaves open the possibility that something was unintentionally omitted.

Standard forms must be identified, refined and printed, so that the standard aspects of the transaction are presented, and consented to, in a uniform manner. This protects the public, as well as the broker and salesperson. Cover letters, clarifying nearly all information presented and the extent of the broker's and agent's roles, are becoming a must. In the face of such potential liability, there is no need for the real estate professional to simply give up and write letters that will discourage the reader when the skillful use of the cover letter can also be a professional selling tool.

There are still buyers and sellers who want to and will consummate transactions through the brokerage network. In fact, it is the very complexity that we all abhor that is entrenching the real estate broker as a necessity in modern life. Just ten years ago real estate transactions were far simpler. All loans were thirty-years fixed; governments did not have planned unit developments (PUD's); down-zoning was unknown; the approval process took three to four weeks; land available for development was plentiful; the air was clean; water, electricity and natural gas were everywhere. This is simply not the case today.

The real estate professional is looked upon by many as an equal to the legal profession. People expect the real estate professional to have access to standard forms and to be able to draft contracts of a much more complex nature than in the past. While we continually encourage people to "see an attorney," we also recognize that many attorneys do not regularly deal in real estate. They have to rely on the draft from the real estate professional.

The skillful creation of a "paper trail" that imparts a feeling of respect for the real estate professional in the eyes of the reader, that fully informs and assists in reinforcing the sale, and presents vital information in a hard-to-dispute form is the core of this work. It is our desire that you take heart from this book and become confident from its use, so that you, too, can draft contracts, forms and letters which will accomplish all this in your own situations.

Comments and sample forms, clauses, letters and e-mails are just that: samples. You should rethink your actual content and not rely solely on the forms we are presenting. Although each case is a little different, try to develop your own standard forms, clauses, letters and habits, so that you always handle a similar situation in the same manner. Careful, planned consistency is the best defense. Establish yourself as a consistent professional.

Recognizing that both sexes are actively represented in the real estate profession, we have tried to write, so that the need to use a particular gender is eliminated. When that is not possible, we have used various genders at random. The use of any particular gender is to save the constant use of his/her, he/she. We have included different variations of the same standard form. Mix and match as you feel appropriate. We wanted to provide several finished options for the reader who desires to just "print" from Adobe Acrobat version.

Please read the sample clauses, forms, cover letters and e-mails in the book before you use them. Do not assume that everything is perfectly the way you want it. Read it carefully.

Real estate must be fun. Enjoy your life. If you are not having fun in real estate, change professions. There is no instant replay. Remember, you are real estate. Join, participate in and support your local, state and national association of REALTORS®. Those organizations maintain the ethics, integrity and continuity of your profession. They truly are the *Voice of Real Estate®*. You are the difference! The collective voices of individual REALTORS® determine the future of the real estate profession. Make your efforts count.

Oliver E. Frascona   Katherine E. Reece

Table of Contents

Chapter 2 31
Listing the Seller's Real Estate 31

Finding, Listing, Representing,
Working With and Retaining Sellers 31

Chapter 3 221
The Buyer Relationship 221

Chapter   4 327

In-Company Sales 327

Selling Your Own Listing 327

Defining the Middle Ground 328

Chapter 5 363

The Contract 363

Chapter 6 459

After the Contract is Signed 459

The Road to a Successful Closing 459

Chapter 1

The Basics

Guidelines for the Entire Office

Pledge of Allegiance to the Broker

- I pledge allegiance to the broker of my office.

- I recognize that I am the agent of that broker.

- I understand that my broker is probably personally liable for my actions and inactions in the real estate business.

- I will conduct my personal life so as to augment the professional standing of my real estate company and associates.

- I will ask questions when I do not know what to do.

- I will continue to learn and advance my knowledge and professionalism.

- I will endeavor to deal honestly with everyone.

- I will provide equal professional service to all prospective clients and customers and endeavor to set an example using the golden rule.

- I will keep my broker informed about every aspect of the transactions with which I am involved.

- I will purchase, sell or lease real estate for my own account only after talking with my broker and obtaining my broker's written permission.

- I obtain my broker's consent before I obligate myself or the company.

- I will keep accurate and timely records of all aspects of every transaction in which I am involved.

- I will practice property management only with the prior written permission of my broker.

- I will conduct all my business as though it were to be reviewed by the Real Estate Commission on a daily basis.

Pledge of Allegiance to the Salesperson

- I will trust my salespeople (associate brokers) and support their efforts.

- I will develop an office policy and continue to update it to reflect the changes in the profession.

- I will develop and provide standard forms for the use of my salespeople.

- I will continue to further my education, so that I can convey accurate and precise information to my salespeople.

- I will provide and maintain an office environment that is conducive to generating real estate business.

- I will recruit and retain salespeople who adhere to the principles outlined in this pledge.

- I will provide assistance and supervision at all times and be available when my salespeople need me.

- I will encourage my salespeople to pursue and continue their professional education.

- I will set an example in my business practices that embodies the spirit of National Association of Realtor® Code of Ethics and the law.

- I will be responsible for training my salespeople in all aspects of the real estate transaction.

- I will conduct all my business as though it were to be reviewed by the Real Estate Commission on a daily basis.

Pledge of Allegiance to Members of the Public

- I pledge to safeguard to the best of my abilities the trust that is placed in me to assist you with your housing needs.

- I promise that I will provide you with all the necessary information available that is pertinent to your individual real estate transaction.

- I promise that I will allow you to make the decisions that affect your real estate needs.

- I am committed to the spirit and letter of the law to provide everyone with equal access to housing.

- I will encourage you to avail yourself of professional attorneys, accountants, surveyors, appraisers, contractors, inspectors and others that are more skilled in their areas of expertise than I am.

- I will not let my personal relationship with others deter me from cooperating with them to accomplish your transaction.

- I will not let my desire to profit from the transaction alter the course that you have selected.

- I will tell you when I do not know the answer to your questions.

- I will accept compensation only from sources that I have first disclosed to you.

- I will continue to stay abreast of those areas where it is reasonable to expect information from a real estate professional.

- I will not inspect property that you are interested in as I am not an inspector, but I will assist you in the selection of an inspector of your choosing and cooperate with you and that inspector.

- I will disclose to you all material facts associated with the property actually known to me.

- I will follow the Code of Ethics of the National Association of REALTORS®.

Rules of the Road for the Office

We will never:

- Enter into oral agreements where only a written agreement would constitute a binding agreement between parties.

- Intentionally misrepresent any aspect of a real estate transaction.

- Serve as the attorney-in-fact for anyone.

- Act in an agency capacity for anyone other than as provided in our agreement with that party.

- Accept a position as an escrow agent.

- Commingle anyone's funds.

- Inspect property for a buyer, seller or any other entity.

- Guarantee the performance of any third party.

The Real Estate Broker in Litigation

Seller and Broker Beware. The old days of "buyer beware" are gone. In their place has come an increasing attempt by the courts to "protect" the consumer from everyone, including, on occasion, himself. In this age of consumerism, everyone dealing with the public is the subject of increased scrutiny. Doctors, lawyers, manufacturers, distributors, retailers and real estate brokers all deal with and provide vital services to the public. The real estate broker is poised in a unique position as the purveyor of one of our most basic needs: shelter. In addition, over the last decade, the real estate profession has been successful in its effort to enhance the image of real estate brokers. The public and the courts have accepted real estate salespeople as professionals, are treating them as such, and are holding them to expectations of top professional practices.

No Inflation and Greater Complexity.   These are the two final nails in the unprepared broker's coffin. First, there is no consistent inflationary blanket to cover the mistakes of the past.   Instead of just selling the home that may have been a mistake, everyone is having to live with them. Second, the world of real estate has become increasingly more complicated. The analysis of the available financing from institutions almost requires a degree in mathematics and the proficient use of a sophisticated calculator, not to mention a crystal ball for each new tax code revision. There is some merit of truth in the theory that tax code revisions are just an ongoing part of the so called "CPA Full Employment and Guaranteed Retirement Act."

Being secure about the type and extent of any financing that may be carried by the seller and being able to anticipate the potential remedies of the various parties in the event of default require a law degree with a specialty in real estate law.   The overlapping rules, including all the association, local, county, state and federal statutes and regulations, are increasing at a rate faster than anyone can even read. These often-conflicting requirements place brokers in the middle of the political arena and leave them vulnerable to lawsuits from all sides.

The Demands Upon The Modern Professional Broker. The sale and acquisition of real estate has become so complex that an untrained person, even one who is a professional in another field, is no longer able to navigate the safe route to a properly closed transaction without a real estate professional as a guide. Into this world steps the real estate professional and her broker with the broker being liable not only for everything that she herself does but also for the actions or inactions of her agents.

In an attempt to protect the public often as not from itself, the court is placing more and more responsibilities on the broker and pulling the fiduciary duty knot tighter and tighter.   Brokers are increasingly being held responsible for their actions, inactions, contract drafting, and other responsibilities related to a real estate transaction. They must learn now how to generate sophisticated paperwork to document the extent of their efforts to a court that is listening to a plaintiff's every word and looking for a mistake, a misrepresentation, an omission, or a way to establish an agency arrangement not previously thought to exist, or a way to provide the basis for assigning liability to both the salesperson and the broker.

The Advent of Buyer Agents. Today, buyer agency is as common as seller agency. In this transaction the buyer looks to the real estate broker with high expectations. Often these expectations are not within the reach of the broker.   The public, unchecked, sees the buyer agent as a guarantor of the transaction. In addition, unlike most seller agency relationships, buyer agency ones are often not written. It is more and more important to obtain written instructions, a written buyer agent listing agreement, or other form of written documentation to delineate the actual duties and responsibilities of the buyer agent. Remember, it is the buyer who will most likely be unhappy with the purchase, not the seller.

Personal Liability. In many states, the broker is held personally liable for everything, regardless of any corporate entity which may exist. Damages from litigation, not to mention the attorney's fees, can run into tens of thousands of dollars, ruining years of work and an otherwise promising and profitable career. It is time to learn from the policies and practices of the large professional companies in other fields of endeavor by creating a professional paper trail.

Disclaimers. Disclaimers or disclosures are here to stay in every business. They have become a fact of life. Think about the information that doctors give their patients before surgery, that auto mechanics give us before they work on our cars and instructors give their students before they attempt to teach.

Disclosure. The broker is now viewed as the source of the information that should be given to the buying and selling public. Documented disclosure is a fixture. Disclosure given with a certain style or flair will enable the broker to present the information in a manner that will assist the public and enhance the broker's reputation. However, first you must know what is required. Then you must document what you did, so that everyone will remember.

Property Condition. The condition of the property remains the most controversial aspect of the transaction. Year after year, we find that at the heart of most disputes is the property condition. Never inspect the property for anyone. Leave inspection of the property to the experts – property inspectors. Always disclose all that you know about a property's physical condition. Never think that seller agency is somehow an excuse to hide a defect. If you know about a defect, disclose the defect if it has to do with the physical condition of the property. "If you know it, tell it to everyone – buyer, seller and lender." Always recommend that the buyer obtain an inspection. Insist on it.

Stigmatized Property. With the advent of the right of the public to know the location of known sexual predators (Megan's Law), drug houses and locations where there was a murder, suicide or other felony, some states direct the real estate professional to remain silent. In other states, brokers are mandated by law to speak only when asked. Finally, in still other states, there is a duty to speak up. Know your state and know it well. As times change, so do these rules, laws and regulations. This is an area where your sympathies may come into conflict with the law, and the results are a disaster. Know the rules for "stigmatized property law" in your state and in your capacity as a buyer agent, seller agent or neutral party (dual agent, limited agent, transaction broker, statutory broker, etc.).

Megan's Law.   This law was enacted after a little girl who moved into a house in New Jersey with her family was sexually molested and killed.   New Jersey enacted the law that bears the name of the little girl, Megan.   The federal government subsequently mandated that states disclose and provide access to an information database containing the location of known sex offenders.   Each state now has a different system and constantly changing procedures for dealing with this issue.   You must know the current procedure and system in your state.

Some states use the internet.   Other states allow the person who feels that s/he is in danger to come in and acquire limited information.   Some cities publish the locations of known sexual predators or offenders in the newspaper.   Some localities provide a list in a limited area, while others make it all available.   The problem is that the data is not verified and not kept accurate.   As one local sheriff is reputed to have said, "Do you want me to take the deputy that guards the prisoners off duty and have him/her verify the data?   How often is enough?   Each day or weekly?   I have no budget for maintaining the database."   Therein lies a large part of the problem.

This is a volatile issue with everyone.   It is imperative to know your state law and address Megan's law in your office policy.   Remember that there are agents who are buyer's agents, others who are seller's agents and finally those who are "dual agents" or transaction brokers, or other non-agency relationship.   Many sellers want to move and not tell the new buyer about the sex offender in the neighborhood, while most buyers want to know if one resides in the immediate area.   An agent will feel a moral duty that will potentially conflict with his or her legal duty.

In general, states indicate that disclosure of this information is not a "material fact." That sounds fine, unless you are a buyer agent.   Then a court could well think that it was material. The best course of action, and the one adopted by almost all locations, is one that requires the licensee to tell the public about Megan's law and the location where the information is to be obtained, but indicates that it is not a licensee's duty to locate or compile that information for the member of the public, buyer or seller.

You do not want to know the location of an offender.   Once you think that you do, you may have different disclosure obligations.   Remember that even though you "know," the studies indicate that the database in most areas is less than 50% accurate.   Stick with the "referral of the buyer or seller to the proper agency" solution, and then do not accompany your buyer or seller to the police station (cities) or sheriff's office (counties). If you do take them to the source of information, wait outside while they make the inquiry.

We have included a reference to Megan's law in the buyer agency agreements. You can use those clauses in any alternative disclosures that you make to a buyer if, in fact, you are not acting as their agent or do not sign a buyer agency contract. This is just another reason to use written buyer agency contracts.

Be glad that these examples of real life sexual offender cases are not yours. There are no answers available to these problems.

Case in Point.
You are the listing agent in a subdivision. Three houses are sold and then number four sells to a known level three sex offender. You are on site the next Saturday and in comes a family with two and a half kids and a Toyota.

You are at the homeowners meeting and someone stands up and wants to go "fix that sucker," the homeowner in their subdivision who is a level three sex offender. Everyone there lives in the subdivision and has little kids who walk to school. People are afraid. Now, add the factor that the subdivision is your farm area.

Clients and Customers as Plaintiffs

The Uniform Care and Feeding of Plaintiffs. Real estate professionals are, by nature, a helpful and trusting group of individuals who spend a small, concentrated amount of time with strangers and then start to treat them like lifelong friends. Treat all clients and customers as if they were going to be plaintiffs. Just because you have bought lunch or dinner for several days or shown someone houses and are now on a first name basis, do not let your guard down. Regard the other person as if he were an FBI agent or government tester. Your treatment of everyone should stand up to the closest scrutiny. Would you like to hear what you have just told someone played back on a tape recording in a court? Would you like to have your daily routine manner of conducting your real estate activities reported in the local newspaper? If the answer is no, maybe you should not say it or do it. This is not to say that you need to be anything other than a uniform, courteous, polite and detail-oriented professional. So often we hear, "but they were my friends. They would never sue me."

Sources of Plaintiffs. Most of the plaintiffs from whom you will be obligated to defend yourself will come from your own list of client, customer, and real estate affiliate contacts. Consider the list of people who may be responsible for your losing your license and livelihood and *think*. Look over your customer, client, and affiliate lists for people with the following characteristics – invariably they make great potential plaintiffs.

Profile of a Potential Plaintiff

- Someone who starts a conversation with "you can trust me."

- Someone who envies the material possessions of others.

- Someone who feels that the world is not fair to them.

- Someone who acts closer to you than they are.

- Someone who tells you that they trust you to "take care of us."

- Someone who tells you about the poor conduct of another real estate professional, lawyer, doctor or lender. You may be next in line.

- Someone who confides in you about things that you really did not need to know.

- Someone who "feels" that they have not been told the truth by others.

- Someone who "feels" cheated in this transaction or in life in general.

- Someone that complains more than is necessary.

- Someone in a position of apparent authority – a loan officer, an attorney, another broker – who suggests that some action or statement is either correct, or incorrect, in direct contradiction to what you know to be true.

- Someone who wants to "get away" with something.

- Someone who tries to avoid paying a legally just obligation, or who thinks there is a way to "get around" the rules, especially loan qualification procedures and financial disclosure requirements.

More often than not plaintiffs fall into two categories. First, plaintiffs often turn out to be people whom you thought were close friends. *Plaintiffs are drawn from the pool of friends.* Ask yourself: Is this because they expected more than you normally deliver, or because you used a standard of practice for friends different from the one you use with your regular clients? With whom would you cancel an appointment first – a new client or an old friend? Second, it should come as no surprise to you that plaintiffs often arise from those people you probably felt were potential trouble. It is rare for a complaint to come from an average customer or client. When in doubt, treat friends like strangers and try not to treat strangers like friends. Remember, there is a reason why there are metal detectors at airports. When the buzzer sounds, listen.

Myths about Disclaimers

- Disclaimers have to be stuffy and dry to be effective.

- Disclaimers, if actually read by the addressee, will kill the deal. "No one will buy this property if I have to tell them all that."

- Oral disclaimers are just as good as written ones.

- A disclaimer is really a contract.

- The buyers and sellers I deal with are my friends; I do not need a disclaimer for them.

- Someone else said it, and even if I know it is false, the fact that someone else made the statement is enough to get me off the hook.

- Only attorneys can or should write appropriate and adequate disclaimers.

- Even though the company policy prescribes the use of this form, I can just change a few words, and it will do the same job.

- Buyers do not need disclaimers.

- I can always give the disclaimer after the showing, after the contract is signed or even at the closing. It will be just as effective.

- No one really cares about or reads a disclaimer.

- An adequate disclaimer will cover any mistake I might make regardless of the severity.

- Disclaimers are like indemnification agreements.

- I do not need a disclaimer because our company has errors and omissions insurance.

- Disclaimers are like an insurance policy. They always provide ample protection.

The Work Habit

Friend or Foe? Are you your own best friend or worst enemy? The manner in which you regularly conduct your business is admissible evidence to demonstrate that there is a pattern of practice – whether it be good or bad – relevant to discrimination, price fixing, negligence, or competence. It is like having good manners. If you have them, they work when you do not think about them. A pattern of good conduct can show a court, judge and jury that you are a careful and consistent professional. Once that has been established, you can win a case using the procedures you always use day to day in the conduct of your business, as demonstrated in other cases.

Pattern of Practice. On the other hand, the most frequently utilized strategy of the opposition is to establish a pattern of practice that tends to discredit the witness. This will compromise your position even if, in this particular transaction, you actually did do and say the things that you claim. No protection system will work unless you establish a pattern of conduct, a reputation and a history of doing things correctly. Believe it or not, professionals who draft comprehensive cover letters are respected by their clients and customers and receive the coveted referral. Their perception of such conduct is one of professionalism and attention to detail. This coveted reputation is better than "he is a real tough person." It becomes, "she is a real stickler and a professional. She will have all her paperwork in order. Suing her is a waste of time." No one wants to start, pay for, work on, or take a losing suit to court. Fifty percent of all lawyers lose. The difference between those who successfully litigate a case is often based solely in aligning oneself with a winning case.

The First Trial. The first place your case will be tried is in the office of the other lawyer. He will never admit defeat to you in front of his client. However, after you leave you want him to make specific comments to his client. "Did you see how organized they were and the paperwork they had," or "I believe they are telling the truth. They were so professional." The opposing counsel will realize that you probably did send the documents you said you sent, that you did explain to his client the areas that you said you explained, and that there is a good possibility that his client is lying. No civil attorney, except possibly the government, wants a client he knows, or fears, is lying. The retainer demanded by opposing counsel after such a meeting, formerly $1,000, is now $3,000.

Company Protection Policies

Brochure. One or more company brochures which include a list of the services offered, the fees charged (if appropriate), and a series of checklists for the client, customer, agent, and the company is quite valuable. It will explain, in a uniform and consistent manner, to everyone which services are, and are not, available, what is expected of each party to a proposed transaction and the amount to be charged for each respective service. This written explanation is especially useful in discouraging unwanted property management, which can be listed as a separate item with its own cost analysis. A set of well drafted company policy statements or brochures with good content and type styles can be a great protection device, ensure uniformity of information being conveyed and serve notice of established company policies. The use of comprehensive checklists for all stages of any transaction removes the sense of uncertainty as to what tasks need to be completed. Having these expectations in writing greatly reduces the level of stress experienced by both the salesperson in the field and the broker. Then it is no longer necessary to rely on memory for all the required steps in a transaction.

Office Manual. Establishing a manual containing specific procedures to be followed in each transaction, as well as routine and formal mechanical treatment of all the company's clients and customers, is the best first line of defense. A manual allows the agents to concentrate on selling real estate, rather than upon worrying about the need for, and the exact wording of, disclaimers, informational letters and contract clauses. It is immediately accessible when the need arises. All well-drafted manuals should be capable of becoming reading material for even the most discriminating individuals, such as regulators, opposing counsel, clients, customers and the Real Estate Commission.

Internet, E-Mail and Web Policy. *The internet never forgets.* While we all use the electronic methods of communication and advertisement, we also need to be aware of the limitations of that use. Everything that you send through the net is caught by someone, often other than the intended recipient, and will be there in the event of a trial or serious controversy. Companies today need a written "electronic computer" policy that governs the use of the Company and personal websites, the use of the company computers and office e-mail for personal and explicit messages, the use of the company and other protected logos and "marks." It does not take a lot of intellect to realize that intellectual property is an area of legitimate concern for all real estate professionals.

Standard Forms. Standard forms are the only answer. Attorneys have used them for years and are consistently developing new ones. This is not because they are lazy or stupid. Quite the contrary, they realize that the thought process that went into the last problem can be utilized on the next similar problem and duplicated without having to rethink and plan for the problems previously presented and solved. Provide your staff with "company approved" standard forms. Insist in your Office Policy that only those forms be used.

Standard Practices. Company wide standardization of practice and procedure is an absolute must. This can be accomplished by creating a complete program that includes the use of only those forms and clauses that have been approved by the state, if applicable, and by the company. The use of a series of approved cover letters for each stage of a transaction should be coupled with a schedule for their step-by-step distribution.

When a transaction does not fit the standard, it must receive broker attention. Discouraging the on-the-spot modification of standard forms and procedures for the unusual transaction is imperative. These transactions have the highest degree of risk. Review by the broker ensures that each client and customer is getting the standard information, the required disclosures and the same set of instructions. In addition, the agent does not have to allow herself to be pressured into making a decision that might not be in anyone's best interests. It removes the need to improvise and allows everyone to concentrate on the listing, sale, and closing of real estate transactions that will not result in future problems.

Sexual Harassment. Each of you and your assistants, secretaries, personal assistants, broker associates and salespeople, employees and even your children, when they are employees of others, all have the right to work in an environment that is free of sexual harassment. Issues in this area of the law are growing for all businesses, not just real estate brokerages.   We believe that real estate professionals have no intention of sexually harassing anyone, whether it be an associate, employee, customer or client, nor allowing anyone to be harassed.

Sometimes the problem person within the company is, in fact, the broker or someone else in a position of power. This can easily include your clients and customers. You have a duty to protect those that work in your real estate office from sexual harassment. Often the offender does not even realize that s/he is violating the law and creating an environment where this sort of abuse exists. Here are a few ideas that will help to protect everyone – the broker, the associates and the employees, as well as the clients and customers.

First, make certain that everyone knows that this conduct will not be tolerated. Hold a short annual presentation attended by the entire office, including the owner, the office support staff, the part time agent and the entry level employee.   This presentation need not be long and can be a part of any regular sales meeting or, better yet, at the annual meeting where the awards are given for performance achievements. At this meeting the company's policy on sexual harassment should be reviewed, and the people to contact in the event of an abuse should be identified. Finally, everyone should know where they can get help outside the office from the state and federal government agencies. Yes, supply a poster with this information for the coffee room where it is readily visible to everyone. The presentation on sexual harassment can be short, but should be serious.   The staff needs to know that management will not tolerate this behavior. That empowers the staff to tell potential offenders to back off, and also lets them know that the company is on their side.

Second, pay attention to the people who are potential offenders. Watch for the person who says, "This is silly and a waste of time," or someone, often a male, who says "I wish that things were the way they used to be. This whole thing is out of hand with these women." That is a problem person, and that person needs special attention after the meeting. Often it is the employing broker and others in management who are the source of violations. Also, keep in mind that most people do not mean to violate the law. They just do not understand it. The top salesperson, the people in the office having affairs, the couples who are married and then decide to split or the office flirt are all individuals who may create potential sexual harassment problems.

Third, make sure that all employment agreements for everyone, whether employee or independent contractor, contain some sort of basic section on sexual harassment, so that everyone has indicated that they will play by the rules when they acknowledge the agreement. You might use the sample clause below.

Finally, take this issue seriously. Make sure that you set an example and are someone who follows the rules. There is no faster way to ruin a great real estate career than to have to defend yourself in one of these actions. It does not matter if you are guilty or innocent. The issue will bury you, professionally and personally.

Following is some sample language for a company sexual harassment policy. We strongly recommend that you speak with your local attorney or a human resources attorney to establish, implement and update your policy. Sometimes the inclusion of the attorney at the meeting can be a showing of the seriousness of the matter.

Clause:

It is the policy of this real estate firm not to condone or tolerate harassment of any individual in the firm. Sexual harassment is defined as unwelcome or unsolicited sexual, physical, or verbal conduct which is made a term or condition of employment explicitly or implicitly, or is used as a basis for employment decisions, or has the purpose or effect of unreasonably interfering with an individual's work or performance or creating an intimidating, hostile, or offensive work environment. We take this very seriously.

Any employee (full or part time), independent contractor (salesperson, broker or associate broker) who believes that s/he is being harassed is encouraged to bring this matter to the immediate attention of the individuals listed below as "contact people." Do not wait to see if you can "fix it." Let us know about the potential or actual problem now. Complaints will receive prompt attention. Investigation will be on a discreet basis to the extent possible. The aggrieved person may take other actions which include filing with the state or federal government. We encourage everyone to know and protect their rights.

All employees and independent contractors agree to fully comply with the letter and spirit of this policy and to assist in all investigations. Failure to follow the policy or cooperate with an investigation will be grounds for immediate discharge without benefits and is a breach of your agreement with this firm.

Contact people : _____

Early Disaster Recognition

Be alert. Watch for the unusual in the usual.

Be consistent. Treat everyone and every transaction in the same manner. No special deals and no "special" treatment.

Keep a copy. Maintain a copy of your communications, e-mails, voice mails, and contract drafts. The draft often shows the history that is all important.

Too good to be true. If it seems too good to be true, it probably is. When things do not seem correct or you do not feel comfortable, talk with your broker or your attorney immediately. Things have a way of moving quickly when they are going the wrong way.

Personal professionals. Have a personal attorney whom you respect, who is above reproach and with whom you can talk available when you feel the need. Know a trusted CPA, insurance agent, Phase I inspector and home inspector (ASHI or NAHI certified and with adequate E&O insurance) upon whom you can call upon to verify tax, insurance and "physical condition of the property" issues.

The "Old" Expert. Just because a procedure was done that way in the past or it is recommended by an "old salt" in the office does not mean that it is proper today. Check it out.

Depart. As soon as the deal starts to look funny, get away from it and make your departure known. If you are leaving a formal meeting, be sure that your departure is noted in the minutes. In other circumstances remember those people who in turn will remember the timing of your departure.

Notes. Make your notes as contemporaneously as possible and retain them. Note what occurs in each transaction and at all meetings. Write letters to your broker, or as a broker, to your salespersons. Document your position and policy in writing, not just by oral conferences. Should you elect to resign, a letter of resignation stating the reasons for your action is important.

If the communication is with a client or a customer, an unrelated witness who is not a relative or associate is invaluable. Make sure that they know that they will be expected to remember what is about to transpire.

Tape Recordings. Tape recordings are very useful. It is unfortunate, but the tape recorder tends to keep honest people's memories in sync. It has literally saved the reputation and fortune of many salespeople. Yes, in many states you can record telephone conversations with at least one party's consent. Remember, you are a party to the call. Some states require both parties to consent.

Be true to yourself. You know when things are wrong. You will remember what happened and worry about the potential repercussions long after the money has been spent.

Remember the government – local, state or federal – has a lot more resources than you do. Even if you win, you lose when you tangle with them. Each transaction should be able to see the light of day and be reviewed by "your mama" and everyone's attorney.

If someone says, "it's the principle of the matter," it is usually the money that really matters. Remember that "principal" earns interest.

The Referral of Third Party Professionals

You will live or die by your referrals of your buyers and sellers to third party professionals. Be sure that whomever you recommend conducts business in the same professional manner and with the same ethical standards that exemplifies your business practices. There is never a need to refer a person to anyone if the association will not be to your direct benefit. If the customer is pleased with your referral, you will occasionally get a little emotional "pat on the back" and a "thank you." If there is any problem, the customer will attempt to hold you responsible, and you will suffer the financial and emotional consequences of the customer's displeasure.

There is no need to be liable for a referral, whether it is an inspector, attorney, broker in another location or loan officer. Here is a great clause that you can use on the reverse of your referral confirmation card. You can also use it as a standard insertion at the bottom of the letter or e-mail to the client or customer indicating the names of the parties that you are referring to them. The clause is better sent with the referral, but, if not, send it after the referral.

Clause:

> There are numerous competitors in the marketplace for this kind of service. Although I cannot be responsible for the several individuals and companies listed on the attached sheet, or listed on the reverse, or listed above, I do know that they have been utilized in the past by other homeowners. Each service provider should be happy to provide you with a list of past clients or customers to assist you in making your decision.
>
> Prior to making your decision, you will want to satisfy yourself that your selection has adequate errors and omission insurance, is licensed, if applicable, and if a home inspector, is a member of ASHI® or NAHI™. For insurance policies, review each policy carefully, as well as consider the reputation of each company.

Tips, Tricks, and Traps

Abbreviations. If at all possible, do not abbreviate anything. Spell it out. Who is the Alex in the statement "Alex and Monica Frascona"? Is this Alex Frascona? It could be Alexander the Great or Alex Hunted. Did you assume that they were married? They are brother and sister. The absence of abbreviations is a sign of professionalism, reduces the need to make assumptions, and avoids misunderstandings.

Adobe Acrobat®. Did you know that you can "encode" (make an Adobe document – create a ".pdf" file) a contract or other computer generated material? Adobe *Reader* is the free download that allows the recipient to view an Adobe document. Adobe *Acrobat* is the program that allows you to make ("encode") your own Adobe documents. With Adobe Acrobat you can generate a contract on your computer and convert it into an Adobe document, which you then attach to an e-mail and send to another party to the transaction. This is the state of the art technique for sending important documents via e-mail. Use it for listing contracts, amend/extends, counter proposals or anything else that you need to get to someone without using a fax. The document arrives in perfect printable form, just like this book appears in Adobe on the disk. For more information, go to www.adobe.com.

Certified Mail vs. Regular Mail. If it is important enough to send by certified or registered mail, you should *also* send it by regular mail. There is a lattice of different regulations for each state. Some subject matters require one form of mail and some allow for the other. In addition, there are a number of cases that indicate that simply sending a letter by certified or registered mail is not sufficient to constitute delivery or notice, especially if the addressee does not claim the letter. A better procedure is to send two identical copies of the letter, one certified or registered and the other by way of regular mail. You may wish to indicate on the original, prior to photocopying, *"Original Sent Certified Mail"* and *"Copy Sent Regular Mail."* If this is your established practice when you send certified or registered mail, it will be seen as proof that, in fact, that is what you did for the matter in question.

Checks and Endorsements. Remember that you become liable for the ultimate payment of the check when you endorse one that is made payable to you. If it is going from you to someone else, endorse it adding these words *"without recourse."* Example: *"pay to the order of Oliver Frascona, without recourse."* When the check includes language that purports to release the payee, you need to remember that endorsements are subject to change. Yes, the restrictive endorsement can be changed by the holder of the check and still the bank will cash the check unless you add the words: *"modification or alteration of this restrictive endorsement makes this check void."*

Confirmation. A good alternative to a letter that requires an affirmative act – such as the signature of the reader which is often difficult to obtain – is the confirming letter. The confirming letter shifts the burden of action to the reader. This is a very convenient method for confirming the content and timeliness of an oral statement. In addition, it firmly places the responsibility to act on the reader if the content does not match his or her understanding of what was said.

Many people who will not take the step of signing the disclosure statement, will also not take the time and effort to deny the facts as outlined in a confirming letter. By simply stating *"This is to confirm our discussion of last Tuesday wherein I indicated...."* you have not only provided good service, but you have established a favorable legal standing if questioned. It helps keep the good deals good and brings the bad, time-wasting or dangerous ones to the forefront.

Cooperating Salespersons. Your association and cooperation with other real estate professionals will enhance the rapid sale of your listings. Build a reputation of being fair but consistent in your representation of your client. Always look for ways to create a winning situation for both parties to the contract. Always be complimentary about the efforts of the cooperating REALTOR®, while at the same time protecting your client's interests. By creating and adhering to a standard of practice that is honest and predictable, cooperating agents will be eager to show and sell your listings. Remember that in representing the Seller you are agreeing to do all that is necessary to sell his home. "Listing stuff" may actually mean showing the home to the buyer for the cooperating salesperson when schedules do not permit otherwise, as well as doing other tasks that may be considered the other salesperson's job. A letter of thanks and addition of the cooperating REALTOR® to your exclusive REALTOR® database for future listing announcements will encourage the salesperson to inquire about your listings first when he has another buyer.

Copies, Letters and E-mails. Copies, policy, and habit are the added plums that give your testimony the credibility that is needed to place the burden of proof on the person who failed to respond. Never let yourself get caught in the position of not responding if such a tactic is used on you. Many people simply do not want to respond if they know the answer is not what they have indicated over the phone or that it will cause the recipient to question the response. People simply try to do what they like to do and leave the unpleasant work for later. This is sudden death when you are utilizing the silent response letter arrangement.

Writing a letter to one addressee, but drafting it knowing that it will be read by those indicated as having received copies, is a useful tactic. Copies to your clients or customers of third party letters serve to inform your client or customer of the progress being made and make them aware of the content of the letter as efficiently as if the letters had been addressed to them.

An indication on the letter of who is to receive copies can be a good record of where copies of the letter were actually sent. You can even include the addresses to which a copy was sent if you wish. This puts the reader on notice that you are letting others know of the activities described in the letter. It can discourage people from contesting the fact that they received the mailing and the truth of its contents. It is also a courtesy since the letter is no longer private. Think of the time-saving advantages of telling everyone exactly the same information at the same time.

Make a habit of including this common notation at the bottom of your letters. Example:

cc: Oliver E. Frascona, Esq.
       4750 Table Mesa Drive
       Boulder, CO 80305

       Hon. Ronald Teck, State Senator

Please note that most elected officials take their mail seriously. Only include them when you actually send a copy to such an individual and then only when the copy has a specific purpose. Sending miscellaneous mail to such offices is a lot like crying wolf.

Blind Copies – Letters and E-mail. There are occasions when you do not want to indicate who received a copy. In such instances you would omit the copy information, but always remember to note on your copy the people who actually received a copy. Remember that you can use a blind copy in your e-mail program. It is noted as bc: instead of cc:. This way you can keep someone else up to date without the recipient knowing. This is a great technique for use with lenders, other agents, brokers and inspectors. People may use it on you also, so remember to save important e-mails.

Color. It is a color world. Try to do everything that you do in color – everything. People are impressed with color; it is now expected. Know how to make color attachments to your e-mails and color presentations. Color digital cameras are expected.

Dates. Regardless of what you write it on, always date all correspondence. It is a good habit to date and initial, or make a mark known only to you, in the lower left or right hand corner of everything you draft, approve or review. The rules vary from state to state. However, unless specified otherwise, references to dates are generally to calendar days. If you want to avoid any possible misunderstandings, specify "calendar," "business" or "banking" days.

Drafts. Try hard never to let your first draft be the final draft. Doing the first draft in pencil will force you to rewrite the letter or the contract at least once. You will always do a better job the second time. Another useful tool is a rubber stamp marked "DRAFT for DISCUSSION PURPOSES ONLY."

The enemy is misunderstanding. Clear and concise documents go a long way to eliminating rather than fostering any potential misunderstanding. Try it for a while and see if your second or third drafts create a better final product.

Exhibits. The wording we prefer is *"The attached Exhibit A – Legal Description, consisting of ___ pages, is incorporated herein and hereby made a part of this document by this reference."* Even if you do not use all of that, try to give each exhibit a title as well as a letter. There can be a lot of legal descriptions marked "Exhibit A" when a stack of documents is dropped. Another useful trick is to number each client or transaction and place that number on all documents that affect the transaction. If in doubt, you can use the street address.

"Exhibit [Letter],[Description of Document], [# of pages]"

Example: Exhibit A, Legal Description, 7 pages

E-mail. Remember that e-mail is not the easiest thing to track for users like us. The FBI and others can track it quite well. Think about sending yourself and/or your broker a copy or a "blind copy" of the e-mail. Then save that copy on your system and do not erase it. Printing an e-mail is a great idea also. One option is to save them all quarterly to a CD marked "e-mails 1st Quarter of 2010." As with all electronic documents, the ability to create false ones exists and therefore your filing method is always suspect. Printing and mailing an e-mail to the recipient is also a great way to keep those that might be tempted to lie from doing so.

Electronic Signatures. Electronic signatures are effective and legal. Know the rules for electronic signatures and how to authenticate them. This is the age of electronics. If you can not take advantage of this form of acceptance as it is available and proven, you will not be in this business for very long. Restrict access to your electronic signature. It is just like the old fashioned real one, anyone who has it has your signing hand.

Facsimile. Are faxes legal? How many times have we heard that? A fax is just a copy, nothing more or less. Think of a fax machine as a copy machine where the input tray and the output tray are located far apart. Yes people have removed or altered the phone number that comes with the fax to mislead people into thinking that the fax originated from a different location. Yes, some recipients are changing the time that is set into the receiving machine in an attempt to convince someone in a multiple contract situation that the subsequent contracts arrived before the first. And we still see a lot of people with "selective" memory about having received the fax in the first place.

There is no substitute for notes and copies of transmissions. In addition, with overnight mail there is no reason not to get the signed original in the mail, or as a minimum original signatures in counterpart when the parties to the transaction are in different geographical locations. Yes, lots of people conduct the entire transaction with faxes and do not insist on the original. We must be held to a higher standard. An original signature on a document can be invaluable in a trial.

When sending or receiving a facsimile, always remember your agency status, if any. Insist that the cooperating agent be ready to personally receive the transmittal and always insist that no one send offers to you without your prior knowledge. Even with cover letters that indicate *"the information that follows is confidential and only intended for the recipient,"* there is no guarantee that others will not review the material. The irony of most fax machines is that the order of transmission is reversed, and the cover sheet ends up on the bottom of all the pages sent, so that any hope of confidentiality is lost.

Consider getting consent to the use of a fax in advance:

Signatures _____ May _____ May Not be evidenced by facsimile.
or
All signatures may be evidenced by facsimile.

Formality.   Everyone wants to be treated like the corporate executive.   People perceive that such individuals always get formal letters.   More importantly, the court will place a greater significance on a formal letter than on an informal one, especially if disclosure is the issue.   Compliment the reader.   Treat him like an ambassador. Formal letters can be written, so that they read in an easy manner.   They need not be stiff.

Frequency.   When in doubt, write a letter or send an e-mail.   It is hard to imagine sending too many letters or e-mails.   Contact is the first step to contentment, and it establishes care and concern.   Most people just want to know what is going on, so that they can adjust their plans accordingly.   Communication is almost always the key. Lack of communication is one of the three most often listed causes of litigation.

Letterhead.   Always write all your letters on letterhead if possible, and always keep a copy for your file.   Like a business card, letterhead exudes credibility and makes a statement about you.   Yes, it is perfectly acceptable to use handwriting on letterhead on occasion.   It is definitely a personal touch.   You may also try the typed letter with a personal note at the bottom.   This gives the impression that you cared enough to personalize the letter with a note rather than just signing the letter.

Trailers on E-mail.   On all your e-mail communications make sure that you have a trailer, a block following your name that contains all the information about how to contact you.   The rules in your state may require that you indicate the state in which you are licensed on all electronic and print advertising.   Remember that "advertising" includes your letterhead, websites, and e-mail.   We are always amazed when we receive a business card or check without an area code, an e-mail address or even a street address for the office.

We can only assume that these individuals only want business from their immediate area where everyone knows them, knows where to reach them, and never plan to receive referrals from another geographical area. Think globally!

Margins and Spacing. These little things accomplish a lot. Ragged right margins are more friendly and less formal. They tend to get more attention and are read more frequently. In addition, they give a personal touch to a standard letter.

Right-justified margins make a form appear more "standard" or "formal". Therefore, the document receives less scrutiny. Right-justified margins are useful to indicate that your office is modern, organized, has a word processor or other automated document-preparation capability, and a standard procedure for completing your professional tasks.

Mechanics – Document Composition. No one will ever know what you know, nor will they be able to open your head and look inside. Most of us will be judged by our paperwork and personality. There is never an excuse for poor grammar or punctuation. They leave the reader with a sense that the author is not a professional.

Whiteout is not only an invitation to modification, but it is personally unacceptable. Whiteout on colored paper gives a very poor impression to the client or customer. If someone cannot prepare a crisp, clean letter, how will they do with contract documents and the important things such as deeds, notes, and the like?

Memorandum of Previous Oral Conversation or E-mail. This is a very useful tool utilized by many attorneys when the cow is not only out of the barn but is hamburger, and you need to cover the tracks. You start your communication with the words, "_This is a memorandum of our previous oral conversation of Friday, June 28th, 1910,_" and follow with the body of what you indicated in that previous oral conversation. This serves to document your disclosure, not as to the date of the memorandum, but as to the date the conversation took place. This is not always a fail-safe system because the other party may refuse to sign, may deny the fact of the previous conversation and/or may even controvert it, which could put you in a more difficult position than had you not tried this tactic. Use it only when the outcome is known.

Notaries and Witnesses. It is possible that if you are merely present during a transaction, no matter how much you disavow your role, someone will hold you responsible for something. Therefore, as a notary never allow anyone to sign whose identity you have not verified and who does not sign in your presence. The number of forged notary signatures, a form of state-approved witness with a seal, would destroy your faith in people.

Case in Point.

A notary testified, under oath, that she saw Nancy sign a document she had notarized. There was no doubt in her mind that Nancy and Fred had appeared before her personally and were the signatories. She could even pick out Nancy now from the present group, standing next to Fred. Imagine her surprise when she was informed that the lady standing next to Fred was really named Roberta, his girlfriend, and not Nancy, Fred's wife.

The story got even better when it was learned that the individual who had signed Nancy's name was a man – not Roberta, not Nancy – and not even present. Once you have been with a stranger for a few days, you too might be tempted to notarize her signature. Require the proper identification with every signature.

Case in Point.

The fax arrived at the lender's office and purported to evidence an inspection report. Imagine the dismay when it was shown that the fax was, in fact, an amalgamation of several different documents, a previous inspection report on another property on the letterhead and with the signature of the inspector. Just a little cut and paste on the computer and out that fax went. Some people still verify with a phone call to be sure that the transmission was received. Result: suspension of the individual's real estate license for 6 months.

Keep copies of all faxes, so that you can prove what you sent, even if the deal does not close. The story got worse when it was found that the sender of the inspection report had, in fact, not sent it and was being accused of sending a false fax. Had the purported sender kept a copy of what was sent, it would have been a lot easier to verify the contents of the now altered fax. Yes, the deal never closed. The file was not in order and the Attorney General was investigating for the Real Estate Commission.

Originals. Any document that has an original signature is an original document. There is no substitute for an original. Even today, with fax signatures, electronic signatures and stamps for signatures, we always let the other people have copies and we keep the original. If everyone wants an original, make duplicate originals (several identical copies all with original signatures). If there are numerous changes to a document, make the changes, photocopy the altered original, and sign the photocopies as originals. Now in effect you have a new original and all the changes are "printed" by the copy machine. You must retain a copy of every letter sent and every signed document that passes through your hands. The good record keepers are hard to discredit. Be one of them.

Personal Touch. If you utilize a word processor, try to make the variables in a letter more than just the name and address of the reader. Include little facts about the transaction or the property to make the form letter as personal to the reader as possible. *Do not change the standard boilerplate language established by your office.* It is there for your protection, as well as for the protection of the firm and the broker.

Printed, Typed and Handwritten. The highest priority is the handwritten remarks. Next comes the typed terms and conditions and finally the printed form. Remember that a printed form could be a photocopy.

For forms, the printed form is the best. For communication, a typed letter or statement is easier to read and more professional. However, a handwritten note or message is faster and may convey personal versus delegated attention to the matter. Remember to proof what you wrote before you send it. The next revisions will be before the jury. Remember to copy yourself on e-mails and faxes, so you know what you sent.

Re: This designator on the letter means "regarding" or "in regard to" and indicates the subject of the content of the correspondence. A general reference, or no reference at all, attracts less attention to the particular matter than a specific reference. Specific references are useful for many letters when you want to be sure the reader's attention is focused on the issue. Alert your readers to the main subject right away and establish the reference for rapid identification when you see the letter later on by leading off your letters with a specific "Re:" line just above the salutation. If you want the letter to receive less significance, eliminate the "Re:" entirely or make it vague and uninviting.

REALTOR®. This is a registered mark belonging to the National Association of REALTORS® (N.A.R.) which may be used by its members in the fashion designated by N.A.R. It should always be followed by the ® symbol. REALTORS® should avoid its use generically in speech, in contracts, in the proper name of their company, or as a synonym for a person who is a real estate licensee, even if such licensee is a member of N.A.R. If you have additional questions or are concerned about the proper use of the mark, an extensive guide dealing with the use of the REALTOR® mark is available from N.A.R.

Receipts. A fast and efficient system to ensure that you can describe the document received by the recipient is to have a self-inking rubber stamp made that looks something like the example below. Simply make a copy of the document, stamp it, and get the signature of the recipient. It is a fast, accurate and efficient system that does not require a lot of thought. This method is also convenient when you are trusting someone else who might not be aware of the importance or the description of the particular document or who does not know what to write on a receipt. Red, with large letters, seems to be the most useful.

Clause:

The undersigned hereby receipts for the original of this document, consisting of ___ pages, on the date indicated.

_____

Recipient   Dated

Now it is not uncommon for someone to send an e-mail that is printed at the other end of the phone line and then faxed back with the signature or electronic signature of the recipient.

Sample Open or Closing Lines. When you finish a letter, keep in mind the many ways to conclude. The following are some sample closing lines. They vary from the simple to the firm and almost offensive.   The last thing you say should be congratulatory, polite, and nice. Always end correspondence with something that is not controversial. Use these separately or combine as needed. Add your own favorites.

Examples:

Please forgive the formality of this letter. It is important for me to document, for everyone concerned, the information [advice is not a good word to use unless you mean it and are willing to stand by it] I have given you and the decisions that you have made. It may seem fastidious, but it is our office policy and helps keep my broker, the Real Estate Commission, and our malpractice carrier happy.

It is my understanding that you completely understand the transaction outlined by both this letter and our previous correspondence; and, after considering all the alternatives as well as the potential risks involved, *you have elected* to proceed along the course outlined herein.

The transaction which you contemplate and which has been outlined in this letter is one that has serious tax, financial, and legal consequences.   Please understand that neither I nor anyone associated with this office is recommending that you complete the transaction in the manner you have elected. *We simply are not responsible* for anything that occurs as a result of your decision.

Again, I would advise you to seek competent legal, accounting, and tax advice before entering into this transaction as you have outlined it.

As I indicated to you earlier, the decision to present the terms you have proposed in the contract and the decision to acquire the property indicated above are your decisions alone. I must send you this letter to verify that you are acting on your own judgment and without any encouragement or advice from me or this office. I know you want to complete the transaction *as you have outlined it*, and I wish you the best of luck.

The property is simply beautiful, and I know both you and Monica will enjoy living in The Meadows. If we can be of service in assisting you in locating other property in the future, *please do not hesitate to inquire.* I have enjoyed showing you property and *admire your ability to make your own decisions.*

Congratulations on your acquisition of another piece of real estate. I wish you the best of luck. Thank you for selecting me and this firm to show you property.

Congratulations on your decision ......

I admire your grasp of the complex issues presented and the business risks involved. Congratulations upon your decision to propose and complete this transaction as you have outlined.

As I have indicated to you all along, and as I know you understand, this letter confirms the fact that you, and you alone, have decided to propose and to complete this transaction with the terms you have outlined. Neither I, nor the office with which I am affiliated, nor the broker for the office can be in any way responsible for the outcome of the transaction. I admire your drive and grasp of the issues and wish you the best of luck.

Silent Response. The silent response cover letter is a useful tool to establish a duty on the part of the recipient either to respond or to accept the consequences. Although not as good as the required response cover letter, it is far better than no letter at all. Coupled with a conversation log which incorporates the name of the party with whom you are talking as well as the date, time and content of the conversation, plus the limited use of certified mail, the silent response letter can put you in a very defensible position. It not only documents the content of the conversation, but also demonstrates the degree of care utilized to bring the information to the client or customer.

Structure. Start every communication, especially a letter, with something pleasant that compliments the reader or makes him feel at ease. Put your reader in the right frame of mind for the content of the letter.

The body of the letter should be polite and tactful but always explicit, especially when a disclaimer is being conveyed. Mix several ideas in a single letter to equalize the content between disclaimer and information. A long letter is a good place to include a lot of serious disclaimers you do not want someone to dwell upon since it will probably never get the reader's full attention and yet will cover the notification process. Several separate letters serve to keep the reader informed but each will receive closer scrutiny. This is a good way to convey good news or routine information. When you want to be sure they read it, keep it short.

The closing should always be polite and offer your assistance: *"If there is anything I can do to assist you, please do not hesitate to let me know." "Thank you for your cooperation and assistance in this matter." "We are happy to be your agents." "It is always a pleasure to have you as a client."* Even if the content of the letter is difficult, always make the closing pleasant.

Telephone Trust. The telephone is used to such an extent that we never even know with whom we speak, or how to verify the information or quotations upon which we rely. Lenders, title companies, inspection services, surveyors, taxing authorities, homeowners associations, ditch and water companies, governmental authorities and similar entities provide us with information that we accept, pass on to our clients and customers and fail to verify or commit to memory. Too often the information changes and the memory of the person to whom we have spoken and upon whom we have relied now fades as time and pressure are applied. A letter to the party confirming the information received or quoted will prompt instant recall.

Term Definition. A convenient way to define a term for later use is to enclose it in parenthesis with quotation marks after the first use of the word; i.e., the real property ("Property"). Thereafter, you can simply refer to it as the Property. This helps your letter be precise without being wordy and gives it that professional appearance.

Chapter 2

Listing the Seller's Real Estate

Finding, Listing, Representing, Working With and Retaining Sellers

General Rules of the Road

Be the Expert in Real Estate – Everyone knows you know real estate.

Recommend an Expert in Other Fields – Let everyone know that you do not do inspections, give tax advice, draft complex contract provisions or give legal advice.

Be the Source – If anyone needs to know something about real estate, they call you.

Be the Professional – "S/He is always working" is the reputation you desire.

Be Recognizable – When anyone sees your name or picture, they know you are "the real estate person." Your business card, website, checks, e-mails, stationery, flyers, postcards – all promotional material – must have your picture.

Be Outgoing – Tell everyone you are in real estate.

Have a Great Memory – People love it when they are remembered by name. Do not expect them to remember you, you remember them.

Be There Always – People list with the last person who talked to them about real estate.

Be the Photographer – Take and send pictures all the time. Pictures of your listings, pictures of yourself, pictures of your sellers outside their home. People love pictures.

Be Computer Literate and Demonstrate – Know how to demonstrate it. People love technology and looking at things that go "WOW!"

Be Persistent and Polite – People may say that they do not want to be bothered, but that is exactly what they want when they are sellers. Supply information or service that they need each time you call.

Searching for the Seller

Where should you look for sellers? Everywhere. Everyone who owns real estate will want to sell it sooner or later. As a new or seasoned real estate licensee, you will always be in constant need of sellers. The secret is to set up sources that continue to produce listings. Often the experienced person will indicate that they follow one source to obtain listings. The very successful people follow many sources.

If this is your "farm" area, geographical or otherwise, you need to maintain communication with the prospective sellers at all times. Personal cover letters spaced at reasonable intervals is one of the best ways to accomplish this. Include everyone's e-mail address in your database, so that you can e-mail things to them. While there are several ways to maintain contact, we will address the "information is more than I can stand" method. It was said well in an old commercial, "when E. F. Hutton talks......"

Sphere of Influence. There are many sources of listings. Sellers can be found everywhere. As a beginning real estate salesperson, look to your family, friends and all those people with whom you do business. Never overlook anyone. Set up a database of contacts from your sphere of influence immediately to let everyone know you are in the business. Get their e-mail addresses, so that you can e-mail to them. Enclose your business card with all your bill payments and, by all means, give your card to everyone whom you meet or with whom you talk. Yes, that means the gas station attendant, the waitress along with the tip and the person who does work for you around the house. A business card is the least expensive form of advertisement you will ever fund.

Letters to your sphere of influence should be sent every 45-60 days. Include those people from whom you receive services, either personal or professional, on a routine basis. This includes your banker, manicurist, barber, tire salesperson, department store clerk, grocery store owner, dry cleaner, social club associations, dentists, physicians and many more.

Business to Business. Everyone is in some business. Farm the businesses that are not exactly related to yours. No one else does. Make sure that you establish contact with the owner of the business as well as those that work there. Let them know that you are in real estate and are working. Compliment them on their place of business and their product or service. Buy from them, trade with them and never let them forget that you are also in business and want their business. Say *"I want your business. How can I get it?"* Offer them a place on your site of preferred businesses. Bring them something when they send someone to you. Send people to them, always with your card. Distribute their promotional material if you can.

If the business has a coupon for their product or service, pass those out to everyone you meet. Be certain to place your name on the back of the coupon, so the owner of the business knows that you are sending them the business. Not only are you promoting another business, any conversation with the card recipient allows you to tell new people what you do, also. It is a great way to start a conversation with someone, and it allows you to give someone something that is not related to your business.

We love to distribute cards for "50 cents off of a large cone" to anyone that we meet. The cards are from a prospective client's business. It is a discount coupon with my name on the back. Everyone likes ice cream. Remember that some businesses are small and do not have advertising budgets. They need you. Network marketing for them will provide mutual results. Remember to give a referral before asking for one.

Where The Sellers Are. Schools are where the kids are. Where there are kids, there are parents. Participate in school activities. Any organization where the sellers are present is a place that you want to be. While it is great to donate money to a good cause, and we do not want to discourage you from such participation, participate in grassroots activities where people that own real estate are present. Habitat for Humanity is a wonderful place to contribute your efforts, and it is real estate related.

The Web. Today literally hundreds of thousands of people browse the internet daily. If you do not have a presence on the internet with your own personal website, do not delay anymore. Create your own home page and do what is necessary to create exposure for your site. Make your home page a vital part of any real estate search by using the appropriate key words. Construct your site, so that the visitor can request additional information from you personally by registering.

Data can be captured with a "get information form," a "registration form" or a "confidential preferred guest form". Always get the e-mail address of anyone who visits your site or with whom you come in contact. Have sections for your personal sellers and buyers that is password protected. Enable them to access their personal real estate files with passwords they set.

Link your site to any other location pertinent to real estate and the needs of your buyers and sellers. You might include the local chamber of commerce, rotary club, an accommodations directory, area attractions, entertainment, school information, lenders, title companies and home inspectors. Also consider an internal page that allows for the calculation of payments and interest rates. There potential buyers can calculate the purchase price range they can afford and the additional loan amount that can be realized with additional down payment. You could include a payment calculator that shows down payments and interest rate variables for 80%, 90% and 95% loan to value in various price ranges for the selected property.

In essence, your website should be **the** site for real estate and community information. You want to encourage traffic. Consider rewarding the person who visits your site with a printable coupon for savings with local merchants or even a market evaluation or other real estate service that you provide.

Geographical Farm. Sellers may be solicited from a geographical "farm" area. The contact with these individuals must be consistent, so that the owners recognize you as the authority on real estate in their area. Include information about the market in the neighborhood as well as mail that shows your activity in other additional areas. These sellers may be "moving up" to a different style home or to a neighborhood in a different location. If you include all your "Just Listed" and "Just Sold" announcements, you will be viewed as a full-time real estate person who takes his job seriously. The best results will be realized if you combine your mail-outs with a "warm" telephone call to establish rapport with people that you know through your correspondence.

Be unique in your selection of printed material to send to your farm area. If your competition is doing newsletters, do letters or postcards instead. If they do small postcards, then send oversized ones. Alternate colors on flyers or stay with black and white. If everyone is sending Christmas cards, then send an "after the holidays and beginning of the New Year" greeting. Coordinate the theme of your mailings with special events, holidays, "how you do business" and always *ask for their business.*

Some people do not like canvassing the neighborhood and others do. For those that do, here are some ideas. If you are on a limited budget and need to get started or get started again, get out and let people see you in your farm area. If you are well known, people are impressed that you stop to say hello in your farm area. Their neighborhood is not just a place to solicit business, but a part of you. Nothing substitutes for showing up in the neighborhood to see people that you know. They will see you always dressed in business attire and always working. They will be impressed that you stopped your busy day to deliver something in the neighborhood. As an icebreaker for the new area, bring something useful or fun. You can coordinate gifts with a special day or event such as home-baked cookies, pumpkins near Halloween, flags near Memorial Day or Fourth of July, or pies near Thanksgiving.

Referrals. Once you have established yourself by a number of successful transactions, you will find that a larger percentage of your business will be derived from past clients and customers and referrals. This is the most satisfying place to be! Always ask for referrals when you close a transaction, when you correspond with your client database, and in any conversation that involves real estate. Let your clients and customers know you are in the business long-term and that you appreciate their future business, as well as the business of their friends and business associates. They will forget to refer people to you unless you ask.

Third Party Referrals – Before the Fact. One source of referrals is from third parties. These entities refer buyers and sellers to you in return for a promised part of your fee. The sequence of events is that the referring party contacts you and agrees to accept a portion of your fee in exchange for referring to you a particular buyer or seller. Utilize a form to secure your commission or confirm payment agreements such as the one on page 283.

After the Fact. In this situation, you already have a brokerage relationship with the buyer or seller, and the third party wants to inject themselves into your brokerage relationship. Please note that you already have a brokerage relationship (listing of the buyer or seller). This third party infection is tortuous interference with your contract and is actionable in most states. Colorado has enacted a law, proposed by Oliver E. Frascona, to prevent such interference and its contents follows:

C.R.S. 12-61-203.5. Referral fees - interference with brokerage relationship.
(1) No licensee under parts 1 to 4 of this article shall pay a referral fee unless reasonable cause for payment of the referral fee exists. A reasonable cause for payment means:
(a)   An actual introduction of business has been made;
(b)   A contractual referral fee relationship exists; or
(c)   A contractual cooperative brokerage relationship exists.

(2)(a)   No person shall interfere with the brokerage relationship of a licensee.
(b)   As used in this subsection (2):
(I)   "Brokerage relationship" means a relationship entered into between a broker or salesperson and a buyer, seller, landlord, or tenant under which the broker or salesperson engages in any of the acts set forth in section 12-61-101 (2). A brokerage relationship is not established until a written brokerage agreement is entered into between the parties or is otherwise established by law.

> *(II)   "Interference with the brokerage relationship" means demanding a referral fee from a licensee without reasonable cause.*
>
> *(III)   "Referral fee" means any fee paid by a licensee to any person or entity, other than a cooperative commission offered by a listing broker to a selling broker or vice versa.*
>
> *(3) Any person aggrieved by a violation of any provision of this section may bring a civil action in a court of competent jurisdiction. The prevailing party in any such action shall be entitled to actual damages and, in addition, the court may award an amount up to three times the amount of actual damages sustained as a result of any such violation plus reasonable attorney fees.*

For Sale by Owner (FSBO).   What better place to find a motivated seller than one who has listed the property himself? If he does not begin with an urgent desire to sell his home, he will soon have one as he becomes more aware of the intricacies associated with finalizing a successful real estate transaction.   With buyer agency becoming more of the norm, it is important to know the inventory of FSBO's in your real estate market, whether you plan to solicit the listing or not. You may find that an introduction based on the honest attempt to gain information about their home, so that you may add it to your personal database of available properties for potential buyers, will open the doors to more communication.

A series of letters that provide both information useful to the seller as well as emphasizing the need for a professional who is in the business full-time will soon impress upon the seller that he can not hope to accomplish the same results by his merely holding an Open House and placing a sign in the yard.

The web is now also a source for FSBO's. Visit their sites and e-mail them the material that will encourage them to work with you. Send them your URL (website address), so that they can click and see what you do for your clients. Make them wish that their property was on your site. Talk about all the sites that are accessed through yours that are not available to them. Also remember to stress the personal service that you provide.   The web is just another newspaper ad.   Think about sending an automatic e-mail with information and a link every time that you list another property, or when one of your listings sells. Create a sense that this seller needs to be part of your system.

Try a link to your website with a personal invitation for a potential seller to go there. It is only a click away. Consider a site that just shows the one property owned by that seller, the one you want to list, so that when the seller goes there and enters the password that you gave her, she can see her property on the net. Think of this as sort of a trial site. Remember to reward the visitor with a coupon that is only available from the site on that date and maybe for that person.

Expired Listings. This seller is either frustrated and anxious for results, or perhaps was never motivated to sell in the first place. The key to getting your foot in the door here is timing. For those who wish to corner this market, you must be on the Multiple Listing computer daily with an immediate call to the seller as soon as the listing shows it has expired. The reasons for the home not selling may not be the fault of the previous listing broker, so it is important to determine the motivation of the seller. You do not want to be in the same situation as the previous broker with money spent on marketing and no sale.

Expired Buyers with a House to Sell. This is a group of people that tried to buy one of your listings and failed. These buyers have not bought anything else, and they are no longer working with the other salesperson. Keep a list of buyers that make offers. Then watch the list of recorded transactions published in the newspaper or online to see if they have bought anything. If they bought something, congratulate them and be alert for their next move. If the other salesperson has abandoned them, they need your expertise and assistance now. In addition, if they have a house to sell, you can assist them with the sale of that house and their new purchase of a new one.

Tell Everyone You are in Real Estate. No matter how successful you are, you need more business. Remember that unless *you* tell people what you do, they will never know. How do you get them to ask you? Simply, ask them what they do for a living. When they answer, they will ask what you do. Tell them, smile and give them a card and say "if you or someone close to you ever needs a good REALTOR®, give me a call." Then wait for them to speak again. Do not start to sell. Let yourself be sold by your approach. Here are some additional thoughts. Give them something that they will keep such as a coupon for something from "one of my clients is in the business, and I want to help him, so I hand these out." Another option is to hand them a flier and say, "this is one of my listings, keep it and maybe you will run into someone who wants to live in the country."

Letter/e-mail – Potential Individual Client

Mr. Pat Potential
Mrs. Pam Potential
420 Anywhere Avenue
Your Town, CO 00000

Dear Mr. and Mrs. Potential:

I just wanted to say thank you once again for the exceptional service I received from you (*or your establishment*). It is always a pleasure doing business with you. Without a doubt you are a professional. The service and quality you provide is consistent and exceptional.

It occurs to me that we might be able to assist each other. As you know, I am a real estate professional. In my daily business of meeting people both new to our area as well as those who have lived here for some time, I find myself routinely referring clients to businesses. I have always been happy to refer people to you. It gives me pleasure to be able to assist my clients in establishing their own network of services where they will be satisfied. This enhances my relationship and rapport with them.

In your daily work you come into contact with a number of people who may wish to buy or sell real estate, or who just have questions about real estate in general. When that happens, I would appreciate your recommending that they talk to me and let me know of their interest. You can rest assured that I will do my very best to justify the trust and confidence that you place in me. My goal is for those people to return to you thanking you for the referral.

For your convenience, I am enclosing several of my business cards. Please give them to those individuals that you feel could use real estate assistance.

Sincerely,
The Real Estate Company

by: Your Name Here,
REALTOR®, CRS, GRI

Letter/e-mail – Potential Business Client

Mr. Mark Potential
The Best Ice Cream There Is
1000 Their Avenue
Your Town, CO 00000

Dear Mark: Try The Link (click here): www.mywebsite.com

It was so nice to see you again today. I just love your ice cream. I tell everyone about your store. As you know, I list and sell real estate for many families here in Your Town. Most of them like ice cream.

I would like to help your business grow and be able to offer something to anyone with whom I come in contact. Obviously, that will help my business and yours to grow.

Are you interested in printing up some certificates that would bring people to your store? I could stamp my name on the back and hand them out to potential customers and clients. That way we could see if I am helping at all and you would know the source of your new customers.

or

I have a website that lots of people visit on a regular basis. I would be willing to let you have a link on my site. If you do not have a website, I could offer the certificates for your products. People could print them from my site and use them at your store.

later

This system of mutual referrals has been so wonderful for us both. I would like to put a poster with my picture on it about Your Town in your store over near the freezer. I would also have one of yo and your store in my office. I have some wall photos of businesses that I particularly like or that are "partners" with me, so that we can boost each others businesses.

Sincerely,
The Real Estate Company

Letter/e-mail – Sphere of Influence

Mr. Frank Friendly
Mrs. Frances Friendly
420 Boy Scout Lane
Boys Town, CO 00000

Dear Frank and Frances:

You and I are both active members in the Boulder Girl Scouts. It is difficult at times to believe we have time for any other activity, but I thought I would give you an idea of what I do with the rest of my life!

I am a real estate broker who assists people with perhaps the largest investment of their lifetime – their personal home. Or it may be the purchase or sale of their second home, vacation home or investment property.   If people have a specific real estate concern, it is my job to provide them with the information they need to make the right decisions for their individual situation.

I am now at a point where I am able to select the people with whom I work. My first choice is to work with people I know and with whom I share similar interests and values. This makes the process for buying and selling real estate more enjoyable and satisfying for everybody. I have found time and time again that when the right people are working together, success happens!

From time to time, I would like to be able to drop you a note to help you stay informed about the market and to remind you that I am in the real estate business. If there is anything that I can do to assist you with your work, please let me know. I come into contact with a large number of people on a daily basis and would be happy to send them your way if you wish.

Sincerely,
The Real Estate Company

by: Your Name Here,
REALTOR®, CRS, GRI

Letter/e-mail – Geographical Farm

Mr. and Mrs. Pat Potential
420 Anywhere Avenue
Your Town, CO 00000

Dear Mr. and Mrs. Potential:

Allow me to introduce myself. I am Your Name with The Real Estate Company During the upcoming months you will be hearing from me about the real estate market in general and as it pertains to your home. I specialize in marketing homes in this area.

One of the most important aspects of marketing a home for a seller is exposure. I like to let the neighborhood know when a home comes on the market. Often, someone right here knows of a friend or associate who might like to live in this area. In addition to local exposure, we market homes throughout the state and nationally.

Below is a partial list of properties that we have sold recently and the price at which they closed.

(*Include a list of homes sold in the neighborhood* – remember "sold" means sold and closed. Should your flyer contain "active listings," remember that you first need the approval of the listing broker to include their listings in your flyer or on your website. This right to advertise a listing generally goes to the listing broker exclusively.)

I look forward to meeting you personally when I am in the neighborhood next time. If you have any present plans for selling your home or know someone that might like to live, here please let me know. Feel free to call me at the office or my home at any time. Also e-mail me at any time.

Real estate is a seven day a week profession. I have enclosed a business card for your convenience, so that you can request information about the various services that I provide.

Thank you for your time. I look forward to serving you. Visit our website at:

Sincerely,
The Real Estate Company

by: Your Name Here,
REALTOR®, CRS, GRI

Please disregard this letter if your home is currently listed with another
REALTOR® or otherwise "on the market"

Letter/e-mail – Geographical Farm
[Keep each e-mail short & consistent and send several – Use a colored background]

Mr. Pat Potential
Mrs. Pam Potential

Your Area Home Owner's Website

Visit this site to see what is going on in your area.: area@neighborhoodlink.com

I am specializing in your area and have developed [linked to] a site that follows the activities in your area. This site is a great place to see homes for sale, homes that have sold and the selling price of each property. As always, the site is not meant to replace one of my market evaluations, but it is a great place to start.

I update this site daily with new information of listings that we have for sale to assist buyers around the world. Please understand that not all properties are on the site. Some of my sellers do not choose to advertise their property on the site or on any website for personal reasons; therefore, we do not show them on this site.

If you would like an e-mail the instant a property is placed on the market for sale or goes under contract, let me know. I provide all my clients with e-mail updates, so that they have the most current information available on the market in this area, as well as others that I participate in here at The Real Estate Company.

One of the most important aspects of marketing a home for a seller is exposure. I like to let the neighborhood know when a home comes on the market. Often someone right here knows of a friend or associate who might like to live in this area. In addition to local exposure, we market homes throughout the state and nationally.

I look forward to meeting you personally when I am in the neighborhood next time. If you have any present plans for selling your home or know someone that might like to live in your area, please let me know.

Please disregard this letter if your home is currently listed with another REALTOR® or otherwise "on the market"

Letter/e-mail – Referral Thank You

Mr. Roger Referral
Mrs. Ruth Referral
420 Reference Lane
Their Town, CO 00000

Dear Roger and Ruthie:

Congratulations on your new home! It has been my pleasure to assist you in finding your new home and monitoring the closing all the way to the end. Even the best paved road has a few bumps, and I know you felt that way a few times along the route. I appreciate your cooperation and perseverance. It has been an honor to work with the two of you.

I know you are happy to be settling into your new home. However, I will miss working with you and obviously, I need to find someone new to help them find a new home. I would love to work with one of your friends or business associates who is looking for a new home. Please keep me in mind when someone mentions real estate. I have enclosed a few business cards. Just hand them out when you get the opportunity.

Don't forget to visit my website at: www.mysite.com from time to time to see what is going on. Please keep me up to date with any changes to your e-mail address, so that you can continue to receive my market data over the next few years. That way when you are ready to sell, you will have an idea of the appreciation. Of course, I look forward to preparing a comprehensive market analysis when the time comes for you to sell.

Thank you for letting me help you with your real estate needs. You made good decisions and that made my job a lot easier.

Sincerely,
The Real Estate Company

[The power of a written letter in addition to an e-mail can never be underestimated. In a world where personal service is disappearing, handwritten addresses and personal letters are a great means to personalize what you do.]

Letter/e-mail – For Sale by Owner

Mr. Sam Seller
Mrs. Sandy Seller
4750 Table Mesa Drive
Boulder, CO 80303

  Re: 4750 Table Mesa Drive

Dear Mr. and Mrs. Seller:

  Congratulations! I see that you have placed your home on the market for sale. Selling real estate is an exciting and challenging endeavor. For your sake, I hope that your real estate experience is brief and successful. However, if you do decide at any time to turn the marketing of your home over to an expert, I hope that you will consider the advantages of allowing my firm, The Real Estate Company, to do the job.

  Selling homes is my profession. Not only is this my full-time job, but more often than not I am working overtime through evenings and weekends to get the job done. Every day I assist people with getting *the price that they select in the shortest amount of time with the least amount of difficulty.*

  Won't you let me help you? There is no obligation. I would be happy to schedule an appointment, so that I may show how I work and share with you everything you will need to monitor in order to secure a successful sale. All I ask is that you consider me in the event that you decide you need help.

      Sincerely,
      The Real Estate Company

      by: Your Name Here
      REALTOR®, CRS, GRI

Letter/e-mail – For Sale by Owner

Mr. Sam Seller
Mrs. Sandy Seller
4750 Table Mesa Drive
Boulder, CO 80303

www.mywebsite.com   **Your House is for sale!**

Visit my website. It shows all the homes in your area that we currently have listed for sale. We display all of our listings on the web as soon as we get them unless the owner elects not to have them on the web. This site will assist you in knowing about your competition.

Congratulations! Although I make a living helping lots of people sell their homes and buy new ones, I understand that you want to try to sell your home yourself without having to pay a commission. I do not blame you at all, but if I can help let me know.

To sell real estate today you need a lot more than just a good REALTOR®. Everything is on the web. Did you know that there are over 100,000 websites displaying real estate? Of course the ones that have 95% of the listings are only accessed by REALTORS® through professional networks. Our business is to expose houses to buyers from anywhere in the world who want to access available homes in our area.

If you find a buyer, you will need some third party help. I will mail you [*unless you want me to send as an attachment to an e-mail*] a copy of the generally accepted contract, and some forms dealing with square footage, hazardous waste, the proximity of known sex offenders, schools, businesses, taxes and other associated materials that the buyers will want to see when they contact you.

Selling homes is my profession. Not only is this my full-time job, but more often than not I am working overtime through evenings and weekends to get the job done. Every day I assist people with getting *the price that they select in the shortest amount of time with the least amount of difficulty.*

Your Trailer here   e-mail/phone

Letter/e-mail – For Sale by Owner

Mr. Sam Seller
Mrs. Sandy Seller
4750 Table Mesa Drive
The Peoples Republic of Boulder, CO 80305

I wish that your home was on this website: *www.mysite.com*

Yes, I want your business. Take a minute and read this short message.

You have a great house! I wish you well in your attempts to sell your home by yourself. However, you have been attempting to market your home on your own for some time now, and your deadline for moving is drawing near.

Let me help. I do this every day for a living, and I am very good at getting homes sold for fair market price. Allow me to come over with a market analysis. Let's talk seriously about getting your home sold professionally.

I am confident that The Real Estate Company can effectively market your home. Part of marketing any home is creating a competitive demand for exactly what you are selling. I do this for a living every day and most evenings; therefore, I do not invest my time in lost causes. I believe in your home and in getting it sold. Once you have reviewed the specific marketing plan for your individual home, I am certain you will be anxious to get started.

We live in a high tech world today, and exposure to the professional real estate sites is important. When you go to my site click on _____ to see what a buyer would see if they were looking for a house in your area. Your home needs to be there.

I certainly understand your desire to save money (i.e., the commission). I have thought about doing my own fillings to save a little money myself, but I also see the wisdom in paying a professional who is experienced in achieving results. Time is money and a professional that can get your home sold for a great net price is worth the small fee that I charge.

It is not as much a question of what professional marketing costs you, but more a question of how much I can put in your pocket. It is not uncommon for

Professional Real Estate Marketing techniques to quickly bring firm offers for considerably more than you have been offered privately. You see, the buyers also expect to save the same commission.

     E-mail me with a time that I can stop by and bring you a professional presentation on the sale of your home. There is no charge for a consultation, and I can even bring the popcorn if you like. Selling your house should be fun.

               Sincerely,
               The Real Estate Company

               By: Your Loyal Agent, CRS, GRI

Letter/e-mail – For Sale by Owner

Mr. Sam Seller
Mrs. Sandy Seller
4750 Table Mesa Drive
Boulder, CO 80305

Re: 4750 Table Mesa Drive   Look at my website: www.mysite.com

Dear Mr. and Mrs. Seller:

Mr. and Mrs. Seller, please know that I wish you well in your attempts to sell your home by yourself. However, you have been attempting to market your home on your own for some time now, and your deadline for moving is drawing near. May I suggest that you allow me to step in and help you. You need your home on a professional website that deals with real estate in your area. I want to put your home on my site and the internet.

Based on my first impression of your home, I am certain that The Real Estate Company can effectively market your home. Part of marketing any home is creating a competitive demand for exactly what you are selling. I do this for a living every day. I believe in your home and in getting it sold. Once you have reviewed the specific marketing plan for your individual home, I am certain you will be anxious to get started.

I certainly understand your desire to save money (i.e., the commission) but I wonder if your overall costs in mortgage payments and extended time on the market may not be more detrimental to your net proceeds. It is not a question of what professional marketing costs you, but more a question of how much I can put in your pocket. It is not uncommon for *Professional Real Estate Marketing* techniques to quickly bring firm offers for considerably more than you have been offered privately. You see, the buyers also expect to save the same commission.

You may have found that negotiating with potential buyers on your own home can be somewhat uncomfortable. Buyers and other agents tend to feel more comfortable with me because they know that once the sale is over and you are long gone, I'll still be here if they have a question or problem. Other agents are eager to show my listings because they can be assured of adequate disclosure and a smooth transaction.

All agents know that I pay them if they have a buyer. That reputation makes me someone with whom everyone likes to cooperate. That means your home is on the list of many more REALTORS®.

                    Sincerely,
                    The Real Estate Company

                    by: Your Name Here,
                    REALTOR®, CRS, GRI

Letter/e-mail – For Sale by Owner

Mr. Sam Seller
Mrs. Sandy Seller
4750 Table Mesa Drive
Boulder, CO 80305

    Re: 4750 Table Mesa Drive

Dear Mr. and Mrs. Seller:

Congratulations! I see that you have placed your home on the market for sale. Selling real estate is an exciting and challenging endeavor. If there is anything that I can do to assist you, do not hesitate to call me.

I am a professional real estate salesperson and know how much there is to be done to get a home ready for a potential buyer. To help you get started I have enclosed some information that might help you prepare for the potential buyers.

First is an MLS information sheet. While you may not have access to the Multiple Listing Service, this sheet will let you know the kinds of information other sellers are making available to buyers through the REALTOR® system. In addition, I have enclosed a Sellers Property Disclosure Statement which informs the potential buyer about the physical condition of the home. Most buyers expect to receive this information to assist them in deciding which home to purchase. Finally, I have enclosed a copy of the contract that our office uses, so that you can prepare to fill in the necessary blanks. I have not included our clauses and addenda as they were developed for us by our attorneys and are for our use only.

Selling homes is my profession. Every day I assist people with getting *the price that they select* in *the shortest amount of time* with *the least amount of difficulty.* It is the way in which I feed my family each and every day. I am committed to finding buyers for sellers and sellers for buyers. Not only is this my full-time job, but more often than not I am working overtime through evenings and weekends to get the job done. Please feel free to call me at any time. This is not an 8:00 a.m. to 5:00 p.m. job. Yes, Saturdays and Sundays are fine, although I usually am conducting a client's Open House part of the day each Sunday.

Sincerely,

Letter/e-mail – Expired Listing

Mr. Sam and Mrs. Sandy Seller
4750 Table Mesa Drive
Boulder, CO 80305

Dear Mr. and Mrs. Seller:

I have watched your property through the Multiple Listing Service and now note that your listing with a competitor has expired. Please consider me and my real estate firm to be the real estate agents who can effectively market and sell your home.

While working with prospective buyers, I have previewed and included your home on my inventory for showing appointments. I would like the opportunity to meet with you to share my insights on marketing your home, as well as to express the objections that buyers had when viewing your home. Please keep in mind that while your home is not the right home for every buyer, there are ways to stage a home for marketing that will enhance its special features.

Selling homes is my profession. Every day I assist people with getting *the price that they select* in *the shortest amount of time* with *the least amount of difficulty*. It is the way in which I feed my family each and every day. I am committed to finding buyers for sellers and sellers for buyers. Not only is this my full-time job, but more often than not I am working overtime through evenings and weekends to get the job done. I believe in Open Houses, community advertising, specialty advertising and "target marketing" to the group of potential buyers that will be able to afford your home.

Enclosed is my personal reference list of satisfied sellers and buyers for your perusal. You will notice many of your neighbors have successfully sold or bought homes with my assistance. Please feel free to call any of the families listed. They will be happy to give you candid answers to any questions you may have.

My real estate office sells real estate. We have agents who carry an inventory of listings as well as several buyer agents working almost exclusively with buyers. While this puts us in the middle of real estate transactions, we *sell* houses. We are always looking for qualified buyers.

I will call you to set an appointment, so that we may discuss the advantages of listing your home with The Real Estate Company Please do not hesitate to call me. My card is enclosed for your convenience. I hope to see you soon.

Sincerely,
The Real Estate Company

by: Your Name Here,
REALTOR®, CRS, GRI

P.S. Here is a recent picture that I took of your home. I think that it came out quite nicely. I will have it duplicated and ready for mailing to my initial target market by the time I see you.

Letter/e-mail – Expired Listing

Dear Mr. and Mrs. Seller:

I have watched your property through the Multiple Listing Service and on the Internet. It appears that your listing has expired. Here is a sample of how your home would look on our site, www.mysite.com. This is only a sample and only available for you to see, so make certain to use your password MYNAME when you see the "how would I look here" symbol on my site.

If you would like me to market your property, I would be happy to discuss our marketing system. Marketing your home involves much more than just the MLS and the Net.

I did see your home when I previewed it for a prospective buyer a few weeks ago and I have some ideas on how I can help you market it more effectively. Please keep in mind that while your home is not the right home for every buyer, there are ways to stage a home for marketing that will enhance its special features.

Selling homes is my profession. Every day I assist people with getting *the price that they select* in *the shortest amount of time* with *the least amount of difficulty*. It is the way in which I feed my family each and every day. I am committed to finding buyers for sellers and sellers for buyers. Not only is this my full-time job, but more often than not I am working overtime through evenings and weekends to get the job done. I believe in Open Houses, community advertising, specialty advertising and "target marketing" to the group of potential buyers that will be able to afford your home. In addition, in this connected world, I find that an effective World Wide Web campaign can encourage buyers and other REALTORS® to show and sell your home.

Enclosed is my personal reference list of satisfied sellers and buyers for your perusal. You will notice many of your neighbors have successfully sold or bought homes with my assistance. Please feel free to call any of the families listed. They will be happy to give you candid answers to any questions you may have.

We have several buyer agents working almost exclusively with buyers. That gives our company the advantage of having ready, willing and qualified buyers for whom your home may be the perfect fit. With both an inventory of homes as well as buyers looking for homes, you can understand that The Real Estate Company sells homes.

Please expect a call from me, so that we may arrange an appointment to discuss the advantages of listing your home with The Real Estate Company.

Sincerely,
The Real Estate Company

by: Your Name Here,
REALTOR®, CRS, GRI

The "Captive Seller". Often the real estate licensee thinks that the seller will list with a "captive" broker, one that has a prior relationship with the seller. The rules for keeping the captive seller and taking the captive seller are the same. Follow the general rules of the road at the beginning of the chapter.

Remember, sellers are looking for professionalism. They want a professional broker to represent them in the sale of their property. The way to keep your "close personal friends" your "captive sellers" is to keep in constant professional contact, not just social contact. *Treat close friends like strangers and work hard for their listing. Treat strangers, other people's close personal friends, professionally.*

Have you ever watched a "For Sale" sign go up at a "good friend's" house? That seller listed with someone else for a variety of reasons. Cards, e-mails and letters are fine, but not enough. You should also endeavor to include in your letters information about real estate and the market. Direct prospective sellers to your website.

Be the reliable source of information on interest rate figures, loan descriptions, the escrow process, how to stage a home for optimum exposure, repairs or improvements that will maximize the seller's net profits and experts they can contact for questions beyond your expertise or liability. The more complex and expansive the information, the better the impression will be. Mix in the complex information with the simple, so that the seller is confident beyond any doubt that *you* are the *expert* in the real estate market and the *only source* of information that s/he needs.

The format of your correspondence may be on letterhead in a sealed envelope with a commemorative stamp or on a bulk rate stamped postage card. Just send it! Make sure that you send e-mail on a regular basis also. Lots of people just read e-mail. Make your e-mail current with links to interesting sites that deal with real estate. For some agents a variety of styles works best, and for others having a consistent piece of mail identifies the individual to the seller. As a minimum, place your name and/or picture on the addressee side of the envelope or postcard, so that the seller always notes the correspondence is from you whether it is read or not. Always use a trailer on your e-mail and include links.

Never take anything for granted. Send pictures of the properties that you have for sale. Send pictures of yourself. Send pictures of the sold property that you or someone in your office has sold. Show them that you are "doing real estate."

Never let them see you sweat and never let them see you casual. Even if you are in a pickup truck, act as if you are looking at ranches. People will tell you that you "work too much" and need to "slow down," but they will list with you because you "are in the business everyday."

Property Management.   Offering to manage property can be a lucrative source of sellers. If you do not wish to manage rental property, you might consider a referral arrangement with property managers who do not like to list and sell property, but like to manage it.

The key to converting landlords into sellers is the property management contract. Is it a given that you will get the listing? Some people think so. However, there is no guarantee. The property management contract should have a clause addressing the potential sale during the management period and provide for a listing opportunity after the management contract expires.

Caution. *There is a potential anti-trust violation with "tying"– a contract for the sale of one product or service on the condition or contingency that another product or service will be sold if you are found to be a "market power." Each product should be sold or offered separately without a condition or contingency requiring the consumer to buy the second product or service.*

The commission structure should have one fee if there is a package including the subsequent listing and another if the fee covers just management. In other words, you can have a fee for management and a fee for listing and a third fee for both. Each must be commercially reasonable. The owner will select the third option because s/he likes you and not just for the amount that you charge.

Rule. *Breach of a fiduciary duty forfeits the entire commission. The Plaintiff need not show they were damaged or lost money, only that you breached your fiduciary duty.*

Not only would it be improper, but it would be a breach of a fiduciary duty to attempt to procure a commission from the sale of property during the property management period if listing or selling the property were not a part of the property management contract. When you enter into the property management contract, insert a clause that protects the managing broker.

Clause:
1. The broker, as partial consideration for managing the property, reserves the right to list the property for a period of _____ months after the termination of

the property management agreement pursuant to the terms of the attached listing contract.

-or-

2. During the term of this property management agreement, owner shall be obligated to pay broker a commission upon any sale of the Property. Such commission arrangement shall be as set forth on the attached listing agreement.

3. As consideration for managing the property at the reduced rate of _____%, Owner grants Broker the exclusive right to list the property pursuant to the terms of the attached listing contract, upon expiration of this management agreement.

Broker Liability

The broker, being responsible for the entire world and, very often, for several well-meaning salespersons, is concerned that the new potential seller understand several principles at the start of what could be a lasting relationship. In most states the listing is the property of the broker, and the broker is personally liable not only for his own actions and inactions, but also for that of the salespersons whose licenses hang under the broker's license.

To that end, the broker wants to make sure that the potential client understands several legal principles and the procedures followed by the broker's firm. Most importantly, the broker desires to limit the apparent authority of the salesperson in the client's eye by defining the extent of such authority early in the relationship.

A nice cover letter or e-mail from the broker before the initial contact by the agent, or immediately thereafter, can accomplish these objectives. If you have a firm brochure or printed statement that can accompany this letter, the letter should include a specific reference to the brochure and the pertinent disclaimer clause or the firm policy statement. Include in your brochure a statement that the broker is the only person that can bind the company by entering into guaranteed sales, establishing commissions, etc., so that it is there for all to see.

The Farm Letter of Introduction

As the salesperson goes out into the field in search of a listing, it would be helpful if he had a letter of introduction to the owner. Specific wording which designates the limitations of the salesperson's ability to bind the company can be included, so that a pattern is established early in the agency relationship. A simple short letter will do. A series of letters could incorporate many additional topics.

This letter of introduction must be one page or less. Try to make the paragraphs short and simple. Start each paragraph with a sentence that immediately grabs the reader's attention. This is the most important line of the paragraph. Use bold type if necessary. If the reader is just skimming the content he will read the bold or italics portion no matter what. However, be cautious about overusing bold and italics or else it will lose its significance and the letter will look too much like a furniture advertisement!

Read and reread your introductory letters. They can be improved over and over again. Watch for redundant statements. Try to make them as personal as possible without sounding generic. Make them as specific as you can to the target market area.

Once the salesperson has made the contact, follow-up with an initial letter from the broker, the salesperson or another salesperson in the office. Talk about the seller's property if there is a potential listing. Otherwise, be thankful and appreciative for his/her time and leave the door open for future contact and business.

Do you believe it will be hard to get your broker to write a letter? Type the letter on the word processor. Insert the new potential seller's name, modify the letter to talk about the specific house and print it ready for the broker's signature. You can mail it. Brokers, sign the letters for your salespeople. Make the letter a standard letter that a salesperson can modify to suit a particular area or project. This system works!

Tip.   *Introductory and follow-up letters are good for the broker also. They limit the liability of the broker for actions of the salesperson/broker associate. They eliminate stress for the salesperson when confronted by the seller about commissions, guaranteed sales, etc.*

Style.   *This is your first letter to this couple. The inside address should have both first names and both last names. Some spouses resent being considered an* *appendage and want their own recognition. The start of the letter should not say Sam and Sandy because we do not know them that well yet.*

Leave a professional impression. It will last longer than the content of the letter. Follow-up with a personal contact as soon as possible.

Web.   *Use the web to impress the potential buyer. Show some fantastic houses with a link, so that they will go there and want their house to be appear there also. Think about a temporary custom site just for them that they access with YOUR NAME as the password. The limited time to visit the site will generate curiosity and a prompt visit.*

Commercial/Industrial. Do not be fooled. A letter of introduction here is critical. The commercial salesperson/broker needs to overcome the affinity between the potential seller and his/her friends. Introductory letters or references are the key. The more personal the letter, the better. Collect letters of introduction from past clients and keep them on file. Letters addressed "To Whom it May Concern" will come in handy in the future.

Remember to mention agency. Most commercial sellers and buyers think of the salesperson that is working with them as "their agent." Mention it often. Also mention your In-Company Sale Policy when you can. Your competition may have no concept of how a proper In-Company sale policy operates.

Letter/e-mail – Introduction of Salesperson to Owner

Mr. Samuel Seller
Mrs. Sandra Seller
4750 Table Mesa Drive
Boulder, CO 80305

Re: 4750 Table Mesa Drive, Boulder

Dear Mr. and Mrs. Seller:

This is to introduce Katherine "Kathy" Reece. She is a salesperson with The Real Estate Company. Kathy has been in real estate for many years and knows the market well. I am very lucky to have her as a member of this office. I have attached a copy of her personal brochure for your review.

Kathy is looking for those individuals who might be interested in a complimentary market evaluation, or comparative market analysis, to determine if it makes sense to sell at this time. Please let Kathy know if you are interested in receiving an analysis of your home when she comes to your home. If not, thank you for your time. In any event, I am sure that you will enjoy meeting Kathy. She knows this area of town quite well.

The Real Estate Company offers services to buyers as buyer agents and to sellers as seller agents. Since we sell a large number of our listings ourselves, ask Kathy about our "In-Company" sale policy.

I supervise each listing and sale personally. In order to grant our salespeople more time for real estate, all contracts that bind The Real Estate Company are signed by me as broker.

Sincerely,
The Real Estate Company

by: Your Name Here,
REALTOR®, CRS, GRI

Letter/e-mail – Introduction of Salesperson to Owner #2

Mr. Samuel Seller
Mrs. Sandra Seller
4750 Table Mesa Drive
Boulder, CO 80305

     Re: 4750 Table Mesa Drive, Boulder

Dear Mr. and Mrs. Seller:

     This is to introduce Katherine "Kathy" Reece. She is a salesperson with The Real Estate Company. Kathy has been in real estate for ten years and knows the market well. I have attached a copy of her personal brochure for your review. I consider myself very fortunate to have her as a member of this office.

     Kathy is looking for those individuals who might be interested in a complimentary market evaluation, or comparative market analysis, to determine if it makes sense to sell at this time. When she comes to your home, please let her know if you are interested. If not, thank you for your time. In any event, I am certain that you will enjoy meeting Kathy. She knows this area of town quite well.

     The Real Estate Company offers services to buyers as buyer agents and to sellers as seller agents. Since we sell a large number of our listings ourselves, ask Kathy about our "In-Company" sale policy. In addition, we have a fully staffed tax deferred exchange department. Tax deferred exchanges allow people with real estate, such as rental property, raw ground and investment property, to sell now, close now, select a new property now, close on the new property in the future and pay the taxes later.

     I supervise each listing and sale personally. This allows our salespeople more time for real estate. All contracts that bind The Real Estate Company are signed by me as the broker. Thank you for taking the time to read this letter. The Real Estate Company looks forward to meeting your real estate needs.

                     Most Sincerely,
                     The Real Estate Company

Letter/e-mail – Introduction Broker Follow-up

Mr. Samuel Seller
Mrs. Sandra Seller
4750 Table Mesa Drive
Boulder, CO 80305

    Re: 4750 Table Mesa Drive, Boulder

Dear Mr. and Mrs. Seller:

    Thank you taking the time to meet and talk with Katherine Reece the other day. She came back with rave reviews about your home. I can hardly wait for the office preview. I know that some of the salespeople around here are already talking about your property to others.

    Should you decide to sell and select The Real Estate Company and Kathy to assist you, we will work hard to ensure that the marketing and sale efforts produce results. As the broker, I am personally responsible for each transaction and take each one very seriously. If there is anything I can do to assist you in the listing stage, please feel free to call me at my office or home number. My business card is enclosed for your convenience.

    I look forward to meeting you when we have our company preview. Again, thank you for taking the time to talk to Kathy.

                Most Sincerely,
                The Real Estate Company

                by: Mr. Right, Broker
                right@therealestatecompany.com

Letter/e-mail – After Contact/Broker Associate

Mr. Samuel Seller
Mrs. Sandra Seller
4750 Table Mesa Drive
Boulder, CO 80305

Re: 4750 Table Mesa Drive, Boulder

Dear Mr. and Mrs. Seller:

Thank you taking the time to meet and talk with Kathy Reece the other day. She came back with rave reviews about your home. I can hardly wait for the office preview. Kathy has been telling us all about the large fenced yard and the wonderful flowers that are everywhere. The office is already talking about your home. Our salespeople are already trying to think of customers and clients that might be interested in the event we are selected to market your home.

Your home sounds wonderful. I look forward to meeting you when we have our company preview. I work with a lot of buyers. This sounds like a property that I would be happy to introduce to some of them.

Most Sincerely,
The Real Estate Company

by: Mr. Right, Broker
right@therealestatecompany.com

Letter/e-mail – After Initial Contact/Broker

Mr. Samuel Seller
Mrs. Sandra Seller
4750 Table Mesa Drive
Boulder, CO 80305

    Re: 4750 Table Mesa Drive, Boulder

Dear Mr. and Mrs. Seller:

    Thank you taking the time to meet and talk with Kathy Reece the other day. We realize that you are not interested in selling your house at this time. However, it was nice of you to allow Kathy to see the interior of your home.

    We are a full service real estate company and will be here in the future if you should have any questions about real estate. Real estate transactions have become so complicated and seem to be getting more so every day. Selling or buying a home is one of the largest transactions many people enter into in their lives and deserves first rate attention.

    Should you know of someone who is interested in a complimentary market evaluation, of his/her house or is thinking about buying a home, Kathy and I would be happy to provide assistance. She is an exceptional salesperson with a long list of happy clients and customers.

    Again, thank you for taking the time to talk to Kathy Reece. [*Add a personal comment here if you can think of one. A reference to a common hobby or particular event that will cement the contact.*]

            Most Sincerely,
            The Real Estate Company

            by: Mr. Right, Broker
            right@therealestatecompany.com

Taxes – The I.R.S.

Exchanges and Tax Deferred Occupied Property Sales. The public is aware that there are tax advantages available, but most people are unaware as to how they can personally take advantage of the tax code. Many are not even familiar with the fact that a tax deferred exchange applies to real estate held for investment purposes only. Many do not know the rules for limiting or avoiding paying taxes on residential sales. Use your knowledge to your advantage carefully. Send out a series of e-mails or letters dealing with taxes, reaffirming what you said. People appreciate information that comes in a series and look forward to the next article.

Failure to discuss the tax implications of a real estate sale is an area of potential liability to the broker. The seller, listed by an aggressive broker, was not told of the possibilities of an exchange. The property sold. Then the seller was made aware of a large tax bill that was due. Can you imagine, that silly seller wanted to hold the broker responsible?

Tax sales make great follow-up e-mails and letters for brokers and salespeople. Sellers tend to repurchase with the same agent that helped them sell the property in tax situations.

Exchange. If the property is not owner occupied, a tax deferred exchange under Section 1031 of the Internal Revenue Code must be mentioned to the owner of the property. These transactions are a great source of business. The results may be not one sale, but two, and maybe a lot more.

Personal Residence Sale. Personal residences do not qualify for tax deferred exchanges. Remember to know the rules for occupancy prior to sale, and only refer people to a C.P.A. for tax advice. Taxes are a critical factor in the ordinary residential sale. Remember that the treatment of the sale of a property owned by an unmarried couple can require consultation with a tax expert, not you. The rules change from year to year, so make sure that you know the current system for the deferral of gain on the sale of a personal residence.

Letter/e-mail – Tax Deferred Exchange Commercial Solicitation

Mr. Samuel Seller, President
The IBM Corporation
4750 Table Mesa Drive
Boulder, CO 80305

Re: 1640 Townsend, Montrose

Dear Mr. Seller:

Allow me to introduce myself. I am Oliver Frascona, broker of The Real Estate Company. Our firm specializes in commercial real estate and investments. One of my salespeople, Kathy Reece is looking for properties that may be ready to come on the market.

Kathy Reece has ten years of experience in the real estate business. I have attached her personal brochure for your review. She has decided to actively search for new listings in this market area as we are not able to meet all of our buyers' demands for commercial real estate. We need more listings.

Kathy will be stopping by to meet you when she is in your area this week. I think you would enjoy meeting her if you have a moment. In the event you are unavailable at that time, she will leave a copy of our company brochure which gives a synopsis of the services we offer to our commercial clients, as well as a biographical sketch of her real estate career. We can appreciate your busy schedule. Therefore, if time does not permit you to talk with Kathy and you desire to have Kathy evaluate your property, please call her directly at (303) 494-3000 ext. 63 for a complimentary market evaluation.

You may wish to examine the benefits of a tax deferred exchange. Ask Kathy to explain the mechanics that may allow you to sell your present property, then select a replacement property and close on it in the future with little or no current tax liability. Does this sound too good to be true? It is called a 1031 Tax Deferred Exchange. These are rapidly becoming standard in the commercial real estate industry.

Thank you for taking a minute to read this letter.

Letter/e-mail – Tax Deferral for Personal Residence

Mr. Samuel Seller
4750 Table Mesa Drive
Boulder, CO 80305

    Re: 2340 Hillsdale Way, Boulder

Dear Mr. Seller:

Did you ever wish that you could sell your home, keep some of the money and then buy a new one for a greater or lesser value and not pay taxes now? The current tax law allows just that sort of situation. While I am not a C.P.A. or tax attorney, I can show you how to use the current tax code to assist you in selling your home and buying a new, one possibly without having to pay Uncle Sam today.

Interested? Allow me to introduce myself. I am Oliver Frascona, broker of The Real Estate Company We specialize in helping home owners, just like you, move up or down with minimal or no tax impact. We work with your accountant, or ours, to make sure that you understand the rules and regulations that surround the sale of a personal home in a manner to eliminate or minimize the tax impact in the current year.

One of my best brokers, Kathy Reece, is looking for properties that may be ready to come on the market. Kathy Reece has ten years of experience in the real estate business. I have attached her personal brochure for your review, or you can see it on our website www.frascona.com. She has decided to actively search for new listings in this market area as we are not able to meet all of our buyers' demands for residential real estate. We need more listings.

Kathy will be in your area this week. I think you would enjoy meeting her if you have a moment. Talk to her about how you can sell your home and not pay the government in the year of sale. In the event you are unavailable at the time that she is there, she will leave a copy of our company brochure which gives a synopsis of the services we offer.

We can appreciate your busy schedule. Therefore, if time does not permit you to talk with Kathy and you desire to have Kathy evaluate your property, please call her directly at (303) 494-3000 ext. 63 or e-mail her at kathy@frascona.com for a complimentary market evaluation.

Sincerely,
The Real Estate Company

by: Your Name Here,
REALTOR®, CRS, GRI

After the Initial Contact

You need to become the "source" for answers about the complex real estate business. You want to leave the seller thinking that if s/he ever has a real estate need s/he will call you. Tell them some of the things that you know.

Not all of the following items need to be addressed in the first letter, but they will serve as a checklist of items that need to be addressed sooner or later. Some are mentioned in different letters since putting them all in the first letter could be overwhelming. Different sellers may require more or fewer of these items in the first letter. As these items are discussed, the seller will start to get a feeling about the agent, the broker, the firm and the complexities of modern real estate. This can be a very good marketing tool because the seller begins to realize that this is an area where a professional is a necessity, and that you are just the professional to employ.

ADA: Americans with Disabilities Act. Yes, this act applies to commercial real estate and also to your office and to the service that you provide to people. You as a person are considered a place of public accommodation. Have the name of the local person that does the education and enforcement for the Federal and State government in this area. Know that person and feel free to give out his/her name and phone number to members of the public with questions.

Agency and Apparent Authority. Establish early the fact that the broker exists and is a party to the transaction, that only the broker binds the firm, and that the broker is available for problem-solving and consultation. Also establish early the extent of the agency relationship which is being created and reinforce it often. Itemize exactly what the broker and salesperson will do for the client, what they will *not* do, and what is expected of the client. Limit or eliminate the apparent authority of the salesperson to bind the broker or the firm. This can be an advantage to the broker, firm and salesperson because the seller now knows the limit of the salesperson's authority to make certain decisions and that the salesperson can not bind the broker in most matters.

The actions or inactions of the salesperson or the broker may serve to override the information and disclaimers given at any point in time. Therefore, the constant reference to the extent of authority or lack thereof is important. You can not say it once, act in direct contradiction to the written statements, and hope to be protected.

Tip.   *Conduct speaks louder than promises and will be the ultimate determining factor. Under promise and over deliver.*

Agency Office Policy. This is the written policy discussing how you will represent or assist sellers, buyers, both or neither. It outlines the procedures that your office will follow for a "normal listing" and for "dual agency," "designated agency" or "no-agency" listings. In some states it is a law that your office must have a written agency policy. Whether it is the law in your state or not, composing an office agency policy is an opportunity to out market your competition. Having your company agency policy in nice, readable brochure format available for the salesperson to leave for the public to see will place you far are ahead of the game. Some sample agency policies are included in this book. Feel free to use them after making the appropriate changes to comply with your firm's objectives.

Agency, Subagency Alternatives and Potential Dual Agency. Describe the MLS compensation system to the seller. Let the seller know and understand with whom you will cooperate, how and why. Explain that there might be: *seller's subagents* (at the time of this publication only one state has this option) and what subagency means (seller being liable for the unknown and unsupervised subagent), or *buyer agents* (people who represent the buyer in the transaction for this property), or *non-agents* (licensees, sometimes called *transaction brokers*, who do not have a buyer agency relationship with the buyer, but are working with a buyer to buy your seller's property), or possibly *non-members* (licensees who are not associated with the board of REALTORS®, or in some locations an open MLS system) who pose certain co-operation and compensation issues in the event an MLS member later brings a procuring cause claim.

Review the compensation amounts that will be offered to each category of licensee working with a buyer. Most consumers are unfamiliar with the REALTOR® system of cooperation among agents and brokers working together. Help them understand. The knowledge gained with your thorough explanation will affirm their confidence in you, as well as in the extensive professional REALTOR® network that is available to assist in the sale of their property. Remember, the selling agent is paid for one reason only – he found the buyer the seller hired you to find! This disclosure of your working relationship with cooperating brokers is a big step to limit your liability when an offer comes from another licensee.

Good, concise, clear and simple agency disclosure may even serve as the beginning of your defense in the case when your seller becomes your buyer. What happens when a seller, whose listing you have or have had, asks to see other real estate? What happens when a buyer with whom you have been working wants to buy your listing? Do you now try to explain to your seller that you are no longer working as his/her agent, but are acting in some other capacity?

Make sure that your seller understands in these situations which services he will retain and which services he will no longer be expecting from you. If done properly, when you sell your own listing, the seller will welcome the *in-company, same salesperson, dual agency* or *transaction broker* relationship when it arises. The seller will understand that you have "advanced" to that relationship and welcome the advancement with excitement. The seller turned buyer will know what to expect and will keep you as his/her REALTOR® with understanding and confidence.

Caution. *Giving a full and proper rendition of the subagency alternative when the property is listed may serve to limit future problems. Some brokers may feel there is no real cause for concern. After all the old seller is now a friend, and we all know that friends are "safe" and do not need the normal disclosures that mere customers and clients would receive. Remember, friends are the pool from which plaintiffs are drawn.*

Tip. *The first salesperson that explains agency openly and easily to the seller will get the listing. Let the competition struggle with the concept.*

Agency – Broker's Agent. See subagency above. Similar, but the selling broker in the "other office" is an agent of the Listing Broker, not a subagent of the Seller. This is not a prevalent option and is only used by a handful of states at best.

Anti-Trust and Commissions. Address any anti-trust commission and cooperative split problems if you feel they might be present. Clearly establish the commission policies of the firm. This will make the salesperson's job of presenting or negotiating the commission much easier and will establish that the broker has the right to split the total commission if the broker so desires. It is important for the broker to indicate to the seller early on that the broker retains the exclusive right to determine if there will be a split, the amount of such a split and the terms upon which the broker will pay the cooperating broker.

Occasionally, after the broker has become obligated to a particular cooperating broker, the seller attempts to intervene and change the obligations created through the MLS system by decreasing the amount that the seller feels should be paid to the cooperating broker or eliminating all compensation to that cooperating broker. We would discourage anyone allowing the seller to enter into this area, except in the instance when the buyer uses the services of a buyer's broker at the buyer's expense.

This is an instance where the buyer agent is being paid a commission from the buyer directly, ("buyer agent fee amount") and, as a result, the buyer lowers the price offered to the seller by the "buyer agent fee amount". In addition, the buyer asks the seller to lower the total commission paid to the listing broker by the "buyer agent fee amount" since there will be no cooperative commission paid by the listing broker to the buyer agent. This is why the seller might request a renegotiation of the total listing fee paid to the listing broker who will not be paying a cooperating commission to the selling broker.

Otherwise, the amount offered and paid by the listing broker to the selling broker, buyer agent or otherwise, should be clearly indicated in the listing contract (see our forms for appropriate wording) and subsequently not within the purview of the seller to attempt to eliminate or modify it. It is imperative that the listing broker not be accused of fixing a cooperative commission or excluding or boycotting a cooperating broker.

"Tying" is when one product must be purchased with another product. An easy example would be if you had to buy a toothbrush to get toothpaste. In real estate it is improper to tie two products together. A broker who indicated that you had to re-list with that broker if you bought a raw lot in a subdivision would have anti-trust tying concerns. The buyer/builder should not have to use the listing services of a particular broker in order to buy the raw lot. Mandatory re-list clauses are probably not proper if your firm is a "market power." Seek a written opinion from your anti-trust attorney before you embark on such a course of action.

Brochure. If you do not have a standard brochure or firm position statement, you might consider drafting one along the lines of the model letters in this book. A brochure is a good medium for standardizing the information that is presented to the public before you have the opportunity to correct or clarify it with a cover letter to any one prospect. Remember to limit the authority of the salesperson or agent to bind the company. *Indicate that all contracts that bind the company must be signed by the broker to be enforceable.*

Comparable "Comps". There is constant discussion about whether or not the selling salesperson should, can or must show comps. There is no need for this matter to be the subject of litigation for you someday. In order to solve the problem of potential litigation, address the use of comparables when listing the seller. It is the seller who should grant the permission to show comparables to prospective buyers. After all, the seller is the principal. Frankly, we would not advise the acceptance of a listing that did not provide for the ultimate selling salesperson, whether within the listing office or otherwise, to be able to show comparables to a prospective buyer. We feel that comps are in the same category as zoning, condition of the property and real property taxes. The buying public is probably "entitled" to see comps.

There are three types of comparable properties. First, there are those that are currently listed. Consider physically showing your seller the competition before you agree on the listing price. Second, there are those homes that are already "sold's." If the data is recent and truly comparable, it is the best reflection of the probable price that will attract the buyer in a short period of time. Finally, there are listings that expired. Some people refer to these as "properties that the market rejected," and we feel that is a more correct label. It tells the seller that this price was not the right price for these properties.

Confidential Information. The seller must know what information he can expect to be kept confidential and what information must be disclosed. Here is a simple checklist for information.

Confidential (Seller's "Personal Secrets"/Motivation) Information:
- The seller's bottom line.
- The price of the last counterproposal.
- The final sales price, until the transaction is actually closed.
- The fact that the seller needs to move rapidly.
- That the seller is being transferred out of the area.
- That the seller is sick.
- Any family emergency that affects the seller's ability to negotiate.
- Seller's acquisition of a "new" home.
- The fact that there is a pending divorce.
- The fact that the property is "stigmatized" by either a psychological or other occurrence, such as the proximity of a known sex offender, (Megan's Law).

Not Confidential (Property Condition):
- The fact that the roof leaks.
- The fact that there is water in the neighborhood or basement.
- Any material fact about the property – *a fact of such importance as to influence a reasonable person's conduct.*
- The fact that the highway is being expanded.
- The proximity of an airport or proposed airport expansion.

- The buyer's ability to qualify for the contract as proposed.
- The proximity to high tension lines.
- The proximity of the property to a known or proposed hazardous waste site.
- The fact that the homeowner's association is going to assess everyone.
- The fact that the homeowner's association is in financial trouble.

Clause: Seller Confidential Information – General

1. You are authorized to indicate that this property is in foreclosure. Seller understands that this statement might encourage the buyer to make a lower offer on the property.

-or-

2. You are authorized to indicate that the "seller is desperate" and willing to consider any reasonable offer. Seller understands that this statement might encourage the buyer to make a lower offer on the property.

-or-

3. You may indicate to prospective buyers that we have been transferred and need to sell fast. Seller understands that this statement might encourage the buyer to make a lower offer on the property.

-or-

4. The fact that the seller has been transferred out of the area is well known. Seller authorizes broker to disclose to any prospective buyer who asks why are the seller is selling, that the seller is "being transferred out of the area". Seller understands that this statement might encourage the buyer to make a lower offer on the property.

-or-

5. The seller hereby authorizes the broker to indicate to prospective buyers that the sellers are involved in a divorce action. Seller understands that this statement might encourage the buyer to make a lower offer on the property.

Clause: Seller Confidential Information – Murder or Suicide

1. Please indicate to all prospective buyers that there was a murder in this house on _____. Also provide them with the newspaper article attached to the listing agreement. Seller understands that this statement might encourage the buyer to make a lower offer on the property.

-or-

1. You are authorized to indicate to buyers that the property was the site of a suicide and provide them with the attached explanation that we have prepared. Seller understands that this statement might encourage the buyer to make a lower offer on the property.

- and/or -

2. I understand that such disclosure may result in fewer buyers who may pay less for the property. I also understand that I am not required by state law to make this disclosure. Nevertheless, I want you to make a disclosure to all buyers indicating "................."

Stigmatized Property.   Each state has a different interpretation on this area of the law. Most salespeople have more of an affinity with the buyer than the seller. So they tend to tell the buyer information that may not be in the seller's best interests. Especially if you are acting as a seller's agent, know your local law. The seller with a stigmatized property is a classic plaintiff. The seller wants to keep this information confidential, regardless of what the law may indicate. Use caution to make sure that, even in the office, you do not disclose information regarding a stigma that is not required to be disclosed to other licensees who may potentially be working with, or communicating with, potential buyers.

Example of Colorado's Law (check your state law and know it):

   (1)   *Facts or suspicions regarding circumstances occurring on a parcel of property which could psychologically impact or stigmatize such property are not material facts subject to a disclosure requirement in a real estate transaction. Such facts or suspicions include, but are not limited to, the following:*

      (a)   *That an occupant of real property is, or was at any time suspected to be, infected or has been infected with Human Immunodeficiency Virus (HIV) or diagnosed with Acquired Immune Deficiency*

Syndrome (AIDS), or any other disease which has been determined by medical evidence to be highly unlikely to be transmitted through the occupancy of a dwelling place; or

(b) *That the property was the site of a homicide or other felony or of a suicide.*

(2) *No cause of action shall arise against a real estate broker or salesperson for failing to disclose such circumstance occurring on the property which might psychologically impact or stigmatize such property.*

Due-on-Transfer ("Due on Sale") Clauses. Be careful not to participate in a transfer of a property secured by an FHA or VA loan that contains due-on-transfer clauses without first obtaining the consent of the lender. "Assumable with qualification" is a due-on-transfer loan. Some people think that it is a violation of the law to participate in a transfer over an FHA or VA due-on-transfer clause. Those people work for the enforcement arm of the federal government. You do not need their business.

Earnest Money. He who holds the earnest money will surely be the center of attention when a dispute arises. Almost without exception, there is nothing you can or should do to distribute the money without a written release. You can not make a determination on the merits of each party's application for the funds, nor determine if a default has occurred. That inability to act will put you in an awkward position. Now is the time to explain to the seller the laws relating to earnest money. Point out the contract wording in the sales contract that deals with earnest money. Explain your limits early.

Control of the earnest money may or may not pose a problem. Generally, it is a contract term; therefore, the parties can designate who will retain the earnest money. As the sellers agent, you want control of the money or the direction to designate on your seller's behalf who shall have control. Except for the good relationship you will have with your bank as the result of the funds sitting in your account, there is little benefit in holding earnest money. Title companies are always willing to accept this type of position. In any event, the preferred repository designated by the seller and the minimum amount that the seller requires with any offer need to be discussed. In many states closing instructions and other agreements relieve the broker of the earnest money retention obligation.

Tip. *We would advise you to try to let someone else hold earnest money. Whoever holds the earnest money will certainly be a defendant in any action* *to obtain the earnest money.   Get permission in the listing contract and again in the sales contract to transfer it to the closing company.*

Clause:

The parties agree that the earnest money may be delivered by the broker to the closing agent, if any, at or before closing.

Fair Housing.   Clear the air and establish the rules early with regard to The Fair Housing Law. People, especially testers, appreciate frankness and will respect you for your knowledge of the law.   You are protecting the seller against potential problems as well as yourself.   If there is going to be a problem here, it is better to know it very early.   Do not tolerate even a tacit or "winky-winky" form of discrimination.   You represent "equal access" to real estate.

FHA Interest Proration.   There is no proration for FHA loan payoffs.   Therefore, the seller will pay a full month's interest for any portion of a month that the loan is in effect.   If the transaction is closing at the end of the month, the mortgage payoff funds must be received by the lender before the first business day of the following month in order to avoid another full month of interest.   FHA loan payoffs do not require 30 days prior notification.

Tip.   *When preparing for a closing that results in an FHA loan payoff, make sure you schedule the closing early enough, so that you can make sure that the payoff gets to the lender before the end of the month.*

Financing.   Start the seller thinking about the ever-increasing list of alternatives. Present to the seller the basic description of certain types of financing that are available that may be suggested by potential buyers.   Describe the potential impact of the general forms of financing on the seller and how each of the alternatives likely to arise in this transaction will affect the saleability of the property.   Documenting the discussion of financing is becoming very important, as financing alternatives vary in complexity and in the effect they may have on sellers in varying situations.

Condition of the Property.   The seller, not the broker, is going to represent the condition of the property.   Most firms have an addendum to the listing contract that allows the seller to designate the current condition of the property.   Adding to this a recitation of one's reliance on the seller's representations may provide an incentive to be more specific and accurate and provide the broker with additional protection.   The trend in some states is to hold the broker responsible for defects s/he could have discovered, even though he did not actually discover them or even know of them.

Hazardous Materials. Long considered a "commercial thing," hazardous waste is now a condition to be addressed in both residential real estate and raw land transactions. With the advent of concerns about radon gas, chemical spills, buried waste materials, lead paint, mold, asbestos and the like, it is often impossible for the broker to know what may be lurking below the surface. The only adequate form of protection is to have experts test the premises – much as is done in many parts of the country for termites – and make the report available to potential purchasers before they contract for the property. The alternative is to wait to see if the buyer will require any tests as a condition precedent to closing. However, a lot of time may pass before you know if you have a deal.

Lead Based Paint. For properties that qualify, you should know the federal and state lead based paint disclosure rules. Generally, the listing broker is required to obtain the seller's signature on the form that is to be presented to the buyer prior to there being a contract. The buyer needs to be given the disclosure form signed by the seller and the listing broker, as well as the HUD booklet, prior to a contract being written. HUD and EPA will be glad to assist you with copies of the booklet.

Mold. Mold is a substance that needs only two things to grow – water and heat. If your market area has these two ingredients, mold is growing. The REALTOR® does not want to make an inspection for mold. If there seems to be a mold issue, call a professional. If the presence of mold is discovered, the disclosure law in most states will require that the buyer be advised of the pre-existing condition, and any repairs that were made. Do not scrimp on mold disclosure. Tell only what you know.

Radon. More and more relocation companies are refusing to purchase properties that have not had a radon test. Many times, in order to take advantage of the company buyout program when the buyer later sells, the buyer will require a radon gas test because the existence of a satisfactory inspection prior to his acquiring ownership will be a requirement for later resale. The proper tests need to be encouraged and performed by recognized experts as soon as possible after the listing is signed. Indicating this to the seller before or immediately after obtaining the listing will add to your credibility as an expert, support the correct perception that marketing a home is complex, and protect you from later – sometimes years later – having to explain why you did not test the property. Such tests are generally a seller's expense; therefore, extracting the money to pay for the test or having the seller agree to pay the tester directly is important.

Tip.   *Do not advance money for anyone. Ever!*

Soil Condition. Much as with the tests for hazardous materials, a soils test or report may alleviate a lot of problems later on. A report from a soils engineer in most states is not too expensive and should be encouraged. If any damage is evident, an inspection and a report indicating what action is recommended should be strongly encouraged. Structural damage that is a result of a soil condition will become a condition later on and possibly result in lost marketing time during a prime season. It goes without saying that the report must be given to all prospective purchasers before they are under contract.

Structural Integrity vs. Mechanical Integrity. Engineers are the experts with regard to the structural integrity of the dwelling. Generally, they do not approve the physical or operating condition of the various mechanical devices located on the property. Mechanical inspections and the subsequent insurance are available from a variety of competitors. The buyer and seller often operate under the misconception, convenient or innocent, that the mechanical inspection also covers the structure. Clear recommendations indicating the talents and scope of the different classes of inspectors and their resultant coverage will limit the valid future claims of a buyer looking for either a way out of the transaction or someone to help with the monthly payments.

Inspections, Engineers and Home Warranties. The use of inspectors to limit the broker's and salesperson's liability for all sorts of potential problems, although not mandatory, is certainly a recommended practice. Acquainting the seller early on with the idea that various other professionals will be required to complete the transaction serves to indicate areas that are not within the purview of the agency relationship and not among the list of tasks that the real estate firm provides. The cost, the availability of home warranty services and the extent of their coverage need to be explained at the outset of the relationship.

Liability for the Premises and Open Houses. Explain the limits of the company's liability and the need to make an inventory of property of unusual value. Give a review of the people who will seek access to the property and the measures that are in place to restrict, limit, or supervise such access. The fact that the broker will not be responsible for anything except gross negligence must be presented.

Discuss the office "Open House" policy and its beneficial use as a marketing tool. Acknowledge the quiet concern people have about having other people in their home. Strangers and neighbors who have not before had access to the home will now potentially have access and possibly become aware of personal items. Present the benefits, liabilities and potential problems and let the client decide. Be clear that the client can always reserve the decision for a later time.

Liability and Lockboxes.   Present the lockbox system used by your office and the possible security problems that exist with any listing that utilizes the lockbox system. People will appreciate your care for their possessions.   Although it may be a system with substantial problems, such as a system with one key for all boxes or one that uses boxes easily opened or destroyed by unauthorized people, it may be a marketing necessity.   The decision to use a lockbox must be clearly the seller's.   If you have a superior system in operation for your company, this would be a good time to point out its comparative advantages.   Still, however, explain the limits of the company's liability.

High technology security and customer tracking has come to the lockbox industry. There are now several lockboxes on the market that are fully electronic.   The keys can be about the size of two books of matches, or look a lot like a credit card or hotel key, and allow the listing broker to track who was in the property and at what time.   There is no need to do anything except let the key read the box and then let the telephone read the key.   Yes, you can limit access during specified times.   Yes, you can ensure that illegal access does not occur as a result of the key being in the possession of an unauthorized user.   The code expires every thirty days.   Authorized users must call an 800 number for an updated code which is good only for the particular key.   Each box can retain almost a hundred showing appointments.

Mortgage Insurance Premiums (MIP).   With the advent of prepaid FHA mortgage insurance, sellers and buyers need to make some decisions about how to incorporate the mortgage insurance premiums into the transaction.   Whether it should be prorated or included as a part of the purchase price – especially in a transaction that calls for an assumption of an existing policy – can mean a substantial amount of money for the seller to receive and from which the buyer must part.   Adequately explaining the alternatives and effects of each selection, as well as the method of proration, is important.   As the amount of the insurance premium comes closer and closer to the total commission, your portion of the commission becomes an obvious source of funds for adjustment in the event of a dispute.

Multiple Listing Service (MLS).   *The Magic Listing Service.*   Explain the broker's membership in, access to, and the operation of the Multiple Listing Service.   Some people still think that the information in the MLS is confidential.   We all know that is no longer true.   Some people wonder if it ever was.   It has never ceased to amaze us that the MLS was thought to be confidential, and yet everyone spent money to advertise the same information in various promotional brochures that are given away to the public.   Also indicate that, although the information in the MLS is for brokers' use, it could be relied upon by the public and therefore must be accurate.   It is the broker's desire that the listing be accurate to the last detail. Encourage the seller's review of the MLS information sheet, which is attached to some states' listing contracts, in order to establish that it accurately presents the facts about the property.

Pricing. The broker should never set the price. One broker used to place a deposit slip on the office wall when she obtained the listing. Her sales presentation was based on the premise "*I sell all of my listings. If you want to test the market, list with someone else. If you want to sell, list with me.*" The advantage was that she wasted very little of her money on listings that did not sell.

The price that you will allow the seller to ask and still accept the listing is a very sensitive area. If you establish the price, you may be liable for its determination. You may also lead the seller to believe that you are an appraiser, and that may set you up for future liability if the market proves you wrong. Therefore, we discourage the broker or the salesperson from attempting to establish the price. If you utilize a "Comparative Market Analysis," make certain that it includes a disclaimer similar to this one or as required by your state.

Clause:
> The preparer of this comparative market analysis ("CMA") is not registered, licensed or certified as a real estate appraiser by the state of .... This is not an appraisal.

Some firms have a limit on the amount of what they feel is "blue sky," or overpricing. They are unwilling to work on listings that are priced so high that the property will probably not sell within the listing period and therefore not be worth the effort and expense. Accepting an overpriced listing, failing to service the listing or disparaging it to fellow real estate agents is asking for trouble. Try to capture the listing at a reasonable price, established by the seller, and boost the professional image of the salesperson and firm. This can be accomplished professionally by providing the seller with the information that you have available about comparable sales and current listings, and letting the seller suggest the listing price. At that time you can determine if in fact it is worth your effort.

Case in Point.
A listing broker took Oliver out to view several "competitively priced" properties in his market area. After Oliver had seen several properties, they all seemed to "blend into one," and it was easier to establish the listing price. Later when an offer was presented, Oliver already knew the market as well as the buyer and could counter with a reasonable price. Yes, the home sold. The final result was that

Oliver was pleased with the price "he selected," as well as the overall efforts of his broker.

Tip.   *You decide at what price it makes sense to take the listing and let the seller decide if they want to list with you.*

One method for educating the seller about the fair market value of his property is to show him other active listings that are similar to his home in the neighborhood.

Personal Property.   So often the broker is on the dime to account for property that was "taken" by the seller after closing. Try to eliminate the risk. We suggest that you take a steno pad or PDA as you go through the house and ask the Seller to be specific about what will remain with the home.

Tip.   *Ask the potential buyer, "If you bought this house would you want the bookshelves, etc.?" As the prospect answers for each major item that you notice on the showing, make a note. Then when you are ready to write the contract, you can list all the property, attached or not, that is included or excluded.*

Jury Talk.
Imagine the attorney for the buyer saying these words to the jury. "Personal property is not covered by the statute of frauds. You are here today to award the buyers, people just like you, who relied upon the broker [buyer agent] to protect them. They trusted their agent and now it is time to make good on those words "we will take care of you and protect you."

Purchasing for Your Own Account.   The seller will never see the sale to a broker as an arm's length transaction. He will always think that the broker had superior market knowledge and took advantage of him. Buying for your own account is very risky. Some offices prohibit it. You only do it because the property is a good deal, and you know it. You know it is a good deal because you think that you can resell it at a profit later.

Rule.   *Self dealing in general is not a good idea. Using the information gleaned while an agent of your seller, to purchase from your seller, your principal, is a breach of your fiduciary duty to the seller.*

Tip.   *If you think that you or someone in your office might like to purchase listed property, reserve the right to buy for your own account when you list, as a term of the listing.*

Caution. *An agent trying to self-deal with a client is the most dangerous type of arrangement. Attorneys get disbarred for such activity.*

The suggestions in this section anticipate your using an attorney to assist the seller. Yes, that means that the attorney may destroy your proposed transaction. There is a hint! Remember, the seller was a former client and relied upon you for advice. Also remember that it was your interest that made all these problems arise. If at all possible, buy it before you list it.

Once you start the listing process you are on the inside. From that point forward, you must treat the potential seller/client as an actual seller/client. The fact that it is not listed yet is irrelevant. While seeking the listing you became privy to the seller's confidential information. Now you must treat this seller just like any other purchase of a company listing.

Tip.   *When listing a particular property and reviewing the terms that are proposed for a particular buyer, Katherine tells the potential seller, "I have just become the buyer, not a listing agent. Let me write a sales contract, not a listing agreement. Take it to your attorney for approval, and this property is SOLD."*

We have provided some rather stringent measures to help assuage your potential risk:
1. Help the seller with the additional legal and appraisal expenses associated with your attempts to purchase the property.
2. Take the process seriously and follow all the steps.
3. Give the seller the chance to get out any time prior to closing.
4. Provide for the seller's attorney to approve the transaction in advance.

Jury Talk.
Imagine the Seller, now plaintiff, telling the jury this story. "We trusted the broker to list our house. Everyone said he was the best. Little did we know that he would not sell our house just so that we would have to sell it at a discount to him after all. He failed in his efforts to sell it because he wanted to buy it from us. He had us so fooled that we actually begged him to buy it. Of course, he knew that we had to close on our new house or lose our deposit."

If your firm allows both buyer representation and seller representation, agents to purchase properties listed with the firm, or other transactions that provide potential conflicts of interest, this is the time to explain in specific detail exactly what the relationship will be in such an event.   Sample dual agency forms and forms that provide for the purchase of a property for one's own account are found in this book.

REALTOR®.   Professional affiliation *is* the difference.   To be a member of the National Association of REALTORS® means that the licensee has agreed to adhere to a strict Code of Ethics. A REALTOR® is a dedicated professional who keeps attuned to the changes in the real estate industry, both locally and nationally. Many complete rigorous educational courses to develop their skills and knowledge and earn special certifications such as the GRI and CRS.   Being a REALTOR® is a commitment to the Code, to arbitration of disputes between REALTORS® and clients, to continuing education and to the protection of the public's right to own and dispose of property.   It is a commitment to excellence. REALTORS® *participate* in real estate; they do not just sell it. Any correspondence to potential clients or customers or to the public at large should always contain the REALTOR® logo and the advantages of having a REALTOR® to guide them successfully through all phases of the transaction.

Tax Deferred Exchange.   With the codification of the rules for tax deferred exchanges, they have become a practical alternative for everyone. No longer are they available only for those who could afford expensive attorneys, these exchanges are open for all to enjoy. The difference in the tax bill is amazing. With this ease of use comes an obligation on the part of the real estate professional, residential or commercial, to know the basics of a tax deferred exchange.

Rule 1 – The property must be "like-kind" which means real estate. Yes, you can trade a commercial property for a piece of vacant ground or an apartment house for a turkey farm. A homeowner who has a rental property can trade it for anything that is real estate. No, you can not trade an owner occupied residence for anything. No, you can not trade a "partnership interest" for another "partnership interest" even if that interest entitles you to occupy a particular property for some defined period of time (used in some time shares). You need a fee interest to take advantage of this IRS code section.

Rule 2 – You do not have to trade "simultaneously." The taxpayer, seller, can sell the property you have listed, leaving the money in escrow, and select another property that you help them buy. Whose agent are you now?

Rule 3 – They must target the replacement property within 45 days of the first closing date. The deadline for identifying a replacement property is calculated from the closing date, not the contract date. The property to be sold could be under contract for a few months, and there still remains 45 days to identify another property.

Rule 4 – They must close on the replacement property within 180 days of the first sale. Who better to help them than you?

Rule 5 – You are probably not a tax accountant or a tax attorney. Let that person do the tax advice and you deal with the real estate. You get paid and they run the risk of getting sued.

Rule 6 – Never indicate "tax free." Always refer to the potentially "tax deferred" exchange.

Clause:

1. Broker shall offer the property under the terms: "Seller will cooperate with a tax deferred exchange."

2. Broker has advised Seller to contact a professional of Seller's choosing to review the prospects of a Section 1031 of the Internal Revenue Code, tax deferred exchanges.

3. Broker has advised Seller that Broker is not a tax expert. Seller should seek a competent attorney or Certified Public Accountant to investigate the possibility of a tax deferred exchange under Section 1031 of the Internal Revenue Code.

4. Seller may be able to defer taxes on all or part of the gain realized by the sale of this property. Broker is not the source of such advice. Seller should seek competent counsel to determine if such a savings or deferral is possible.

5. Seller shall cooperate with any buyer desiring to facilitate a tax-deferred exchange so long as it is not to the economic detriment of Seller.

Company Office Policy

General Provisions

In order to better serve the public, our customers and clients, we have adopted the following policy for our business. Each salesperson needs to be familiar with and follow these procedures.

The Company is committed to providing professional service for all sellers, buyers, landlords and tenants whom we elect to serve without regard to race, creed, color, religion, sex, national origin, familial status, marital status or disability (handicap). Our primary function is to assist the public with the acquisition, disposition and leasing of real property.

In addition, we are strong supporters of the right of all people to work at our firm. We do not discriminate in our employment procedures and practices. Moreover, this office is committed to providing an environment free of sexual harassment for all people who work in, or visit, our office.

This Company consists of a licensed real estate broker, sometimes referred to as the "designated" or "employing" broker, and licensed salespersons, including salespersons who have broker's licenses (broker associates or associate brokers) and who have elected to operate in a salesperson's capacity and hang their licenses under the broker. In the event that we have multiple offices or locations, now or in the future, all locations are considered as a single entity. Each office is not a separate company or brokerage company. It is a separate branch of a single entity.

"The Company," or "The Brokerage Firm", is defined to include all licensees and the broker. By law, we are all "fingers on the hand of the broker," a single entity, and all listings belong to, and are in the name of, the broker. If The Company is, or becomes a part of, a franchise, then "The Company" only refers to our franchised office(s), as a single entity, and not those owned by other franchisees. This is true even if we offer "designated agency," "split agency" or "designated brokerage."

When any licensee accepts a listing for a seller's house or a listing for a buyer, a "Company Listing," the entire Company becomes the agent of the seller or buyer [alternatively, only that agent becomes the agent of the buyer or seller. This is called "designated agency."]. The "Broker" means the broker of record with the state regulatory agency that is in charge of the office. In a large multi-office company, "Broker" shall mean the broker or managing broker for each individual office.

In the event a member of the public asks to have a copy of this policy, any salesperson may, after checking with the Broker, provide that person with a current copy.

The Company is proud to be committed to the letter and spirit of the Federal, State and Local Fair Housing law, rules and regulations. Regardless of the capacity in which we serve, we will always work for "equal access" to all property and employment at our firm for all people.

List specific provisions that only apply in your office.

Subject Matter Cover Letters

The following are sample cover letters for specific topics. Not everyone will use every letter. Some may be consolidated and some done in a series. They may be written by the broker to all listings on a once a month basis, or sent by the salesperson on a listing by listing basis. Remember if you want them to read it, keep it short. If you do not want them to read it, make it long.

These letters are not only intended to provide information to the prospective seller but also to impress upon him that real estate is for professionals only. Each talks about a different aspect of a proposed transfer that is second nature to the listing broker or salesperson. However, for someone who does not deal in real estate on a daily basis ie., a potential for sale by owner, the topics addressed may amount to several good reasons to list with you.

Part of your efforts is to list the property for sale. In addition, you do a lot of work after the sale to get things closed. Many prospective sellers discount those efforts. These letters emphasize all the aspects of real estate transactions. In order to save space these letters will not be reproduced in a later section. A simple revision should suffice to use them after the listing is signed, or even during a pending transaction.

Letter/e-mail – Agency Alternatives
[Sent by the Broker]
(Subagency/Buyer Agency/Transaction Broker or other non-agent system)

Mr. Sam Seller and
Mrs. Sandy Seller
4750 Table Mesa Drive
Boulder, CO 80305

    Re: 4750 Table Mesa Drive, Boulder

Dear Sam and Sandy:

It is my desire that each seller be fully aware of the agency options that are available. While Kathy either has explained or will explain them to you, and give you a copy of the state mandated agency disclosure form and our company office policy, I want to take a moment to drop you a letter since this is a very important issue.

This firm lists property as agents of the seller. That means that we represent you in the sale of your property. In addition we represent buyers looking for property as buyer's agents. A good example would be when you go out with Kathy to look for your next home. In that event we would probably be acting on your behalf as your buyer agent. Yes, there is a separate listing agreement. Kathy will probably give it to you when she lists your home as a seller's agent. In this firm we like all agreements to be written, so that everyone knows what to expect from each other.

Other firms become exposed to your home as the result of our advertising in various publications, through marketing meetings and breakfasts, as a result of the Multiple Listing Service, or *Magic Listing Service* as I like to call it, and as a result of the efforts of all the salespeople in the firm. We need to make sure that we offer these "cooperating" firms some direction as to the types of agency offering we will acknowledge. There are essentially these choices:

First, Subagents. Subagents work with a buyer but represent you, the Seller, and owe you duties of utmost good faith, loyalty and fidelity. Unfortunately, you may be vicariously liable for the acts of these Subagents when they are acting in the scope of the agency relationship. That is why we carry malpractice insurance.

[Check your state law, some states still have subagency, but without vicarious liability. A few others now have "Broker's agents."]

Second, [use in states where it is applicable only] Transaction Brokers. These are people licensed to sell real estate that are not your subagent, not my agent [broker's agents] and not buyer's agents. They simply have a real estate license and are assisting, not representing, buyers in the purchase of real estate.

Third, Buyer Agents. Buyer Agents represent the Buyer and owe duties of utmost good faith, loyalty and fidelity to the Buyer only. Do not worry. We will not let them know any confidential information about you and your sale. (Examples of confidential information would include that you are in a divorce, need to sell and move with a job transfer or are buying a new house through our office.) We provide only the information regarding the physical condition of the property to every cooperating broker. The good news is that you are not vicariously liable for the acts of buyer agents. Although buyer agents work with the Buyer, we agree to pay them a portion of our commission to encourage them to show and sell your home. In a similar manner, when we are acting as your agent for the purchase of your next house, we will try to collect our fee from that seller.

In most cases the cooperative broker, regardless of what designation she claims, is much more closely aligned with the buyer anyway. It is important to be careful about the information you make available to those that you might meet at the property site or encounter during a showing. We encourage you not to meet and talk with prospective buyers, as you might give them or their agent information that they could use to your detriment. This often happens when the buyer asks an innocent question such as, "Were you transferred?" Sometimes it is hard to answer without giving away information that should remain confidential.

It is for that reason that we want you to know that any inquiry about your home, from anyone, should be referred to us immediately. We will step in and protect that vital personal information and assist that buyer with a showing and offer. In this manner we save you from being bombarded with questions that will demure your bargaining position.

In our office we have _____ types of agents [and non-agents]. In fact, it may be one of our salespersons acting as a buyer agent that sells your house. In that situation we follow our "In-Company" sale policy. Kathy will provide you with a copy for attachment to the listing contract. We want you to be fully aware of how we assist both parties in order to get your house sold for a price, and on terms, that you select and with which you are happy.

Finally, in an effort to procure as many qualified buyers as possible, we shall seek assistance from and offer compensation to brokers, licensed by any state, located outside our market area, in the form of a "referral fee..." While nobody seems to know, we do not consider these referring brokers as subagents of the seller, nor do we accept liability for their conduct. They are simply licensed brokers who are paid a referral fee to send a buyer to us for your home. There is no additional charge to you. We simply absorb that "referral fee" cost.

Sincerely,
The Real Estate Company

by: Your Name Here,
REALTOR®, CRS, GRI

Letter/e-mail – Agency Alternatives (No Subagency/Buyer Agency)

Mr. Sam Seller and
Mrs. Sandy Seller
4750 Table Mesa Drive
Boulder, CO 80305

    Re: 4750 Table Mesa Drive, Boulder

Dear Sam and Sandy:

It is our desire that each seller be fully aware of the agency options that are available. While Kathy either has explained or will explain them to you, and give you a copy of the state mandated agency disclosure form and our company office policy, I want to take a moment to drop you a letter since this is a very important issue.

This firm lists property as agents of the seller. That means that we represent you in the sale of your property. In addition we represent buyers looking for property. A good example would be when you go out with Kathy to look for your next home. In that event we would probably be acting on your behalf as your buyer agent. Yes, there is a separate listing agreement. Kathy will probably give it to you when she lists your home as a seller's agent. In this firm we like all agreements to be written, so that everyone knows what to expect from each other.

Other firms may become exposed to your home as the result of our advertising in various publications, through marketing meetings and breakfasts, as a result of the Multiple Listing Service, and as a result of the efforts of all the salespeople in the firm. We need to make sure that we offer these "cooperating" firms some direction as to the types of agency offering we will acknowledge. There are essentially two choices:

First, Subagents. Subagents work with a buyer but represent you, the Seller, and owe you duties of utmost good faith, loyalty and fidelity. Unfortunately, you may be vicariously liable for the acts of these Subagents when acting in the scope of the agency relationship. That is why we do not offer compensation and co-operation to subagents. We will always pay a referral fee, described later, to any licensed real estate broker if he procures a buyer for your property. ***We simply can*** *not agree to be liable nor to subject you to the liability of a subagent whom we know nothing about.*

Second, Buyer Agents. Buyer Agents represent the Buyer and owe duties of utmost good faith, loyalty and fidelity to the Buyer only. Do not worry. We will not let them know any confidential information about you and your sale. We provide only the information regarding the physical condition of the property to every cooperating broker. The good news is that you are probably not vicariously liable for the acts of buyer agents. Although buyer agents work with the Buyer, we agree to pay them a portion of our commission to encourage them to show and sell your home. In a similar manner, when we are acting as your agent for the purchase of your next house, we will try to collect our fee from that seller.

In most cases the cooperative broker is much more closely aligned with the buyer anyway. It is important to be careful about the information you make available to those that you might meet at the property site. We encourage you not to meet and talk with prospective buyers as you might give them or their agent information that they could use to your detriment. This often happens when the buyer asks an innocent question such as, "Were you transferred?" Sometimes it is difficult to answer without giving away information that should remain confidential.

In our office we have both seller and buyer agents. In fact, it may be one of our salespersons acting as a buyer agent that sells your house. In that situation we follow our "In-Company" sale policy. Kathy will provide you with a copy for attachment to the listing contract.

In an effort to procure as many qualified buyers as possible, we shall seek assistance from, and offer compensation in the form of a referral fee to, brokers licensed by any state, located within or outside of our market area. A condition of this referral fee is an acknowledgment that the other broker and salespersons are not acting as our agent which would make them your subagents.

We treat all inquiries regarding your property as if they come from a buyer agent. That way you can be assured that no confidential information is unintentionally passed along to a potential buyer for your home. We cooperate with every person we legally can to get your property sold without subjecting this firm or you, our seller, to any additional liability.

Finally, we reserve the right to cooperate and compensate any licensed real estate broker that shows and sells your home, so long as they will agree to bound by the National Association of REALTORS® Arbitration system and rules for determination of "Procuring Cause." This gives the flexibility to compensate as many other brokers as possible to help sell your property.

Most Sincerely,
The Real Estate Company

By: Your Broker, CRS, GRI

Letter/e-mail – Broker to Potential Subagent

Mr. Ed Schmale, Broker
Pacific United Realty
21 North Center Green
Denver, CO 80213

     Re: Subagency Relationship
             Smith Road Property

Dear Ed:

     Thank you for calling this office to inquire about acting as our subagents with regard to the above property. We are offering a commission equal to ____% of the total sales price of the property to the successful subagent who procures the buyer, ready, willing and able to complete the transaction as proposed by the seller, our principal. This obligation to pay you (your broker) such a commission, and the payment of commission itself, are subject to the following terms and conditions:

     First, you are the agent (licensee) who procures the buyer who ultimately purchases the property. To ensure that there is no confusion, the names of all prospective buyers must be submitted to this office, either before you show the property or within twenty-four hours after the scheduled showing. We intend to give those names to the seller, our client, in order to provide protection for both of us in the event that a buyer should try to circumvent our listing agreement.

     Second, our obligation to pay you a commission is predicated upon our receipt of our commission in cash. Should we be forced to accept conditional payment, which we may in our sole discretion elect to do, we will not be obligated to pay you until we are paid. In addition, we shall have no obligation to institute any form of collection procedure, including litigation, to collect the commission due. Should such action be necessary, you will be expected to share, in advance and on demand, in the expense of collection, including attorney's fees for the attorney I select, or forfeit your right to any portion of the proceeds of such an effort.

     Third, that you do not compromise the interests of the seller, our principal, by your actions or inactions. We require that you provide us, in a timely fashion, with any information that you possess as to the financial qualifications of the prospective buyer, his intentions, and the amount that he will ultimately be willing to offer for the property. We understand that you will use your best efforts on behalf of the seller to obtain the highest and best offer possible.

Finally, you agree that you will be bound by the National Association of REALTOR® Ethics and Arbitration Manual ("Manual"), or its successor, as adopted by the National Association, as of the date that your buyer's contract is signed by the seller should there be an issue regarding who is the "Procuring Cause" of the sale. This obligates you to arbitrate in the event that another licensee demands the advertised and agreed "co-op" commission indicating that such claimant is the "procuring cause of the sale" pursuant to the rules and regulations set forth in the Manual. You will be treated, and agree to arbitrate, as if you were a member of the local Board/Association of REALTORS®.

Your acceptance of this proposal is evidenced by your taking any action with regard to the real estate without first giving us a written statement to indicate that you are not accepting the proposal. You will be responsible for your own actions and inactions not consistent with the laws of agency in this state and the terms of this letter.

It is a pleasure to have you as a subagent for the potential sale of this property. Please understand that this commission split is not offered with the intention that you split any listing commissions which you may independently have originated and upon which we become your subagents in the same fashion.

Sincerely,
The Real Estate Company

by: Your Name Here
REALTOR®, CRS, GRI

Letter/e-mail – Other Brokers Rejecting Subagency

Mr./Ms. Other Broker
Super Buyer Realty
30000 Sales Boulevard
Commission, CO 99999-9999

    Re: Compensation Schedule for Cooperating Brokers

Dear Other Broker:

We will pay you if you sell one of our listings. With all the confusion about agency and compensation, we have decided to write to everyone and explain what we think is very good news. It is our desire to cooperate fully with all offices and still limit both the listing broker's risk and the selling broker's risk. I hope that you are as excited about this as we are.

We want to stimulate cooperation and ensure confidence that your office is going to be compensated when you sell one of our listings. This information overrides any information provided in the MLS book.

Listings. We have determined that it is in the best interests of this firm and the sellers that we represent to offer the following compensation alternatives:

1. **Cooperating Brokers and Buyer Brokers or Buyer Agents.** We want to cooperate with everyone possible. In the event that your office is licensed by the state and is not trying to act as our "subagent," we will immediately pay to your office _____% of the final sales price upon receipt of payment in full from the seller. The only requirement is that your office have a licensed broker. That is all that it takes. You do not need to be a buyer broker, buyer agent or represent anyone. In order to be paid, all you need is a broker's license and be the procuring cause of the sale.

2. **Subagents.** Like so many brokers across the country, we have decided that subagency is not in the best interests of the seller or this office. Our sellers just can not understand how you can represent them when you do not even know who they are. While we have assured our sellers that you will tell us everything that your buyer tells you, our sellers are still skeptical. Therefore, we make no offers of, nor accept subagency and do not pay

subagents. ***Do not worry. If you are the procuring cause, we will pay you.*** Please read the first option (#1) above.

This offer is made unilaterally to all brokers in the area. You do not need to agree to reciprocate to take advantage of this offer of compensation and cooperation. If you decide to treat us differently, that decision is totally up to you. We want no bilateral commission splits or agreements. We simply offer what we have decided is in the best interests of this firm and our sellers to encourage you to show and sell our listings.

Sales. When we have procured the buyer and are cooperating with your office, you are no longer potentially liable for the actions or inactions of our salespersons. In order to avoid potential conflicts of interest, we no longer are acting as subagents for sellers. We do, however, need to be compensated for working with a buyer. We indicate to our buyers and sellers that each is paying a portion of the commission which is reflected in the purchase price and is, in fact, paid by the seller to the listing broker at settlement.

1. **Compensation.** When we show and sell your listings, we will first be asking for compensation from your office. We will expect to be compensated in the amount that you indicate in the MLS book for subagents or buyer's agents or otherwise, whichever is greater. Absent such an offering in the MLS, we will be contacting you on each showing to verify the commission amount. We do not collect twice, "double commissions," or once from you and once from the buyer.

We wish to leave the extent of commissions to an agreement between offices. In the unlikely event that your office and our office can not reach an agreement which is satisfactory to compensate our office, either through the MLS or between offices, we will ask that the buyer insert a clause in the contract providing that the seller pay our commission.

2. **Agency Status.** We will be acting as either buyer brokers, representing the buyer, or licensed brokers who do not represent the seller or the buyer. We will not be acting as your agents; that is, as subagents of your sellers.

If you feel that the proper alternative is not addressed here, please call me immediately as we are committed to working with all brokers in the area. In order to maintain a consistent approach to all offices, this policy can be modified only by me personally, and no one else in my office. If you have questions, please call me.

Letter/e-mail – Buyer Agency Relationship

Ms. Sharon Reichman, Broker
Pacific United Realty
21 North Center Green
Denver, CO 80305

    Re: Buyer Agency Relationship

Dear Sharon:

    Thank you for you inquiry. This letter is to confirm the extent of cooperation and terms upon which you may show and sell property that we have listed. Subject to the terms and conditions of this letter, we will pay you a commission equal to ____% of the total sales price of any property that is sold and closed with a buyer that you procure. Such procurement, of course, must be during our listing period and any proper extensions or protection periods that may exist thereafter. This obligation to pay you (your broker) such a commission, and the payment of commission itself, are subject to the following terms and conditions:

    First, you are the agent who procures the buyer who ultimately purchases the property. To ensure that there is no confusion, the names of all prospective buyers must be submitted to this office, either before you show the property or within twenty four hours after the scheduled showing. We intend to give those names to the seller, our client, in order to provide protection for both of us in the event that a buyer should try to circumvent our listing agreement.

    Second, our obligation to pay you a commission is predicated upon our receipt of our commission. Should we be forced to accept conditional payment, which we may in our sole discretion elect to do, we will not be obligated to pay you until we are paid. In addition, we shall have no obligation to institute any form of collection procedure, including litigation, to collect the commission due. Should such action be necessary, you will be expected to share, in advance and on demand, in the expense of collection, including attorney's fees for the attorney I select, or forfeit your right to any portion of the proceeds of such an effort.

    Third, so that you and I do not waste our time and the time of our clients, we require that you provide us, in a timely fashion, with any information that you possess as to the financial qualifications of the purchaser for this property. We understand that you will use your best efforts on behalf of the buyer to obtain the best offer possible.

Finally, you agree that you will be bound by the National Association of REALTOR® Ethics and Arbitration Manual ("Manual"), or its successor, as adopted by the National Association, as of the date that your buyer's contract is signed by the seller should there be an issue regarding who is the "Procuring Cause" of the sale. This obligates you to arbitrate in the event that another licensee demands the advertised and agreed "co-op" commission indicating that such claimant is the "procuring cause of the sale" pursuant to the rules and regulations set forth in the Manual. You will be treated, and agree to arbitrate, as if you were a member of the local Board/Association of REALTORS®.

Showing our listings is all the verification that we need that you will abide by the terms of this agreement. Anticipating that you will accept, let me tell you that we are glad to have you as a competitor. Please sell all the property that you can that is listed with this office. You will, of course, be responsible for your own actions and inactions. We both understand that we are free to make the same, similar, and different agreements with other potential cooperating offices, without regard to the contents of this agreement, upon such terms and conditions that we alone determine are adequate, without regard for or notification to you.

Please understand that this is not a proposal for a reciprocal agreement, and no such agreement is sought by this letter. In the event you wish to discuss the terms under which you will allow us to act as buyer agents for property that you have listed, please let me know. You are under no obligation to pay us upon the same terms or conditions that are agreed upon here for your payment. This agreement supersedes any offer in the Magic Listing Service.

Sincerely,
The Real Estate Company

by: Your Name Here
REALTOR®, CRS, GRI

Letter/e-mail – Potential Buyer's Agent

Mr. LaVerne Davis
SanVern Realty Consultants
Boulder, CO 80305

    Re: Buyer's Brokerage Arrangement

Dear LaVerne:

    Thank you for your inquiry regarding our policy for dealing with potential buyers' brokers. As you know, we are very interested in marketing our seller's property to all interested buyers. We welcome the participation of buyers' agents and, subject to the qualifications outlined in this letter, are happy to acknowledge your agency relationship with your buyers.

    Upon your initial contact, please advise us that you are acting as a buyer's agent. You will be paid the amount indicated in the Magic Listing System book in the event that you are the procuring cause for the ultimate sale. That agreement to pay you is not subject to any conditions. In the event that you are also receiving money from your client, please indicate that fact. There is no need to indicate the amount. That agreement is between you and your client in the same manner our listing commission is between our office and the seller.

    Upon initial contact, we do not need to know the name of your buyer. However, you agree to provide us with that name immediately upon request should we need to disclose it to our seller to protect our rights to receive a commission during any holdover period indicated in our listing. That will protect us both should the listing expire while the buyer is still interested in the property.

    Our obligation to pay a commission is predicated upon our receipt of our commission. Should we be forced to accept conditional payment, which we may in our sole discretion elect to do, we will not be obligated to pay you until we are paid. In addition, we shall have no obligation to institute any form of collection procedure, including litigation to collect the commission due.

    Should such action be necessary, you will be expected to share, in advance and on demand, in the expense of collection, including attorney's fees for the attorney I select, or forfeit your right to any portion of the proceeds of such an effort. We reserve the right to require, as a condition precedent to payment, a statement from your principal outlining the fact that you are not receiving anything of value from that principal as a result of this transaction, i.e., that you are not also being paid by the buyer.

Finally, you agree that you will be bound by the National Association of REALTOR® Ethics and Arbitration Manual ("Manual"), or its successor, as adopted by the National Association, as of the date that your buyer's contract is signed by the seller should there be an issue regarding who is the "Procuring Cause" of the sale. This obligates you to arbitrate in the event that another licensee demands the advertised and agreed "co-op" commission indicating that such claimant is the "procuring cause of the sale" pursuant to the rules and regulations set forth in the Manual. You will be treated, and agree to arbitrate, as if you were a member of the local Board/Association of REALTORS®.

Your acceptance of this proposal is evidenced by your calling this office and obtaining information about a listing or scheduling a showing. We are happy to have you as a competitor and to provide you with access to the properties that we have listed. We expect you to exercise due care and at all times to safeguard the property and possessions of the sellers we represent. Please sell all the property that you can that is listed with this office. You will, of course, be responsible for your own actions and inactions. You understand that we are free to make the same, similar, and different agreements with other potential buyers' brokers and subagents, without regard to the contents of this agreement, upon such terms and conditions that we alone determine are adequate, without any obligation to notify you.

Please understand that this is not a proposal for a reciprocal agreement, and no such agreement is sought by this letter. In the event you wish to discuss the terms under which you will allow us to act as buyer agents or non-agents, for the sale of your listings, please let me know. You are under no obligation to pay us upon the same terms or conditions that are agreed upon here for your payment.

Sincerely,
The Real Estate Company

by: Your Name Here
REALTOR®, CRS, GRI

Letter/e-mail – Anti-Trust

Mr. Sam Seller and
Mrs. Sandy Seller
4750 Table Mesa Drive
Boulder, CO 80305

    Re: 4750 Table Mesa Drive, Boulder

Dear Mr. and Mrs. Seller:

You will see in our listing agreement a section which addresses the commission that our office charges and several items dealing with the commission that we offer and pay to a "cooperating" brokerage office. All commissions are payable to the broker. Some people think that "everyone charges the same fee" or that "all the fees are pretty much standard." Nothing could be further from the truth.

While it may appear that a lot of the commissions charged are similar, there are no "standard" commissions. The "cooperative" commissions that our firm offers and pays to other brokerage firms are set by this firm. Neither the Multiple Listing Service, nor the Board or Association of REALTORS®, establish or set commissions or cooperative commissions. Each office independently determines what they will charge, whom they will pay and how much.

The value of our services is based on many things: the quality of service we provide, the number of listings that we feel we can properly and successfully market in a given period, the time estimated for the sale of various listings, the price ranges of listings that we hope to market, and the overall cost of doing business in today's market. If other firms price their services at a similar or equal rate, that is a result of their own analysis and is solely their concern. We feel that the level of professionalism and the degree of success that we attain for our clients justifies our commission rate.

I know that after you have had the opportunity to experience our services you will agree. The amount of commission we charge is one of the items for which I alone am responsible, and I would be glad to discuss it at length with you if you so desire.

Letter/e-mail – Pre-Listing Company Brochure

Mr. Sam Seller and
Mrs. Sandy Seller
4750 Table Mesa Drive
Boulder, CO 80305

     Re: 4750 Table Mesa Drive, Boulder

Dear Mr. and Mrs. Seller:

Please allow me to introduce myself. I am the licensed broker for The Real Estate Company. I have just spoken with Katherine Reece who has been describing your home in detail to me. I must say she is very excited and feels that as the agent for this office, she can market it successfully, on the terms and conditions you have established, if we are selected to be your listing agent.

When you list your home through Kathy with this company you also obtain the cooperative efforts of the rest of our professionally trained agents and our entire office staff of support personnel. I have included a brochure describing the services that we provide to our clients as a team. Please look it over since it describes all of the various services that we provide, the areas for which you are responsible, the areas over which we both have no control, some valuable information about the complexities involved in modern real estate, and why I am proud to be the responsible broker for this office. As I am sure you know, all contracts that bind the brokerage firm must be signed by me pursuant to state law.

If I can be of any assistance, please do not hesitate to give me a call anytime. Thank you.

                    Most Sincerely,
                    The Real Estate Company

                    by: Your Friendly, Broker

Letter/e-mail – Due-On-Transfer

Mr. Sam Seller and
Mrs. Sandy Seller
4750 Table Mesa Drive
Boulder, CO 80305

   Re: 4750 Table Mesa Drive, Boulder

Dear Mr. and Mrs. Seller:

   Once you make the decision to list your property with The Real Estate
Company, one of the first items on our agenda will be to request information on the
terms of your current mortgage. Your mortgage may contain what is generally
called a "due-on-sale" clause. Basically, this clause gives the mortgage lender the
right to call the entire loan due if you transfer the property to a buyer. Relax, this is
not the end of the world.

   The due-on-sale clause simply means that in the event you elect to sell your
home by allowing the purchaser to assume your existing mortgage or take the
property subject to the mortgage, the existing mortgage lender will have to be
consulted. The buyer will have to qualify to assume the loan. Should the mortgage
lender determine that the buyer "qualifies," s/he will allow the transfer and
assumption. We assist people with this type of financing problem every day. We
must take the necessary steps to ensure that we have time to obtain the approval,
and that any buyer who seeks to assume your loan is indeed qualified.

   Yes, you could elect to transfer the title to a buyer without notifying the
mortgage lender. However, that would enable the lender, at the lender's election,
to accelerate the loan and potentially force a refinancing or foreclosure. In such
instances, we require that the seller and buyer seek and obtain written approval
from their respective attorneys prior to entering into the contract.

   As with all assumptions, we can not be responsible for the ability of the
buyer to make all the payments. That determination is yours. We will help you
obtain a credit report and financial statement, if you so desire, to assist you with
this decision. In addition, we have found that consulting your banker is one of the
best ways to determine the financial capabilities of a prospective buyer. Lenders
make these decisions every day.

Letter/e-mail – Earnest Money

Mr. Sam Seller and
Mrs. Sandy Seller
4750 Table Mesa Drive
Boulder, CO 80305

    Re: 4750 Table Mesa Drive, Boulder

Dear Mr. and Mrs. Seller:

    The policy of most of the offices in this state is that any entity selected by the parties can be the holder of the earnest money deposit. It is the policy of this firm that we, as the listing brokerage company, in the absence of direction from you to the contrary, either hold the earnest money or select the escrow agent to hold the earnest money. These funds are placed in a separate bank account segregated from our operating accounts.

    Unless everyone agrees to the contrary, the earnest money is not placed in an interest-bearing account. The need to have the interest accrue to a specific social security number or federal identification number from the date the account is set up makes the routine setup and payout from such an account a nightmare. In addition, the amount involved and subsequent interest which would accrue are insufficient to warrant the effort. If, however, the amount is large or the term of its retention is long in duration, an interest-bearing account is an alternative we are happy to provide for either the buyer or seller. In such a circumstance it is normal that the interest accrue as additional earnest money.

    Over the years this company has adopted a policy of encouraging the parties to select an escrow agent or title company to hold the earnest money deposit. This independent escrow agent will accept, retain and disburse any funds that are associated with your real estate transactions. This procedure ensures an impartial stakeholder, reduces bookkeeping and removes us from any dispute that may arise with regard to the disposition of any such funds in the future.

    By law we are not authorized to make any determination with regard to the entitlement of anyone to any portion of the earnest money in the event of a dispute.

Letter/e-mail – Fair Housing

Mr. Sam Seller
4750 Table Mesa Drive
Boulder, CO 80305

  Re: Federal, State and Local Fair Housing

Dear Mr. and Mrs. Seller:

  This firm is committed to the principles and practices of fair housing. We support equal access to the American dream – housing. We want to be sure that every individual who is financially able to qualify for your home has an opportunity to see it and attempt to purchase it. At a time when some people feel that they are excluded, for whatever reason, we want to do everything possible to provide equal access to housing for everyone.

  We are proud to display the Housing and Urban Development (HUD) Equal Housing Opportunity Poster, "*We do business in accordance with the letter and spirit of the Federal, State and Local Fair Housing Law.*" It is illegal to discriminate against any person because of race, creed, color, sex, religion, national origin, handicap or familial status [local additional classes]. Some states and cities add additional categories. In order to comply fully with the letter of the law and its spirit, we simply do not discriminate against anyone, period.

  As real estate professionals, we are pledged to providing equal access for every potential purchaser to all locations and types of housing that are available in this area, that may be selected by the potential customers or clients who inquire about housing. I know you are happy to know that we, as your agents, will show your home to anyone who shows an interest and has the financial ability to buy it. We make sure that every potential customer knows that your house is available and is made aware of the features that it offers. This helps protect you as a seller since the Federal, State and Local Fair Housing Law applies to all of us.

       Most Sincerely,
       The Real Estate Company

       by: Your Agent, CRS, GRI

Letter/e-mail – FHA Interest Payoff

Mr. Sam Seller and
Mrs. Sandy Seller
4750 Table Mesa Drive
Boulder, CO 80305

     Re: 4750 Table Mesa Drive, Boulder

Dear Mr. and Mrs. Seller:

    Once you make the decision to list your property with The Real Estate Company, one of the first items on our agenda will be to request information on the terms of your current mortgage. If it is an FHA mortgage, we need to be careful about the date and time of closing for your home. The FHA mortgage probably provides that in the event of a payoff an entire month of interest will be charged for any portion of the month that the loan remains outstanding. In short, you may not want to close on the last day of the month with the final payoff credited with the lender after the first of the following month, and be required to pay another full month of interest.

    We work with the closing agents to ensure the proper calculation of interest due. In addition, we make sure that there is time to get the payment to the mortgage lender before another month's interest is added on. In the event we are forced to close on or near the last day of the month through no fault of yours, we endeavor to provide in the contract that the buyer will pay the interest for the following month. We also make sure that the closing agent sends the payoff to the lender, via overnight mail, to try to save you a month's interest.

    While this is not always possible, I will attempt to arrange the transaction so as to save you as much interest as possible.

                      Most Sincerely,
                      The Real Estate Company

                      by: Your Agent, Broker Associate

Letter/e-mail – Hazardous Materials and Inspections

Mr. Sam Seller and
Mrs. Sandy Seller
4750 Table Mesa Drive
Boulder, CO 80305

    Re: 4750 Table Mesa Drive

Dear Mr. and Mrs. Seller:

We are all aware of the potential for contamination. Radon, lead based paint, mold and/or asbestos can exist in any home. More serious waste problems crop up at the most inopportune times. If we are selected to market your home, one of the first things that we do is discuss with you any possibility that a hazardous situation exists in your home. Such things as close proximity to high tension lines, a power plant, or waste disposal site can discourage a potential buyer.

We comply with the Federal Lead Based Paint Disclosure rules and will provide you with the requisite forms for proper disclosure. Yes, if the building permit for your home was issued prior to January 1, 1978 you need to comply. We assist in that compliance effort.

While most people are inclined to inspect and review a property thoroughly after making an offer, some cautious buyers will want to have the property inspected for the presence of radon gas, mold and other hazardous materials, and to verify the condition of the soil prior to being obligated to purchase. Today, many lenders and relocation companies make such verifications a must for their participation in a transaction.

Most importantly, a potential purchaser will probably inquire about and subsequently require that a test be conducted prior to his final purchase of your home. All this takes time when you can least afford it, that is, after the buyer has bound your home with a signed contract, but before the closing has occurred. This is a critical period when you will want to have as few problems as possible.

The solution that we recommend is to have every home that we list tested as soon as possible for the condition of the soil and the presence and extent of radon gas and other hazardous materials. In this way, we can have the test results available for potential purchasers who can review them *prior* to making their decision to purchase. Hopefully, we can then eliminate the need for the contract to be conditional upon the results of a subsequent test.

A list of firms that provide these services is enclosed. Please discuss your options, make a selection and order the tests. I would be glad to assist the tester of your choice by meeting her at the property during the day, as I realize that you are both quite busy. In fact, after you make the selection and give me a budget of how much you wish to spend, I would be glad to arrange for the test on your behalf.

I can see no reason why both tests should not be simply a matter of course. Having them ready might just be the factor that helps that buyer decide on your home. Buyers, once they see what they want, usually are in a hurry to move in. The inspections would eliminate one more delay.

I work with the various inspectors and agencies to make sure that the inspections that you select are completed. This frees you to live your life and lets me stay on top of the sale of your home.

Most Sincerely,
The Real Estate Company

by: Your Real Estate Agent

Letter/e-mail – Hazardous Waste and Inspections Commercial

Mr. Sam Seller and Mrs. Sandy Seller
4750 Table Mesa Drive
Boulder, CO 80305

   Re: 4750 Table Mesa Drive

Dear Mr. and Mrs. Seller:

   Commercial real estate is often affected by hazardous waste. No potential buyer wishes to acquire a location that has existing waste issues, or the potential of waste issues, without knowing these facts as part of the initial disclosure. Therefore, one of the first things that we do when we get a listing is to encourage the seller to obtain or update a phase one audit or, as is becoming common, an insurance policy indicating coverage for such items.

   While most people are inclined to inspect and review a property thoroughly after making an offer, buyers will also want to have the property inspected for the presence of radon gas and other hazardous materials and to verify the condition of the soil prior to being obligated to purchase. Today, many lenders make such verifications a must for their participation in a transaction.

   If there is a problem, we want to know early. One of our objectives is that you complete the sale without any lingering fears of later repercussions from the ultimate buyer, someone that you most probably do not even know yet. We like to have the phase one audit and engineering results available for potential purchasers, who can review them *prior* to making their decision to purchase. Hopefully, we can then eliminate the need for the contract to be conditional upon the results of a subsequent test.

   I know you want to complete this sale with a minimum of delay and potential problems. Therefore, I am willing to do whatever you direct to expedite the process and to coordinate the people you choose to make the necessary repairs and inspections.

                  Most Sincerely,
                  The Real Estate Company

Letter/e-mail – Lockboxes

Mr. Sam Seller
Mrs. Sandy Seller
4750 Table Mesa Drive
Boulder, CO 80305

Re: 4750 Table Mesa Drive

Dear Sam and Sandy:

The electronic lockbox is one of the most valuable marketing tools available today. This electronic system allows those that are participants, but not the public at large, accessibility to your home. It also allows us to track the date, time and identification of each entry, including the name of the person to whom the key is issued. People can see your home easily, and we can maintain accurate records detailing each person who saw your home.

These key safes contain a key to your home which can be accessed by other members of the Multiple Listing Service. Once the listing has been finalized, we can review the Lockbox Authorization Form. You can make the decision as to whether or not you want to take advantage of this sophisticated security and entry system.

While this is not a "security service" it does allow us to "lock out" any entry during certain times of the day or days of the week, so that your privacy is more assured. In addition, we can adjust it as your needs change.

Most Sincerely,
The Real Estate Company

by: Your Broker Associate

Letter/e-mail – Mortgage Insurance (MIP) FHA/Conventional

Mr. Sam and Mrs. Sandy Seller
4750 Table Mesa Drive
Boulder, CO 80305

  Re: 4750 Table Mesa Drive

Dear Sam and Sandy:

  When I explain a mortgage insurance policy to my clients, I always feel it would be nice to have a written explanation for your review now and in the future. Mortgage insurance represents a significant amount of money and the alternatives are not always clear to brokers, lawyers or closing agents, let alone sellers and buyers. This is a little overview for you to keep handy throughout your listing with me. If you want to discuss it at any time, just let me know, and I will try to explain it further.

  Private mortgage insurance consists of a small initial premium and monthly premiums that are reflected in the interest rate of the loan. There are no prorations upon sale and no refunds. It is a simple system.

  FHA mortgage insurance can consist of two premiums. One is calculated as a percentage of your loan balance and collected each month. There is nothing that we can do about that. The other is collected in advance and runs for a term longer than a year. If a new loan is obtained, there is a possibility that you might get a credit for the amount of your unused premium upon the sale of your home.

  The general rule for items that have been prepaid by the seller is that the buyer purchases the unused portion of such expenses since the buyer will enjoy the benefits of the unused portion of the contract. Fire insurance is a typical example. The buyer either buys the balance of the seller's fire insurance policy, since the new buyer will be covered as the owner for the remainder of the term, or the buyer obtains his own insurance and the seller is allowed to cancel his policy and receive a refund from the insurance company.

  Mortgage insurance, absent an agreement to the contrary, should be treated in the same manner. The problem that occurs with FHA mortgage insurance is twofold. First, unlike most expenses, this is not an annual policy; it is a multi-year policy fully paid in advance. The proration, that is, the division between the buyer and the seller of the unused portion of the prepaid premium, would substantially increase the amount of money that a buyer would need, and the amount that the seller would receive, upon the closing of the transaction.

Second, the prepaid premium is not easily prorated. The computation tables that are available from the Department of Housing and Urban Development essentially load more of the premium into the first years of the life of the policy. This means that in the event of cancellation the amount available for a refund diminishes rapidly with each passing year. Essentially, the proration is calculated as if the buyer, who would be the owner of the mortgage insurance policy, cashed it in for a refund on the date of closing. The amount the buyer would receive is the amount that would be allocated to the seller at the closing.

As I have indicated previously, in the event there is an offer that entails the assumption of your FHA loan, it is often not possible for the buyer to also bear the burden of the proration. Therefore, the buyer may ask that the prepaid insurance not be prorated. That would not be an equitable proposition. I shall continue to indicate that, even on a full price contract, the FHA insurance must be prorated. Much like our discussion of assumptions, this presents a decision that ultimately must be made by you when you receive an offer to purchase.

Thank you for letting me take the time to review this complex little area. Feel free to call if you want to talk it over some more.

Most Sincerely,
The Real Estate Company

by: Your Confused, Broker

Letter/e-mail – Multiple Listing Service
(Information Verification)

Mr. Sam Seller and
Mrs. Sandy Seller
4750 Table Mesa Drive
Boulder, CO 80305

Re: 4750 Table Mesa Drive, Boulder

Dear Sam and Sandy:

Yes, we are members of the Multiple Listing Service or "MLS." We will place your property listing in the Multiple Listing System – the book, the computer and on the internet – for review by numerous other licensed salespeople who are MLS participants. Before we do this, we will submit to you the information as it will appear in the MLS, so that you can review it to ensure its accuracy.

We want to be sure that everything we publish will detail your home's available options and features as accurately as we both can make them. Even though the MLS may contain a statement indicating that the information is for the exclusive use of member brokers and that the information contained therein is not to be strictly relied upon, we want our listings to be as accurate as possible.

Some people request that their property not be exposed to the MLS. We do not encourage such a practice. By not allowing us to market your home through the MLS, you severely limit our ability to expose your property to a multitude of potential buyers in order that we might find that one buyer who will buy your home. In addition, our competitors will think that we reserved the listing, so that we could sell the property ourselves and deprive them of the opportunity to sell it to their buyers. That is not good for either of us.

We realize that there are extenuating circumstances that may warrant not utilizing the MLS, and we would be happy to discuss your particular situation with you. With your informed consent and my approval, as the broker, we could make an exception to accommodate your individual marketing needs.

Most Sincerely,

Letter/e-mail – Internet Web Advertising
(Information Verification)

Mr. Sam Seller and
Mrs. Sandy Seller
4750 Table Mesa Drive
Boulder, CO 80305

    Re: 4750 Table Mesa Drive, Boulder

Dear Sam and Sandy:

    In addition to our membership in the Multiple Listing Service or "MLS," we are participants in one or more services which automatically upload that MLS data to the internet and various websites. The selection of these sites is at the discretion of the Board of Directors of the MLS and/or REALTORS® to which we belong.

    You will note an authorization in the listing contract to place your property on such internet sites as we, in our sole discretion, determine are effective. This authorization permits us to advertise your home on the internet. We will provide you with those website links, so that you can view your home and confirm the data that is associated with that listing. If there are any errors, please notify us immediately.

    In addition to the sites that are automatically uploaded from the MLS, your listing may appear on websites of different housing entities with which we are affiliated, and on websites where we advertise. There is no additional charge for this service.

                        Most Sincerely,
                        The Real Estate Company

                        By: Your Loyal Agent

Letter/e-mail – Purchase for Your Own Account
(Purchase Encouraged)

Mrs. Sandy Seller
4750 Table Mesa Drive
Boulder, CO 80305

Re: 4750 Table Mesa Drive

Dear Mr. and Mrs. Seller:

We are in the business of selling real estate for our sellers. Should a salesperson affiliated with this company desire to buy property for his/her own account, s/he is encouraged to do so. In order to avoid issues that may breach our duties of utmost loyalty and confidentiality, please do not discuss your personal motivation for selling with any agent in this office as s/he may ultimately become the buyer of your home.

To effectuate this system, you were provided with an additional authorization form with your listing agreement. If you did not get one, or if you have only now decided to avail yourself of this program, please let me know immediately. We must have that form signed prior to allowing any agent in this office to attempt to buy your property.

Under this program, the office and I remain your agents, and the buyer who is also licensed with this office acts as the buyer, period. We will treat that buyer as it s/he were represented by an independent third party broker and is not associated with this office. In either event, you will need to have an attorney review any proposed offer. That will be at our expense, of course. We do limit that expense to $300.00, which we feel is a reasonable amount to be charged by an attorney with real estate expertise in this area.

We realize that we are exposing ourselves to potential litigation. However, we feel that your review of the addendum to the listing contract, as well as your attorney's subsequent written approval of any offer, ensures that all your terms are met and our liability is reduced. The successful sale of your home makes the risk worth the reward.

We look forward to having your home in our inventory of available homes. It is always a pleasure to have a well-kept and well-maintained home such as yours in our inventory of available listings.

Most Sincerely,
The Real Estate Company

Letter/e-mail – REALTOR® Professional Affiliation

Mr. Sam Seller and
Mrs. Sandy Seller
4750 Table Mesa Drive
Boulder, CO 80305

   Re: 4750 Table Mesa Drive, Boulder

Dear Sam and Sandy:

   Not every real estate licensee is a REALTOR®. Once someone obtains a
real estate broker's or salesperson's license, he or she may apply for membership in
the board or association of REALTORS®. We think that REALTORS® are
striving to be the best that they can be.

   We are proud to be members of the National Association of REALTORS®
through our affiliation with our Board or Association of REALTORS®. This
means that we adhere to the Code of Ethics and participate in the various
educational opportunities that are available to members of the board. I have
included a copy of the Code of Ethics for your perusal. If you would like to discuss
it with me, I would be only to happy to review the code with you.

   Being REALTORS® means we are concerned with the state of real estate in
our area. We support the private ownership of real estate and the ability to convey
it. If you would like more information about the REALTOR® organization, please
let me know.

                                   Most Sincerely,
                                   The Real Estate Company

                                   by: Ethical Real Estate Agent

Letter/e-mail – Tax Deferred Exchange

Mr. Sam Seller and
Mrs. Sandy Seller
4750 Table Mesa Drive
Boulder, CO 80305

    Re: Tax Deferred Exchanges under
          Section 1031 of the Internal Revenue Code

Dear Mr. and Mrs. Seller:

If the property you are selling is your personal residence, then this letter is not applicable. However, should the house that you are selling be other than your personal residence, or should you own other real estate property that you are thinking of selling, this letter will provide you with some very interesting information. There is no way to eliminate taxes. There *is* a way to potentially defer taxes into the future. The transaction is called a tax deferred exchange.

This information is not intended to substitute for advice from your accountant or attorney. It is only intended to give you some insight into the potential savings that are available to everyone through the use of this Internal Revenue Service Code section. If you are interested after you read this letter, we can set up a time to review a tax deferred exchange in more detail. A brief explanation follows:

You must be dealing with "like-kind" property. That means real estate. Apartments, single family houses, farms, ranches, industrial buildings, warehouses, raw land are all examples of like-kind property. It is my understanding that ownership in partnerships, limited liability companies or shares in an entity can not be traded in a tax deferred exchange. You can trade any piece of like-kind property for another, but all entities must be real estate. In fact, you can trade one piece of property for many, or many for one.

Difficult? Not in the least. First, you sell your property in the normal fashion. We will provide you with the clause that can be inserted into your contract. It will not affect your sale. Nor will the clause place any additional demands upon the buyer. In fact, the sale occurs in the normal fashion.

A "qualifying intermediary" such as a title company, friend, broker or attorney holds the proceeds of sale. It is important to select someone whom you can trust for that position who is familiar with the tax deferred transaction. We can assist you with that selection should you desire. If in doubt, the title company seems to do a pretty good job.

You have 45 days to indicate to the "qualifying intermediary" up to three properties that you think you might like to own. There are provisions for designating more than three properties. If you need additional information on those provisions, we can discuss your particular needs in detail. Yes, you might already have the new property or properties under contract.

Finally, you have to close the property or properties within 180 days of the initial tax deferred closing. That is all. We will be glad to examine the effect and potential savings that you may be able to obtain. If you are thinking about selling one property and buying another, this could be an alternative you may wish to consider.

Tax deferred exchanges are fun, easy and can save you a substantial amount of money now. We are happy to assist you without practicing law or accounting. We charge no additional fees. It is just another service to our sellers.

Most Sincerely,
The Real Estate Company

by: Your Broker

Transaction Broker Alternative – The "Non-Agent" Option

Assistance vs. Representation. Here you "assist" a seller or buyer. You do not "represent" a buyer or seller. In order to demonstrate that in fact a seller can list a property with a broker without entering into an agency relationship, we have included a copy of a generally accepted Exclusive Right-to-Sell (Transaction Broker) Listing Contract. This is the Colorado Real Estate Commission approved form and is not copyrighted. You can see all Colorado Real Estate Commission approved forms on its website – http://www.dora.state.co.us/Real-Estate/

This form demonstrates that the basic real estate listing services the seller desires can be accomplished without creating an "agency" relationship in some states. Check your state before trying to use this method of providing professional assistance. This is the form of choice for the authors when they list their personal real estate for sale with a brokerage company. Utilizing a transaction broker has the distinct advantage of eliminating vicarious liability since there is no agency relationship. The seller is not liable for the actions or inactions of the broker and all the salespeople in the broker's office.

- Yes, you still need to be a licensed salesperson working for a licensed broker.

- Yes, you still have a long list of duties to be provided to the seller and the buyer.

- Yes, you should annex a form indicating the services that you provide to the buyer and the seller.

- Yes, the seller must understand that you are not his/her "agent." However, this method of working for the seller does not relieve you of your duty to treat the seller honestly and perform the itemized duties.

- Yes, you can still offer a cooperative fee to another broker (agent or not) that is assisting or representing the buyer.

On the following pages is an example of a Transaction Broker Listing Contract. Feel free to add other sections that are appropriate to your practice or jurisdiction.

Exclusive Right-to-Sell Listing Contract
Transaction Broker – Designated Brokerage
(Residential)

Date: _____/200____

1. Agreement. The parties agree that Seller irrevocably engages Brokerage Firm as Seller's exclusive broker and Broker as Seller's Designated Broker, under the terms and conditions of this Listing Contract, except as stated herein. Broker is not an agent or advocate of Seller or buyer. Seller shall not be vicariously liable for the acts of Broker. Seller agrees to conduct all negotiations for the Sale of the Property only through Broker, and to refer to Broker all communications received in any form from real estate brokers, prospective buyers, tenants or any other source during this Listing Period. Seller and Broker agree to the terms and conditions set forth in this contract.

2. Defined terms.

   a. Seller: _____.

   b. Brokerage Firm: _____.
   Listing Company

   c. Broker: _____.

   c. Property: _____.

   d. Sale. The voluntary transfer or exchange of any interest in the Property or the voluntary creation of the obligation to convey any interest in the Property, including a contract or lease.

   e. Listing Period. Shall be from _____through _____.

3. Broker's services.

   a. Broker shall exercise reasonable skill and care for Seller including, but not limited to:

   (1)   Presenting all offers to and from Seller in a timely manner regardless of whether the Property is subject to a contract for sale;

   (2)   Disclosing to Seller adverse material facts actually known by Broker;

     (3)   Advising Seller to obtain expert advice as to material matters about which Broker knows but the specifics of which are beyond the expertise of Broker;

     (4)   Accounting in a timely manner for all money and property received;

     (5)   Keeping Seller and Buyer fully informed regarding the transaction;

     (6)   Assisting Seller and Buyer in complying with the terms and conditions of any contract for Sale including closing the transaction; and

     (7)   Informing Seller and Buyer that, in their respective capacities, they shall not be vicariously liable for the acts of Broker.

b. Broker shall not disclose the following information without the informed consent of Seller:

     (1)   That Seller is willing to accept less than the asking price for the Property;

     (2)   What the motivating factors are for Seller to sell the Property;

     (3)   That Seller will agree to financing terms other than those offered;

     (4)   Any material information about Seller unless the disclosure is required by law or failure to disclose such information would constitute fraud or dishonest dealing; or

     (5)   Any facts or suspicions regarding circumstances which may psychologically impact or stigmatize any real property pursuant to Colorado law.

4. Price and terms.

a. Price: U.S.$_____

b. Terms: _____ Cash _____ Conventional Loan _____ FHA _____ VA
_____ Other _____.

c. Loan discount points: _____.

d. Seller agrees to Pay, Buyer-Disallowable Closing Costs (FHA/VA):
_____.

e. The minimum earnest money deposit shall be: $_____.

f. Seller will receive net proceeds of closing as indicated: ___ Cashier's Check at Seller's expense; ___ Funds Electronically Transferred (Wire Transfer) to an account specified by Seller, at Seller's expense; or _____ Closing Company's Trust Account Check.

g. The Internal Revenue Service may require Closing Company to withhold a substantial portion of the proceeds of this sale when Seller is a foreign person after closing. Seller should inquire of Seller's tax advisor to determine if withholding applies or if an exemption exists.

5. Deposits. Brokerage Firm is authorized to accept earnest money deposits pursuant to a proposed Sale contract. Broker is authorized to deliver the earnest money deposit to the closing agent, if any, at or before the closing of the Sale contract.

6. Inclusions and exclusions.
   a. The Purchase Price includes the following items (Inclusions):
      (1) Fixtures. If attached to the Property on the date of this contract, lighting, heating, plumbing, ventilating and air conditioning fixtures, TV antennas, inside telephone wiring and connecting blocks/jacks, plants, mirrors, floor coverings, intercom systems, built-in kitchen appliances, sprinkler systems and controls, built-in vacuum systems (including accessories), garage door openers including ___ remote controls; and _____
      _____.
      (2) Other Inclusions. If on the Property whether attached or not on the date of this contract: storm windows, storm doors, window and porch shades, awnings, blinds, screens, window coverings, curtain rods, drapery rods, fireplace inserts, fireplace screens, fireplace grates, heating stoves, storage sheds and all keys. If checked, the following are included: ___Water Softeners, _____ Smoke/Fire Detectors, _____ Security Systems, _____ Satellite Systems (including satellite dishes and accessories); and
      _____
      _____.
      (3) Parking and Storage Facilities. The use of the following parking facilities: _____; and the following storage facilities:_____.
      (4) Water Rights. The following legally described water rights:
      _____ _____.

b. Instruments of Transfer. The Inclusions are to be conveyed at closing free and clear of all taxes, except personal property taxes for the year of Closing, liens and encumbrances, except as provided herein. Conveyance shall be by bill of sale or other applicable legal instrument(s). Any water rights shall be conveyed by a _____ _____ deed or other applicable legal instrument(s).

c. Exclusions. The following attached fixtures are excluded:
_____
_____
_____
_____.

7. Title and encumbrances. Seller represents to Broker that title to the Property is solely in Seller's name. Seller shall deliver to Broker true copies of all relevant title materials, lease(s), improvement location certificates(s) and survey(s) in Seller's possession and shall disclose to Broker all easements, liens and other encumbrances, if any, on the Property, of which Seller has knowledge. Seller authorizes the holder of any obligation secured by an encumbrance on the Property to disclose to Broker the amount owing on said encumbrance and the terms thereof. In case of Sale, Seller agrees to convey, by a _____ deed, only that title Seller has in the Property. Property will be conveyed free and clear of all taxes except the general taxes for the year of Closing.

All monetary encumbrances (such as mortgages, deeds of trust, liens, financing statements) shall be paid by Seller and released except as Seller and buyer may otherwise agree. Existing monetary encumbrances are as follows: _____
_____.
The Property is subject to the following leases and tenancies: _____
_____.
If the Property has been or will be subject to any governmental liens for special improvements installed at the time of signing a sale contract, Seller will be responsible for payment of same unless otherwise agreed. Broker may terminate this Listing Contract upon written notice to Seller that title is not satisfactory to Broker.

8. Evidence of title. Seller agrees to furnish buyer, at Seller's expense, a current commitment for owner's title insurance policy in an amount equal to the

Purchase Price in the form specified in the sale contract, or if this blank is checked, _____ an Abstract of Title certified to a current date.

9. Association assessments. Seller represents that the amount of the regular owners' association assessment is currently payable at $_____ per _____ and that there are no unpaid regular or special assessments against the Property except the current regular assessments and except: _____
_____.
Seller agrees to promptly request the owners' association to deliver to buyer before date of closing a current statement of assessments against the Property.

10. Possession. Possession of the Property shall be delivered to buyer as follows: _____,
subject to leases and tenancies as described herein.

11. Material defects – disclosures – inspection.
    a. Broker's Obligations. State law requires Broker to disclose to any prospective buyer all adverse material facts actually known by Broker including, but not limited to, adverse material facts pertaining to the title to the Property which shall survive closing and delivery of deed, the physical condition of the Property, any material defects in the Property, any environmental hazards affecting the Property which are required by law to be disclosed. These types of disclosures may include such matters as structural defects, soil conditions, violations of health, zoning or building laws and nonconforming uses and zoning variances. Seller agrees that any buyer may have the Property and Inclusions inspected and authorizes Broker to disclose any facts actually known by Broker about the Property.

    b. Seller's Obligations. Seller shall complete:
      (1) Seller's Property Disclosure Form attached to this listing agreement, completed to the best of Seller's current, actual knowledge.
      (2) Lead-Based Paint. Unless exempt, if the improvements on the Property include one or more residential dwelling(s) for which a building permit was issued prior to January 1, 1978, a completed Lead-Based Paint Disclosure (Sales) form must be signed by Seller, the real estate licensee(s) and given to any

potential buyer prior to the buyer and Seller signing a sales contract.

12.   Compensation to broker. Seller agrees that any broker compensation which is conditioned upon the sale of the Property shall be earned by Broker as set forth herein without any discount or allowance for any efforts made by Seller or by any other person in connection with the sale of the Property.

    a. Amount. In consideration of the services to be performed by Broker, Seller agrees to pay Broker a sale commission equal to _____% of the gross sales price in U.S. dollars.

    b. Such commission shall be earned upon the happening of any of the following:
        (1)   Any Sale of the Property within the Listing Period by Seller, by Broker or by any other person;
        (2)   Broker finding a buyer who is ready, willing and able to complete the transaction as specified herein by Seller; or
        (3)   Any Sale of the Property within _____ calendar days subsequent to the expiration of the Listing Period (Holdover Period) to anyone with whom Broker negotiated and whose name was submitted, in writing, to Seller by Broker during the Listing Period (including any extensions thereof).

13.   Limitation on third-party compensation. Broker shall not accept compensation from Buyer or the Selling Company, without the written consent of Seller. Additionally, Broker shall not be permitted to assess and receive mark-ups or other compensation for services performed by any third party or affiliated business entity unless Seller signs a separate written consent for such service(s).

14.   Other brokers, multiple listing service, marketing. Seller has been advised by Broker of the advantages and disadvantages of various marketing methods, the use of multiple listing services and various methods of making the Property accessible by other brokers (e.g., using lockboxes, by-appointment-only showings, etc.), and whether some methods may limit the ability of a selling broker to show the Property. After having been so advised, Seller has chosen the following (check all that apply):

Broker shall seek assistance from and offer compensation to the following brokers outside of the Listing Company:

_____ Buyer Agents: _____ % of the gross sales price
_____ Transaction-Brokers (non-agent licensees): _____ % of the gross sales price

15. In-Company transaction(s). When this Brokerage Firm assists or represents both parties to a transaction, an In-Company Transaction, Broker shall continue to function as a Transaction-Broker.

16. Other sellers. Seller acknowledges that under state law Broker may have agreements with other sellers to market and sell their properties.

Seller:

_____   _____
            date   date

Brokerage Firm hereby designates the undersigned Broker.
Brokerage Firm by Broker:

_____
            date

After the Listing is Signed

Now that you have the seller's acknowledgment on the listing agreement, the work has really begun. Communication is even more important now by telephone, written correspondence and e-mail. Send a confirmation letter or e-mail of any significant communication discussed by telephone and keep an accurate and concise telephone log. In addition, save those e-mails to and from the seller. A good practice to follow is written market updates by letter, fax or e-mail attachment to the seller, on a previously agreed upon basis. *Sellers have no concept of the time you actually spend on their transaction, but expect that you should spend every waking moment working for them, regardless of the number of listings you service.* After all, their listing is the most important.

The Seller's Checklist. When you are busy with multiple transactions, checklists become imperative to a smoothly running day. It is much simpler to follow a checklist for routine tasks, so that you do not have to reinvent the wheel for the same process each time. If you employ an administrative assistant, the checklist becomes even more critical to ensure that you are indeed "cloned" in your approach to procedures. You can arrive at your listing appointments confident in knowing that all the forms are properly completed with the necessary information and that all are indeed there! Being organized and prepared will give the immediate impression of being a professional in the real estate field. Even if you are not organized, give the appearance of organization.

Included in this chapter is a sample listing checklist. Use this checklist, personalize it with your own additions, or create your own. The important thing is to have a checklist and live by it.

Continued Correspondence. Send the seller a letter, postcard, e-mail or fax describing what you are doing to sell their home no matter how routine the procedure may seem to you – entering into the Multiple Listing Service, sending announcements to their neighbors, sending flyers to cooperating REALTORS®, calling buyers' agents, distributing flyers at your local REALTOR® meetings, putting their home in a web advertisement or placing the listing data on the internet. Reconfirm the office policy on key issues such as inspections, lockboxes, agency, disclosures and all other aspects of marketing the seller's home in your continuous correspondence. Stay in touch. Informed sellers are not plaintiffs. They are teammates. Real estate is a team sport.

These letters and e-mails can be more personal. "Dear Sam and Sandy" is more appropriate now. Standard letters, postcards or e-mails can be used to suggest items not selected. It is sometimes difficult to tell a seller to "clean" the house. Oftentimes, by just seeing the item listed on the standard form, the seller will get the idea without the need to check the box.

E-mail can be a very effective manner of conveying both good news, as well as events in the transaction that may not be progressing as well as anticipated. The succinctness of email allows business matters to be discussed without the emotional overplay. Perhaps it is the very remoteness of e-mail that allows both the sender and recipient to detach from emotional overtones. Each may be more inclined to be open and direct which will facilitate the successful completion of the transaction.

Another idea is to provide the seller an extensive checklist for preparing the home for sale with the knowledge that, of course, not all items will apply to him. You will find that he will have a tendency to make certain all are complete.

Tip.   *Walk through the home with the seller with "buyer's eyes." Ask him to note any changes he feels he should make to the home in order to sell it. Emphasize that you are on his team, but as the professional chosen to market his home, you will note any objections you would anticipate a potential buyer would have. Decide at the onset how the seller will address any such objections to the condition of the home. Katherine has used a tape recorder effectively for the walk through with a written list provided to the seller. By doing this, you have already "paved the way" to discussion of any objections to the home.*

Market Updates. No matter how many times you tell a client or customer, either Seller or Buyer, a specific piece of information regarding his transaction, he will tend to have "selective memory" when the occasion fits. In the client's defense, it is impossible to remember the volumes of information, not to mention the content of all the forms he has signed in today's real estate transaction. Remember, the very complexity of real estate transactions is why he hired a real estate professional in the first place.

The practice of using a written update to keep the client informed and happy just makes common sense. Not only does it keep her informed of items which have been accomplished and eliminate confusion of what needs to be done, but a written update gives her a realistic impression of all that you are doing on her behalf to sell the property. Seldom will you receive a call demanding to know why the home has not sold or implying you are not doing your job.

The last paragraph of the update should always request the client to call you or e-mail you within a specific period of time if s/he has questions. This places the burden on the client to speak up now with any suggestions or changes s/he wishes to make. If none is proposed, you at least have a record of having made suggestions yourself. This again helps to establish that standard of practice common to all your transactions if your client should become a plaintiff.

Do not hesitate to be as detailed as possible with daily entries. There will be a tendency not to include those items you consider routine to any transaction. Those items may be routine to you, but a daily log shows your clients that you are doing something for them every day. It will show that you are "working all the time" for them. They may even call to apologize to you for their house not selling when you are working so hard for them, and offer the price reduction themselves! It has happened.

Personal Follow-up. In today's world, everyone is busy. As the listing agent, you need to take time to make personal follow-up communications. Drop off baked goods. Remember kids' birthdays. Know when the family members are participating in sports or plays. Be there to support your sellers outside of your role as a real estate professional, and they will support you. Stay in contact with them, no matter what.

Open Houses and Celebrations. Have a party once the home is listed. You might schedule several – one for brokers only, one for friends of the seller and one for the neighborhood. Neighbors especially know who wants to live where they live, so let them help you sell their neighbor's home. Can you think of a better way to convince them that they should call you when they decide to sell their own home?

Listing Checklist

Date:_____20____

Name:_____ RES Phone:_____

Address:_____ OFF Phone:_____

_____ CELL Phone:_____

_____ E-mail:_____

Title Company:_____ File No:_____

Contact:_____ Phone:_____

Cell:_____

E-mail:_____

LISTING PROCEDURE

____1.   Mail broker introduction letter
____2.   Assemble listing presentation packet
____3.   Send introduction e-mail and website for listings
      a. Include a color graphic of the house
      b. Direct the seller to your website with a special password just for him/her (Temp Client Password)
      c. E-mail "just listed" information if your MLS rules allow it, so that they can see what is on the market
____4.   Visit the seller in person
____5.   Mail follow-up personal letter to seller
____6.   Send follow-up e-mail
____7.   Mail/e-mail selected subject matter letters
____8.   Actual listing presentation date:_____
      a. Take digital picture and print some envelopes with it in the return address
      b. Put the picture on the top of the proposed listing contract or
      c. Put the picture in your laptop on the top of the listing contract
____9.   When listing documents are signed by Seller:
      a. Broker's signature on Listing Agreement (if req'd)

  b. Enter into the MLS computer
  c. Write MLS# on property profile sheet
  d. Write the URLs (websites) on the property sheet
  e. Deliver copy of MLS sheet to seller with confirming letter or by e-mail attachment in color
  f. Put the listing on the net and send the location to the seller

____10. Mail selected post-listing letters and e-mails
____11. Notify seller about home warranty programs by e-mail
____12. Assemble office showing instructions
____13. Mortgage info request letter mailed to lender _____
____14. Request association documents, covenants, etc. for common interest properties
____15. Target market
  a. Assemble showing sheet draft and make package for property
  b. Take picture with your sign in the yard; send one to seller
  c. Mail photos to market area (down 50%)
  d. Photo plus picture to shopping center boards
____16. Assemble neighborhood "just listed" letter and mail
____17. Assemble REALTOR® network "new on market" letter
____18. Make open house appointment with seller
____19. Hang the lockbox and obtain the seller consent form
____20. Schedule broker's open (confirmation to seller)
____21. Schedule first public open house
  a. Seller's friends only
  b. The neighborhood with food
____22. Make pro-forma Marketing Update Sheet master

WHEN LISTING SELLS
____1. Original/FAX of contract to file
____2. Original/FAX of contract to title company
____3. Prepare and deliver escrow instructions
____4. Prepare letter designating tasks to be completed
  a. Mail/e-mail to seller
  b. Mail/e-mail to buyer (via other broker)
____5. Prepare performance deadlines sheet
____6. Revise listing status in MLS and the Net
____7. Revise status in floor book and on company website
____8. Begin to assemble appraisal package for appraiser
____9. Designate and start to mail the letters/e-mails that will flow through the pre-closing period
____10. Mail/e-mail lender selection letter

WHEN LOAN IS "APPROVED"

____1. Mail loan confirmation letter
     a. To the buyer
     b. To the lender (reminds them what they said)
____2. Confirm loan status with lender and title company
____3. Make a project checklist to delegate outstanding tasks

WHEN TRANSACTION CLOSES and RECORDS

____1. Purge office file, prepare MLS sold change form
____2. Enter MLS status change
____3. Pull from the Net
____4. Give office file to accountant
____5. Complete entry for client database
____6. Input into personal farm database
____7. Send note and gift to client
____8. Send follow-up letters or e-mails (color) to all parties
____9. Ask for referral to new client!
____10. Schedule "get acquainted party" for buyer and new neighbors at the house
____11. Clean the file to save needed documents
____12. Make digital copy of closing statement
____13. Send delayed delivery of closing statement to seller and buyer for end of the year(copy to you)

THE MONEY

____1. Note 1099 for all "referral" fees
____2. Calculate the value of gifts and bonuses paid
____3. Quarterly payments

Marketing Update

Today's Date:_____ Date of Last Report:_____
Reporting Period:_____ Months __ Days

Listing Date:_____ Days on the Market:_____
Original   Current
List Price: $_____ List Price: $_____

ACTIVITY

_____ Showings from other offices
_____ Showings from our office
_____ Open houses:_____
_____ Written proposals received

Comments from other salespeople/buyers:
_____
_____
_____.

My Comments:
_____
_____
_____.

[Add your personal comments about the progress of the marketing. Include any future appointment dates such as inspections, performance deadlines on contracts, escrow or loan progress concerns that you want the client to remember. Offer suggestions for any change in marketing strategy, such as improving the property condition, offering additional incentives to potential buyers or price reductions. Be upbeat, but honest about any difficulties encountered in the marketing or escrow process.]

Please call me within 48 hours of receipt of this report if you have any questions, specific needs, comments or suggestions concerning the sale/marketing process of your home. I shall continue my work and dedication as we progress towards a completed sale of your home. Thank you.

SHOWING REPORT

To: _____

Property Address:_____

Your home was shown on the date(s) indicated below. Included are some of the comments that our office received. I thought that you might like to see them.

Date(s) Shown:_____

Comments:
☐ Exterior needs to be painted   ☐ Interior needs to be painted
☐ Carpets need to be cleaned   ☐ Animals made showing difficult
☐ House seemed cluttered   ☐ Children made showing difficult
☐ Garage seemed cluttered   ☐ Tenants made showing difficult
☐ I would rather show homes without the owners being home
☐_____
☐_____

I checked some suggestions that might assist us in showing your home in the future. Review them when you have a minute and I will give you a call.

Suggestions to enhance future showings:
☐ Offering incentives so tenants would cooperate with showings
☐ Paying "points" to a new lender to assist a buyer with a loan
☐ Remove or store some items, so that your home looks even larger
☐ Leave fresh baked bread in the oven before showings
☐ Leave a fire in the fireplace
☐ Place potpourri in your home
☐_____
☐_____
☐ Please call me at _____ when it is convenient

Salesperson:_____ Date: _____

Thank you for selecting us to market your home

Letter/e-mail – After Listing is Signed (Broker)

Mr. Sam Seller
Mrs. Sandra Seller
4750 Table Mesa Drive
Boulder, CO 80305

 Re: 4750 Table Mesa Drive, Boulder

Dear Sam and Sandy:

 Kathy and I and all the members of this firm are happy and proud to have been selected to market your home. Kathy has been an agent with this company for many years and has assisted many people in both marketing their existing property and in selecting new real estate. As I am sure she indicated to you, in order for all contractual obligations of The Real Estate Company to be effective under the law, they must be formally approved by me as the licensed broker. This policy allows agents to concentrate on the marketing of your home and leaves the obligations of this firm to the broker.

 I am happy to inform you that I, as the broker of The Real Estate Company, have just accepted and countersigned your proposed Listing Agreement, including the Seller's Property Disclosure Addendum, as submitted by Katherine Reece. A copy of the fully executed Listing Agreement is enclosed for your records. Welcome to our list of clients.

 Kathy has been describing your home, including your beautiful master bedroom, extensive well-cared-for garden and oversized garage with a shop area, in detail to everyone in the office as she prepares us for our office tour. I look forward to seeing your home personally on the tour.

 Please feel free to contact me at any time should you wish to discuss your relationship with this company. I am always happy to discuss any aspect of your real estate needs or your relationship with this company or real estate in general.

     Most sincerely,
     The Real Estate Company

Letter/e-mail – After Listing is Signed (Salesperson)

Mr. Sam Seller
Mrs. Sandy Seller
4750 Table Mesa Drive
Boulder, Colorado 80305

    Re: 4750 Table Mesa Drive

Dear Sam and Sandy:

    I want to thank you for selecting me and The Real Estate Company to market your home. I will be working hard to get your home SOLD upon the terms you have selected in the shortest amount of time possible.

    I will begin to market your home through the Multiple Listing Service (MLS) as soon as I have your approval of the "MLS Information Sheet." The listing information will then be entered in the MLS computer, and any REALTOR® from any member company can access that information twenty-four hours every day. In addition, everyone knows they can reach me at home, on my cellular phone or by digital pager if they need assistance.

    Finally, look for your home on the web. Yes, we will e-mail you with the location of your home on the internet. Please view it as soon as you can and proof the advertisement. You know the home better than anyone.

    I have delivered information about your property to each salesperson in the office. Additionally, I will be talking about your listing at our upcoming office meeting and other REALTOR® events. Should you see anyone that you think might be a possible buyer, just let me know. We are all searching together.

    Sam and Sandy, I know that selling real estate can sometimes be overwhelming. If you have any questions, comments or criticisms, please give me a call. I believe the marketing of your home is a team effort, and open communication is the best way to solve any problems that may arise.

                        Sincerely,
                        The Real Estate Company

Letter/e-mail – Listing Price Verification

Mr. Sam Seller
Mrs. Sandy Seller
4750 Table Mesa Drive
Boulder, CO 80305

     Re: 4750 Table Mesa Drive

Dear Sam and Sandy:

As I indicated when we listed your home, we want to be sure that you arrive at a price that reflects your understanding of the market. That has been done, and we congratulate you on pricing the property within a range that allowed us to accept the listing. Of course, no one knows the final sales price and terms.

As I indicated when we listed your home, the Competitive Market Analysis is yours to keep. It showed you those homes that had either sold, been rejected by the market or were still available as competition that we were able to locate that were similar to yours . Those are the same comparable properties that we indicated we would provide to an interested buyer when they inquire about the relative value of your home. Buyers must go through the same process that you experienced as they try to determine the price of your home.

I am so glad that I am a REALTOR® and not an appraiser. As a Realtor®, I can provide the data regarding relative value to the public and let the buyer and seller determine the price they feel is correct. Then once the contract is signed, we can all see if the appraiser agrees with the parties. We simply can not set, nor be responsible for, the price of real estate. We decide if the price determined by the seller is close enough to the market in our minds to warrant marketing the property at the selected price.

                            Most sincerely,
                            The Real Estate Company

                            by: My Name, Broker-Owner, Realtor®

Letter/e-mail – Listing MLS Information Verification

Mr. Sam Seller
Mrs. Sandy Seller
4750 Table Mesa Drive
Boulder, CO 80305

     Re: 4750 Table Mesa Drive

Dear Sam and Sandy:

    As I indicated when we listed your home, we want to submit your home to the Multiple Listing Service as soon as possible. Enclosed is the Multiple Listing Service data input form that I have completed for your home. Please review it as soon as possible. Also, enclosed is a sample of how the information on your home will appear on the web. Suggestions are welcome.

    If you desire to change or correct anything, let me know immediately. We are eager to represent your home accurately. Unless there are a number of changes, a phone call will do the job nicely. I know you are busy. If I do not hear to the contrary by Friday, I will assume that everything is correct and will submit the listing to the MLS in its present form. Remember that the internet uploads a sub-set of the data from the MLS to the web automatically on a periodic basis, so your home should hit the net soon.

                Most sincerely,
                The Real Estate Company

                by: Your Local REALTOR®, CRS, GRI

Letter/e-mail – Copy of Showings Report

Mr. Sam Seller
Mrs. Sandy Seller
4750 Table Mesa Drive
Boulder, CO 80305

    Re: 4750 Table Mesa Drive

Dear Sam and Sandy:

    Enclosed for your records is a copy of the feature Showings Report which has been mailed to all the real estate brokers who routinely have buyers for homes such as your home. This helps to keep your home first in salespersons' minds when they meet buyers and helps to trigger their remembrance of your home for those clients looking for homes now.

    Of course, this exposure is in addition to that already received from the Multiple Listing Service and internet site. This is just one of the extra things I do to ensure that your home is exposed to the largest number of salespersons and potential buyers.

    Should you have any questions or suggestions, please do not hesitate to call me. It is the team approach that will help us both toward a mutually beneficial business relationship.

                    Sincerely,
                    The Real Estate Company

                    by: Your Name Here,
                    REALTOR®, CRS, GRI

Letter/e-mail – Just Listed Neighbor's Home

Mr. Noisy Neighbor
Mrs. Nosey Neighbor
4760 Table Mesa Drive
Boulder, Colorado 80305

    Re: 4750 Table Mesa Drive

Dear Noisy and Nosey:

    Your neighbors at 4750 Table Mesa Drive have just listed their home with my company, The Real Estate Company. I will be doing my best to market the home to obtain a successful sale in the shortest amount of time.

    I would like to ask for your assistance. If you know of any friends or neighbors who may be renting at this time, or business associates who may have expressed an interest in living in your neighborhood, please have them contact me. I have enclosed a brochure on the home for your information.

    We will be having our first Open House this Sunday, September 10, between the hours of two and five in the afternoon [just for the neighbors]. I do hope you will stop by to see how lovely and well maintained your neighbors have kept their home.

    If you have any questions about the property, please do not hesitate to call me. My card is enclosed for your convenience.

                 Sincerely,
                 The Real Estate Company

                 By: Your Associate Broker, REALTOR®

The Real Estate Company

PRIVATE PARTY

Just Listed in Your Neighborhood

Your neighbors, Sam and Sally Seller, have just listed their nice home at 4750 Table Mesa Drive with me and my company. We will be doing everything we can to market their home in the shortest possible time. You may have seen this home on our website, www.therealestatecompany.com/4750

You are invited to an exclusive Open House just for the neighbors. You may already know someone who has expressed an interest in living in your nice neighborhood, so we want you to come and see this home. Often the residents who live here are the best sources of qualified buyers. Maybe you have a friend or business acquaintance who you always wanted to live near you.

Our Private Party Open House is: _____

We would appreciate an RSVP since we will be serving afternoon food and beverages. If you have special dietary needs, please let us know.

This Open House is for neighbors and their personal friends only. Regular Open Houses will be scheduled in a few days.

Name: _____

Address: _____

Phone: _____ Number Attending; _____

You Local Person, REALTOR®, CRS, GRI

Home: _____ Office: _____ Mobile: _____

E-mail: _____

The Real Estate Company

Just Listed in Your Neighborhood

Your neighbors Sam and Sally Seller have just listed their nice home at 4750 Table Mesa Drive with me and my company. We will be doing everything we can to market that home in the shortest possible time. You may already have seen their home on our website, www.therealestatecompany.com/4750

You can help. If you have any friends, relatives or business associates who have either expressed an interest in living in this neighborhood or whom you believe would enjoy living here, please let me know.

Our first Open House is:_____

Please fell free to stop in and bring interested friends.

I am always available should you have questions about Sam and Sandy's house, or real estate in general. With constantly changing financing rates, you may have thought of refinancing. I would be glad to give you the names of the lenders that we use for our clients.

Your Local Hardworking, REALTOR®, CRS, GRI

Home:_____ Office:_____ Mobile:_____

E-mail:_____

Letter/e-mail – Hazardous Waste and Soil Condition

Mr. Sam Seller
Mrs. Sandy Seller
4750 Table Mesa Drive
Boulder, CO 80305

    Re: 4750 Table Mesa Drive

Dear Sam and Sandy:

As we discussed when I presented our company's policies prior to your selecting our firm and me to represent you, there are many outside factors that need to be determined or confirmed, so that buyers can make informed decisions about the home they are buying. One of our objectives is that you complete the sale of you home without any lingering fears of later repercussions from the ultimate buyer, someone that you most probably do not even know yet.

While most people are inclined to inspect and review a property thoroughly before making an offer, some cautious buyers will want to have the property inspected for the presence of radon gas, mold and other hazardous materials and to verify the condition of the soil prior to being obligated to purchase. Today many lenders and relocation companies make such verifications a must for their participation in a transaction.

As I indicated, the information that I have been reading suggests that all homes have some radon gas present. The key issue is to determine the amount. In addition, the composition of the soil on which the house is built concerns many buyers. In this area, bentonite, an expanding clay soil, is common. The key is to determine the composition of the soil, the extent to which it is composed of bentonite, whether the soil is a factor that needs to be addressed, and the extent of any hazardous substances, such as radon gas, lead based paint or mold.

Most importantly, a potential purchaser will probably inquire about, and subsequently require, that a test be conducted prior to his final purchase of your home. All this takes time when you can least afford it; that is, after the buyer has bound your home with a signed contract, but before the closing has occurred. This is a critical period when I like to have as few problems as possible.

The solution that we recommend is to have every home that we list tested as soon as possible for the condition of the soil and the presence and extent of radon gas and other hazardous materials. In this way, we can have the test results available for potential purchasers who can review them *prior* to making their decision to purchase; therefore, hopefully eliminating the need for the contract to be conditional upon the results of a subsequent test.

A list of firms that provide these services is enclosed. Please talk it over, make a selection and order the tests. I would be glad to assist the tester of your choice by meeting her at the property during the day, as I realize that you are both quite busy. In fact, after you make the selection and give me a budget of how much you wish to spend, I would be glad to arrange for the test on your behalf.

I can see no reason why both tests should not be simply a matter of course. Having them ready might just be the factor that helps that buyer decide on your home. Buyers, once they see what they want, usually are in a hurry to move in. The inspections would eliminate one more delay.

As I mentioned in my initial meeting with you, there are a number of areas that would tend to indicate to a potential purchaser that the property has some form of structural defect. Once this is known to me, I have to point out the presence of such a defect. Having an engineer's report to show that the repairs you have elected to perform will totally take care of the potential problem, or that you have already performed the repairs satisfactorily to eliminate the problem, will help market what otherwise could be a slower moving property.

When you have made your selection, just indicate it on the bottom of this letter and drop it back to my office. I have enclosed a stamped, self-addressed envelope for your convenience. Thank you for selecting me as your agent. I am proud to have your home in my inventory of listings and to represent you as your real estate agent. I know you want to complete this sale with a minimum of delay and potential problems. Therefore, I am willing to do whatever you direct to expedite that and to coordinate the people you choose to make the necessary repairs and inspections.

Sincerely,
The Real Estate Company

Enclosure: List of Radon/Mold Inspectors
                 List of Soils Engineers

Letter/e-mail – Structural/Mechanical Inspections/Home Warranty

Mr. Sam Seller
Mrs. Sandy Seller
4750 Table Mesa Drive
Boulder, CO 80305

    Re: 4750 Table Mesa Drive

Dear Sam and Sandy:

The acquisition of a home is the largest purchase the average person will attempt in a lifetime. Real estate transactions are becoming more and more complex. Most people are convinced that the cautious buyer will make inquiry into the structural condition and mechanical condition of all prospective properties. To avoid making what might be interpreted by some as "the mistake of a lifetime," many buyers are reviewing reports that indicate the structural and mechanical integrity of properties they are considering buying.

Having the requested information available when a prospective buyer inquires allows us a better chance of capturing a sale, while other sellers are still trying to determine whether they will allow an inspection and at whose expense. While other sellers are unsure about who will select the various inspectors and the timing of the inspections, we will have the results available. This requires making a decision with regard to the type of inspection, the extent to which it will be performed and who will be selected to perform it within your budget. Should any defects come to light, we will have the opportunity to make corrections or obtain adequate insurance before the discovery of some minor defect destroys a potential sale.

Structural Inspection – Engineer's Report

While we can use a friend or builder, engineers have the greatest impact upon a prospective buyer. Engineers are licensed by the state. I am not, and never want to be, an engineer. As with all professions, the degree of expertise varies from individual to individual. If you have someone with whom you feel confident, I would recommend you contact her soon. Most engineers will write a report indicating their opinion with regard to the structural integrity of the home in general. These professionals generally do not indicate the condition or life expectancy of the mechanical systems in your home. Although this can be expensive, it also is very useful to demonstrate to a prospective purchaser that an engineer has inspected the home. This will discourage the buyer from obtaining a separate inspection; thus, potentially saving time and expense.

Mechanical Inspection – Home Warranty Companies

There are a number of companies offering a service which generally includes an inspection of the mechanical systems and appliances located in a home. The report will indicate whether they are in good working order or if any repairs are necessary. In addition, many of these companies offer an insurance policy that protects the insured, usually the buyer, against failure of the indicated components within the terms of the policy. This may seem expensive; however, it is part of the marketing package included with a new home. New homes are definitely part of our competition.

There are numerous competitors in the marketplace for this kind of service. Although I cannot be responsible for the several individuals and companies listed on the attached sheet, or listed on the reverse, I do know that they have been utilized in the past by other homeowners. Each should be happy to provide you with a list of past clients or customers to assist you in making your decision.

Prior to making your decision, you will want to satisfy yourself that your selection has adequate errors and omissions insurance, is licensed, if applicable, and if a home inspector, is a member of ASHI® or NAHI™. For insurance policies, review each policy carefully, as well as consider the reputation of each company.

Our firm acts as an agent for the attached Home Warranty company. We feel confident that its policy is one of the best in the marketplace. To date, buyers have indicated that they have received excellent and prompt service. A copy of its policy is attached for your review. Please feel free to select any home warranty provider. Our list of providers and recommendations is to be considered as a service to you, and not as an endorsement or guarantee of the services they provide.

I will be happy to work with the professionals you select by providing access to your home, in the event it is necessary to schedule their visit at a time when you will not be present. If you wish, after your selection and negotiation of the fee with the inspector, I will arrange for the scheduling of the inspection.

I will meet the home inspector at your home. I will let the inspector in the property. I do not accompany the home inspector through the property, so that the inspector can make an impartial assessment of your home without input from me. I am not an inspector, and I want this to be an impartial home inspection without even the appearance of impropriety.

Sincerely,
The Real Estate Company

by: Your Name Here, REALTOR®

cc: Oliver Twist, Broker

Direction to Obtain Inspections

You are hereby instructed to contact and employ, on my behalf, the following entities that I have selected, within the cost guidelines indicated, to accomplish their respective inspections. Please inform each to provide you with a written report as soon as possible after the job is completed. Where indicated on this form, I want an estimate prior to employment. Please request that the proper entity provide us with an estimate of the premium for a Home Warranty Policy for a one-year period.

Entity:		Phone:	
Min Fee: $	Max Fee: $	Estimate First: (yes) (no)	

Entity:		Phone:	
Min Fee: $	Max Fee: $	Estimate First: (yes) (no)	

Entity:		Phone:	
Min Fee: $	Max Fee: $	Estimate First: (yes) (no)	

Entity:		Phone:	
Min Fee: $	Max Fee: $	Estimate First: (yes) (no)	

I understand that there are numerous competitors in the marketplace for this kind of service and that you are not responsible for the several individuals and companies I have selected.

I hereby authorize and direct you to present the results of all inspections to any and all prospective buyers and to forward them to me. This will help to eliminate any potential liability either of us might incur. Please indicate to each inspector that he should send the statement for his services directly to me for payment.

Thank you for your efforts on my behalf.

_____   _____
Seller   Date

Letter/e-mail – Confirming Action

Mr. Sam Seller
Mrs. Sandy Seller
4750 Table Mesa Drive
Boulder, CO 80305

> Re: 4750 Table Mesa Drive
> Inspection Selection

Dear Sam and Sandy:

It was nice to get your call today. This is just a note to tell you that I was able to contact the inspector. S/he agreed to complete the engineer's report within the next two weeks for a fee not to exceed $350. In addition, I also contacted Radon Gas Associates and requested that they come over next Thursday to perform the test for the flat fee of $125.00 to which you agreed.

I compliment you on your selection of these experts for the inspections. As you are aware, I am not personally responsible for their actions or inactions. I am happy that I was able to obtain their services within the budget you set. I do not want to spend any more of your money than absolutely necessary. Both specialists indicated that they would bill you directly at the end of the job.

You have completed one more step to a well-planned sale. It never ceases to amaze me what it takes to properly market a property in these complicated times. If you have any questions, please give me a call. It is a pleasure to act as your listing agent. I hope that your wife is feeling better.

Sincerely,
The Real Estate Company

by: Your Name Here,
REALTOR®, CRS, GRI

cc: Oliver Twist, Broker

Liability for the Premises

The Key. The seller usually gives the agent a key to the house. This starts a series of delegations of the right to enter the property. The number of reported thefts and other problems grow as agents become more involved in the servicing of many different listings and touring houses with various buyers. Unfortunately, the mere fact that a person has obtained a real estate license and possibly joined a board or multiple listing service is no indication of the reputation, degree of care, integrity or ability of that agent. More importantly, unknown to some agents, customers use this showing procedure as an opportunity to case vacant houses and view possible entry systems, or to set up open windows or doors for accomplices. There are even some agents that let the purchaser have the key to view the property.

You need not concern your client with all these particulars. However, maintain an awareness yourself, so that you will always remember to assist your client in understanding his or her side of the responsibility inherent in letting others into the home. _Be clear and be safe._

Other Selling Licensees. Automatically assume that you need a higher degree of concern and care for any showing request other than your own. This should be paramount in the listing broker's mind, and the decision to allow an unaccompanied showing should be examined closely. The broker is becoming responsible for the manner in which he protects the property of his client, the seller. Ask yourself, "Could I demonstrate a high degree of care in court? To whom did I give the key, lockbox combination or electronic keycard? Was it to someone I did not even know?"

Personal Unlocking Service. There is absolutely no substitute for opening the home for each prospective purchaser, whether or not accompanied by any other form of agent. The practice of personally opening the home for each showing appointment is rare and difficult when coordinating a convenient time for all parties, but may be appropriate for unknown selling licensees. This does not suggest interfering with the relationship between the prospective purchaser and the agent showing that prospective purchaser the home.

There is an absolute duty to take care of the house when you get the key and a responsibility to ensure that others who acquire entry to the house and/or use of the key be scrutinized carefully. Remember, duplication of keys is a very easy procedure.

Tip.   *Decide how much of the risk you can reasonably accept and let your client know your limits. You decide how you do business and let them decide if they want to do business with you.*

Expensive Items and Limit of Liability. The seller is someone that you know very little about and who may have an insurance claim in mind for items that were never on the property. Establish the extent of liability and the degree of care that is expected. In addition, ask the seller to make an inventory of expensive items. Simply and politely state that the firm is not responsible for furs, jewelry, gun collections and the like. Recommend that the seller temporarily store these items elsewhere during the marketing of the home.

The Lockbox. Lockboxes can vary from the rudimentary, single key and uniform key, to the electronic recording key safe. While some people are still using a single key system, the pressure upon the entity responsible for the operation of the system is mounting to provide a more security oriented and accountable use access system. Yes, there are many keys outstanding and unaccounted for. Yes, HUD does utilize such a single key lockbox access system. Remember, as a governmental entity, it generally deal with vacant houses.

Next is the combination box system. Supra Products, Inc. manufactured many of these boxes, which came with the combination of S-P-I. To this date there are literally thousands of these boxes on houses that still use that same S-P-I code. In fact, that same box is sold at hardware stores and is even fitted for vehicular use for a spare key. The updated version has a touch pad code system, but it is essentially the same box that has been used for years and years. The careful REALTOR® inputs a personalized code for each home and frequently changes the combinations of each box. The problems with this old technology are well known. The box can be picked or drilled.

The state of the art is the electronic lockbox or "key safe." This electronic lockbox actually retains the date, time and identity of each person that accesses the box. The information is instantly available through the key for security and marketing purposes. Run by a computer, access is regulated, and keys generally expire every thirty days, as indicated by the respective issuing agency, the board or MLS. While there is still room for unauthorized entry, it is greatly reduced. Systems now use infrared signal transmission, are compatible with PDA's and even upload and update nightly.

Great care should be taken in the selection of a system and in giving access to the key, combination or electronic recording system. Not even the cover letter will protect you from the negligence of your own agents, nor that of the plethora of others waiting to see or preview the house.

Nothing protects you from gross negligence, such as giving out the lockbox combination or key to any person assumed to be a real estate agent, or the dissemination of the information over a mobile phone or an e-mail. It goes without saying that no one should allow anyone to know the access code or to "borrow" the key or the electronic key pad. Neither the firm nor the agent should have a standard combination. Be demonstrably cautious. Never use the same combination for more than one property at any given point in time. Change the combination between listings and certainly see that the combination is changed at least monthly, if not weekly. A lockbox authorization or release form must be in your files.

Case in Point. *The owner of a condominium in a large complex allows the agent to put the key to the entire building in a lockbox placed at the main entry. There is a theft, and the broker is held responsible for encouraging the thief by the placement of the lockbox; thereby, indicating that a vacant unit in the building is for sale. To make matters worse, the agent also placed a lockbox on the unit entry door. This was a nice way of pointing to the unit that was for sale and, in the mind of at least one hearing panel member, of making the unit vulnerable. That was held to be negligence since there was a theft in the unit for sale and in two other units in the building in a single day.*

Interestingly enough, there was no accurate record of the individuals who had access to the combination, nor of those who had shown the property in the preceding two weeks. The few names that were available proved to include one person that was not a member of any board, held no license, and had no operable local phone number.

The listed unit was robbed without the use of force. It is so easy when you have the combination. I wonder what a court would have decided. The broker was very happy to write a few checks.

Periodic Inventory. If there are a lot of valuable items left in a listed home, a periodic inventory by the seller and/or agent may help to eliminate the allegations of negligence or theft that may arise in such situations. Some people, after claiming that they were robbed while the property was listed, have been extremely lucky to be able to locate items almost identical to those that were stolen in their post-theft, post-settlement with some insurance company. There is no need for you to be the victim of such practices.

Letter/e-mail – Post Listing General Lockbox

Mr. Sam Seller
Mrs. Sandy Seller
4750 Table Mesa Drive
Boulder, CO 80305

    Re: 4750 Table Mesa Drive

Dear Sam and Sandy:

As I indicated, one of the available marketing methods to allow fast access to other cooperating and in-house salespersons is to place a lockbox on your door. This is a key safe that contains a key to your home and is accessed by other members of the Board or Multiple Listing Service. Please read the Lockbox Authorization Form, sign and return it to me if you wish to utilize this system.

I look forward to previewing your home with the entire office staff in the next few days when your home is scheduled as part of our weekly office tour. I am proud to have my name affiliated with the marketing of your home.   If you have any questions, please feel free to call me or my broker at any time.

           Sincerely,
           The Real Estate Company

           by: Your Name Here,
           REALTOR®, CRS, GRI

Lockbox Authorization Form

We, the undersigned owner(s) of the following described real estate, hereby authorize you, subject to the conditions indicated below, to place a lockbox on our property. In addition, we understand that you will not be responsible or liable to us for the unauthorized use of the lockbox or the key located therein, as long as you are in compliance with the terms of this agreement. We understand that potential cooperating licensed salespeople will enter our property through the use of the lockbox. While we understand that you will try to limit such access, we realize that there is no way that you can be responsible for unauthorized access through the lockbox. We thank you for your suggestion that we inventory our household possessions.

Property Address: _____

Type of Lockbox: _____

Special Conditions: _____

_____

_____

Access to be given to (*please initial all that apply*):

Appraisers: _____   Inspectors: _____

Other:_____

Owner: Owner:

_____   _____
                date   date

Letter/e-mail – Post Listing Combination Lockbox

Mr. Sam Seller
Mrs. Sandy Seller
4750 Table Mesa Drive
Boulder, CO 80305

Re: 4750 Table Mesa Drive

Dear Sam and Sandy:

There are several methods for showing your home. Our preferred method is for any salesperson from our office or another office to have an opportunity to talk with me prior to any showings. The salespeople in our office are constantly encouraged to talk to the listing salesperson prior to a showing. There are many instances where this is simply not possible.

If you desire, we will place a lockbox on your home. This presents special risks for the unauthorized entry to your home and requires your written authorization prior to its placement. The advantage of having a key placed in the lockbox is that other salespeople can view the home after making a telephone appointment, without the need to travel to several offices to obtain keys and then repeat the journey after each series of showings. In a metro area such as ours, the distance between offices can be great. By providing more accessibility for showings to potential cooperating agents, you will ultimately receive more showings and exposure for your home.

In spite of all our efforts, we feel that it is always in your best interest to place valuable jewelry, coins, currency and other easily-removable items in your safe deposit box at your bank or to store these items, as well as expensive tools, furs and the like, at another location. We simply can not be responsible for such items. If you have any large items of value, other than your ordinary furniture, such as expensive televisions, computers, video equipment and the like, we encourage you to mark these items with an identity number. Complete an inventory including the value of each item for your insurance company. We have included a simple form given us by the insurance agency to assist you in taking such an inventory.

Most sincerely,

Letter/e-mail – Post Listing Combination Lockbox #2

Mr. Sam Seller
Mrs. Sandy Seller
4750 Table Mesa Drive
Boulder, CO 80305

Re: 4750 Table Mesa Drive

Dear Sam and Sandy:

There are several methods for showing your home. Our preferred method is for any salesperson from our office or another office to have an opportunity to talk with me prior to any showings. The salespeople in our office are constantly encouraged to talk to the listing salesperson prior to a showing. There are many instances where this is simply not possible.

In order to facilitate all possible showings, we can provide a lockbox, or key safe, for your property. This device is attached to the property and contains the key to your home. When the proper combination is entered, the key is released. In order to provide more security, we change the combination frequently and do not use the same combination for all our listings. Nevertheless, there is risk associated with such a box. The combination could become known to a prospective purchaser or others.

In spite of all our efforts, we feel that it is always in your best interest to place valuable jewelry, coins, currency and other easily-removable items in your safe deposit box at your bank or to store these items, as well as expensive tools, furs and the like, at another location. We simply can not be responsible for such items. If you have any large items of value, other than your ordinary furniture, such as expensive televisions, computers, video equipment and the like, we encourage you to mark these items with an identity number. Complete an inventory including the value of each item for your insurance company. We have included a simple form given us by the insurance agency to assist you in taking such an inventory.

Thank you again for listing your home with our agency. We are happy to be marketing your property for you.

Combination Lockbox Authorization Form

We, the undersigned owner(s) of the following referenced property, hereby authorize you, subject to the conditions indicated below, to place a lockbox on our door. We fully understand that the combination will be set by you, and changed by you, at intervals you determine. In addition, we understand that you will not be responsible or liable to us for the unauthorized use of the lockbox or the key located therein, so long as you are in compliance with the terms of this agreement.

We understand that potential cooperating licensed salespeople will contact you and request the combination, which you are authorized to provide to them, so that they can view our property without your presence. We realize that there is a risk that the combination will be discovered by parties with interests adverse to ours, and that it may encourage people to consider this property for illegal entry. While we understand that you will try to limit such access, we realize that there is no way that you can be responsible for unauthorized access through the lockbox. We thank you for your suggestion that we inventory our household possessions.

Property Address: _____

Type of Lockbox: _____

Special Conditions: _____
_____
_____

Access to be given to (*please initial all that apply*):

Appraisers: _____   Inspectors: _____

Other:_____

Owner: Owner:

_____   _____
Dated:_____   Dated:_____

Letter/e-mail – Electronic Lockbox/Key Safe

Mr. Sam Seller
Mrs. Sandy Seller
4750 Table Mesa Drive
Boulder, CO 80305

     Re: 4750 Table Mesa Drive

Dear Sam and Sandy:

    There are several methods for showing your home. Our preferred method is for any salesperson from our office or another office to have an opportunity to talk with me prior to any showings. The salespeople in our office are constantly encouraged to talk to the listing salesperson prior to a showing. There are many instances where this is simply not possible.

    In order to facilitate all possible showings, we can provide an electronic lockbox, or key safe, for your property. This device is attached to the property and contains the key to your home. It is accessed by an electronic card that is issued to each member of the Multiple Listing Service. The box will register which key accessed the box and indicate the time and date of the entry. In addition, I can set the box, so that it will not allow access before or after certain hours and on special occasions. When the electronic key is placed in the box, the key to your home is released. While we feel that this is the best available system, there is still room for illegal or unauthorized entry. We simply can not be responsible for that risk.

    For any showing made by appointment through our office, we contact the other salesperson for a report once the showing has been completed. We access the box periodically to determine who is showing the property and contact them for feedback, in the event showings are made without an appointment.

    In spite of all our efforts, we feel that it is always in your best interest to place valuable jewelry, coins, currency and other easily-removable items in your safe deposit box at your bank or to store these items, as well as expensive tools, furs and the like, at another location. We simply can not be responsible for such items. If you have any large items of value, other than your ordinary furniture, such as expensive televisions, computers, video equipment and the like, we encourage you to mark these items with an identity number. Complete an inventory including the value of each item for your insurance company. We have included a simple form given us by the insurance agency to assist you in taking such an inventory.

Sincerely,
The Real Estate Company

by: Your Name Here,
REALTOR®, CRS, GRI

Letter/e-mail – Electronic Lockbox/Key Safe #2

Mr. Sam Seller
Mrs. Sandy Seller
4750 Table Mesa Drive
Boulder, CO 80305

        Re: 4750 Table Mesa Drive

Dear Sam and Sandy:

        There are several methods for showing your home. Our preferred method is for any salesperson from our office or another office to have an opportunity to talk with me prior to any showings. The salespeople in our office are constantly encouraged to talk to the listing salesperson prior to a showing. There are many instances where this is simply not possible.

        We utilize the electronic key safe that I demonstrated when we first listed your home. This system allows me to immediately determine which salesperson has accessed your home, as well as the exact time of entry. This helps to provide more security for your home, and allows me to track potential buyers immediately. Valuable marketing information can be obtained from the potential buyer, and any objections to the home can be relayed to you, so that we can market your home effectively.

        Although it is impossible to personally know all of the salespeople who might potentially show your home, we will not let anyone unknown to us show your home unaccompanied. We have informed all other prospective salespeople that we reserve the right to accompany anyone who displays an interest in viewing your home.

        In spite of all our efforts, we feel that it is always in your best interest to place valuable jewelry, coins, currency and other easily-removable items in your safe deposit box at your bank or to store these items, as well as expensive tools, furs and the like, at another location. We simply can not be responsible for such items. If you have any large items of value, other than your ordinary furniture, such as expensive televisions, computers, video equipment and the like, we encourage you to mark these items with an identity number. Complete an inventory including the value of each item for your insurance company. We have included a simple form given us by the insurance agency to assist you in taking such an inventory.

Thank you again for listing your home with our firm. We are happy to be marketing your property for you.

Sincerely,
The Real Estate Company

by: Your Name Here,
REALTOR®, CRS, GRI

Electronic Recording Key Safe (Lockbox) Authorization

We, the undersigned owner(s) of the following described real estate, hereby authorize you, subject to the conditions indicated below, to place an electronic recording key safe (lockbox) on our door. We understand that the box will record each entry. We also understand that many individuals have electronic keys to the box. In addition, we understand that you will not be responsible or liable to us for the unauthorized use of the key safe, or the key located therein, so long as you are in compliance with the terms of this agreement.

We understand that potential cooperating licensed salespeople will contact you and request permission to show the property without your presence. While we understand that you will try to limit such access, we realize that there is no way that you can be responsible for unauthorized access through the key safe. We have indicated the times that we do not want any access in the special conditions section. Please program the key safe accordingly. We thank you for your suggestion that we inventory our household possessions.

Property Address: _____

Type of Key Safe: _____

Special Conditions:_____ __

_____

_____

Access to be given to (*please initial all that apply*):

Appraisers: _____   Inspectors: _____

Other:_____

Owner: Owner:

_____   _____
Dated:_____   Dated:_____

Letter/e-mail – Open House

Mr. Sam Seller
Mrs. Sandy Seller
4750 Table Mesa Drive
Boulder, CO 80305

    Re: 4750 Table Mesa Drive

Dear Sam and Sandy:

With a house that is as nice as yours or that has a location such as yours, we have found that having it open to the public on a Saturday, Sunday or evening gives people an opportunity to look through your home in a relaxed atmosphere. Warm bread in the oven, a fire in the fireplace or cut flowers can enhance the sense that your home is perfect for them.

We would have an agent on the premises at all times and would encourage you to take the day off and go somewhere else, so that the house is available for inspection by interested persons. This allows the home to look larger and more spacious than it would if we were all there and also reduces the intimidation factor when a prospective purchaser enters.

I will be contacting you to schedule some tentative times for an Open House. I want to plan an advertising strategy in advance to try to maximize the number of prospects we can anticipate.

Sincerely,
The Real Estate Company

by: Your Name Here,
REALTOR®, CRS, GRI

Open House Request/Authorization Form

Property
Address:_____

Please consider this as our request for your office to hold our house "open to the public." We understand that you will provide equal access to everyone, regardless of their potential membership in a "protected class," as defined by the laws, rules and regulations of the federal, state and local governments.

We understand that there is a risk that the public, when viewing our home, may damage it or steal some of our property. To prevent or reduce our potential loss, we have obtained insurance on our possessions in an amount we feel is appropriate and/or removed and stored those items about which we are concerned. We know that it is impossible for you to be physically present with everyone when more than one person is walking through our home. Therefore, we will not hold you responsible for any loss occasioned by having our house open to the public.

We understand that you will notify us within _____ days in advance of the open house date to verify the exact date and time for the open house. We agree to have the house clean and prepared to show to the public. In addition, if we have pets, we will remove our pets from the property during the open house period.

Our special requests follow:

_____

_____

_____

Thank you.

Date:_____

Owner(s):_____

Property Management

By Design. Property management seems to flow from two distinct sources. First, the arrangement is set up by design. The owner and the agent enter into a comprehensive agreement dealing with the rights, duties and obligations of both the owner and the agent. These vary from simple rent collection and mortgage payment application, to full rental and management authority, including the right to offer, negotiate and lease the premises, bring eviction actions, contract and pay for repairs and generally deal with the real property.

By Default. Second, a property management arrangement simply happens. This occurs when the real estate professional, while in the course of her normal listing duties, is called upon to be the agent for the owner in a capacity not anticipated or delineated in the original listing agreement. The agent then unwittingly becomes a more comprehensive agent for the owner for leasing, repair, maintenance, eviction and so forth, without the proper agreement. The result is that the owner denies the relationship when it suits him, and the agent and broker are left with expenses, tenant suits and other problems without any assistance from the owner. See to it early that your duties are made clear, so that you will not be victimized by either an owner's exaggerated expectations or by your own desire to be helpful.

Confirmation of the Tenancy. If you should decide to accept the job of property manager, we would suggest a nice little letter to each tenant to verify the current status of that particular tenant's tenancy. This will serve to verify any information you were fortunate enough to have received from the landlord and establish a rapport with the tenants. This type of letter can also be useful at the start of a new year, just so that the tenant does not start to feel he is the owner.

Eviction. There are those that need excitement in the world, and eviction is the place to get it. If you are going to act as the agent for the eviction of a tenant, we would recommend a series of cover letters to confirm each step in the procedure and to request instructions often. When the counterclaim comes, it will be nice to be able to hide under the agency cloak. To be entitled to that protection, you must have been acting within the scope of your agency. Yes, that means more than a standard listing agreement.

Equity Skimming.   While you would never participate in an equity skimming scheme, it is a good idea to be familiar with the meaning of the term. In this situation, the owner, intending from the outset to make money and not payments, acquires a property with the intent to rent it and keep the rent paid by the tenants. Such a person pays the utility companies and often any association fees, but neglects to pay the taxes or mortgage payments. It is important to note that intent is a key element in this definition in many states.

Equity skimming is not a term that would generally apply to the owner of a single property who, after owning it for some time, finds that s/he can no longer subsidize the rent to make all the required payments. Often the real estate broker is collecting the rental amounts and turning the rent over to the owner.

To avoid even the appearance of impropriety in such circumstances, we suggest that the broker cease to manage any property that he/she knows is in such a situation. The owner or someone else can handle the rental payments. Maintain the listing but cease managing the property.

Tenant Mentality. Tenants are important people in real estate. It is the tenant and his all-important rental payments that drive the income property market. Good tenants are invaluable and deserve an owner's best. Recognize that many tenants are red flags. These others fit part of our plaintiff profile. They do not generally have a lot of assets, wish they owned a house, are jealous of the owner and his real estate agent, have little downside risk in litigation, and very often no ability to stick around after you win the suit, let alone pay the amount of the judgment against them. It is next to impossible to recover the what it "cost you to play in court" from a tenant.

Tip.   *Yes, your principles are important. Just as with the other kind of principal, they need to be placed where they will compound interest, not compound problems.*

If, for whatever reason, you must function as a manager, get a written agreement and get paid separately and adequately for it.

Protection. As the broker and/or agent, you are interested in protecting yourself from the perils and pitfalls of becoming a volunteer management agent. At the same time, you want to keep the listing and assist the owner as much as necessary, so that the property can be marketed. At first this may seem impossible, but it is really quite easy. All that is required is that you define the relationship as it exists, and as it may evolve.

Caution. *It is important to note that property management is not covered by many of the professional liability insurers. This is because of the extreme exposure and loss that occurs in this field when it is practiced by the inexperienced real estate agent, generally without any documentation as to the extent of the agent's authority. A quick review of your policy might be helpful.*

Tenancy Agreements. The tendency to suggest or use a lease agreement that was used in the last deal, or is a standard form, can be very strong. Resist the urge. Have the owner select and designate a form. Do not proffer your form; that is practicing law and not necessary to accomplish the objective. Leases, even in the most mundane residential transaction, are very complex and often devoid of what might later prove to be important clauses.

Timing. As with all notices and agreements, agreement before the fact is the preferred route. In this case, however, the memorandum of previous oral conversation or agreement is a useful bootstrapping tool. If you sense that any of your relationships might be cloudy on this matter, fire off some memoranda of your previous oral agreements or conversations immediately.

Payment. You work hard enough to earn your normal commission. Charge a fee for the additional management services you may be induced to perform. Fees are a good way to either eliminate the request for management or to open the door for a satisfactory comprehensive management agreement.

Withdrawal. Any management agreement – in addition to a multitude of other agreements not to be discussed in this book – should contain a provision allowing you to withdraw, turn the damage deposits over to the owner, with tenant confirmation of course, and stop managing the property when you have had enough.

Ask for A Signed Copy. You can guarantee a signed copy for your files of any agreement with the tenant if you make duplicate copies of all written agreements. Make a copy of the agreement on pink paper and send one white copy and one pink copy to the tenant. Mark the white copy, "tenant copy – retain for your records," and the pink one, "return in self addressed envelope." Most people will comply and return the pink copy.

Letter/e-mail – Verification of the Terms of the Tenancy/Owner

Mr. Robert S. Caplan
750 Prospect Lane
Colorado Springs, CO 80903

     Re: Unit 203 B

Dear Mr. Caplan:

     Another year has ended, and it is time to get everything ready for the accountant and the dreaded tax return. I hope that last year was all that you hoped it would be, and that next year meets your expectations.

     Each year the accountant requests that I verify the terms of each tenancy. Please take a minute to confirm for the accountant that you are the tenants in the property indicated above and are occupying this property under a rental arrangement that does not include any option to purchase.

Family:	Robert, Laurian, Monica and Adam		
Pets:	No pets are allowed		
Tenancy:	Month to month		
Monthly rent:	$450.00	Deposit:	$400.00
Late on the:	15th	Late Charge	$50.00
Rent due on:	The 1st of each month in advance		
Rent paid through:	December		

Thank you for your efforts. It makes the accounting so much easier.

     Most sincerely,
     The Real Estate Company
     Agents for the Owner of the Property

     by: Oliver E. Frascona, Broker

Approved: *(Only one approval is needed. Any tenant may approve for all tenants.)*

_____

Robert S. Caplan
Please return pink copy in the enclosed stamped self addressed envelope.

Letter/e-mail – Verification of the Terms of the Tenancy

Mr. Robert S. Caplan
Mrs. Laurian Greening
750 Prospect Lane
Colorado Springs, CO 80903

　　　Re: Unit 203 B

Dear Mr. Caplan and Mrs. Greening:

　　Please allow me to introduce myself as the as the new property manager for the owner of this building. I enjoy assisting people with their living needs and want you to know that I am available during normal working hours at the above office. Please feel free to contact me there for the payment of rent and other business related to the building. I too have a family, and have promised my wife that I will not work after 5:00 P.M. unless it is an emergency. I know you will understand that in an emergency I would want you, by all means to contact me at home at 303-494-6661.

　　My records indicate that the following is a correct status report of your account:

Your family consists of:	Robert, Laurian, Monica and Adam
Pets:	No pets are allowed
Tenancy:	Month to month
Monthly rent:	$450.00
Deposit:	$400.00
Rent is due on:	the 1st of each month
Late on the:	15th
Late Charge:	$50.00
Rent is paid:	In advance on the first of each month
Rent paid through:	March

　　If any one of the above terms is incorrect, please call me and send me a written letter indicating what you feel is in error. You must do both. If it is easier, just make a notation on this letter and sign your name. If I do not hear to the contrary within five days of the date of this letter, I will understand that the above information is correct.

Letter/e-mail – Verification of the Terms of the Tenancy – *Just for Fun*

Mr. Robert S. Caplan
Mrs. Laurian Greening
750 Prospect Lane
Colorado Springs, CO 80903

    Re: Unit 203 B

Dear Mr. Caplan and Mrs. Greening:

    Let me introduce myself. In order to obtain the listing for the sale of the building where you are now a tenant, I have grudgingly decided to manage the property. Please refrain from making statements that would hinder the sale of the property as I am showing it at odd hours of the day and night. The only reason that I am taking this job is that I hope it will help me retain the listing on the property.

    I have heard that you are a difficult tenant, and I intend to run a tight ship. If you even think about causing trouble, I will have to file a legal action for the owner. No, I do not want to be bothered at home in the evenings or on the weekend. Just call the office if you need to talk to me.

    Yes, there will be other agents showing the property that have no clue about its features. Just keep a low profile and do not make disparaging statements about the property. There are no leaks. There is no problem with the heat. The electric wiring is not aluminum, as some think.

    I know that you think that the property is located in close proximity to a nuclear waste site that is yet to be identified, but you need not share that belief with the prospective buyers. You might even think that if you give each buyer enough trouble you will be allowed to stay here. Wrong, you will be evicted immediately.

    Finally, as an inducement for you to cooperate I will pay you $500.00 if the property is sold within the first month of my listing or $250.00 if it sells in the second month. You will be given thirty days prior notice of any sale, so that you can arrange for a new place to live. If things work out okay, I will even act as your agent to locate a home for you to buy or rent.

                        Most sincerely,

Letter/e-mail – Property Management

Mr. Sam Seller
Mrs. Sandy Seller
4750 Table Mesa Drive
Boulder, CO 80305

    Re: 4750 Table Mesa Drive

Dear Sam and Sandy:

Thank you for telling me that you will be moving out by the end of the month. I had hoped that your home would sell by this time. I know that you intend to rent the property for a few months on a month-to-month basis, and thought I should explain the firm's position with regard to our property management services.

Property that is occupied by people other than the owner often raises concern about the extent of management that the owner may expect from us as a listing office. Property management is not covered in our listing contract. Therefore, we do not render any property management services without the express prior written approval of both our broker and the owner. We have long felt that the listing of a property for sale and the management of real estate are very different tasks and should be covered separately. We have two levels of service available.

First, our limited service. Under this plan, we do not take an active role in the management of the property. We limit ourselves to responding to your instructions, preferably in letter form, requesting that we accomplish certain specific tasks. Such items include: the collection of rents; paying specific payments; arranging for work to be done or confirming that the work has, in fact, been performed; showing the property to prospective tenants; cooperating with the attorney of your selection – in the event eviction becomes necessary; and generally working on a case-by-case basis, with no duty to manage the property, except as indicated.

We are not responsible for policing the property or the tenants. We do not initiate action, nor are we responsible for "management" of the property. We do not execute leases on your behalf, nor do we commence any litigation regarding the property or any tenant on your behalf or in your name. We feel that these items are best done by your attorney. Our fee is $_____ per hour spent while following your instructions.

Second is our full-service management service. This is the subject of our Management Agreement, a copy of which is enclosed for your review. We would be happy to provide you with full-service management. Before we can accept the responsibility of full-service management, this agreement needs to be completed, signed both by you as owner and by the broker, and returned to this office with the indicated retainer deposit.

As you can see, the full-service management agreement provides that we will use our best efforts to lease, maintain, supervise and care for your property on your behalf. This involves much more than simply collecting the rents. Therefore, it is the subject of a separate, comprehensive, agreement.

Please send us a letter to confirm the limited service, or simply sign at the bottom of this letter and return it. To engage in the full service system, execute the Management Agreement and return it. Unless we receive your written selection of the method of service that you desire, we will assume that we are not responsible for the management and maintenance of the property under either system. Should you later direct us to perform certain tasks, we will assume that we are operating under the provisions outlined above under the first option.

If I can be of any further assistance, please do not hesitate to let me know. We are proud to have your property listed for sale with this office and feel that we can complete the marketing of your real estate, with or without regard to our being party to the property's management.

Most sincerely,
The Real Estate Company

by: Your Friendly, Broker

cc: Owner

Letter/e-mail – Property Management Referral

Mr. Sam Seller
Mrs. Sandy Seller
4750 Table Mesa Drive
Boulder, CO 80305

      Re: 4750 Table Mesa Drive

Dear Sam and Sandy:

Thank you for telling me that you will be moving out by the end of the month. I had hoped that your home would sell by this time. I know that you intend to rent the property for a few months on a month-to-month basis, and thought I should explain the firm's position with regard to our property management services.

As I indicated to you earlier, neither this firm nor any of the salespeople are allowed to engage in the property management business. Our broker feels that we are in the business of representing sellers by professionally marketing of our clients' homes for sale, as well as representing buyers interested in the purchase of real estate – not in the management of real property. Property management can be very time-consuming and could distract us from our primary goal. I wish I could help you, but it is simply not possible.

Often a friend or neighbor is adequate for the isolated short-term case of property management. If that does not appeal to you, there are a lot of people whose exclusive business is property management   Although I can not be responsible for the several individuals and companies listed on the attached sheet, I do know that they have been utilized in the past by other homeowners. Each should be happy to provide you with a list of past clients to assist you in making your decision.

I will assist your property manager any way that I can. By working together, we can help each other and effectuate the rental and sale of your property.

                  Sincerely,
                  The Real Estate Company

Letter/e-mail – Property Management Equity Skimming

Mr. Sam Seller
Mrs. Sandy Seller
4750 Table Mesa Drive
Boulder, CO 80305

    Re: 4750 Table Mesas Drive

Dear Sam and Sandy:

We are happy to have your property listed for sale. While collecting the rents and turning them over to you promptly, we have noticed that the mortgage payments on the property are not being made in a timely manner. While you are welcome to do as you wish with your rental receipts, we do not wish to be involved with the collection of rent that does not go to maintain the mortgage.

We will continue to list your property for sale and endeavor to obtain a buyer before the property goes into foreclosure. However, we can not continue to collect the rental amounts that come due. It might be a good idea to collect them yourself, or have a friend or other professional collect them for you. Our fear stems from the concept of "equity skimming."

In this situation, the owner, *intending from the outset* to make money and not payments, acquires a property with the intent to rent it and keep the rent paid by the tenants. Such a person does not pay the taxes or the mortgage payments. As a result, the property goes into foreclosure.

In your case we do not have any idea what your intent is, but we do not think that you acquired the property with the intent of letting it go to foreclosure. Equity skimming is not a term that would generally apply to the owner of a single property who, after owning it for some time, finds that he can no longer subsidize the rent to make all the required payments.

To avoid even the appearance of impropriety in circumstances where we, in our own discretion, feel that such is the case, we will not release any money to the owner unless we are satisfied that it is being applied to the payment of the utilities, association dues, the mortgage and the like and that all such payments are being made in full. To avoid this potential problem, we will not be collecting the rent anymore. I am sure that you understand our position.

Sincerely,
The Real Estate Company

by: Your Name Here,
REALTOR®, CRS, GRI

Seller Financial Status

Liens and Loans. As early as possible, you need to ascertain the liquidity of the property you are trying to sell. You are going to make commitments to cooperating brokers for a portion of the commission. Let's find out early if there is enough equity to pay the commission. Many people do not tell their broker that they are behind in their loan payments, the property is in foreclosure or that there are tax or judgment liens against the property.

Owners and Encumbrances Report. Referenced by many names across the country, this is a report similar to a preliminary commitment from a title company that indicates the defects, encumbrances and clouds on the title. Smart brokers are ordering "to be determined" title insurance commitments to verify the information often verbally conveyed in an owners and encumbrances report. Get the seller to pay the fee if you can.

Loan Status. Regardless of how certain you are that the property will not be sold by way of an assumption, it happens. You need to know the status of the existing loan. Information on the underlying mortgage on the seller's property should be obtained as soon as possible to determine if there is any chance the loan may be in default. Having a home go into foreclosure is often very personal and embarrassing to the seller. They may not provide that information initially in hopes that the home will sell before anyone knows. It is critical to know in which stage of foreclosure the seller may be involved.

Tip. *Resist the temptation to advance the funds yourself to obtain this information. In addition, never, we mean never, take the sellers' word for their loan balance.*

In some instances you can verify the loan balance by telephone with the loan number. Other times just looking at the latest mortgage receipt stub, if one is available, is sufficient. Many people have "troubled" real estate, and they have a hard time acknowledging that fact internally, let alone disclosing it to a stranger. Be sensitive and professional but insist on ordering a payoff and an assumption statement. You just never know which you might need.

The best system is to write a letter to the lender asking for the appropriate information. A sample follows. You can modify it to suit your needs. The key elements are the loan number and that the information can be delivered, faxed or sent to the broker or salesperson. Do it early. The pressure may mount as the problem becomes more evident. Get the information as early as you can.

Caution. *Many times the lending institution will offer to "cooperate" with the homeowner to give him time to sell or reduce his payments while the home is on the market. At the same time, the lender is discovering the location and financial capability of the borrower, your seller. Should things not work out, the lender will have all the information it needs to pursue the seller. Consult with the attorney for the seller before you give out information to the lender.*

It will also become critical for you as the seller's agent to carefully monitor the contract performance deadlines, so that obligations in a foreclosure sale may be met. Be careful – remember whom you represent. Disclosing that the property is in foreclosure is rarely in the seller's best interest. Do not do this without the seller's prior written, *informed* consent.

Other information gleaned from the mortgage information will assist you in offering the correct financing terms. Will the loan be "due-on-sale" if sold by way of seller financing or by an installment land contract? Is there a possibility of an assumption without notifying the lender? Is there a possibility of an assumption with, or without substitution of liability?

Caution. *A transfer that violates the lender's due-on-sale clause could cause serious trouble for everyone. If one party contemplates a transfer that violates the due-on-sale clause, make sure the buyer, seller and you have an attorney to guide you through the proposed transaction.*

Caution. *FHA and VA loans that contain a "due-on-sale" or "due-on-transfer" clause are a more serious problem. Consult with an attorney first. Never attempt to transfer the title to a property that contains an FHA or VA due-on-sale clause without written lender consent.*

Does the lender require that the new buyer qualify with an assumption and will the interest rate change with an assumption? Having a ready answer to these questions will enhance your ability to assist any new buyer or his agent with the proper financing terms and arrangements.

Letter/e-mail – Existing Lender for Loan Status

Mr. and/or Ms. Bobby Fisher
Seal Mortgage and Loan
250 Anywhere Street
Next Door, CO 00000

     Re: Loan Number:
              Borrower:

Dear Sir or Madam:

    We have just listed our house for sale with the real estate company indicated on this letterhead and, in particular, with the salesperson whose card is attached. Please consider this as our request that you immediately send to our real estate firm an assumption statement and a payoff statement indicating the balances that are current for our loan.

    We have authorized our real estate salesperson, indicated below, to contact you directly to facilitate either the transfer and assumption of the loan or the payoff of the loan. Please offer them your cooperation. Should you wish to contact us, we can be reached at:

    Thank you for your consideration. We have enclosed our check to your order in the amount of $_____ for your preparation fee.

                        Sincerely,

                        _____
                        Sam Seller

                        _____
                        Sandy Seller

cc: The Real Estate Company
        Your name here, REALTOR®, CRS, GRI

Letter/e-mail – Existing Lender for Loan Status #2

BancBoston Mortgage Corp.
P. O. Box 0000000
Boston, MA 02241

    Re: Your loan number:_____
    Borrowers: Sam and Sandy Seller
    SSN: _____-_____-_____
    Property: 4750 Table Mesa Drive, Boulder, CO 80305-5575

Dear Sirs:

    Enclosed you will find a mortgage information release form signed by the
above referenced owners for the property indicated.

    Please provide me with the following information at your earliest
convenience.

    Current mortgage balance:_____
    Current interest rate:_____
    Type and class of mortgage:_____
    Assumption terms and conditions:_____
    Prepayment penalty:_____

    I have enclosed a check to your order in the amount of $_____, and
would ask that you forward an assumption and payoff statement.   I have enclosed a
self addressed, stamped envelope for your convenience.

                    Sincerely,
                    The Real Estate Company

                    by: Your Name Here,
                    REALTOR®, CRS, GRI

Standard Owner's Authorization and Request for Loan Information and Verification

To: _____

Mortgage Company Name

_____

Mortgage Company Address

_____

City, State, Zip

Loan Number: _____
Property Address:

_____

_____

_____

Please release to:

_____

_____

all information regarding my/our loan with your company.

Sincerely,

_____
Owner
SSN: _____ - _____ - _____

_____
Owner
SSN: _____ - _____ - _____

Terminated and Withdrawn Listings
Post Listing Period Protection

Termination. The listing period may terminate for various reasons. First, the listing expires. Second, the seller cancels the listing. There are cases that seem to indicate that since the listing agreement is a consensual agency relationship between the principal and the agent, it is terminable at will by the principal, the seller. This does not imply that the broker is not entitled to some compensation; only that the listing can be cancelled. Third, the broker could decide that s/he does not want the listing anymore. However, it is much more difficult for the agent to cancel than the principal. Broker cancellations are rare and can be difficult if the principal is opposed. Seek local counsel before consenting to the attempted termination of any listing agreement by the seller.

The seller hears termination and thinks that the listing is over, and that there is no need to pay a commission. The broker hears termination and thinks that s/he is protected for some sort of "holdover" period. The execution of a simple form with "Amend/Extend Listing Contract" written across the top will help to ensure that everyone thinks the same. The form is a written amendment to the listing, and it is much better to outline the terms in a form rather than a letter. Following is a sample holdover clause to be included in the listing agreement to protect the broker.

Clause:
   Commission shall be earned upon the occurrence of any of the following:
   a. Sale of the Property within the Listing Period by any person; or,

   b. Broker finding a buyer who is ready, willing and able to complete the transaction as specified herein by Seller; or,

   c. Sale of the Property within _____ calendar days subsequent to the expiration of the Listing Period to anyone with whom Broker negotiated and whose name was submitted to Seller by Broker during the Listing Period.

There is a lot of discussion about how long the protection period should be in the contract. We recommend the protection period be as long as you can get. Do not tolerate clauses that purport to extinguish the holdover rights if the property is re-listed with another broker.

Tip.   *Delete such clauses similar to the one indicated below in italics before you present the proposed listing agreement to the seller.*

Clause:

Commission shall be earned upon the occurrence of any of the following:

a. Sale of the Property within the Listing Period by any person; or,

b. Broker finding a buyer who is ready, willing and able to complete the transaction as specified herein by Seller; or,

c. Sale of the Property within _____ calendar days subsequent to the expiration of the Listing Period to anyone with whom Broker negotiated and whose name was submitted to Seller by Broker during the Listing Period. *[Provided, however, that Seller shall owe no commission to Broker under this subsection if a commission is earned by another licensed real estate broker acting pursuant to an exclusive right-to-sell listing contract or an exclusive agency listing contract entered into during this period.]*

In order to protect yourself under the terms of the Listing Agreement, you must disclose to the seller the names of all persons with whom you have negotiated (talked about the property) for the sale of the property during the listing period. Note that a showing is not a requirement, only negotiations. Contrary to some opinions, the presentation of a contract from a prospective purchaser during the listing period does satisfy this requirement. The disclosure of the list of possible buyers must also be made during the listing period. Written disclosures are all that we are concerned with here since a seller is unlikely to acknowledge an oral disclosure if there is litigation.

Clause:

The listing agreement is hereby terminated as if the expiration date were today. All other terms and conditions, except the expiration date, specifically including those that provide for compensation in the event of a subsequent sale to one who was disclosed properly to Seller, shall remain in full force and effect.

Seller warrants that Seller is not seeking this termination with the intent of selling the Property to a prospective purchaser procured or discovered during the term of this listing. If such is the case, the indicated commission shall still be due to Broker.

Performance Criteria Listing Option. This option is designed for new and large construction where the project will conceivably take longer to fully sell all units than your regular listing period normally allows, or a high end or unique property which appeals to a smaller, specific target market. One solution is to list for a "normal" period of time (each office establishes its own time frame as there is no standard listing period) and, as the expiration date approaches, attempt to renew the listing. Another option is to work with the seller's oral promise that "if you are working okay, I will renew."

The seller is legitimately concerned about a long listing. The seller wants to see sales before committing to extensions. The listing broker is also concerned that s/he may work hard to get the project started, only to have the seller then list with another licensee, perhaps even a family member, once the listing term expires. This has happened far too often. The solution is a performance criteria in the original long term listing. Edit the following clause as is appropriate for your use.

Since initial marketing expenses, to include project brochures, newspaper and magazine advertisements, can be extensive for a new project or unique property, it might be wise, but difficult, to request a retainer with the original listing. This retainer can be subsequently deducted from the final commission when the listing closes. In the event the listing is not extended, at least marketing costs are not a total loss.

Clause:

Seller may cancel this listing only after the listing has been in effect for _____ months, on any _____ month anniversary of the listing date, by giving the Broker 30 days prior written notice indicating the specific aspects of the Performance Criteria that have not been met. During the 30 day period, Broker and Seller shall review the alleged failure of Broker to adhere to the Performance Criteria.

Performance Criteria are:

Broker shall during each _____ month period, starting with the date of the listing, present to Seller _____ proposed contracts for the sale of units of the Property.

Sales of _____ units during any _____ month period.

Broker shall during each _____ month period, starting with the date of the listing, show the Property to _____ buyers.

Broker hereby receipts for a non-refundable retainer of $_____. In the event that the Property sells during the term of this listing, or any extension thereof, the retainer shall be deducted from the total commission due.

- or -

Broker hereby receipts for a retainer of $_____. The broker shall credit Seller with an amount equal to _____% of the retainer amount on each closing that takes place after _____ units are sold and closed, until the entire retainer is accounted for.

Withdrawn or "Off the Market". The seller hears, "I am free of the listing now and can sell it myself and save that money." The broker hears, "The property is still listed; and if it sells, I will get paid." Withdrawn is one of the most misunderstood concepts in the real estate business. To make matters worse, the Multiple Listing Service rules can also modify this "status." Use caution to make sure that the full ramifications of a subsequent sale are clear.

Clause:
1. The Property is "off the market" which means ....

-or-

2. The Property is "off the market" for a period of ____ days. During that period, the Property remains subject to the listing contract, except that Broker shall not advertise. Should the Property sell during this period, a full commission will be due to Broker. Seller will not solicit any other brokers to list or sell the Property during this period and shall refer all inquiries to Broker.

Subagents. This practice is all but extinct. If you still utilize subagents, they are working for you, the listing broker. They owe the full range of fiduciary duties to you, their immediate principal, as well as to the seller, their ultimate principal. Subagents are required to tell their principal, the listing broker, the name, address and phone numbers of all interested buyers. That might bother some selling agents, but then they would not be subagents. They would be buyer brokers. Should the subagent refuse to divulge such information to the listing broker, the listing broker might have a cause of action against the subagent for breach of a fiduciary duty resulting in loss of a commission. Remember, you are liable for the actions of these subagents.

Cooperating Selling Agents. The difficult task is to protect yourself with regard to the negotiations conducted with prospective purchasers by your cooperating selling agents because they will generally not have disclosed the names of their customers to you. This is where an accurate and concise record of showings and interest in the property will allow you to contact those cooperating agents and politely request that they provide you with the needed information.

Potential Post Listing Seller FSBO. Try to impress upon the seller the complexity of the sale of real estate today, so that the seller will feel that he truly does need your services, even if a potential buyer were to approach him the day after the expiration of the listing. The letter to the seller should attempt to emphasize some facet of the transaction with which you feel he is most uncomfortable, such as sources of new financing, the need to accept a home in trade or a guaranteed sale, the need for a home warranty program or other service that he cannot get from the local attorney who probably has no idea how to market a home properly anyway. That attorney will be your competition once the buyer is located.

Procuring Cause. You may have a non-contractual claim for a commission if you can show you were the "procuring cause" of an ultimate sale. Do not place too much faith in this or any other "equitable" remedies. The limited success of those claims has generally been in the absence of a listing contract. When there is a contract, the court will look to it for the agreement of the parties.

Lien for Commission. Under current law in most states, neither the broker nor the salesperson has any right to file any document that effectively places a lien upon the property. Brokers do not have a security interest in the seller's property to secure the payment of their commissions. The broker listing contract is a "personal services" contract, not a contract dealing with an interest in land. Wish you had lien rights? Well, here is the clause. It is doubtful that too many sellers will sign it. Do not be afraid to ask for it in a commercial or ranch transaction, where you will expend a lot of money for a long period of time. The clause is also useful with absentee owners.

Clause:

Seller hereby grants broker a security interest in the Property to the extent of, and to secure payment of, the broker's commission.

Termination Time Limit and Confidential Information. Once the listing is terminated, you may still be obligated to retain the personal information about the seller that you obtained while an agent. That is to say, after the listing has terminated, if you become a buyer agent or are "working with" a buyer, you may still have to keep the seller's personal secrets secret. Here is a potential clause to try to alleviate that situation. Good luck.

Clause:

Upon termination of this listing agreement, Broker shall not be an agent of seller. Broker shall be released from any and all fiduciary duties and may represent any buyer attempting to purchase Seller's property without any obligation to keep confidential any of Seller's previously confidential information.

Re-listing Broker. If you are the subsequent listing broker who is listing after an expired or terminated listing, you should ask to examine the previous listing agreement. You need to determine, if in fact, there are buyers that are covered by a holdover period. This practice of protection for a buyer obtained during a listing period is common in many states. The mere fact that a buyer was shown the home through the listing broker's marketing efforts entitles the broker to a commission on the sale to any prospect whose name was properly given to the seller during the term of the listing.

Showing Data Report

Seller's Name:_____

Address:_____

Date	Time	Agent	Company	Phone #	Comments

Letter/e-mail – List of Buyers on Termination of a Listing - Subagents

Mr. Tina B. Daniel, Broker
American Real Estate Service
915 East Race
Scary, CO 80305

    Re: 4750 Table Mesa Drive

Dear Tina:

    Our records indicate that you scheduled and completed a showing of the above referenced property as our subagents. Please provide me with the names of the purchasers that viewed the property, so that we can deliver those names to the seller. This will protect both offices in the event the buyer buys the property after the expiration of the listing period. While I hope that your buyers purchase the property during the listing period, one can never be too careful.

    I understand that you may be reluctant to provide us with that information for fear that we might attempt to sell your buyers this or another property. I can assure you that we will not attempt to solicit your customers. We want you to show us the same courtesy when we have shown property that you have listed. The important issue is that we are both compensated if the buyer buys the property.

    If you want to discuss this matter with me personally, please call me. If you wish, you can fax the information back on the bottom of this letter. Any comments that would help market the property would be appreciated. You can be candid.

Date: Buyer's Name:

_____   _____

_____   _____

_____   _____

    I look forward to working with you in the future, appreciate you as a cooperating broker and further appreciate your association with us and your attempts to market this property.

                         Most sincerely,
                         The Real Estate Company

Letter/e-mail – List of Buyers on Termination of a Listing – Subagents #2

Mr. Tina B. Daniel, Broker
American Real Estate Service
915 East Race
Scary, CO 80305

     Re: 4750 Table Mesa Drive

Dear Tina:

     Our records indicate that you recently showed this property. While I think that the sellers will renew their listing with this office, I like to try to protect all of the brokers who have acted as our subagents during the listing period. Should your buyer ultimately purchase the property and, with or without the knowledge and assistance of the seller, attempt to avoid paying us our commission, I want to be ready. In order to avoid such a result, I need to indicate to the seller the names of those individuals with whom you may have negotiated or have shown the property, as well as the dates of your negotiations and/or showings.

     I understand that you may be reluctant to provide us with that information for fear that we will then try to sell this property or other listings to those individuals you have indicated to us are interested in buying this property. I promise you that we will not attempt to solicit your customers in any fashion. There is simply no reason for us both to lose the right to an earned commission if these buyers buy.

     Time is short and your cooperation is greatly appreciated. Thank you for your assistance. In the event you ever need the same assistance from this office upon the expiration of one of your listings, please do not hesitate to ask and we will comply promptly. We are competitors, but there is no need to allow a seller to profit from our failure to protect ourselves as the standard listing provides.

     I look forward to working with you in the future, appreciate you as a cooperating broker and further appreciate your association with us and your attempts to market this property.

                                 Most sincerely,
                                 The Real Estate Company

Letter/e-mail – List of Buyers on Termination of a Listing/General

Mr. Tina B. Daniel, Broker
American Real Estate Service
915 East Race
Searcy, CO 80305

Re: 4750 Table Mesa Drive

Dear Tina:

Thank you for showing this property. Our listing agreement with the seller provides that in the event a buyer who was shown the property during the listing period buys the property after the listing expires, we will still be owed a commission. Of course, we cooperate with your brokerage office by splitting the commission as indicated in the MLS system. All that we need to do is provide the seller with the names of the buyers who have seen the property.

I understand that you may be reluctant to provide us with that information for fear that we might attempt to sell your buyers this or another property. I promise you that we will not attempt to solicit your clients or customers. We extend to you the same courtesy we would expect when we have shown property that you have listed. The important issue is that we both get paid if the buyer buys the property.

If you want to discuss this matter with me personally, please call me. If you wish you can fax the information back on the bottom of this letter. Any comments that would help market the property would be appreciated. You can be candid.

Date: Buyer's Name:

_____   _____

_____   _____

I look forward to working with you in the future, appreciate you as a cooperating broker and further appreciate your association with us and your attempts to market this property.

Letter/e-mail – Expiration of the Listing Period – Seller

Mr. Sam Seller
Mrs. Sandy Seller
4750 Table Mesa Drive
Boulder, CO 80305

　　　Re: 4750 Table Mesa Drive

Dear Sam and Sandy:

　　　In spite of all of our marketing efforts, our listing period is nearing expiration. It has been a pleasure to serve as your agents. We have been happy to receive so many nice compliments from the numerous cooperating brokers who have had the opportunity to show your home. Your willingness to always have your house ready for last minute showings has certainly been helpful. We all want to commend you on your efforts.

　　　Try as we have, we seem to have been unable to locate a buyer who is ready, willing, and able to complete the purchase of your home as proposed in your instructions in the listing agreement. I will be contacting you to encourage you to extend your listing with this firm. We are all very eager to locate a suitable buyer for you. We know your home better than anyone else and have invested quite a lot of time and money in the marketing of your home.

　　　The following is a list of the persons with whom we, or those brokers to whom we offered cooperation and compensation, have been negotiating and who have not yet made an acceptable offer to purchase your home. Should any of these individuals purchase your home during the post listing period indicated in the listing agreement, they would be considered to have been located and procured through our efforts. We therefore would be entitled to payment of the indicated commission.

　　　As always, the sale of your home on terms acceptable to you is our primary concern. We hope that some of these people do in fact purchase your home within the allotted time since it will accomplish your goals and help us to recover the expenses we have incurred in our efforts to market your home. Since these parties are "protected buyers," we will be glad to assist you with the sale. Just contact us when you need our assistance.

Prospective purchasers obtained directly through this office:

In addition, the following cooperating brokers have shown the property and have negotiated with their buyers:

Thank you for allowing us the opportunity to market your home. I trust you will re-list with Kathy when she meets with you. If there is anything I can do to assist you or clarify our position, please do not hesitate to call me.

Most sincerely,
The Real Estate Company

by: Your Name Here, Broker

Letter/e-mail – Expiration of the Listing Period – Seller #2

Mr. Sam Seller
Mrs. Sandy Seller
4750 Table Mesa Drive
Boulder, CO 80305

    Re: 4750 Table Mesa Drive

Dear Sam and Sandy:

The initial term of your listing with our office will soon expire. Enclosed is a listing extension form extending the listing for an additional period of time. Often the basis for the ultimate decision to purchase begins with the introduction to the property by one of our agents or a cooperating salesperson, but there is simply not enough time to bring the buyer to the final decision prior to the expiration of the listing.

Should any of these buyers contact you personally, please give me a call immediately, so that I can complete the sale in a professional manner. With real estate being as complicated as it is today, there is a lot more to be done than just drafting a contract for sale. A continuation of our services will ensure that you, as the seller, are properly represented, and the buyer is made aware of all of the disclosures that the law now requires, as well as the different sources of financing that are available.

I have prepared a new listing form for the MLS containing the information about your property. Sometimes a "reintroduction" will encourage someone to make the decision to buy. A copy is enclosed. In addition I have included the comparable sales in your area. This might be a good time to consider offering terms more in line with those offered for the properties that have sold. I will call you tomorrow to discuss the entire re-listing process.

It has been a pleasure to serve as your agent. We have been happy to receive so many nice compliments from the numerous cooperating brokers who have had the opportunity to show your home. Your willingness to always have your house ready for last minute showings has certainly been helpful. We all want to commend you on your efforts.

Here is a list of the persons with whom we, or those brokers to whom we offered cooperation and compensation, have been negotiating, and who have not yet made an acceptable offer to purchase your home. Should any of these individuals purchase your home during the post listing period indicated in the listing agreement, they would be considered to have been located and procured through our efforts. We therefore would be entitled to payment of the indicated commission.

As always, the sale of your home on terms acceptable to you is our primary concern. We hope that one of these people does in fact purchase your home within the allotted time since it will accomplish your goals and help us to recover the expenses we have incurred in our efforts to market your home. Since these parties are "protected buyers," we will be glad to assist you with the sale. Just contact us when you need our assistance.

Prospective purchasers obtained directly through this office:

In addition, the following cooperating brokers have shown the property and have negotiated with their buyers:

Thank you for allowing us the opportunity to market your home. I trust you will re-list with Kathy when she meets with you. If there is anything I can do to assist you or clarify our position, please do not hesitate to call me.

Most sincerely,
The Real Estate Company

by: Your Name Here, Broker

Additional Listing Agreement Clauses and Addenda

The listing agreement sets the stage for the entire relationship with the seller. We have compiled several clauses and some explanation of those clauses to assist you with the preparation of the listing agreement. As usual, try to determine not only what will transpire but also who will be in charge of making decisions. The seller may want you to think that you are in charge, but the seller is always in charge. This is an agency requirement and good business judgment.

Tip. *People are always trying to get someone else to make decisions for them. The decisions will be made to the seller's liking. All that remains is to determine whom the seller can blame or sue in the future.*

It is much better to include a clause that would cover any future possible issue, even though it may not seem applicable at the time of the listing. It is much more difficult to negotiate an agreement with the seller as an issue arises later in the listing period. Some brokers believe it is better to "leave well enough alone in the beginning" and just deal with things as they come up. Contrary to that belief, it is much better for all parties to have established criteria for potential issues. When they do arise, you will then be able to go merrily along without conflict or misunderstanding.

Clause Regarding Use of Professionals:
1. This form has important legal consequences and the parties should consult legal and tax or other counsel before signing.

-or-

2. Brokers and salespeople are not licensed to practice law. They can not give legal advice. You are advised to seek such legal, tax, environmental and other counsel as you determine appropriate.

-or-

3. The real estate contract may have significant legal remedies. The broker and salesperson can not give you legal, tax or other advice. You are advised to obtain the advice that you deem appropriate.

-or-

4. Do not rely upon the salesperson or broker assisting you. Neither is licensed to practice law or accounting. Consult with competent legal, tax or other counsel before signing.

-or-

5. The property may qualify for a tax deferred exchange under Section 1031 of the Internal Revenue Code. We recommend that you seek tax or legal counsel to assist you with such an exchange.

-or-

6. Broker shall offer the property "Seller will cooperate with a tax deferred exchange so long as it is not to the financial detriment of Seller."

-or-

7. Broker has advised Seller to contact a professional of Seller's choosing to review the prospects of a Section 1031 tax deferred exchange.

-or-

8. You may be entitled to a "homestead" in your state, or you may qualify for beneficial tax treatment on the sale of your personal residence. There may be rules and regulations with which you will need to comply. We advise you to seek competent tax advice.

-or-

9. If you sell this home and have occupied it as an owner, you may be able to avoid paying some or all of the tax on your gain. We encourage you to seek competent tax advice regarding this matter.

Clause Regarding the Physical Condition of the Property:
1. Seller hereby authorizes Broker to indicate to all prospective buyers, "The property is located within 50 miles of a nuclear weapons facility."

-or-

2. Seller hereby authorizes Broker to indicate to all prospective buyers, "The property is within a line of sight to high tension power lines."

-or-

3. Seller hereby authorizes Broker to indicate to all prospective buyers, "The property next door is being utilized as a shelter for paroled criminals."

-or-

4. Seller hereby authorizes Broker to indicate to buyers, "Seller and Broker strongly encourage you to have the home inspected by an ASHI® or NAHI™ inspector."

It would be improper to indicate that the house next door was anything other than just another house if the occupants are a protected class indicated by the federal or state fair housing laws. Remember, the law covers such things as group homes for the handicapped or mentally challenged.

Clause Regarding Title Status:
1. Seller authorizes and instructs Broker to obtain a title commitment to determine the status of the title to Seller's property. Broker shall order and obtain the commitment from a company that will not charge the seller unless the property is sold.

-or-

2. Seller authorizes Broker to obtain a title insurance commitment at Seller's expense.

-or-

3. Broker is authorized to contact all lien holders and obtain payoff statements for all liens upon the property.

-or-

4. Seller shall provide "extended coverage" title insurance.

-or-

5. Seller shall comply with the reasonable requirements of the title insurance company and pay the premium to obtain Form 130 endorsement.

Clause Regarding Prepaid FHA Mortgage Insurance Premiums:

1. Prepaid FHA mortgage insurance premiums shall be prorated to the date of delivery of deed, using the schedule attached to this Listing Agreement.

-or-

2. Prepaid FHA mortgage insurance premiums shall be prorated to the date of delivery of deed, using the schedule provided to the closing agent by HUD.

-or-

3. The unused portion of any prepaid FHA mortgage insurance premiums will be purchased by the buyer at closing. The amount will be determined utilizing a form provided by HUD for such prorations.

Clause Regarding FHA Mortgage Interest:

Seller is hereby made aware that FHA mortgage interest is not prorated for the month of the loan payoff. Seller will owe a full month's interest if the loan is in effect for one day of the following month. There is no guarantee that the loan payoff will reach the lender prior to the end of the month. This may cause Seller to be responsible for an additional month's interest.

Clause Regarding Hazard Insurance:

1. Broker has advised the seller that his existing hazard insurance policy may not cover the period of time between the closing and delivery of deed and the actual surrender of possession by the seller. The seller is advised to seek the counsel of his insurance agent and obtain a written assurance satisfactory to the seller as to the extent of his coverage on, and after, closing.

-or-

2. Seller is hereby advised that in the event he allows someone other than himself to occupy the property, either during the pendency of the listing or after the sale has closed, the existing hazard insurance policy may not cover the premises or the possessions of the seller or the occupant.

-or-

3. Seller is advised that in the event the seller remains in the property after closing, the seller's homeowner's policy may not cover the property nor its contents, as the insurance company may deem the former seller to be a tenant, and not insured under a "homeowner's" policy.

Clause Regarding Liability Upon Loan Assumption:
1. The seller, in the absence of a written release signed by the lender to the contrary, will remain liable for the repayment of the loan on the property in the event the seller allows it to be assumed. In the event of an assumption and subsequent default by the buyer, the seller will not be able to reacquire the property.

-or-

2. The broker, her agents, subagents and employees are not liable for any event that occurs after the delivery of the deed, including, but not limited to, a failure on the part of the buyer, or subsequent buyers, to make any payments after assuming the mortgage or after a subsequent transfer without an assumption. We are not responsible for the actions of the buyer after the property is transferred.

-or-

3. Seller acknowledges that, although a purchaser may assume the existing note and mortgage, Seller shall remain personally liable for the ultimate re-payment of the loan.

Clause Regarding Reservation of the Right to Purchase Property for Own Account:
1. Broker, and any licensees associated with Broker, reserve the right to purchase Seller's property at the listed price, or such price as Seller may accept, at any time during the term of the listing. This reservation shall apply to all the salespeople in Broker's office.

Seller waives any claim for a conflict of interest regarding such sale. Seller agrees that neither Broker nor any salesperson assisted Seller in the determination of the listing price.   In the event a salesperson purchases the Property, the following procedures shall be followed:

a. The seller and broker shall terminate the listing agreement for the subject property; and,

b. The broker or a salesperson in the broker's office ("salesperson") will submit a written offer to purchase the seller's property; and,

c. The price may, at the discretion of the salesperson, be reduced by any commission due as a result of the former listing agreement; and,

d. The offer shall be conditional upon the seller's attorney reviewing and approving in writing the offer prior to it becoming a contract; and,

e. The salesperson shall contribute $_____ to the seller's actual attorney fees at closing; and,

f. The seller shall be entitled to rescind the contract of sale at any time prior to closing and the salesperson shall immediately make the contract terminated; and,

g. Seller may be required by salesperson to obtain an independent appraisal of the property.   In such an event salesperson shall pay $_____ toward seller's expense for the appraisal at closing.

Addendum to Listing Contract
(Purchase by Licensee)

This addendum is a part of the Listing Contract between the indicated Seller and the Real Estate Broker ("Broker"), dated _____, 20_____, concerning Seller's real estate ("Property") located at: _____
_____.

1. Broker and Seller agree that Broker and Broker's salespeople ("Buyer-Salesperson") have the right to purchase the Property for their own account.
2. The parties acknowledge that this creates a potential conflict of interest. Broker shall use Broker's best efforts to obtain a buyer not associated with Broker upon the terms and conditions outlined by seller.
3. Seller has consulted with an attorney of Seller's selection prior to the execution of this Listing Contract. The signature of that attorney approving this addendum as to form is evidenced below.
4. In the event Buyer-Salesperson decides to attempt to purchase the Property, Broker and Seller will first negotiate the termination of this Listing Contract. Seller is under no obligation to terminate the listing and allow Buyer-Salesperson to purchase the property.
5. Subsequently, Buyer-Salesperson will submit an offer. This offer will not be effective unless approved by Seller's attorney in writing as to form. Buyer-Salesperson shall pay Seller, upon the transfer of title, the sum of $_____ as a contribution to Seller's legal fees.
6. Buyer-Salesperson will suggest that Seller obtain an independent appraisal prior to accepting Buyer-Salesperson's offer. Buyer-Salesperson will contribute $_____ to the cost of such an appraisal upon transfer of title.
7. Any such offer shall contain language that allows Seller to accept another contract and terminate this contract at any time prior to the date and time indicated for the transfer of deed and closing.

In the event of a conflict between these terms and those in the body of the Listing Contract, the terms on this Addendum shall prevail.

_____   _____
Seller   date   Seller   date
Real Estate Broker: Approved as to form:

_____   _____
by   date   Attorney for seller   date

                                          _____
                                          Print Name of Attorney/Phone

Clause Regarding Determination of the Listing Price:

Seller has considered the Competitive Market Analysis, which indicates the price of other similar properties that have sold, are listed or were rejected by the market, provided by Broker in the determination by Seller of the listing price. Broker is not responsible for determination of the listing price.

Clause Regarding Comparable Properties:

1. I hereby authorize you to provide data about comparable listed, sold and rejected properties, available through the MLS or otherwise, to prospective buyers, in order to assist them in valuing my property.

-or-

2. It is okay with me for you to show comps to a potential buyer, even if they undermine the listed price of my property.

Clause Regarding a Broker Guaranteed Sale:

Seller and Broker have agreed that Broker will purchase the Property under the terms of a separate Guaranteed Sale Agreement.

If you are trying to lose your real estate license, a guaranteed sale has got to be a great start. Most real estate commissions carefully scrutinize attempts by the "agent" to guarantee the sale. They often feel, as the consumer does, that the "agent" was not trying hard enough to facilitate the ultimate sale of the home to a qualified buyer at fair market value. Use extreme caution. Get local legal advice and assistance in drafting any guaranteed sale program documents.

Clause Regarding Schedule of Rents and Deposits:

The Seller/Owner warrants that the attached schedule of rents and deposits is a true and correct representation of the rents and deposits actually collected, and currently due. In addition, Seller/Owner represents that each individual listed as a tenant is actually occupying the property according to the terms indicated. Seller/Owner shall transfer all deposits and prorate all rents as of the date of delivery of deed. There are no incentives or rent preferences in effect that would alter, or amend, the rental information contained on the attached list.

Clause Regarding Commission Rates:

1. Compensation – commissions and fees – charged by real estate brokers is not set by law nor by the Board/Association of REALTORS®. Such charges are established by each real estate broker independently.

-or-

2. There are no standard commissions. Each broker establishes his own fee structure and the amount that will be offered to cooperating brokers.

-or-

3. No entity is allowed to set or establish commission or fee structures. Each broker determines the fees that he will charge, and the amounts that he will offer to cooperating brokers.

-or-

4. Commissions charged by real estate brokers are not set by the state, the board or association of REALTORS® nor by law. These fees are established by each real estate broker independently.

Cooperative Commissions. These are the amounts that you will be paying to cooperating brokers for their efforts in finding a buyer for your listing.

Rule. *Breach of a fiduciary duty forfeits the commission regardless of loss.*

Even if you successfully achieved the sale of the house, you could lose the entire commission if you breached your fiduciary duty – the duty to tell the seller what you were doing on the seller's behalf.

Tip. *Tell the seller how you do business, and let the seller determine if he wants to do business with you.*

There are many potential relationships between the listing broker and the selling broker, and between the selling broker and the buyer. It is imperative that the listing broker address, in the listing agreement, the various options offered by the broker's company. Indicate who will be paid and how much. With what type of selling brokers will we work? Adequate treatment should avoid the broker's hearing some of these statements for the first time at the same time they are heard by the jury.

Jury Talk.

"They did not work on my property very hard. They refused to cooperate with other brokers. They kept my property a secret in their office, hoping to sell it themselves, instead of exposing it to all the brokers in their market area."

"They only offered other brokers _____%, and that was not enough."

"I never knew that I was liable for these other brokers, these subagents. They should have told me when I listed the property that I would be liable for all the brokers in my area."

"When I heard that they were not cooperating with buyer brokers, I was furious. Those are the people that have buyers. Why would we not work with them to get my house sold?"

Clauses and Addenda for Cooperative Commissions.   The following sample addenda and clauses address the commission options facing the listing broker. It is suggested that the seller consent to the cooperative commission schedule. The forms and clauses are basic and intended to be reviewed by the reader, edited where necessary and a selection made. The paragraphs with the same number are alternative paragraphs.

There are several different addenda from which to choose. We have tried to provide different forms that contain the terms for each alternate way of doing business. Read them carefully and then select the one that best suits your current needs. They will be right here when you decide to change the way you do things.

Addendum to Listing Contract

This addendum is hereby made a part of the Listing Contract between the indicated Seller and the Brokerage Firm ("Broker"), dated _____, 20__, concerning Seller's real estate ("Property") located at:_____
_____.

1. **Use of Professionals.** Seller is advised to seek the advice of professionals, such as attorneys, accountants, appraisers, surveyors, contractors, engineers, property inspectors, environmental hazard and radon gas experts. Broker does not render services provided by such professionals.

2. **Homeowner Warranty.** Seller is aware of the existence of pre-owned home warranty programs which may be purchased and may cover the repair or replacement of some Inclusions. Broker is not liable for the financial integrity of such companies.

3. **Buyer's Financial Ability.** Seller shall independently determine buyer's financial qualifications. Such review may include: the form and amount of earnest money, the amount and source of down payment, the ability of the buyer to obtain financing, buyer's credit reports, tax returns and financial statements. Broker is not responsible for the financial integrity of the buyer, including the payment or collection of any notes and any checks tendered in connection with the real estate transaction, or subsequent payments as part of an owner financed transaction.

4. **Possession, Lease and Insurance.** If the Possession Date and Time are other than Closing Date, Seller, to protect Seller's real and personal property interests, should consider obtaining casualty and liability insurance and a lease for the period between Possession Date and Time and the Closing Date.

5. **Facsimile.** Signatures may be evidenced by facsimile.

6. **Advertising.** Broker is authorized to advertise and market the Property, to the extent determined by Broker, in Broker's sole and absolute discretion, through any means, including newspaper advertisements, Multiple Listing Services of which Broker is a member and electronic network(s), including internet site(s). Multiple Listing Services may provide a prospective buyer with

property history information which includes prior listing and sales prices. Public records also provide buyers with prior sales prices.

7. **Compensation for Cooperating Brokers.** Broker is a member of the _____ Association of REALTORS® and, as such, is bound to arbitrate compensation (cooperative commission) disputes with competing selling brokers who are also members. Broker shall offer assistance to, but is not required to offer compensation to, brokers who are not either bound to REALTOR® arbitration (before either the local Board/Association of REALTORS® or Multiple Listing Service), or who agree in writing to such arbitration in advance of any contract negotiations or showings.

8. **Compensation for Out of Area Cooperating Brokers.** Broker shall offer compensation to brokers who are REALTORS®, but not members of Broker's MLS, Board or Association, the indicated cooperative commission or, if this box is checked, ☐ a reduced cooperative fee of ____% of the gross sales price.

9. **Broker as Buyer.** Broker, and licensees associated with Broker, may purchase the Property, upon such price and terms as Seller may accept, at any time during the term of this listing. Such a purchase creates a conflict of interest. Any such contract shall be conditioned upon prior written approval of the offer by Seller's attorney.

10. **Tax Consequences.** The sale of real estate has tax consequences. Seller may be able to defer or avoid paying taxes (e.g. § 1031). Seller is advised to seek professional tax counsel (e.g. accountant and/or attorney). Broker does not give tax advice.

11. **Advisory-Tax Withholding.** The Internal Revenue Service and the _____ Department of Revenue may require Closing Company to withhold a substantial portion of the proceeds of this sale when Seller either a foreign person or will not be a _____ resident after closing. Seller should inquire of Seller's tax advisor to determine if withholding applies, or if an exemption exists.

12. **Referral Fees – Buyers**. Broker, in an effort to procure as many qualified buyers as possible, shall seek assistance from, and offer compensation in the form of a referral fee, to brokers, licensed by another state located outside Broker's market area. Broker shall pay to the referring licensee, a referral fee, equal to, but not less than _____% nor more than _____% of that portion of the total commission received by Broker. No payment shall be due in the

event that such payment violates the Real Estate Settlement Procedures Act ("RESPA").

Seller:

_____   _____
Seller   date   Seller   date

Broker:

_____
by   date

Addendum to Listing Contract
(Cooperative Compensation and Commission Structure)

This addendum is a part of the Listing Contract between the indicated Seller and Brokerage Firm ("Broker"), dated _____, 20___, concerning Seller's real estate ("Property") located at: _____
_____.

1. **Cooperating Commission.** Broker shall seek assistance from, and offer _____ % of the gross selling price to, all brokers (subagents, buyer agents or otherwise) licensed by this state, located within the market area of Broker, whose licenses are with a company other than Broker's company.

2. **Referral Fees – Buyers.** Broker, in an effort to procure as many qualified buyers as possible, shall seek assistance from, and offer compensation to, brokers, licensed by any state, located outside Broker's market area in the form of a referral fee. Depending upon the referring licensee, Broker is authorized to pay other brokers a portion of Broker's total commission, determined by Broker in Broker's sole discretion, for the referral of prospective buyers for Seller's property.

In the event of a conflict between these terms and those in the body of the Listing Contract, the terms on this Addendum shall prevail.

Seller:

_____   _____
Seller   date   Seller   date

Broker:

_____
by   date

Addendum to Listing Contract
(Cooperative Compensation and Commission Structure)

This addendum is a part of the Listing Contract between the indicated Seller and Brokerage Firm ("Broker"), dated _____, 20____, concerning Seller's real estate ("Property") located at: _____ _____ _____.

1. **Cooperating Commission**. Broker shall seek assistance from, and offer _____ % of the gross selling price to, all brokers licensed by this state, located within the market area of Broker, whose licenses are with a company other than Broker's company. This offer shall include Subagents and Buyer Agents.

-or-

1. **Cooperating Commission**. Broker shall seek assistance from, and offer _____ % of the gross selling price to, all brokers (subagents, buyer agents or others) licensed by this state, located within the market area of Broker, whose licenses are with a company other than Broker's company.

-or-

1. **Cooperating Commission**. Broker shall seek assistance from, and offer _____ % of the gross selling price to, all brokers licensed by this state, except brokers attempting to act as subagents, located within the market area of Broker, whose licenses are with a company other than Broker's company. Subagents work with a buyer, but represent Seller and owe duties of utmost good faith, loyalty and fidelity to Seller only. Seller may be vicariously liable for the acts of subagents when acting in the scope of the agency relationship. Buyer agents representing the buyer owe duties of utmost good faith, loyalty and fidelity to buyer only. Seller is probably not vicariously liable for the acts of buyer agents.

2. **Referral Fees – Buyers**. Broker, in an effort to procure as many qualified buyers as possible, shall seek assistance from, and offer compensation in the form of a referral fee to, brokers licensed by any state located outside Broker's market area. Broker shall pay to the referring licensee, a referral fee, equal to, but not less than _____% nor more than _____% of that

portion of the total commission received by Broker. No payment shall be due in the event that such payment violates the Real Estate Settlement Procedures Act ("RESPA").

-or-

2. **Referral Fees – Buyers**. Broker, in an effort to procure as many qualified buyers as possible, shall seek assistance from and offer compensation in the form of a referral fee to brokers, licensed by any state located outside Broker's market area. Depending upon the referring licensee, Broker is authorized to pay other brokers a portion of Broker's total commission, determined by Broker in Broker's sole discretion, for the referral of prospective buyers for Seller's property.

-or-

2. **Referral Fees – General**. Broker, in an effort to cooperate with as many other brokers as possible, is authorized to pay other brokers a portion of Broker's total commission, determined by Broker in Broker's sole discretion, for the referral to Broker of prospective buyers for Seller's property.

In the event of a conflict between these terms and those in the body of the Listing Contract, the terms on this Addendum shall prevail.

Seller:

_____   _____
Seller   date   Seller   date

Broker:

_____
by   date

Addendum to Listing Contract
Commission Division
(Cooperative Compensation and Commission Structure)

This addendum is a part of the Listing Contract between the indicated "Seller" and Brokerage Firm ("Broker"), dated _____,20____, concerning Seller's real estate ("Property") located at: _____
_____.

1. Broker shall seek assistance from, and offer the indicated compensation as a percentage of the gross selling price to, the following brokers licensed by this state, located within the market area of Broker, whose licenses are with a company other than Broker's company.

   ☐ (a)_____ % to other brokers representing Seller ("Subagents"). Subagents work with a buyer, but represent Seller, and owe duties of utmost good faith, loyalty and fidelity to Seller only. Seller may be vicariously liable for the acts of Subagents when acting in the scope of their subagency relationship.

   ☐ (b)_____ % to brokers representing the buyer ("Buyer Agents"). Buyer Agents representing the buyer owe duties of utmost good faith, loyalty and fidelity to buyer only. Seller is not vicariously liable for the acts of Buyer Agents.

2. Broker, in an effort to cooperate with as many other brokers as possible, is authorized to pay other brokers a portion of Broker's total commission, determined by Broker in Broker's sole discretion, for the referral to Broker of prospective buyers for Seller's property.

In the event of a conflict between these terms and those in the body of the Listing Contract, the terms on this Addendum shall prevail.

_____   _____
Seller   date   Seller   date

Broker:

_____
by   date

Addendum to Listing Contract
Commission Division
(Cooperative Compensation and Commission Structure)

This addendum is hereby made a part of the Listing Contract, dated _____, 20___, between the indicated "Seller" and Brokerage Firm ("Broker") concerning Seller's real estate ("Property") located at: _____ _____.

1. Broker shall seek assistance from, and offer the indicated compensation as a percentage of the gross selling price to, the following brokers licensed by this state, located within the market area of Broker, whose licenses are with a company other than Broker's company.

   □ (a)_____ % to other brokers representing Seller ("Subagents"). Subagents work with a buyer, but represent Seller, and owe duties of utmost good faith, loyalty and fidelity to Seller only. Seller may be vicariously liable for the acts of Subagents when acting in the scope of their subagency relationship.

   □ (b)_____ % to brokers representing the buyer ("Buyer Agents"). Buyer Agents representing the buyer owe duties of utmost good faith, loyalty and fidelity to buyer only. Seller is not vicariously liable for the acts of Buyer Agents.

   □ (c)_____ % to other licensed brokers assisting the buyer in the transaction, but not acting as agents of either the buyer or seller. Such licensees must exercise reasonable skill and care for the parties. Seller is not vicariously liable for the acts of these brokers.

2. Broker, in an effort to cooperate with as many other brokers as possible, is authorized to pay other brokers a portion of Broker's total commission, determined by Broker in Broker's sole discretion, for the referral to Broker of prospective buyers for Seller's property.

In the event of a conflict between these terms and those in the body of the Listing Contract, the terms on this Addendum shall prevail.

_____   _____
Seller   date   Seller   date
Broker:

_____
by   date

Addendum to Listing Contract
Commission Division
(Cooperative Compensation and Commission Structure)

1. Broker shall seek assistance from, and offer the indicated compensation as a percentage of the gross selling price to, the following brokers licensed by this state, located within the market area of Broker, whose licenses are with a company other than Broker's company.

   □ (a)_____ % to other brokers representing Seller ("Subagents"). Subagents work with a buyer, but represent Seller, and owe duties of utmost good faith, loyalty and fidelity to Seller only. Seller may be vicariously liable for the acts of Subagents when acting in the scope of their subagency relationship.

   □ (b)_____ % to brokers representing the buyer ("Buyer Agents"). Buyer Agents representing the buyer owe duties of utmost good faith, loyalty and fidelity to buyer only. Seller is probably not vicariously liable for the acts of Buyer Agents.

   □ (c)_____ % to other licensed brokers assisting the buyer in the transaction, but not acting as agents of either the buyer or seller.

   Seller recognizes that there may be some brokers licensed by the state that are not acting as buyer agents, and whom the seller does not want as subagents because of the potential vicarious liability. Seller hereby authorizes Broker to cooperate with every conceivable other broker licensed by this state to accomplish the sale of the property without incurring vicarious liability. Such Broker should, but may not, exercise reasonable skill and care for both buyer and seller. Seller is probably not vicariously liable for the acts of these licensed brokers.

2. Broker, in an effort to cooperate with as many other brokers as possible, is authorized to pay other brokers a portion of Broker's total commission, determined by Broker in Broker's sole discretion, for the referral to Broker of prospective buyers for Seller's property.

In the event of a conflict between these terms and those in the body of the Listing Contract, the terms on this Addendum shall prevail.

_____   _____
Seller   date   Seller   date
Broker:

by _____   Date: _____

Addendum to Listing Contract
Commission Division
(Cooperative Compensation and Commission Structure)

1. Broker shall seek assistance from, and offer the indicated compensation as a percentage of the gross selling price to, the following brokers licensed by this state, located within the market area of Broker, whose licenses are with a company other than Broker's company.

   ☐ (a)_____ % to other brokers representing Seller ("Subagents"). Subagents work with a buyer, but represent Seller, and owe duties of utmost good faith, loyalty and fidelity to Seller only. Seller may be vicariously liable for the acts of Subagents when acting in the scope of their subagency relationship.

   ☐ (b)_____ % to brokers representing the buyer ("Buyer Agents"). Buyer Agents representing the buyer owe duties of utmost good faith, loyalty and fidelity to buyer only. Seller is not vicariously liable for the acts of Buyer Agents.

   ☐ (c)_____ % to brokers assisting the buyer in the transaction, but not acting as agents of either the buyer or the seller ("Transaction Brokers"). Transaction Brokers should exercise reasonable skill and care for the parties. Seller is not vicariously liable for the acts of Transaction-Brokers.

2. Broker, in an effort to cooperate with as many other brokers as possible, is authorized to pay other brokers a portion of Broker's total commission, determined by Broker in Broker's sole discretion, for the referral to Broker of prospective buyers for Seller's property.

In the event of a conflict between these terms and those in the body of the Listing Contract, the terms on this Addendum shall prevail.

_____   _____
Seller   date   Seller   date

Broker:

_____
by   date

Chapter 3

The Buyer Relationship

Doing What
Comes Naturally

The Nature of Buyers

1. Buyers are the ones who will own the property after the closing.

2. A large percentage of buyers think that you are their "agent," even if you are not. They say things like "my REALTOR®" or sometimes "my Rea-la-tor."

3. The law is moving quickly to protect buyers by requiring a myriad of disclosures regarding all aspects of a real estate transaction.

4. The informed buyer is the buyer of the future. Buyers do not always know what they want. Give them information.

5. Buyers will be around after the sale and will remember who helped them acquire this new piece of real estate. You may have represented the seller, the buyer, neither or both. The buyer is the one who will probably start the suit.

6. Buyers who are dissatisfied with their new acquisition will be searching for a way to extricate themselves from the transaction. Protect yourself against the buyer.

7. Sellers, lacking a seller-financing situation, will generally take their money and be gone. As a practical matter sellers may not be available to help with the post closing problems. Sellers often do not remember the key points that were so easy to express only months before. They become afflicted with "selective memory."

8. Buyer representation is here to stay. Once novel, this concept is now mainstream. The definitions of words like "exclusive" buyer agent and "dual" agent now take on more significant meanings. The industry is struggling to present a common image of the buyer agent, while the public continues to expect more and more from their "agent." Your company will provide some type of buyer agency services. What remains to be determined is who will provide those services and the type of documentation that will be required. "Oral" buyer agency is currently the most common method of representation; however, written exclusive buyer agency agreements are the new frontier and becoming standard.   Professional buyer's agents already utilize a written buyer agency agreement.

9. Everyone must understand the concept of buyer agency and be prepared to explain it and deal with it in some fashion

Pledge of Service to the Buyer

- I will provide you with all the information that I have in my possession regarding any home that you may select.

- I will search all Multiple Listing Services of which I am a member for property you designate.

- I will provide you with all information that I have concerning the physical condition of any property that you select.

- I will provide you with the agency disclosure forms and explain the options available to you, including the manner in which we sell our own listings.

- I will allow **you** to make the decisions that affect **your** real estate needs. I will not make decisions for you, even at your request.

- I am committed to the spirit and letter of the law to provide everyone with equal access to housing.

- I will encourage you to avail yourself of attorneys, accountants, surveyors, appraisers, contractors, inspectors and other experts that you desire.

- I will encourage you to have the property inspected as a part of your contract.

- I will not inspect any property for you. I am not a property inspector.

- I will not let my personal relationship with others deter me from cooperating with them to accomplish your transaction.

- I will keep you informed about the changing financing market, so that you can make an intelligent selection of a lender to assist you with financing.

- I will tell you when I do not know the answers to your questions.

- I will accept compensation only from sources that I have first disclosed to you.

- I will continue to stay current in those areas where it is reasonable to expect information from a real estate professional.

- I will treat you honestly at all times.

Passive Defense Techniques

1. In a lawsuit, it is always nice to have someone who has the ability to pay. Attorneys call this the "deep pocket" theory. Be the poorest in the group. The first rule of litigation is "only sue people with money."

2. Wealth is a personal thing. There is no need to explain to potential plaintiffs that you have a lot of money. Advertisements that say, "I did $10 million last year," can be detrimental to you.

3. The perception that you are not much of an adversary, are poorly organized, do not pay attention to details, do not keep good records, or have something to hide may encourage someone to include you in litigation.

4. Lawsuits are a spectator sport. Try to avoid being a player. Be prepared to demonstrate through your paperwork that you have disclosed properly and treated the buyer in the appropriate manner.

5. Try not to discuss other transactions that you have completed in order to indicate that a risky transaction will work. The more you describe other transactions, the more you may have the opportunity to defend a tenuous perception of what happened.

6. Display the image of an organized, detail-oriented, highly professional agent who *always* follows the rules and is above reproach. No one likes a well organized defendant. She is too credible.

7. Be someone your kids can respect. Be someone who does not make a derogatory comment about others.

8. Try to limit the amount of unimportant information you give to a buyer, client, or other potential plaintiff. Stick to the facts about the property.

9. Limit your liability by explaining alternatives, rules, local sources of information, the extent of your abilities and agency status in written form from the beginning.

10.   Use cover letters, faxes and e-mails to confirm actions taken by yourself and others.

11.   Do the right thing. Do not be swayed because the information seems important. Is it confidential? Did you promise someone that you would not tell? Do you have a fiduciary duty to the buyer?

12.   Unless you are a buyer's agent, you have no duty to the buyer other than honesty. If you are the seller's agent, honesty does not include telling the seller's personal secrets. If you are the buyer's agent, then it is your duty to tell your buyer all information about the property and any confidential information you may have about the seller.

13.   Stay in constant communication with your broker on your real estate transactions. You are both in this together, especially if anything goes wrong. Do not withhold information.

Myths about Buyer Agency

- *You can not look in the Magic Listing System for property.* Sellers put their listings in the MLS because they are looking for buyers. You have buyers.

- *Buyers must pay their agents to be legal.* Anyone can pay anyone in most states. People have the right to contract as they please. People can agree on paying points. Why not agree on paying the brokers? Anyone can agree to pay the Buyer Agent, but it is best coming from the listing broker.

- *Banks will not recognize a buyer agent.* Banks do not care. They want to loan money to the buyer. FHA and VA may present some unusual problems. If you charge a reasonable fee and disclose it in the beginning, problems are limited.

- *No one understands it.* The buyer understands it very well. S/he wants someone who is on his/her side, not the seller's side. Many buyers always thought they had their own advocate when, in reality, they only had a "subagent."

- *You can't show and sell your own listings.* Of course you can. Yes, it requires defining in advance what you will and will not do. Remember, the seller wants to sell the house. That is why he hired you as the listing broker. Most sellers think that you will sell the home yourself when they list with you. Most sellers who become buyers will want to see your listings also. Explain the rules in advance, so that they can enjoy the game.

Myths about Transaction (Real Estate) Broker

- *You can not look in the Magic Listing System for property.* Sellers put their listings in the MLS because they are looking for buyers. You have buyers. You are not a seller's agent or buyer's agent. You simply are a licensed broker selling the house. You are neutral, just like a stockbroker. Disclose information about the property and not about the people.

- *Buyers must pay the broker to be legal.* Anyone can pay anyone in most states. All that is required is a real estate broker's license. People are free to hire a licensed broker to assist them with a real estate transaction. People can agree on paying points. Why not agree on paying the brokers?

- *Banks will not recognize a transaction broker.* Banks do not care. They want to loan money to the buyer. FHA and VA may present some unusual problems. If you charge a reasonable fee and disclose it in the beginning, problems are limited. Act like a broker and you will get paid like a broker.

- *No one understands it.* That is the first thing people think. Brokerage is easier than agency to understand. You discuss the real estate and not the people. Transaction Brokerage offers an option for those buyers who do not want to sign a buyer agency contract, but want to see and buy real estate. They simply do not want an agent. The buyer understands it very well. He wants someone who is neutral who can show and sell real estate.

- *You can't show and sell your own listings.* Of course you can. Yes, it requires defining in advance what you will and will not do. Remember, the seller wants to sell the house. That is why he hired you as the listing broker. Most sellers think that you will sell it yourself when they list with you. Most sellers turned buyers will want to see your listings also. Explain the rules in advance, so that they can enjoy the game. The new name for "dual agency" is more properly Transaction Broker.

- *It is illegal.* Check your state laws. While some states specifically endorse it, others specifically say that you can not do it. Most do not have an opinion.

They license people as brokers and salespersons and have never thought about agency or non-agency. What is a referral fee?

What to Tell, What to Keep Secret

	Buyer Clients	Buyers (Non Clients)
Facts about the property	Yes	Yes
Personal facts about the seller	Yes	No
Motivation of seller to sell	Yes	No
Seller sickness or death	Yes	No
Seller in divorce	Yes	No
Seller building new house	Yes	No
The terms of previous offers to buy	Yes	No
Terms of counteroffers that failed	Yes	No
What "price" to offer	No	No
What "price" to counter	No	No
Which form to use (state with no forms)	No	No
Which form to use (state req'd forms)	Yes	Yes
Which inspector to use	No	No
Which lender is the "best"	No	No

Finding and Working With a Buyer

Searching for the Buyer. Where do buyers come from? Everywhere! If you think back to prospecting for sellers, you will note that all the sources for buyers are identical with those for sellers. The sphere of influence, geographical farm, referrals from satisfied past and present clients or customers and property management tenants have an overflowing pool of buyers just waiting for professional assistance to find the right home.

FSBO. Don't overlook the For Sale By Owner. The owner of the "For Sale By Owner" may initially be unwilling to pay a real estate fee to someone working with a buyer on the sale of his property. Remember, this is the same person who will be searching for professional assistance when searching for a replacement home. At that time, the seller turned buyer will be less hesitant to allow that seller to pay a commission to the buyer agent.

It is likely that a professional real estate licensee will sell the FSBO, and the commission will be included in the price, regardless of who is perceived to pay it. The salesperson must be careful to disclose the buyer relationship to everyone. It might be a good idea for someone who was "working with" or "representing" a buyer to attempt to obtain a "one party" listing as a seller's agent. Your buyer might wonder how negotiating a "one party listing" with the seller, as a seller's agent, is in the buyer's best interests. Remind the buyer that he wants the seller to pay the fee, so that the buyer does not have to pay it. The one party listing will accomplish that objective.

What you might want is a "fee agreement" (see page 282), not a "listing," so that the seller agrees to pay your commission, and you can remain a buyer's agent. Now your commission is part of the total price and, therefore, part of the loan to value calculation. In this way your commission does not cause the buyer to have additional cash requirements in excess of the down payment.

Sellers. Where there is a seller, there will be a buyer. Do not forget to ask the sellers that you represent if you can assist them in the purchase of their next home. They will be looking for a new home the instant that you sell their property. Let's hope that they want you to continue as their REALTOR®. Some agents think that they own these sellers and are aghast when they find that "their seller" has gone out and bought a new property without them. Can you think of a easier way to acquire a new buyer than when you are listing a seller? Even if they are moving to a different location, you can obtain a fee by referring them to another broker. Keep in contact with the seller who moves to a different location, even out of state. Katherine has received a number of buyer referrals from a seller who knows a business associate or friend moving to the area he has left.

Always be on the alert and listening for the opportunities to assist a first time buyer, the buyer who is "moving up" and also needs to sell his present home, and buyers looking for investment properties. That might mean another property to sell and one or more to help them purchase. Buyers looking for second homes and vacation homes represent a growing market. Maybe they could pool their resources with another couple. Where there is a buyer, there will be a seller in the future. When you approach your real estate business as a long term endeavor, you will be there for the same individuals as buyer or sellers for all their real estate transactions. If you pattern each transaction with the idea that you want repeat business, you will indirectly conduct your daily activities in the professional manner to ensure that end.

Farms. "Farm" for buyers the same way you do for sellers. In fact, any and all correspondence should include references to buying or selling real estate if you are assisting the public with both types of transactions. Talk about real estate by telling stories about a couple or individual that you helped purchase a property. Never put the buyer down or make light of his attributes. Set the stage, so that the transaction is productive for the buyer because of your skills. Leave the people thinking, "If I ever want to buy, that is the person that I should call." Everyone should know that you are working with buyers, as well as sellers, in real estate.

Broker referrals. Networking with brokers within your local association or board, as well as intrastate, interstate, and even internationally, will supply a steady stream of referrals for relocating clients. Many of the large franchise companies furnish a relocation network of referrals within their structure. If you are not a member of this type of real estate firm, you can start your own network database. Keep all those cards you collect at REALTOR® events – whether local, state, or national.

Get to know the people to whom you contemplate sending a referral. Remember, that person is not only a direct reflection on you, but is the only way of holding on to the buyers you send to them and the only way you will get paid. No matter how loyal the client may have been to you, loyalty will not overcome the lack of service on the other end. When you are the recipient of another broker's client, keep in contact with the broker with regular updates.

Utilize the benefits of your professional designations. The Certified Residential Specialist (CRS®) directory offers you the assurance of networking with other REALTORS®, who see the importance of specialized continuing education. These individuals have invested in attaining a higher level of professionalism and will conduct their business accordingly. They also complete more of their transactions and make more money than the average salesperson. You are referring your buyer to a professional who will make you look good.

Always create a Paper Trail or Electronic Paperless Trail to verify the payment agreement that you made with the other REALTOR® for the referral. In the event of a dispute, that agreement will be paramount. Remember to indicate in the agreement that all disputes can only be brought in your town and state. Lawyers call this jurisdiction. You want to have all disagreements with referring brokers heard in your local area.

Buyer Contact Card

Date of Initial Contact: _____

Buying Date: _____

Name:_____

Address:_____

City, State, Zip:_____

Phone: Work_____ Home_____

Cell _____ Other_____

Source of Buyer: ___ Open House   ___ Advertisement

___ Walk in   ___ Referral   ___ The Web

___ Franchise   ___ Broker   ___ Other

Buyer is a Tenant:

Current Rent:_____ Lease Expires:_____

Buyer is an Owner:

Value:_____ House Listed with:_____

Debt: _____

Buyer's Price Range:_____

Has been looking for _____ Months

Occupancy Date: _____

Follow-up on:_____ Info:_____

Follow-up on:_____ Info:_____

Follow-up on:_____ Info:_____

Disclosures: ____ Fair Housing   ___ In-Company Sale

____ Agency   ___ Lead Based Paint Booklet

Notes:_____

_____

_____

Letter/e-mail – Fair Housing

Mr. Bill Buyer and
Mrs. Betty Buyer
Apartment 610 A
12th and Main Street
Tenant City, CO 00001

    Re: Fair Housing

Dear Mr. and Mrs. Buyer:

    Let me be the first to welcome you to Ownersville, Colorado, and to our office. We have a small cadre of professional agents and support staff who have been doing business at this location for fourteen months. Satisfied clients and customers are our primary concern.

    Real estate is the American Dream. My company wants to ensure that all buyers know that they have equal access to all the real estate in our market area. We are anxious to show you property that suits your needs.

    We are very proud to adhere to spirit and letter of the Department of Housing and Urban Development's Fair Housing Standards, as well as those of our state and local governments. We want you to realize that you are free to view and make an offer on any house that you select. In fact, we encourage you to do so. The only limiting factors to your selection are the amount of money you have available to spend for a down payment, the amount that you can or will borrow and the size of the monthly payments that you desire.

    Neighborhood mix or makeup are impossible for us to determine. Please do not ask us to try to give you an estimate of the makeup of any neighborhood. We simply can not do that, even if known. Things are changing so fast in today's market that it is impossible for us to know the makeup of any neighborhood. This is a totally open market with equal access to everyone. I am sure that you will be able to select a home that meets your needs from a wide variety of available homes, either listed with our firm or through the Multiple Listing Service.

    We are happy to show you and your family as many homes as you desire in any part of the city and surrounding county. We will provide you with the information at our disposal to aid you in determining the right new home for you to acquire. The different available locations vary from the urban-city-center to the rural county locations. Only you can decide which home is located in the area you desire, is best suited to your physical needs, and meets the financial requirements you determine are within your budget.

If you are ever unable to reach me, or just want to talk to the broker for this company, please feel free to contact the managing broker of this office:

at (_____) _____-_____, office direct or
    (_____) _____-_____, home number or
    (_____) _____-_____, cell phone

He is a well respected broker, and I am proud to work for him. I am sure that he and I will be able to assist you in your selection of a new home in this area.

Enclosed you will find copy of the HUD Lead Based Paint booklet to review. In the days before 1978, some homes used paint that was lead based. Lead based paint was not to be used in houses for which a building permit was issued after January 1, 1978. We want you to be aware of all the issues that may affect any home you decide to purchase.

Thank you for selecting me to assist you with your real estate needs. Searching for housing is fun. Helping people find housing is like a treasure hunt. Let's get started!

Sincerely,
The Real Estate Company

by: Your Name Here,
REALTOR®, CRS, GRI

Motivation of the Buyer and Qualification. Before you ever allow a buyer in your car to see properties, you must first determine the urgency of her desire to buy and if, in fact, she has any money to do so. Urgency alone does not make a buyer. One of the most difficult things to tell someone who really wants to own her home is that there just is not any way she can currently qualify to make her dream a reality. Of course, that presupposes that you have investigated all the possibilities available, to include family assistance with loan qualification or the down payment, co-signors or co-mortgagors. Nothing compares to the sense of accomplishment felt when you can help a struggling buyer realize her dream through creative efforts and financing. On the other hand, if the impossibility of buying a home is approached with honesty and with empathy, the buyer will return to you when her financial situation improves.

During the initial interview, be certain to determine if the buyers sitting across from you are the final decision makers. The ultimate decision of which home to select may rest with another family member or third party, especially if that entity will be responsible for a portion or all of the down payment or qualification. Establish the parameters that the buyer desires in his home.   These include the location or neighborhood, the desired price range and monthly mortgage payment, age of home, style of home (single or multi-level), importance of proximity to schools, entertainment, shopping malls, transportation and any special needs if the buyer is handicapped.

Selecting the right people to work with will make you money every time.   Some salespeople work with whomever comes to town. A few minutes of questions at the initial interview lets the buyer know that you are a professional salesperson who only works with qualified people. S/he will *want* to become your buyer. S/he will want the best.

Determine Your Agency Status.   Prior to the buyer revealing any confidential information, you must verify what your relationship will be with that buyer. Explain verbally to the buyer the services you can provide as a buyer agent, subagent, or neutral real estate broker.   Discuss the fees relative to each and the methods for payment for your fees or commission.   Once the buyer determines the degree of representation he wishes to have, acknowledge the agreement with a written employment contract. Do not be afraid to charge people for your services. You are worth it.

Agency is not the issue. You will make a selection, as we will discuss later. What is important is that you understand the basic functions associated with working with the buyer. Regardless of your status, the buyer is expecting you to provide service before the contract, during the contract and after it is signed. Know the basic duties and follow a checklist.

Signing the Agreement. Once you have decided that these people are worth your effort, you need to sign a contract with them that details your services and how you will be paid. Remember these factors that apply to all buyers:

- The buyer wants to buy a home. That is why he is talking to you.

- You do this for a living. This is not a hobby.

- Someone has to pay you for your services. That is how you pay your bills.

- Indicate some of the services that you provide.

- Professionals talk about their fees just as you do.

- No one wants to pay you if they can help it.

- The buyer will help you get paid if you ask him.

- The buyer will insist that you get paid once you explain the facts of life to them.

- Your commission is part of the transaction.

- Written agreements cement your relationship, impose loyalty from the buyer and define the parameters under which you will work.

- Ask for the order. Then sign up the buyer!

The duration of the agreement can be a key element in obtaining the buyer's consent. If it is a seller whose home you already have listed, you have rapport. That seller turned buyer will sign whatever you place in front of him.

If the buyer is not well known to you, he will be more reluctant to sign a long term agreement. Do not be hesitant to ask for a few days or a week instead of a long term listing. Maybe he will not be the right person with whom you will want to spend valuable time. Protect yourself for the property that you do show him, but leave the listing short and the buyer will be more agreeable to sign. He does not know you either. After a few days with you, he will be happy to extend. You will see extension clauses in some of our forms.

Inventory of Homes to Show. Once you clearly have parameters for the buyer's desired home, search your inventory of homes. Do not neglect to check recently expired listings, the newspaper advertisements, For Sale by Owners and other REALTORS® for homes expected to come on the market, in addition to researching the current listings in the Magic Listing Service. Your research can extend to letters or door knocking in areas where the buyer has expressed an interest to live. If you have a written agreement, you know your method of payment has been covered even if you show a FSBO. Remember to indicate in your agreement exactly the extent of the inventory you are willing to research in order to try to locate the desired home.

Pricing/Market Value. Too often the buyer wants to rely upon you, as the real estate professional, for advice on what price to offer for the home. Do not fall into this trap. Your job is to provide information and let the buyer decide. That means you will have supplied the buyer, whether he is a customer or client, comparable sales for similar homes in the neighborhood. A letter of confirmation may be wise after the offer is accepted. One follows this text.

You can also assist the buyer by explaining the advantages and disadvantages of specific terms, amount of earnest money, financing alternatives and closing dates as they relate to the buyer's personal needs and desires. If this is the "only" house for the buyer, then his offer will be very different from one for a home that is one of several selected. Never forget that your job is to "provide" and let your buyer "decide." That will keep you out of court. People are always looking for someone to blame for "their" decision. It should not be you.

Prepare the Offer. Your technical expertise must be thorough when drafting and preparing an offer for the buyer. Provide the buyer with a detailed market analysis for the neighborhood where he has selected the home, so that he can make an informed decision on pricing. You will also need to be knowledgeable of market trends for the area. Are new developments anticipated that may flood the inventory? Are there plans for road widening projects, or are other city, county or association assessments imminent? Do not rely on the information provided by the listing agent in ascertaining whether you have given full disclosure of material facts to your buyer. Once the price and terms have been determined, review all other aspects of the contract with the buyer. Review the necessity for inspections and the significance of any contingencies included in the contract. When the contract and addenda are completed, reviewed and approved by the buyer, attach a copy of the lender's pre-qualification letter (validating the offering price only) and a cover letter of introduction before presenting the offer to the listing agent or seller. A sample cover letter can be found in the following chapter on contracts.

Home Warranty. (See also page 422) Sometimes a salesperson may inadvertently provide an opportunity for the buyer to litigate. The only way to ensure that all parties understand what is offered, rejected or waived is to provide a written form. This also applies to the cost and availability of a home warranty program. If you get a commission on the sale of a home warranty policy, inform them of that fact. If there are several companies that offer the service, provide a list, just as you would with any other service provider.

Case in Point. *Out of town buyers are referred to the salesperson by their son-in-law, your close personal friend. Everyone looks at the home, which obviously needs a lot of work. The salesperson tells them about home warranties. They decide not to buy one. The contract is written and includes an inspection clause. The buyers have the home inspected and verify the defects. The buyers are fully aware of the defects and decide to purchase the home anyway at a price that reflects the work to be done. The defects are clearly disclosed in written form. Everything seems great. After closing, the buyers testify that they were sure that the salesperson "guaranteed the home" and agreed to do whatever it took to make it "right" for them. They indicate that the salesperson said he would "take care of everything." Now they feel that such a statement meant fix the property. They indicate that they were never told about a home warranty!*

Square Footage. Square footage can be the source of litigation. We have added a form which has stood the test of time for your use (see page 241). It should be filled out by the listing broker or salesperson and then given to the selling agent or the buyer. However, if that did not occur, it could be filled out by the selling agent, also. One solution utilized by several firms is to employ the services of an appraiser who does a "limited appraisal" which only indicates the square footage of the property. These are usually inexpensive and definitely a seller expense. Think of using them when the property is hard to measure, has large open second floor areas allowing you to see the lower floor, or interior spaces under eaves, which may be susceptible to differing interpretations of usable square footage.

Stigmatized Property. Each state has a different interpretation on this area of the law. Most salespeople working with a buyer have more of an affinity with the buyer than the seller. So they tend to tell the buyer information about any stigma that affects the property. If you are not a buyer agent, this could be an error in judgment. The prime example would be a subagent, an extension of the seller, who would need to keep the information confidential.

Know your state law. Some states indicate that disclosures are required for items that "affect the value," while others distinguish between the duties of a buyer agent, a seller subagent and a non-agent. Use caution when you become a dual agent or other In-Company relationship.

Many want to know "what does a buyer agent do?" Well, the first answer is right here. If you are a buyer agent, you would tell what you knew. That is what the buyer is getting when they get an agent. If you are a seller's subagent, check the listing to see what you are authorized to disclose. If you are a transaction broker or other non-agency licensee, this information is probably confidential and should not be disclosed to the buyer. If the buyer needs this information, they need a buyer agent. The disclosure of stigmatized property status is generally not in the seller's best interests.

Example of Colorado's Law (check your state law and know it):

(1)   *Facts or suspicions regarding circumstances occurring on a parcel of property which could psychologically impact or stigmatize such property are not material facts subject to a disclosure requirement in a real estate transaction. Such facts or suspicions include, but are not limited to, the following:*

    (a)   *That an occupant of real property is, or was at any time suspected to be, infected or has been infected with Human Immunodeficiency Virus (HIV) or diagnosed with Acquired Immune Deficiency Syndrome (AIDS), or any other disease which has been determined by medical evidence to be highly unlikely to be transmitted through the occupancy of a dwelling place; or*

    (b)   *That the property was the site of a homicide or other felony or of a suicide.*

(2)   *No cause of action shall arise against a real estate broker or salesperson for failing to disclose such circumstance occurring on the property which might psychologically impact or stigmatize such property.*

Once the Offer is Accepted. A continuation of the research begun prior to writing the offer may be necessary to remove contingencies and conditions. Offer to be present for all inspections and assist with scheduling the appointments. Insist on the buyer being present, so that the information he receives is firsthand and not misrepresented by subsequent explanations. It is important to monitor impending deadlines for contingencies which must be performed by the buyer or from which the buyer will benefit. Offer to accompany the buyer when applying for a loan, or supply the buyer with a list of items that are necessary for the lender's file. Prepare a package for the appraiser to consist of a comparative market analysis, special features of the home and neighborhood statistics if the listing agent does not. Be prepared to meet with the appraiser. Monitor the escrow, title and mortgage processes to ensure a timely closing.

Inspectors, Buyers, The Property and Litigation. If there are problems with the transaction, most will involve the condition of the property. All real property has defects, and some will not be found right away. Can you imagine that some sellers may actually conceal defects. If you wish to limit your personal and professional liability, heed these words of advice. ***Never go through the home with the inspector!***

Think of how you would answer these questions on cross examination:

Clerk of the Court:	*"Do you swear to tell the truth, the whole truth and nothing but the truth?"*
REALTOR®:	*"Yes, I do."*
Attorney:	*"Do you care about your buyer?"*
REALTOR®:	*"Yes, I do."*
Attorney:	*"If you saw something during the inspection that the buyer missed, would you point it out to them, or keep quiet?"*
REALTOR®:	*"I would point it out, of course."*
Attorney:	*"I admire you for that. I knew you would. Now, what if you saw something that the inspector missed. Would you point that out to your buyer, or keep it to yourself?"*
REALTOR®:	*"I would point it out, of course!"*

Attorney: *"So, ladies and gentlemen of the jury, I think that you can see that the buyers, my clients, were justified in relying on the REALTOR®. Not only was he inspecting the property, but he was supervising the buyer and the inspector."*

Oliver E. Frascona, Esq. represented the REALTOR®, and settlement was fast. The issue is not that the REALTOR® is dishonest, or will not tell the truth. In fact, the reverse is true, and that very fact will pose real problems as the opposing attorney tries to hang you. Remember, in most states the inspector's liability is limited by contract. The REALTOR® is present in the litigation as the player with the deep pockets.

Closing. Even the smoothest transaction can fall to pieces in the end. The emotions of both the buyer and seller are the most frayed at this stage. Many facets of the transaction must come together in the final hour. Remind the buyer of the necessity for a cashier's check to close, if applicable in your state. The hazard insurance binder must be in the lender's file. Review the closing documents, including the settlement statement, for any errors on names, addresses, or prorations. *Do not forget to ask for the referral!*

Insurance. Remember, if your buyer is moving in early or letting the seller remain on the property after closing, there may not be the proper insurance coverage. The "homeowner's" policy in most states covers the homeowner only. People who move in early, or stay after closing, are tenants and not covered by the "homeowner's" policy. If you are helping the buyer, remember to make sure that her property is insured. She will remember the service and send you potential buyers as a result.

The availability of a hazard/casualty insurance policy for a prospective buyer has become a major issue. Properties with have claim histories that are accessible by a prospective insurance company (C.L.U.E. Reports) may not be insurable at a cost that is reasonable to a new buyer. Buyers who have a claims history on a previous home may also find it difficult to obtain a new policy on their next home. (See clause at page 421)

The New Owner Has Possession. And you have been paid! Now the buyer has hopefully become a long term client and a source of constant referrals. It is a good idea to send or deliver a housewarming gift once the buyer has had an opportunity to settle in her new surroundings. Contact after the closing can be maintained by a reminder to re-key the home, place important documents in a safe place and by supplying a mortgage amortization schedule. Be sure you place them in your client database and stay in contact!

Letter/e-mail – Selling Price Verification

Mr. Bob Buyer
Mrs. Betty Buyer
47 Park View Lane
Boulder, CO 80305

Re: #4 Dream House Lane

Dear Bob and Betty:

Congratulations! You new home is under contract. It has been a delight to assist you with the location and purchase of your new home. As I have told you before, I need to clarify the way in which you determined the price that you finally decided to offer on this property.

A Competitive Market Analysis for this property was provided. It was comprised of properties which seemed to be similar to the property you wished to buy that I located through the Multiple Listing Service. We used current listings of properties, properties that had sold and properties that had been rejected from the market. As you know, the MLS does not represent all properties that are in these categories.

I am glad that I am a REALTOR® and not an appraiser. As REALTOR® I can provide you with the data regarding the relative value as indicated, but I can not determine the ultimate value. That is a job for the appraiser. When we receive the final appraisal, we will see how close you were.

Thank you for selecting me to help you with the selection and acquisition of your new home.

Sincerely,
The Real Estate Company

by: Max A. Loyalty, Broker-Owner

Square Footage Disclosure

Property Address: _____

1. Licensee Measurement.
Listing Licensee ___ Has ___ Has Not measured the square footage of the residence according to the following standard, methodology or manner:

Standard/Method/Manner	**Date Measured**	**Square Footage**
___ Exterior measurement	_____	_____
___ FHA	_____	_____
___ ANSI	_____	_____
Local Standard _____	_____	_____
Other _____	_____	_____

2. Other Source of Measurement:
Listing Licensee ___ Is ___ Is Not providing information on square footage of the residence from another source(s) as indicated below:

Source of Square Footage Information

	Dated	**Square Footage**
___ Prior Appraisal ___ Attached	_____	_____
___ Building plans from _____	_____	_____
___ Assessor's Office	_____	_____
___ Other _____	_____	_____

These sources may be unreliable. Measurement is for the purpose of marketing, may not be exact and is not for loan, valuation or other purposes. If exact square footage is a concern, the property should be independently measured. Do not rely upon the square footage indicated. Broker is not liable for square footage measurement.

Buyer and Seller are advised to verify this information. Buyer is advised to obtain an independent measurement or investigation on, or before, the Inspection Objection Deadline of the contract.

By_____

_____ Listing Licensee   Date _____

_____ Selling Licensee   Date _____

Checklists

Professional airline pilots who have flown thousands of hours never memorize any of the checklists. They must use a checklist. They are required to read it and check it each time before, during and after each flight. There is a reason. If there is a checklist and it is followed, the chance of failure is greatly reduced. Nothing takes the place of a good checklist outlining the tasks to be performed and the division of labor. Define at every possible juncture what is expected of everyone, and most people will either comply with their appointed tasks or alter the checklist. Either way, you are happy. A checklist of, and for, your own actions is a good example of a precise standard method of operation, a good defense, and a superb credibility builder.

A 3 x 5 card, a standard form, a Rolodex card, or a computer entry system can be used to track all stages of working with the buyer. Personal attention to detail is the only solution to a smooth closing with no after closing blues. Here is a sample buyer checklist. Make your own. Put it in the word processor and add to it each time you think of an additional item that you need to report or accomplish.

Buyer Data

Date:_____

Name:_____ RES Phone: _____

Address:_____ OFF Phone: _____

_____ CELL Phone: _____

e-mail: _____

Other: _____

Title Company:_____ File No: _____

Contact:_____ Phone: _____

Cell: _____

e-mail: _____

Mortgage Company:_____ File No: _____

Contact:_____Phone:_____

Fax: _____

Cell: _____

e-mail:_____

Other REALTOR®:_____

Contact Information:_____

e-mail:_____

Appraiser:_____

Contact Information:_____

e-mail:_____

Performance Deadline Checklist

Property Address: _____

Sellers: _____

Buyers: _____

Event	Deadline Date	Done
Offer Acceptance Deadline Date		
Offer Acceptance Deadline Time		
I. Document Delivery		
Loan Application (New Loan/Assumption)		
Buyer's Credit Info (Owner Carry)		
Existing Loan Documents (Assumption)		
Governing Documents Delivered		
Title Documents Delivered		
Seller's Property Disclosure Delivered		
Document Request Deadline		
Off-Record Matters Disclosure Deadline		
Attorney Review Date		
II. Objection Deadlines		
Loan Commitment Deadline (New/Assn)		
Disapproval of Buyer's Credit Deadline		
Objection to Existing Loan Deadline		
Approval of Loan Transfer Deadline		
Title Objection Deadline		
Governing Documents Objection Date		
Insurance Availability Deadline		
Inspection Objection Deadline		
Resolution Deadline		
III. Off Record Issues		
Appraisal Deadline		
Survey/Improvement Location Certificate Delivered to Buyer		
Off-Record Matters Objection Deadline		
Right Of First Refusal Deadline		
IV. Closing Date		
Possession Date		
Possession Time		

Buyer Checklist

BUYER LISTING PROCEDURE

_____1. Mail broker introduction letter to buyer
_____2. E-mail buyer website for real estate office
_____3. E-mail buyer website for financing, etc.
_____4. Assemble buyer listing agreement packet
    a. Lead Based Paint Booklet
    b. Agency disclosure
    c. Listing contract ready to go
    a. List of past clients as references
    e. Home inspector guidelines
_____5. Appointment with the buyer
    a. Motivation _____Hot_____Warm_____"Looky-Lou"
    b. Determine agency status
    c. Written buyer listing agreement
    b. Pre-qualify the buyer
    d. Commitment to appoint with a lender
    e. Items for lender checklist
        1). Need for tax returns
        2). Employment verification
        3). _____
    f. Determine property parameters
        1). Price_____
        2). Age_____
        3). Square footage_____
        4). Bedrooms/Baths_____
        5). Kids ages _____
        6). Schools_____
        7). Special Needs _____
        8). Worship _____
    g. Broker's signature on Listing Agreement
    h. Copy for the buyer with everyone's signatures
_____6. Search for properties that suit buyer's needs
_____7. Set appointment to show properties to buyer
_____8. Mail follow-up Letter/e-mail to buyer
_____9. Mail selected subject matter letters
_____10. E-mail websites for properties (schools, etc) to buyer
_____11. Confirm mortgage qualification with lender
_____12. Obtain written letter of pre-qualification from lender
_____13. Start the showing process

SHOWING PROCEDURE

_____1. Prepare show inventory
     a. Research MLS actives and expired listings
     b. Call REALTOR® network for new listings
     c. Research newspaper advertisements
     d. Contact FSBO owners
_____2. Preview homes without buyer
_____3. Select homes that meet the buyer criteria
_____4. Set appointments for showing buyer
_____5. Showing day:
     a. Allow adequate time
     b. Allow with breaks for rest and meals
     c. Schedule the properties in the correct order for a sale
     d. Turn off your cell phone and pager

WRITING THE OFFER

_____1. Collect all data needed
     a. Price
     b. Terms
     c. Possession issues
     d. Inclusions
     e. Exclusions (will they be hauled off by seller)
_____2. Review contract and addenda with buyer in detail
_____3. Attach lender pre-qualification letter
_____4. Attach cover letter explaining and selling the offer

WHEN THE OFFER IS ACCEPTED

_____1. Original of contract to file
_____2. Original of contract to title company
_____3. Original or copy to new hazard insurance company
_____4. Prepare and deliver escrow instructions
_____5. Prepare letter designating tasks to be completed
     a. Mail to buyer
     b. Mail to seller (via other broker)
_____6. Prepare performance deadlines sheet
_____7. Assemble appraisal package for appraiser
_____8. Designate and start to mail letters or e-mails that will flow through the pre-closing period
_____9. Obtain closing company's secure website for this transaction, title work and exceptions. Get it and give to buyer

_____10. Mail/e-mail lender selection letter
_____11. Mail/e-mail inspector selection form or cover e-mail
_____12. Schedule inspection appointments
_____13. Accompany buyer **TO** inspections, but **DO NOT GO THROUGH THE HOME** with the Buyer and Inspector
_____14. Confirm New Homeowner's Insurance is Available/Cost Effective

WHEN LOAN IS APPROVED
_____1. Mail, e-mail attachment or fax loan confirmation letter
_____2. Confirm in a cover letter that you are not liable for lender non-performance.
_____3. Confirm loan status with lender and title company (e-mail)
_____4. Make a project checklist to get through closing
_____5. Verify that inspection report was received and given to buyer and/or seller as contract provides (receipt)
_____6. Congratulatory letter for inspection (offer home warranty)

WHEN TRANSACTION CLOSES and RECORDS
_____1. Copy the settlement sheets (Adobe® or photo copy) for your personal file.
_____2. Copy the contract and other important papers for your personal records.
_____3. Purge office file as appropriate
_____4. Prepare and submit MLS sold change form
_____5. Give office file to accountant
_____6. Complete database or 4x5 index card for client database
_____7. Input in contact management a list of 3-6-9-12 month follow-up correspondence
_____8. Plan "welcome to the neighborhood party" with names of neighbors and friends from the new and the old neighborhood
_____9. Input into personal farm database
_____10. Send note and gift to client
_____11. Send follow-up letters to all parties
_____12. Ask for referral to new client!
_____13. Send delayed delivery e-mail (calendar) to yourself for Dec 15th to send out the closing statements to the parties for their taxes
_____14. Copy and Deposit your check

Loan Application Checklist

1. Relocation paperwork
   a. Military
      i. Orders
      ii. Current leave and earnings statement
   b. Corporate relocation package
   c. Home guarantee information for relocation buyer

2. Buyer's checkbook to pay for appraisal and credit report

3. Work address and telephone number

4. Deposit verification information for each account (Social Security No)
   a. Bank name/address
   c. Bank phone number
   d. Account number
   e. Latest bank statement

5. Credit card and loan information
   a. Creditor name
   b. Creditor address
   c. Creditor account number
   d. Nature of debt
   e. Balance
   f. Payment schedule

6. Addresses for last three years

7. Tax returns for past two years (be ready to sign them)

8. Personal financial statement or list of major assets with respective values – Cars, Boats, Trucks, Vacation homes, etc

9. VA loans – Certificate of Eligibility

10. Copy of lease or rental agreement

11. Copy of sale contract on existing property

12. Copy of closing statement and deed for previous houses that still have you on the loan

The Use of Professionals

Delegation. There is no need to be all things to all people. If there is someone else who can preform the required task, their services need to be recommended and encouraged. Should the buyer be reluctant, a cover letter is an appropriate way to indicate the importance of your suggestion. You may say, "You realize that I must give you a letter indicating that I thought you should seek an independent appraisal or a structural inspection prior to signing the contract." By this time, they are ready for that statement. Follow it up with a letter.

The Referral. The salesperson exposes herself to great danger with the recommendation of a friend or associate. You will not only look bad if there is ever a problem, but you may have placed yourself in a lose-lose position. If you are going to recommend the services of a professional, mentioning that other clients have seemed satisfied or have told you that they were pleased with the service might be a tactful way to indicate that one person is, in fact, better than the other. If you provide a list, most people use the rule of "three." Remember that the number "three" does not limit any liability for the performance of any one of the three. Use a cover letter for any referral that specifically indicates you are not liable for the individual(s).

Referrals are a good way to lose a customer, and rarely make any money. Agents live with a referral long after the transaction is closed, and the money spent.

Complexity. The status of the modern real estate transaction today simply does not lend itself to the general broker who is an expert in everything. The buyer will buy without your having to obligate yourself. Let the buyer decide on the expert and employ the expert personally. Do not arrange for, or contract for, the expert.

Opinions. Too often salespersons give title insurance opinions by saying something like, "Sure the title is OK. Those are just standard exceptions." You might hear a new agent or an agent helping a good friend say, "This is the best loan available," or "Charles Raudonis at Denver Funding is the best. Whatever he says is what you should do," feeling compelled to have an opinion or the need to "keep the deal together."

Inflation is never as much as anyone wants when he is thinking of selling and always too high when he is thinking of buying. Neither you nor a buyer can simply sell a mistake. The parties are going to rely on your statements. Should your statements prove to be in error, you will be responsible and so will the broker. The use of standard letters can help clear the air and explain in specific detail the duties you have and have not assumed. This will help to limit the liability of everyone including your broker. Stay out of the glib opinion business and just offer responsible service.

Home Inspectors. Always recommend the use of a home inspector. Whether you have made one or more referrals to the buyer, or he has found one on his own, you may wish to send a confirming note in a letter or card to the buyer. Note that this clause is a confirmation on his selection. (See Referral at page 18) Below is a standard FHA form clause.

Clause:

"FHA believes that homebuyers are best served when they are aware of their own responsibilities for assuring that the property is acceptable to them, and that FHA does not warrant the condition of the home. Homebuyers are also encouraged to obtain an inspection service to make the determination that the house is free of defects"

Clause:

Congratulations on your selection of _____ to act as your home inspector. There are numerous competitors in the marketplace for this kind of service. Although I cannot be responsible for the individuals and companies that I provided to you, I had other buyers use this entity and they seemed satisfied. I am glad that the inspector was able to provide you with a list of past clients or customers to assist you in making your decision.

Remember to verify that in fact the inspector has adequate errors and omission insurance, is licensed, if applicable, and is a member of ASHI® or NAHI™.

Use similar language for the referral and confirmation letter or e-mail for the selected lender, the termite inspector, the roof inspector or accountant, etc. The key to reducing your liability are the introductory words, "Congratulations on your selection....."

Caution. *The Buyer Agent is "All Powerful Expert Theory." In the eyes of the public, the Buyer Agent is all things to all people. S/he is an expert on all matters and, in fact, obviates the use of other inspectors. When you are a buyer's agent, or assisting a buyer in any form, you must emphatically and repeatedly stress that you are not an expert beyond the scope of your* *professional real estate duties. Do so nicely with cards, e-mails and brief cover letters. Remember, the buyer is usually the one who will bring the suit, and you are the number one person auditioning for the position of defendant.*

Professional Services Form. With the buyer's perception that the buyer agent is an expert on everything, it is imperative that you provide the buyer with a form that indicates what you do and what you do not do. All that the buyer really wants is to know that someone is handling those aspects of the transaction that the buyer does not want to handle or does not know how to handle. This will dispel the myth that the buyer agent knows all and does all.

Professional Services Provided

To better assist our sellers and buyers we have a list of the various services that we provide and the ones that are provided by other professionals.

Service	Provider
Assistance with Showings	Realtor® – Any MLS Property
Market Evaluation	Realtor® – Not appraisal
Appraisal of the Property	Licensed Appraiser (recommended)
Contract Preparation	Realtor® – Fill in blanks
Contract Drafting	Attorney at law
Contract Acceptance	Buyer/Seller determine terms of the Contract
Legal Advice	Attorney (Prohibited for Realtor®)
Negotiations	Realtor®
List of Lenders	Realtor® helps to shop rates
New Loan	Bank or Your Mortgage Company
Lender Selection	Buyer
Loan Rate/Term Decision	Buyer
Condition of the Property	Buyer/Inspector (Not Realtor®)
List of Home Inspectors	Realtor® (Inspectors not licensed by state)
Inspection	Inspector (recommended)
Inspector Selection	Buyer
Termites	Termite Inspector
Home Warranty	Home warranty company
Title Examination	Title Company or Your Attorney
Survey	Surveyor (Improvement Location Certificate is not a survey)
Neighborhood Crime	Local Police or Sheriff (all areas have some)
Megan's Law (sex offenders)	Buyer and local law enforcement
Mold Inspection	Mold Inspector – Environmental Professional

I have been given a copy of this Professional Services Provided sheet.

_____   _____
Buyer   Date   Buyer   Date

Broker:

_____
Licensee   Date

Mold Disclosure Form

✓ Properties in _____ may have either toxic (harmful) or non-toxic (not harmful) mold.

✓ There is a probability that mold exists in the next property that you will buy or rent.

✓ Some homeowner's and renter's insurance policies are excluding loss due to mold.

✓ Some mold can cause serious health problems, and even death for certain individuals.

✓ Not all types of mold are visible on the surface as a lot of mold exists behind the drywall, in an attic, in duct work or in a crawl space.

✓ Neither a buyer nor his REALTOR® is qualified to inspect a house for mold. Neither is trained to recognize mold. The REALTOR® is not liable for the inspection of the property or for the presence of mold specifically.

✓ REALTOR® strongly recommends that a buyer obtain an inspection of the property by an engineer or home inspector who will look to the extent s/he can for mold and other potential defects, before expiration of the Inspection Objection Deadline indicated in a Contract to Buy and Sell Real Estate.

✓ If a more thorough inspection is required, then a buyer or tenant may elect to have an environmental expert inspect the house.

✓ Some hints of the possible existence of mold are: standing water, prior water problems or leaks, floods or construction of improvements with rain or snow present.

We have received a copy of this Mold Disclosure Form.

REALTOR®:   **Buyer:**

by:_____   _____
            date   date

Letter/e-mail – Buyer's Use of Professionals

Mr. and Mrs. Brilliant Buyer
Apartment 610 A
12th and Main Street
Denver, CO 80305

   Re: 909 First Street

Dear Mr. and Mrs. Buyer:

    As you know, our firm is comprised of professional real estate people whose job it is to assist sellers and buyers with their real estate needs. I will be happy to help you locate a house that you feel not only suits your needs, but which also fits your budget.

    Prior to obtaining a series of inspections, I encourage you to make sure that the property is insurable. This means that you will need to contact your insurance agent and verify that you can obtain a policy on terms that are acceptable to you and your budget.

    Once that is done, we encourage the selection and use of the services of other professionals to satisfy the requirements indicated in the contract. Your satisfaction is important, and you will certainly want to avail yourself of the assurances you desire. We are not in the lending, title insurance, termite inspection, structural inspection, radon testing, mold discovery, home inspection or home warranty businesses; nor are we in the business of providing legal or accounting services. Being real estate agents is a full-time job in itself. There are numerous professionals who are experts in these areas, who are ready to assist buyers just like you with your decisions.

    Although we all have received recommendations from previous clients and customers regarding their selections and favorites, and have a list of our own professionals, we cannot be responsible for any firm or person whom we think will fill your needs. That selection is a personal one and left up to you. However, to provide you with a place to start, I will provide you with a list of people who have been utilized by other buyers in the past or who have done work for us. Of course, I can not accept responsibility for the work product of any of these firms or individuals. I do know that other buyers have been happy with them in the past, and that each entity will provide you with a list of their past customers to assist you in your decision.

I hope the list will be helpful in making your choice. If I can be of any further assistance, please do not hesitate to let me know. But first, we have to find the right house.

Sincerely,
The Real Estate Company

by: Your Name Here,
REALTOR®, CRS, GRI

Letter/e-mail – Buyer – Professionals – Older Home

Mr. and Mrs. John Happy
Apartment 610 A
12th and Main Street
Denver, CO 80305

    Re: 909 First Street

Dear John and Sue Happy:

    Congratulations on your decision to make an offer to purchase this property. I am pleased that we were able to locate an older home you feel is affordable, and that you think you will enjoy. As you know, with all older homes, there are a number of areas that may require special attention.

    Prior to obtaining a series of inspections, I encourage you to make sure that the property is insurable. This means that you will need to contact your insurance agent and verify that you can obtain a policy on terms that are acceptable to you and your budget.

    We recommend that in addition to obtaining the normal radon gas, septic system and water quality tests you requested, you also consult a structural engineer and a termite inspector. These are terms we included in the contract at your direction, and you will need to get started as soon as possible after the offer is accepted since there is often a delay between the time a test is requested and the time the results are obtained.

    I want to try to stay within the dates outlined in your contract, so that there is no chance that you will lose the property. In addition, your prompt attention will allow us to indicate to our sellers the status of the contract, so that they can make decisions on other proposals, which they may elect to accept as alternative contracts if and when they arrive.

    The contract indicates that you must give written notice of any dissatisfaction directly to the seller, with a copy delivered to the seller's agent, prior to noon on Wednesday the 12th. Otherwise the condition, requiring a satisfactory inspection will be deemed to have been satisfied. You need to retain an inspector as soon as possible to allow for enough time to complete the inspection. I am ready to help you.

Our firm is comprised of professional real estate people who are familiar with properties in this area. Please know that we are not soil engineers nor structural engineers. Therefore, we cannot be responsible for the physical condition of the property, nor the soil it rests upon. The services of other professionals are required to satisfy these questions in your mind as well as the other requirements indicated in the contract, and to provide you with the assurances you desire. Transactions today are complex and require the talents of lending institutions, title insurance companies, termite inspectors, radon testers and sometimes home warranty underwriters, not to mention the services of a lawyer or accountant.

We encourage you to seek and select the counsel of the experts of your choice in order to ensure that you are satisfied with all of the complex aspects of the purchase of your new home. Please understand that we can not accept responsibility for the work product of any of these firms or individuals. Even I must rely on professionals when I acquire real property because the talents they possess are just not within my area of expertise. If I can be of any further assistance, please do not hesitate to let me know.

Sincerely,
The Real Estate Company

by: Your Name Here,
REALTOR®, CRS, GRI

Agency Basics for the Company

Company Agency Policy. Each company must have a company agency policy. This document should set forth the position statement for the *entire* company. We feel that it should be a document which informs the prospective buyer or seller regarding all aspects of the company agency selections. While it will not suffice for agency disclosure in most states, it will ensure that all members of the public are getting the same information for all the salespeople in the office.

Entire Company – Even in Designated Agency States. Salespeople (Associate Brokers) are agents of the broker, period. From a liability point of view they are treated as an entity – one company – even if the broker can designate one agent to "represent" a buyer, and another agent to "represent" the seller. All listings are with the broker. Basic agency laws dictate that the Broker is liable (vicarious liability) for the conduct of his/her agents. The first step is to get the entire company together and solicit their understanding about how they currently do business, and how they want to do business. If you can formulate a policy that incorporates as much of the current practice as possible, it will make the transition easier. *Everyone must follow the same policy. There can be no exceptions.*

After receiving input, the managers should meet away from the office distractions and agree on the policy that they will follow. Try out various scenarios with role playing and determine if the policy truly covers all aspects of your market. Do not be overly influenced by the actions of other offices. Everyone must have a policy that works for him or her office. Be prepared to role play the agency disclosure discussion as it would be presented to potential customers or clients in a manner that is acceptable in your state and in your office. The broker needs to be able to demonstrate the procedure and answer questions from his agents.

Company Forms. If you are looking for a good place to implement company forms, we can think of no better area than agency. Develop a set of company agency forms. Have them printed and require compliance with the policy. Make certain that the forms follow the administrative and statutory rules of your jurisdiction. There is no allowance for mistakes here. You must be absolutely certain you are in compliance with the statute. Do the research and consult competent legal advice, preferably from a real estate attorney.

Training. At each sales meeting have a new set of salespeople do some role playing as buyers, sellers and salespeople. Do not be critical. Emphasize the strong points. Encourage participation, right down to the words to be said to the buyer. Do not interrupt. As the broker, you must let the salespeople try, fail and try again. Remember, if it is not in the meeting, the role playing will be real life. Once said in public, the script can not be rewritten. Your salespeople will ask you how to do each presentation, so be ready with the proper answers. You can role play with them. If they do not know a system, they will quickly emulate yours. Make sure that you know the options cold.

Agency Selection Alternatives

Subagents. *[Almost all states have eliminated sub-agency. Hawaii has not required subagency for decades. In Colorado it is now illegal. Perhaps the following disclosure will encourage a revision of the policy in your office and state.]* The listing office, *the entire office, broker and salespeople*, is an entity working as an agent of the seller. The selling office, *the entire office, broker and salespeople*, as an entity, acts as the agent of the listing office, thus becoming the subagent of the seller. Subagents owe their duties of fidelity, loyalty, confidentiality, etc., to the listing office and the seller. Yes, subagents owe fiduciary duties to a seller whom they have not met, instead of to the buyers with whom they are working. If subagency seems a little awkward, it is.

Subagents are on the seller's "side" and do not represent the best interests of the buyer. Subagents must disclose this fact clearly to all buyers. This disclosure has never been done by a majority of the real estate salespeople. It was very difficult to accomplish. It is difficult for the authors, and many judges and jurors, to imagine a buyer who, after being told *"everything that you tell me, I will promptly tell the seller,"* would be anxious to utilize a subagent. The conclusion is that a reasonable person would not make that election; therefore, the disclosure was not made or was made improperly.

Eventually, the concept will not exist. Few salespeople actually tell the buyer "whatever you tell me, throughout this entire transaction, I will tell the seller." Few tell their seller, now turned buyer, looking for a new home, "I used to be your agent, but now I am an agent for sellers that I do not know. I will be telling them all that I know about you." The buying public wants someone who is at least not on the seller's team. *The courts are having a field day with brokers who are failing to inform the customer of the nature of the relationship that exists between buyer and broker.*

Letter/e-mail – Buyer's Agent Rejecting Subagency – *Just for Fun*

Mr. Larry Listing Broker
Seller's Realty and Insurance
23 West Coop Lane
Commission City, WA 80000

  Re: No. 7 Benthaven Way

Dear Larry:

  Thank you for taking the time to talk with me today about the above referenced property. As I indicated to you, I am rejecting your kind offer of subagency with regard to this property. In this particular instance, I am operating as a buyer's agent and do not want to have any fiduciary duty to either you or the seller.

  I was initially rather confused when you indicated that your sellers were not interested in my showing the property if they could not be liable for me as a subagent. Now that the liability issue is cleared up, and we both realize that one benefit of buyer agency is that the seller, your client, and you are not responsible for me, I feel more confident that we can work together. Some other listing offices have indicated that we were not to show their sellers' properties. I suppose they were afraid that we might sell them. That would certainly not please the sellers. Maybe they felt that if the buyer had representation, the sides would be too equal.

  I am happy that you did not take such an announcement too seriously and were still able to confide in me the secrets that the seller had confided in you. The indication that the seller would take a lesser price will be very advantageous in my representation of the purchaser and will probably expedite a fast sale. I appreciate your comment that the sellers are moving out of the area due to a company transfer. That information, coupled with your statement that they have only a month until the company buyout guarantee kicks in, should give us time to take advantage of them. Finally, the information about the divorce was most helpful. With you as their agent, they should do well.

  Thank you for arranging the showing for tomorrow. I will expect a constant flow of confidential information. It is always a pleasure to work with you in a real estate transaction.

Broker's Agents. A few states have decided that the selling office is not a subagent of the seller, but instead is an agent of the listing broker. No matter what anyone says, this looks a lot like subagency. The goal of this designation is to remove any vicarious liability of the seller for errors made by the selling office, the "broker's agent." The selling office is not an agent (subagent) of the seller, but was an agent of the listing broker. This type of agency is not mainstream.

Buyer Agents and "Exclusive Buyer Agents." This battle is raging. What is an "exclusive buyer agent?" Is it someone who does not take any listings; ever? Is it someone who works with buyers one day as a buyer agent, and sellers as a listing broker on another day? The definition will not be settled for sometime. While we recognize that a "true exclusive buyer's agent" does not take listings and only represents one buyer at a time, in this book we will use the term "exclusive buyer's agent" as it is used in actual practice. An "exclusive buyer's agent" is an individual (generally not the entire company) who is representing the buyer in the transaction at hand. That person may, in fact, represent other buyers and sellers in different transactions. The individual may have been an exclusive seller's agent for the seller. Then the same agent became an exclusive buyer's agent for the buyer. Now the buyer wants to buy the agent's listing and the agent serves as a dual agent or transaction broker.

Whole Office Concept. The entire office, as a unit, represents a buyer, a seller or some form of both. The representation of both the buyer and seller in the same transaction may be dual agency or transaction Broker, or some other form of "neutral." Although rapidly disappearing throughout the country as it is replaced by "Split, Designated or Assigned Agency or Brokerage Relationships," this system follows the principle that the entire office is one entity to all people in a transaction. This is a myth to be certain, and a dying one at that.

Exclusive Buyer Agency Offices. These are entire offices that do not take listings. The agents only represent buyers. If you were listing a property, would you want your broker to contact these offices – ones with only buyers as clients – to see if they had a buyer for your home? Of course! The fact that these offices do not take listings suggests that this form of business is not for everyone. These offices will always be able to indicate that they have no conflict of interest because they never act as "dual agents."

Designated, Split, Assigned Agency and Designated Brokerage. These are all names for the developing, and we believe, mainstream form of real estate in the next 100 years. In this situation, the Broker, the Employing Broker, the "Broker" Broker, remains the owner for all the company's listings. This is no different from the way it always has been. The Broker is also liable for the actions and inactions of those whose licenses hang under him/her. The Broker still is the master of the ship and responsible for "supervision" under the various real estate commission regulatory entities.

Through various methods the Broker "designates" a licensee in the office to act as a "buyer's agent," and one to act as a "seller's agent." In some states the designation may be for either licensee to act as a "transaction broker," or other non-agency relationship established in that particular state, if that is the selection of the customer.

The advantage of designated brokerage/agency is that "dual agency," "transaction broker" or "statutory broker," or any other "neutral" fallback position, only occurs when the same licensee finds him/herself representing both the buyer and seller in a particular transaction. While this does happen, it is not prevalent and allows firms more flexibility for In-Company sales. The old system, "whole office" concept, was a killer as it promulgated the myth that all licensees in the firm represented the buyer, seller or both as in the In-Company sale.

Buyer Agency Option. With the advent of Designated Brokerage/Agency, Buyer Agency is on the rise. More and more offices now offer the option of buyer agency if the buyer so desires. They recognize that the buyer may want representation, or at least be able to have a salesperson who is "neutral" and not the agent for some seller whose property is listed with the office, or stranger yet, some seller whose home is listed with another company. These brokers decided that their salespeople can represent or assist either the buyer or the seller, and sometimes both, with the proper advance written disclosure and, if possible, a written agreement.

Buyer Agency, Optional or Mandatory? There are some people you "should" represent, some you "must" represent, some you "might" represent, some you will "wish you had" represented, and some that you know you should have sent to your worst enemy. Do the following people require a buyer agent? (think about it)

> **You are the Buyer.** When you are buying a property for your own account, are you your own agent? No, you *are* the buyer. Hopefully, you are not buying one of your company's listings. Although you are the principal, many people will refer to you, and regard you, as a buyer's agent. You *are* the buyer. Of course, you could never be a subagent of the seller, but some will try to convince you otherwise. Just smile and write the contract.

Relatives Near and Far. Parents, brothers and sisters, brothers-in-law, uncles, aunts, children and spouses are all people with whom you enjoy a special blood relationship. You are on the buyer's team here, whether you like it or not. You are not a subagent of the seller – period. You may try, in some states, to be a Transaction Broker or some other "neutral" licensee. That is a state by state question.

Buddies and Business Associates. The person with whom you play golf each Saturday, the pastor of your church, the banker who knows all your financial dealings, as well as you know hers, the roommate from college, the partner at work or the other owner in the boat are all people who are close to you. You should *probably* be a buyer agent. Yes, these could be Transaction Broker relationships if your state allows this method of selling. You would not be an agent of the seller, nor would you represent the buyer either. You could just sell them some real estate. Yes, you would keep the personal secrets of both sides to yourself. The goal is to just talk real estate, not people. Isn't that exactly what a "dual agent" does?

Sellers Ready to Buy. If you do not think that you are "their" REALTOR®, ask them. They consider you as their real estate person. That was the plan, remember?

Relocation Referrals. These companies have made it very clear that they want their buyers to have agency representation. Maybe you could convince them that you would be neutral. Seller subagency is definitely not what relocation companies want.

Non-Agency Options. Many states are offering the buyer and seller another option. Some call it transaction broker, facilitator, limited agent or statutory broker. One state even calls it "another relationship." The motivation is the same, no matter the name. The licensee provides real estate service without being an agent. This is an alternative that consumers find a little easier to understand than "dual agent." It is typically used in the In-Company transaction as an alternative to "dual agent."

Regardless of the title, this is a system to provide professional services to the buying public without forcing the consumer to accept the seller's subagent or employ an agent. Suppose the buyer does not want you to act for the seller and is unwilling to have you as a buyer agent. In a growing number of states, buyer agency requires a written agreement. Some buyers may not want to sign an agreement, yet they still desire to use the services of a professional REALTOR® to buy a home.

Buyers are vicariously liable in many states for the actions of their agent. That is a basic agency principle. The non-agency option is used a lot in states where the state mandates a written agency agreement. When the buyer is reluctant to sign a written agreement there needs to be an option that allows the licensee to sell real estate without a written agreement. In this situation only a disclosure telling the buyer that you are not the agent of seller or the buyer is required.

No matter how the relationship between the buyer and salesperson is defined, the salesperson has several duties that relate to the transaction. The buyer now has someone who is interested in creating a win/win transaction. The salesperson provides all the information necessary to her customer, so that the customer can make informed decisions on each aspect of the sale. The key here is to provide information, but leave the final decision to the buyer. The salesperson must be willing to investigate all resources, to include the building department, tax office, any pertinent public records and local schools in the area, to gain information on the material facts about the property. Keep in mind the differences between investigating material facts relating to the property, a duty of all licensees, and the need to direct the buyer to other sources of information, such as locations to determine the addresses of known sex offenders (Megan's Law), where the licensee has no duty to investigate.

A comprehensive evaluation of the comparable listings and sales in the neighborhood should be supplied to the buyer, so that s/he can determine the price s/he wishes to offer. The salesperson should have the technical expertise to prepare the applicable documentation for securing the purchase. A good salesperson not only gets the offer accepted, but is able to see the transaction through to closing. The salesperson should keep the buyer's personal information confidential. Finally, the broker must be competent in accounting for all funds.

In-Company and "Out of Company" Sales. With buyer agency comes the need to address the In-Company or "In-House" Sale – the sale of a company listing – and the "Out of Company" or "Cooperative Sale" rules. These are two very different relationships. The public does not want to be bothered; yet, they have expectations that need to be addressed. The buyer must know the difference between buying one of your company's listings and buying a property listed with another firm.

Letter/e-mail – Rules of the Road for the Buyer
(Read this carefully. Is this your office?)

Mr. Bill Buyer and
Mrs. Betty Buyer
Apartment 610 A
12th and Main Street
Tenant City, CO 00001

     Re: Buyer Agency Services for Purchasers
              Seller Agency Services of Sellers

Dear Mr. and Mrs. Buyer:

    Let me be the first to welcome you to Ownersville, MyState, and to our office. We have a small cadre of professional agents and support staff, who have been doing business at this location for fourteen months. Satisfied clients and customers are our primary concern.

    Each state has its own set of laws, rules and regulations concerning real estate in general, and real estate salespersons, brokers, lenders, title companies and other real estate affiliates, specifically. I sometimes wonder how so many different systems evolve.

    In this state, the state licenses a broker for each office, and all contracts or agreements that bind the company must be signed by the broker to be effective. Salespeople are licensed under the broker and act as agents of the broker. I am happy to work for John Under Whelmed, the licensed broker for The Real Estate Company

    It is important to us that you understand all the aspects of a potential real estate transaction. In addition to the state mandated disclosure forms for lead based paint, square footage, physical condition of the property and others, we need to address the agency issue first.

    Our company acts as agents for, and represents, many owners who have listed their properties with us for sale. In addition, as members of the Multiple Listing Service, we have access to, and can show you, literally hundreds of additional properties, encompassing all the properties listed by other member brokers.

As one of the licensed agents here, I work hard to assist buyers with their real estate needs. I am sure that I will be able to provide you with the information you request concerning almost all of the aspects of the local real estate market, to include a comparable market analysis (not an appraisal) and sources of available financing, so that you will be able to make an informed selection of a new home.

Regardless of which real estate company has listed the home you select, we will always disclose to you all that we know about the physical condition of the property and its proximity to schools, shopping, transportation. In addition, we will promptly inform you regarding proximity to any potential hazards such as high tension lines, nuclear weapons plants, waste disposal sites and landfills of which the salesperson working with you is aware.

We are proud to adhere to the Department of Housing and Urban Development's Fair Housing Standards. We want you to realize that you are free to, and in fact we encourage you to, make an offer on any house that you select. The only factors limiting your selection are: the amount of money you have available to spend for a down payment, the amount that you can or will borrow, and the size of the monthly payments that you desire.

Neighborhood mix or makeup are impossible for us to determine. This is a totally open market with equal access to everyone. I am sure that you will be able to select a home that meets your needs from a wide variety of available homes, either listed with our firm or through the Multiple Listing Service.

We are happy to show you and your family as many homes as you desire in any part of the city and surrounding county. We will provide you with the information at our disposal to assist you in determining the right new home for you to acquire. The different available locations vary from the urban-city-center to the rural country locations. Only you can decide which home is located in the area you desire, is best suited to your physical needs, and meets the financial requirements you determine are within your budget.

In this state, there are different options available to buyers for the acquisition of our services. It is our company policy to act as sellers' agents on properties listed with this office. That means that we work for the seller all the time on properties that we have listed. You need to be aware that we must tell the seller everything that we learn from or about you. This applies even if you ask that we keep information confidential.

When we show you properties listed by other offices, we act as buyers' agents. In that situation, personal information that you share with us remains confidential as long as you are buying a property that is not listed with this office. Should you later decide to buy a property listed with this office, we revert to sellers' agents and will convey any and all information that we have learned about you to our sellers, so that they are better able to obtain the listed price. I know that this is confusing, and you probably want to use another office to represent you as a buyer, so that your personal motivation remains confidential. I totally understand.

If you are ever unable to reach me or just want to talk to the broker for this company, please feel free to contact Mary Might Worry:

at (_____) _____-_____, office direct or
(_____) _____-_____, home number or
(_____) _____-_____, cell phone

Mary is a well-respected broker and I am proud to work for her. I am sure that she and I will be able to assist you in your selection of a new home in this area.

Enclosed you will find copy of the HUD Lead Based Paint booklet to review. In the days before 1978, some homes used paint that was lead based. Lead based paint was not to be used in houses for which a building permit was issued after January 1, 1978. We want you to be aware of all the issues that may affect any home you decide to purchase.

Sincerely,
The Real Estate Company

by: Your Name Here,
REALTOR®, CRS, GRI

Letter/e-mail – Exclusive Buyer Agency – Rules of the Road for the Buyer
(This Office Does Not Take Listings)

Mr. Bill Buyer and
Mrs. Betty Buyer
Apartment 610 A
12th and Main Street
Tenant City, CO 00001

      Re: Buyer Agency Services for Purchasers

Dear Mr. and Mrs. Buyer:

      Let me be the first to welcome you to Ownersville, MyTown, and to our office. We have a small cadre of professional agents and support staff who have been doing business at this location for fourteen months. Satisfied clients and customers are our primary concern.

      Each state has its own set of laws, rules, regulations concerning real estate in general, and real estate salespersons, brokers, lenders, title companies and other real estate affiliates, specifically. I sometimes wonder how so many different systems could evolve.

      In this state, the state licenses a broker for each office, and all contracts or agreements that bind the company must be signed by the broker to be effective. Salespeople are licensed under the broker and act as agents of the broker. I am happy to work for Mary Perfection, the licensed broker for The Real Estate Company

      It is important to us that you understand all the aspects of a potential real estate transaction. In addition to the state mandated disclosure forms for lead based paint, square footage, physical condition of the property and others, we need to address the agency issue first.

      In this state, there are a few different options available to buyers for the acquisition of our services. It is our company policy to act as exclusive buyers' agents on all property that we show you. We only represent the buyer in a transaction. We will keep everything we learn about you confidential. I will explain the details when we meet. We feel that by working exclusively for the buyer, and not being on the seller's side or neutral, we are more effectively representing you throughout the transaction. Since we do not take listings, there is never a possibility that we will be also representing the seller and get stuck in this "dual agency" thing.

As an exclusive buyer agent, we will *not* disclose the following information without your informed consent:

- That you are willing to pay more than what you offer;
- What the motivating factors are for you in buying or leasing the property;
- That you will agree to financing terms other than those offered;
- Any material information about you, unless disclosure is required by law, or if lack of disclosure would constitute dishonest dealing or fraud; except that we are required to disclose all adverse material facts pertaining to your financial ability to perform the terms of the transaction and whether you intend to occupy the property as a principal residence.

Our company does not act as agents for, nor represent, any homeowners who have their properties for sale. We do not take listings. We will never have a conflict of interest between a seller and buyer. We are members of the Multiple Listing Service. We have access to, and can show you, literally hundreds of properties, encompassing all the properties listed by other member brokers. Since listing agents are looking for buyers, they are generally glad to know that we have a qualified buyer as a client who wants to see the home that they have for sale.

As one of the licensed agents here, I work hard to represent buyers with their real estate needs. I am sure that I will be able to provide you with the information you request concerning almost all of the aspects of the local real estate market, to include a comparable market analysis (not an appraisal) and sources of available financing, so that you will be able to make an informed selection of a new home. Regardless of which real estate company has listed the home you select, we will always disclose to you all that we know about the physical condition of the property and its proximity to schools, shopping, transportation. In addition, we will promptly inform you regarding proximity to any potential hazards such as high tension lines, nuclear weapons plants, waste disposal sites and landfills of which the salesperson working with you is aware.

There are so many aspects of a real estate transaction that involve professionals these days. I am including a "Services Provided" list for your perusal. It shows some of the extensive professional associations that we use to ensure you have all the information you need in order to make your new housing decisions.

We are proud to adhere to the Department of Housing and Urban Development's Fair Housing Standards. We want you to realize that you are free, and in fact we encourage you, to make an offer on any house that you select. The only factors limiting your selection are: the amount of money you have available to spend for a down payment, the amount that you can or will borrow, and the size of the monthly payments that you desire.

Neighborhood mix or makeup are impossible for us to determine. This is a totally open market with equal access to everyone. I am sure that you will be able to select a home that meets your needs from a wide variety of available homes, either listed with our firm or through the Multiple Listing Service.

We are happy to show you and your family as many homes as you desire, in any part of the city and surrounding county, and provide you with the information at our disposal to aid you in determining the right new home for you to acquire. The different available locations vary from the urban-city-center to the rural country locations. Only you can decide which home is located in the area you desire, is best suited to your physical needs, and meets the financial requirements you determine are within your budget.

Enclosed you will find copy of the HUD Lead Based Paint booklet to review. In the days before 1978, some homes used paint that was lead based. Lead based paint was not to be used in houses for which a building permit was issued after January 1, 1978. We want you to be aware of all the issues that may affect any home you decide to purchase.

If you are ever unable to reach me, or just want to talk to the broker for this company, please feel free to contact Mary Perfection either in the office, (___) ___-_____, or at her home, (___) ___-_____. She is a well-respected broker and I am proud to work for her. I am sure that she and I will be able to assist you in your selection of a new home in this area.

Sincerely,
The Real Estate Company

by: Your Name Here,
REALTOR®, CRS, GRI

Letter/e-mail – Transaction Broker – Rules of the Road for the Buyer

Mr. Bill Buyer and
Mrs. Betty Buyer
Apartment 610 A
12th and Main Street
Tenant City, CO 00001

   Re: Real Estate Services for Purchasers

Dear Mr. and Mrs. Buyer:

   Let me be the first to welcome you to Ownersville, Colorado, and to our office. We have a small cadre of professional agents and support staff who have been doing business at this location for fourteen months. Satisfied clients and customers are our primary concern.

   Each state has its own set of laws, rules, and regulations concerning real estate in general, and real estate salespersons, brokers, lenders, title companies and other real estate affiliates, specifically. I sometimes wonder how so many different systems could evolve.

   In this state, the state licenses a broker for each office, and all contracts or agreements that bind the company must be signed by the broker to be effective. Salespeople are licensed under the broker and act as agents of the broker. I am happy to work for Mary Perfection, the licensed broker for The Real Estate Company

   It is important to us that you understand all the aspects of a potential real estate transaction. In addition to the state mandated disclosure forms for lead based paint, square footage, physical condition of the property and others, we need to address the agency issue first.

   We have elected to work as transaction brokers for our customers. As transaction brokers, we assist you throughout all aspects of the real estate transaction with communication, advice, negotiation, contracting and closing, without being an agent or advocate for you or the seller. You are not vicariously liable (legally responsible) for our actions, and a written contract with us is not required.

As a transaction brokers we will:
- Disclose to you any adverse material facts which we actually know about the property;

- Perform any oral or written agreement made with you;

- Exercise reasonable skill and care;

- Present all offers in a timely manner;

- Advise you regarding the transaction, including suggesting that you obtain expert advice on material matters about which we know but the specifics of which are beyond our expertise;

- Account to you promptly for all money or property we receive;

- Assist you in complying with the terms and conditions of any contract and with the closing of the transaction;

- Assist you and the seller without regard to race, creed, sex, religion, national origin, familial status, marital status, or handicap.

As a transaction broker we will not disclose the following information without your informed consent:
- That you are willing to pay more than what you offer;

- What the motivating factors are for you in buying or leasing the property;

- That you will agree to financing terms other than those offered;

- Any material information about you unless disclosure is required by law or if lack of disclosure would constitute dishonest dealing or fraud; except that we are required to disclose all adverse material facts pertaining to your financial ability to perform the terms of the transaction and whether you intend to occupy the property as a principal residence.

I will answer any questions or concerns you may have when we meet. As your Transaction Broker, we are not on anyone's "side." We just professionally assist both parties with their real estate needs. Your secrets, personal motivations are safe with us. We assist you throughout the transaction. This allows us to take listings, sell those sellers a new house and assist buyers with buying houses that we have listed. We never become "dual agents."

Whenever we show you any property, listed with our firm or another firm, we will be transaction brokers. We will never have a conflict of interest between a seller and buyer. We are members of the Multiple Listing Service. We have access to and can show you literally hundreds of properties encompassing all the properties listed by other member brokers. Since listing agents are looking for buyers, they are generally glad to know that we have a qualified buyer who wants to see the home that they have for sale.

As one of the licensed agents here, I work hard to assist my buyers with their real estate needs. I am sure that I will be able to provide you with the information you request concerning almost all of the aspects of the local real estate market. That would include a comparable market analysis (not an appraisal) which shows you property that has sold, when it sold and for how much money, as well as sources of available financing. With that information you will be able to make an informed selection of a new home.

Regardless of which real estate company has listed the home you select, we will always disclose to you all that we know about the physical condition of the property and its proximity to schools, shopping, transportation. In addition, we will promptly inform you regarding proximity to any potential hazards such as high tension lines, nuclear weapons plants, waste disposal sites and landfills of which we are aware.

There are so many aspects of a real estate transaction that involve professionals these days. I am including a "Services Provided" list for your perusal. It shows some of the extensive professional associations that we use to ensure you have all the information you need in order to make your new housing decisions.

We are proud to adhere to the Department of Housing and Urban Development's Fair Housing Standards. We want you to realize that you are free to, and in fact we encourage you to, make an offer on any house that you select. The only factors limiting your selection are: the amount of money you have available to spend for a down payment, the amount that you can or will borrow, and the size of the monthly payments that you desire.

Neighborhood mix or makeup are impossible for us to determine. This is a totally open market with equal access to everyone. I am sure that you will be able to select a home that meets your needs from a wide variety of available homes, either listed with our firm or through the Multiple Listing Service.

We are happy to show you and your family as many homes as you desire, in any part of the city and surrounding county, and provide you with the information at our disposal to aid you in determining the right new home for you to acquire. The different available locations vary from the urban-city-center to the rural country locations. Only you can decide which home is located in the area you desire, is best suited to your physical needs, and meets the financial requirements you determine are within your budget.

Enclosed you will find copy of the HUD Lead Based Paint booklet to review. In the days before 1978, some homes used paint that was lead based. Lead based paint was not to be used in houses for which a building permit was issued after January 1, 1978. We want you to be aware of all the issues that may affect any home you decide to purchase.

If you are ever unable to reach me, or just want to talk to the broker for this company, please feel free to contact Mary Perfection:

     at (_____) _____-_____, office direct or
        (_____) _____-_____, home number or
        (_____) _____- _____, cell phone

Mary is a well-respected broker and I am proud to work for her. I am sure that she and I will be able to assist you in your selection of a new home in this area.

Sincerely,
The Real Estate Company

by: Your Name Here,
REALTOR®, CRS, GRI

Getting Paid When Working with the Buyer

Fees. The salesperson and the buyer must know what the agreements are regarding the fee that the salesperson expects to be paid for his/her services. This is an uncomfortable situation. We have included some forms that will help. *There is no substitute for a written contract with the buyer* – none. The salesperson and broker need to know that they will be paid for their efforts.

Cooperative Commission. *Real Estate is a team sport.* The days of differentiating between how much a listing broker pays subagents, buyer agents, transaction brokers, real estate brokers and confused salespeople are over. A cooperative commission is exactly that. It is a commission for the cooperating real estate office. Do not let agency get in the way. Everyone will be a buyer agent, a seller agent or on neutral ground at some point in time. Cooperate with each other, so that you will always get paid when you are on the other side. Some Multiple Listing Services have made the jump to the future and eliminated any indication of agency in their services. They have also eliminated subagents. They refer to the selling office as the selling office or the cooperating office. The commission that is offered and paid is for the cooperating office – period.

MLS Cooperation Provision. The use or placement of listings in the Multiple Listing Service shall not create any agency relationship between offices. Any agency relationship between offices shall be established outside of the Multiple Listing Service. Listing offices, in order to place a listing in the Magic (Multiple) Listing Service, shall offer the selling office a cooperating fee.

MLS services that have opted to operate without references to agency have just one box for the compensation to be paid to the cooperating broker. Think about it. It is good for the seller and good for the salespeople. Everyone knows that if they procure the buyer, they can get the cooperative commission when the property closes. Careful, it is simple.

Imagine a system where there were no agency distinctions in the MLS. Think how easy it would be to list a buyer and say, *"If the property is in the MLS, I will be paid through the listing broker. It is only when we find a FSBO that you need to realize that you may have to pay me for my work."*

Getting paid by Listing Agents Who are not REALTORS®. An item of concern for a buyer agent is ensuring a cooperative commission when selling a "non-listed" property or property that is listed with a licensee who is not a participant in the Board/Association or MLS. Since you represent the buyer, you need to show and tell him about such properties that match the desired parameters indicated by your buyer client. However, you also need to get paid.

A written buyer agency contract will provide (see samples in this book) that you can ask the seller for payment. In fact, you are directed to ask the seller, so that your client does not have to pay you. Yes, you need that authorization from your client. Once you make an agreement, you need a form to complete to make it a written contract. Several forms follow this text.

For Sale by Owner. There are two schools of thought on dealing with the For Sale by Owner. One holds that it is easier to get the buyer to pay you if you are neutral. In that situation, you approach the seller as, "I am working with the buyer, and the buyer is interested in your property, Mr. Seller. If the buyer buys your home, I will be acting as a "dual agent" or "transaction broker," a neutral party, and your secrets (motivation to sell) are safe with me." This school of thought rests on the idea that it is easier to get the seller to pay you if you are not to deep in the "buyer agency" role. It also presupposes that if the buyer does not select this property, you will try to list the seller anyway. In this scenario, you have a better chance of listing the For Sale by Owner, as you have not alienated the seller with a strong buyer agency disclosure.

The second option, which we feel is less effective, is to remain a buyer's agent throughout the transaction. When you approach the For Sale by Owner acting as a buyer agent, you must tell that seller that you will tell your buyer all that you learn about the seller's motivation to sell. Then you need to tell him that he will be asked to pay you for representing the buyer against him. Think about it.

You need a clause in the sales contract to ensure that you get paid. Insert this clause in the contract at the direction of your buyer. The "direction of your buyer" is critical. The buyer wants this clause in the contract because the buyer is committed in your agency agreement to pay you. The buyer wants to ensure that the seller will satisfy that obligation as a term of the contract. If it is done in this manner, there is no violation of the Code of Ethics. However, should you just add the clause without the buyer's direction, you will have violated the Code of Ethics, and probably your state's regulations also.

Clause:

> Buyer's obligation to buy is expressly conditional upon seller paying buyer's agent, simultaneous with closing, the sum of ___% of the sales price as a commission.

Buyer Agency Listing Agreements. This area is so cluttered with forms and ideas that nothing is standard at all. We have included some contracts that we recommend you seriously consider. Use parts of them, or all of them, as you desire. Our current favorite is the "plain language" form for which we received numerous requests to include in this revision. In some states the "entire office" (office representation) represents the buyer and may ultimately become "dual agents" or "transaction brokers." In other states the system provides that only the actual person representing the buyer is the agent, "designated agency." There are forms for both options. Use with care, but get a written listing agreement with the buyer.

Buyer Agency Script. Prior to listing a buyer as a "client," you need to address his fears and concerns about the pending relationship. The buyer has two basic concerns about signing a buyer agency contract. First, s/he thinks that s/he does not want to pay the broker. Second, s/he is nervous about a long term commitment that leaves him "trapped" with a particular broker.

The better you present your proposal, the better your chances are of getting an exclusive buyer agency contract on terms that are as they should be. There are times when listing the buyer is easier. For example, you just listed the sellers' home, and now they are real buyers who have a sense of urgency in finding a replacement home. In another instance, the buyers are transferees who were recommended to you specifically to represent them by the home relocation company, a good mutual friend or a former client.

The following script is designed to overcome objections. You must address the two concerns of the buyer at the first meeting – payment and term. Below is a five point process which is designed to explain the compensation system, your role in that system and help the buyer gain an understanding of why you need to be paid. Following that process is a nonthreatening approach to the issue of term. Each point is followed by the _script_ to use, and then an explanation of the understanding you wish to achieve.

Payment – Getting them to be happy with the concept of paying you.
   1. **Real estate brokerage is my job.**
      "So, tell me what do you do for a living?"

We are retired [or whatever]. The purpose of the question was to open the field, so that it is ok for you to say....

"I am a professional real estate broker. My goal is to help 3 or 4 families buy or sell a home each month. If I can do that, I can make a living [or feed my family, or be able to afford to send my kids to school, or take a vacation, or buy a new car..........etc.]"

Now you have established that real estate is your profession. You work in real estate for a living, and your time is limited and valuable.

2. Permission to get paid.
"Is it all right with you if I make money as a result of helping you buy a home?"

The purpose of this dialogue is to get their permission to make money. This may seem silly, but the conversation confirms that the buyer has agreed that you should make money, that your service is valuable to her and that you are worth the fees that you charge. You have permission to charge the buyer. An analogy would be reading the menu at a restaurant to see what each meal costs. If discussed ahead of time, there is no argument when the bill comes.

3. Buyer should not have to pay you.
"Is it ok with you if you do not have to pay me?"

They respond with a "yes" or "we can't or won't pay you" or "I should hope so" or "it has to be that way."

"As your agent, it is my job to see that you don't have to pay me. The system generally provides that the listing broker will pay me if the property is listed in the MLS [Magic Listing System]."

4. The System.
"Will you help me get paid?"

Then they will ask, or you just explain the cooperative system.

"If the property is listed in the MLS, and the listing broker offers me a cooperative commission which allows me to make a living, and almost all of them [99.9%] do, then I am fine as I will get paid by the listing company. On some listings [I have yet to deal with one] the cooperative fee offered is too low,

so that I can not make a living or there is no fee offered at all, such as a for-sale-by-owner or a new home builder. In those instances I need your help. Ok?"

Sure.

"Ok, then you can instruct me to insert a clause in your contract that provides: "Buyer's obligation to buy is expressly conditional upon seller paying buyer's agent, simultaneous with closing, the sum of ___% of the sales price as a commission."

5. The Closing.
"Finally, if I help you purchase the house of your dreams, at a price that was terrific and no one else would pay me, would you pay me, or do you expect me to do that one for free?"

Then be quiet and wait for them to answer. If they press you, remind them,

"This is how I make a living. I just can't afford to work without getting paid."

Term – Getting them to realize that your time has value.
1. Fear of Commitment.
Understand that this issue is a real concern for the buyer. Address it up front and be pro-active. Do not wait for this issue to surface on its own. The buyer is nervous. Be direct and lead him into a recommendation with which he will be comfortable.

"I am not sure how well we will work together. Why don't we start with just today [you can use any time limit]. If at the end of the day you want to work with me, and I want to work with you, we can extend. That way we are not locked in or stuck. Is that ok with you?"

This takes the objection from them and makes them feel comfortable. It also tells the buyer that you are a valued commodity, and they are lucky to have you helping them.

2. Your time is valuable.
At the end of the initial time period, remember that you are a valuable asset to them. They need you. They want to work with you. They trust you to help

them find a house. Your time is valuable to you. Remember, you need to do 3-4 transactions a month to make a living.

"I have enjoyed working with you. How much longer do you think you will need me to help you find your new home?

We want them to say "I think that in three [or whatever] days we can get this done." Watch one of the buyers look at the other. That is a great sign.

"Ok then, let's agree to a _____ day extension. By then I am sure we can get a great home for you. After that I am not sure if I can give you the amount of time I am now. I devote my time and attention to only one buyer at a time, and I need to attend to some other people who are indicating that they want me to help them with a new home."

3. The cell phone. Constantly receiving cell phone calls, **that you do not answer – no matter what**, while you are working with these buyers, alerts them to the fact that you are in demand. It also prepares them for your not answering their call when you are busy with other buyers. These buyers will feel important knowing they have your undivided attention when working with them.

Compensation Agreement Among Brokers

Date of agreement:_____/_____/_____
Agreement made by: ___ e-mail _____ letter ____ telephone _____ fax
Property
Address:_____

**Listing
Office:**_____

Salesperson's
Name:_____
Contact
Information:_____

Listing Office is acting as ____ Seller's Agent _____ Other _____

**Selling
Office:**_____

Salesperson:_____
Contact
Information:_____

Selling Office is, for the sale of this Property, acting as:
_____ Buyer Agent _____ Subagents of the Seller
_____ Other _____

This confirms that the Listing Office has a listing on the Property. The Listing and Selling Offices agree that the Listing Office shall pay a commission upon closing to the Selling Office, so long as the Selling Office is the Procuring Cause as defined by the National Association of REALTORS®. Any dispute shall be arbitrated before the applicable local/state Board/Association of REALTORS®.

Compensation shall be (select one):
1) _____ % of the final sales price, 2) a fixed fee of $_____, or
3) Other:_____

Approved:
Listing Office   **Selling Office**

by :_____   by :_____

Thank you for your assistance
Please sign, then fax/e-mail to the other office and send one original U.S. Mail

Compensation Agreement – For Sale By Owner

Date of agreement:_____/_____/_____
Agreement made by: __ e-mail ____ letter ___ telephone ____ fax

Property
Address:_____

Seller/Owner:_____

Contact
Information:_____

Broker:_____

Salesperson:_____
Contact
Information:_____

Broker is, for the sale of this Property, acting as a:
_____ Buyer Agent ___ Dual Agent _____ Real Estate Broker Only
_____ Other _____

This confirms our agreement that the Seller shall pay the sum indicated below to Broker, simultaneous with closing of the transaction, for any buyer procured by Broker. Seller's acceptance of an offer procured by Broker entitles Broker to the fee indicated below. In the event of legal action to enforce this agreement, the winner shall be awarded actual attorney's fees and costs. The Seller authorizes Broker to incorporate a term in the buy/sell contract evidencing this agreement.
(Select one option.)

1) _____ % of the final sales price   2) a fixed fee of $_____

3) Other: _____

Approved:
Seller/Owner   **Broker**

by :_____   by :_____

Referral Fee Agreement

Date of agreement:_____/_____/_____
"Prospect:" ____ Buyer or ____ Seller
Name _____
Address _____
Seeking Real Estate Broker for ("Location") _____
"Referring Party":
Full Name _____
Company _____
Address _____
Phone _____ Fax _____
e-mail _____
States where licensed: _____
"Broker" – Broker Associate/Salesperson Receiving the Referral:
Full Name _____
Company _____
Address _____
Phone _____ Fax _____
e-mail _____
States where licensed: _____

This confirms our agreement that Broker shall pay the sum indicated to the Referring Party, so long as payment is legal under the law of the Location, simultaneous with closing of the first transaction in which the Prospect acquires or sells property through Broker. Disputes shall be resolved through binding arbitration in the case of REALTORS®, or in a court of competent jurisdiction in the event the Referring Party is not a REALTOR®, venue being proper in or near the Location. The winner shall be awarded actual attorney's fees and costs. Referral fee is: (make one selection)
_____ % of net commission actually received by Broker Associate or Salesperson, or a fixed fee of $_____ or
Other _____

Agreement made by: ___ e-mail ___ letter ___ fax ___telephone
(Duplicate originals receipted for by each party)

_____   _____
Referring Party   Date   Broker   Date

Exclusive Right-to-Buy Contract
(Buyer Agency)

Date:_____

1.   Agreement. The parties agree that Buyer irrevocably engages Broker as Buyer's exclusive agent to represent Buyer in acquiring real estate as described herein. Broker is the limited agent of Buyer and will represent only Buyer, except as stated herein. Buyer agrees to conduct all negotiations for the Property only through Broker, and to refer to Broker all communications received in any form from real estate brokers, prospective sellers, or any other source during the Term of this contract. Buyer and Broker agree to the terms and conditions set forth in this contract.

2.   Defined Terms.
a. Buyer:_____,
and any other person or entity on whose behalf the named party acts, directly or indirectly to Purchase the Property.

b. Broker:_____,
Name of Company

c. Property. Broker shall search the Multiple Listing Services of which Broker is a member ("MLS") and make submissions to Buyer describing and identifying properties contained therein, and property actually known to the salesperson assisting Buyer, appearing to Broker to substantially meet the requirements on the attached Property Preference Sheet.

d. Purchase. Purchase means the voluntary acquisition of any interest in the Property or the voluntary creation of the right to acquire any interest in the Property (including a contract or lease).

e. Term.   The Term of this contract shall begin on the date of your signature below and shall continue until the earlier of (i) completion of the Purchase of the Property or (ii)_____. Broker shall continue to assist in the completion of any transaction for which a Success Fee is payable to Broker.

Buyer: ___ ___ ___   Broker: ___ ___ ___   Page ___ of ___
   initial initial date   initial initial date

3. Showing Properties. Buyer is aware that there are various methods of showing property, seller present, listing office provides a key, lockbox, etc. Broker has no showing limitations.

4. In-Company Transaction(s). When the same brokerage company [licensee] represents or assists both parties to a transaction, it is called an In-Company Transaction. The following attached addendum applies to In-Company Transaction(s)

5. Broker's Services. Broker will exercise reasonable skill and care for Buyer, and make reasonable efforts to locate the Property.

a. Broker will promote the interests of Buyer with the utmost good faith, loyalty and fidelity, including but not limited to:

(1) Seeking a price and terms which are acceptable to Buyer, except that Broker shall not be obligated to seek other properties while Buyer is a party to a contract to purchase the Property;

(2) Procuring acceptance of any offer to purchase the Property and to assist in the completion of the transaction;

(3) Presenting all offers to and from Buyer in a timely manner, regardless of whether Buyer is already a party to a contract to purchase the Property;

(4) Disclosing to Buyer adverse material facts actually known to Broker;

(5) Counseling Buyer as to any material benefits or risks of the transaction which are actually known to Broker;

(6) Advising Buyer to obtain expert advice as to material matters about which Broker knows but the specifics of which are beyond the expertise of Broker;

(7) Accounting in a timely manner for all money and property received, and

(8) Informing Buyer that Buyer may be vicariously liable for the acts of Broker when Broker is acting within the scope of the agency relationship.

b. Broker shall not disclose to the seller or any other third party, without the informed written consent of Buyer:

(1) That Buyer is willing to pay more than the purchase price for the Property;

(2) What Buyer's motivating factor(s) are;

Buyer: _____ _____ _____   Broker: _____ _____ _____   Page ____ of ____
    initial initial date   initial initial date

(3) That Buyer will agree to financing terms other than those offered;

(4) Any material information about Buyer unless disclosure is required by law or failure to disclose such information would constitute fraud or dishonest dealing; and

(5) Any facts or suspicions regarding circumstances which would psychologically impact or stigmatize the Property.

c. Broker shall disclose to any prospective seller all adverse material facts actually known by Broker, including but not limited to adverse material facts concerning Buyer's financial ability to perform the terms of the transaction and whether Buyer intends to occupy the Property as a principal residence.

d. Broker shall make submissions to Buyer describing and identifying properties appearing to substantially meet the criteria set forth herein.

6. Costs of Services or Products Obtained from Outside Sources. Broker will not obtain or order products or services from outside sources unless Buyer has agreed to pay for them promptly when due (examples: surveys, soil tests, radon tests, title reports, engineering studies, property inspections). Broker shall not be obligated to advance funds for Buyer. Buyer shall reimburse Broker for payments made by Broker for such other products or services authorized by Buyer.

7. Compensation to Broker. In consideration of the services to be performed by Broker, Buyer shall pay Broker as set forth in this Section. In the event no one else pays Broker at or before closing, Buyer shall, in consideration of the services to be performed by Broker, be obligated to pay Broker a "Fee" as follows:

a. Price of the Property ("Price"). Price as used in this paragraph shall mean: ☐ the price of the property indicated in the purchase and sale contract, or ☐ the price established by the seller on the first day the property is introduced to Buyer, or ☐ the lesser of the two, or ☐ the greater of the two.

b. Property Listed in MLS. In the event the Property is listed with the MLS, Broker's Fee shall be the greater of the amount actually paid by the Listing Broker or _____% of the Price.

---

c. Property Not Listed in MLS. In the event the Property is not listed with the MLS, Broker's Fee shall be _____% of the Price. Buyer shall insert a clause if buyer so desires that indicates buyer's obligation to buy is expressly conditional upon seller paying buyer's agent, simultaneous with closing, the sum of ____% of the sales price as a commission.

d. Source of Funds. Broker is authorized and instructed to request payment of Broker's Fee, on behalf of Buyer, from the following sources: ☐ Listing Broker ☐ Seller ☐ Other _____.

e. General. The Fee is conditioned upon the Purchase of the Property or the acquisition by Buyer of property not in compliance with the requirements specified above but within the purview of this contract. This Fee is payable upon closing of the transaction, unless the seller fails to close through no fault of Buyer, in which event no Fee shall be due. In the event Buyer fails to close, the Fee shall be due and payable immediately. Broker shall not advance funds for Buyer. This Fee applies to Property contracted for during the original term of this contract or any extension(s) and shall also apply to Property contracted for within _____ days after this contract expires or is terminated if the Property was shown or specifically presented in writing to Buyer by Broker during the original term or any extension(s) of the term of this contract.

f. Retainer. Buyer shall pay Broker a non-refundable retainer Fee of $_____ upon the signing of this contract, which amount ☐ shall ☐ shall not be credited against the Fee indicated above.

8. Limitation on Third-Party Compensation. Except as set forth herein, Broker shall not accept compensation from the seller or the Listing Company, without the written consent of Buyer. Additionally, Broker shall not assess and receive mark-ups or other compensation for services performed by any third party or affiliated business entity unless Buyer signs a separate written consent for such services.

9. Disclosure of Buyer's Identity. Broker ☐ **Does** ☐ **Does Not** have Buyer's permission to disclose Buyer's identity to third parties without prior written consent of Buyer. At the earliest reasonable opportunity, Broker shall inform all prospective sellers or their brokers with whom Broker negotiates pursuant to this contract that Broker is acting as an agent on behalf of Buyer.

Buyer: ___ ___ ___　　Broker: ___ ___ ___　　　　Page ___ of ___
　initial initial date　　　　initial initial date

10. Other Buyers. Broker may show properties in which Buyer is interested to other prospective buyers without breaching any obligation, duty or responsibility to Buyer. In the event Broker is assisting multiple buyers all of whom are interested in the same property, Broker shall keep all information regarding each buyer and their proposed transaction confidential and shall not disclose any elements of any offer made by or to any buyer to any other buyer.

11. Assignment by Buyer. Neither Buyer nor Broker shall not assign this contract without the other parties prior written consent.

12. Nondiscrimination. The parties agree not to discriminate unlawfully against any prospective seller because of the race, creed, color, sex, marital status, national origin, familial status, physical or mental handicap, religion or ancestry of such person.

13. "Megan's Law". If the presence of a registered sex offender is a matter of concern to Buyer, Buyer understands that Buyer must contact local law enforcement officials regarding obtaining such information.

14. Recommendation of Legal and Tax Counsel. By signing this document, Buyer acknowledges that Broker has advised Buyer that this document has important legal consequences and has recommended consultation with legal, tax or other counsel, before signing this contract.

15. Mediation. If a dispute arises relating to this contract, prior to or after Closing, and is not resolved, the parties shall first proceed in good faith to submit the matter to mediation. Mediation is a process in which the parties meet with an impartial person who helps to resolve the dispute informally and confidentially. Mediators cannot impose binding decisions. The parties to the dispute must agree before any settlement is binding. The parties will jointly appoint an acceptable mediator and will share equally in the cost of such mediation. The mediation, unless otherwise agreed, shall terminate in the event the entire dispute is not resolved within thirty (30) calendar days from the date written notice requesting mediation is sent by one party to the other(s).

16. Property Condition. Broker has no duty to conduct an independent inspection of the Property, the Inclusions, Seller's Property Disclosure form or the Title Documents (Abstract of Title, Title Commitment and related Documents) for the benefit of Buyer. Broker has no duty to independently

Buyer: ___ ___ ___   Broker: ___ ___ ___   Page ___ of ___
    initial initial date   initial initial date

verify the accuracy or completeness of statements made by seller, seller's broker, independent inspectors, or other third parties, regarding: the actual lot size, location and square footage of improvements, building, zoning and allowed use regulations, well (flow rate, capacity, depth, recovery rate, suitability for Buyer's needs, exempt status such as household, domestic, etc., water quality, potability, location on property, etc.), septic (useful life of the system, capacity and suitability for size of house, pumping needs, location on property, etc.), leach field (adequacy, location on property, percolation, etc.), radiant heating systems (e.g. Entran II), electromagnetic fields (proximity to power lines), termites or other infestations and the presence of various types of mold, exterior insulation and finish systems (e.g. artificial stucco), polybutylene plumbing materials, roofing materials (e.g. Woodruf shingles), proximity to a flood plain or hazardous waste site and the quality of the schools, crime statistics (such as "Megan's Law" which provides that information concerning the location of known sex offenders be available from local law enforcement) and other similar matters.

17. Use of Professionals. Buyer is advised to seek the advice of professionals, such as: attorneys, accountants, appraisers, surveyors, contractors, engineers, septic inspectors, well testers, water engineers, property inspectors, environmental hazard and radon gas experts. Broker recommends that Buyer obtain a written inspection report covering the Property and Inclusions, an improvement location certificate or survey to determine lot size, location of improvements and any encroachments. Buyer should verify all information using experts of Buyer's own choosing

18. Property Repairs/Improvements. Buyer should obtain written cost quotations (bids) for all work Buyer intends to have done to the Property to be fully aware of the costs of such repairs, maintenance, improvements and/or upgrades. Broker is not responsible for any recommendations as to professionals. Each professional should be able to provide Buyer with a list of past customers to assist Buyer in making his/her own decision and selection. Buyer is advised that all work done on the Property as part of any contract should be done by licensed contractors where possible, and inspected by the governmental authority.

19. Homeowner's Warranty. Buyer is aware of the existence of pre-owned home warranty programs which may be purchased and may cover the repair or replacement of some Inclusions. Broker is not liable for the financial integrity of such companies. Buyer is encouraged to evaluate the terms of coverage and financial strength of any company offering to issue such a warranty.

20. Price Determination. Broker shall prepare a Competitive Market Analysis, for potential properties selected by Buyer, comprised of similar properties that have sold, are listed for sale or were rejected from the market, as reported to the MLS of which Broker is a member. This may not comprise all of the properties in the market area. Buyer is solely responsible for the determination of the contract price. Broker is not responsible for the determination of the contract price.

21. Possession, Lease and Insurance. If the Possession Date and **Time** are other than Closing Date, Buyer, to protect Buyer's real and personal property interests, should consider obtaining casualty and liability insurance and a lease for the period between Possession Date and Time and the Closing Date.

22. Broker Purchases. Broker or Broker's agents may, for their own account, purchase property that is available for sale, including property that may or may not have been shown to Buyer.

23. Attorney Fees. In case of arbitration or litigation between Buyer and Broker in their respective capacities, the parties agree that costs and reasonable attorney fees shall be awarded to the prevailing party. Any dispute shall be properly filed only in the State and County wherein Broker has its main offices.

24. Facsimile and Electronic Signatures. Signatures ❑ **May** ❑ **May Not** be evidenced by facsimile, and ❑ **May** ❑ **May Not** be evidenced by electronic signatures. Documents with original signatures shall be provided upon request of any party.

25. Modification of this Contract. No subsequent modification of any of the terms of this contract shall be valid, binding upon the parties, or enforceable unless in writing and signed by the parties.

26. Counterparts. If more than one person is named as a Buyer herein, this contract may be executed by each Buyer, individually, and when so executed, such copies taken together with one executed by Broker shall be deemed to be a full and complete contract between the parties.

Buyer: _____ _____ _____   Broker: _____ _____ _____   Page ___ of ____
      initial initial date   initial initial date

27. Entire Agreement. This contract constitutes the entire agreement between the parties and any prior agreements, whether oral or written, have been merged and integrated into this contract.

28. Copy of Contract. Buyer acknowledges receipt of a copy of this contract signed by Broker, including all attachments.

29. Attachments. The following exhibits, attachments, and addenda are a part of this contract:

30. Additional Provisions.

_____

_____

_____

Buyer: _____   **Buyer:** _____

_____   _____

Name   Date   Name   Date
Buyers Address:_____
Buyers Phone: _____   E-mail:_____
Broker:

By:_____

                               Date
Brokers Address:_____
Brokers Phone: _____ E-mail:_____

Extension. This contract is extended and shall continue until the earlier of _____,20___, or completion of the acquisition of the Property.

Buyer: _____   **Buyer:** _____

_____   _____

Name   Date   Name   Date
Broker:

By:_____   Date: _____

Buyer: ____ ____ ____   Broker: ____ ____ ____   Page ___ of ____
initial initial date   initial initial date

Exclusive Right-to-Buy Contract
(Buyer Agency)

_____, 20_____

_____ ("Buyer")

appoints _____("Broker")
as Buyer's exclusive limited agent for the purpose of representing Buyer to acquire interests in real property ("Property") as indicated below under the terms specified herein.

1. **Effect.** Broker is hereby engaged as Buyer's exclusive limited agent. Buyer shall conduct all negotiations for Property through Broker and refer to Broker all inquiries received from real estate brokers, salespersons, prospective sellers, or any other source during the time this contract is in effect. Buyer agrees that any compensation to Broker which is conditioned upon the acquisition by Buyer of interests in real property, whether by lease or purchase (collectively "Purchase"), will be earned by Broker whenever such interests are acquired by Buyer directly or indirectly, without any discount or allowance for any efforts made by Buyer or any other person in connection with the acquisition of such interests by Buyer.

2. **Purchase.** "Purchase of the Property" or "Purchase" means the voluntary acquisition of any interest in the Property or the voluntary creation of the right to acquire any interest in the Property (including a contract or lease).

3. **Property.** Broker shall search the Multiple Listing Services of which Broker is a member ("MLS") and make submissions to Buyer describing and identifying properties contained therein, and property actually known to the salesperson assisting Buyer, appearing to Broker to substantially meet the requirements on the attached Property Preference Sheet.

4. **Duration.** Broker's authority as Buyer's exclusive agent shall commence _____, 20___, and shall continue until the earlier of _____, 20___, or completion of the acquisition of the Property unless extended as indicated below.

Buyer: _____   Broker: _____   Page ___ of ____
    initial initial date   initial initial date

5. **Broker's Services.** Broker will exercise reasonable skill and care for Buyer, and make reasonable efforts to locate property.

   a. Broker will promote the interests of Buyer with the utmost good faith, loyalty and fidelity, by:

      (1) seeking a price and terms which are acceptable to Buyer, except that Broker shall not be obligated to seek other properties while Buyer is a party to a contract to purchase Property;

      (2) procuring acceptance of any offer to purchase property and to assist in the completion of the transaction;

      (3) presenting all offers to and from Buyer in a timely manner, regardless of whether Buyer is already a party to a contract to purchase Property;

      (4) disclosing to Buyer adverse material facts actually known to Broker;

      (5) counseling Buyer as to any material benefits or risks of the transaction which are actually known to Broker;

      (6) advising Buyer to obtain expert advice as to material matters about which Broker knows but the specifics of which are beyond the expertise of Broker;

      (7) accounting in a timely manner for all money and property received; and

      (8) informing Buyer that Buyer may be vicariously liable for the acts of Broker when Broker is acting within the scope of the agency relationship.

   b. Broker shall not disclose to the seller or any other third party, without the informed consent of Buyer:

      (1) that Buyer is willing to pay more than the purchase price for Property;

      (2) what Buyer's motivating factor(s) is;

      (3) that Buyer will agree to financing terms other than those offered;

      (4) any material information about Buyer unless disclosure is required by law or failure to disclose such information would constitute fraud or dishonest dealing; and

      (5) any facts or suspicions regarding circumstances which would psychologically impact or stigmatize Property.

   c. Broker shall disclose to any prospective seller all adverse material facts actually known by Broker, including, but not limited to adverse material facts concerning Buyer's financial ability to perform the terms of the transaction and whether Buyer intends to occupy Property as a principal residence.

d. Broker shall search the Multiple Listing Services of which Broker is a member and inform Buyer of other property actually known to the salesperson assisting Buyer that Broker feels substantially meets the criteria identified above.

e. Broker has no duty to Buyer to conduct an independent inspection of Property for the benefit of Buyer and has no duty to independently verify the accuracy or completeness of statements made by the seller or independent inspectors.

6. **Costs of Services or Products Obtained from Outside Sources.** Broker will not obtain or order products or services from outside sources without Buyer's written authorization and unless Buyer has agreed to pay for them promptly when due. (Examples: surveys, soil tests, radon tests, title reports, property inspections.)

7. **Compensation to Broker.** In the event no one else pays Broker at or before closing, Buyer shall, in consideration of the services to be performed by Broker, be obligated to pay Broker a "Fee" as follows:
   a. **Price of the Property ("Price").** Price as used in this paragraph shall mean: ☐ the price of the property indicated in the purchase and sale contract, or ☐ the price established by the seller on the first day the property is introduced to Buyer, or ☐ the lesser of the two, or ☐ the greater of the two.

   b. **Property Listed in MLS.** In the event the Property is listed with the MLS, Broker's Fee shall be the greater of the amount actually paid by the Listing Broker or _____% of the Price.

   c. **Property Not Listed in MLS.** In the event the Property is not listed with the MLS, Broker's Fee shall be _____% of the Price.

   d. **Source of Funds.** Broker is authorized and instructed to request payment of Broker's Fee, on behalf of Buyer, from the following sources: ☐ Listing Broker ☐ Seller ☐ Other_____.

Buyer: _____ _____ _____   Broker: _____ _____ _____   Page ___ of ___
    initial   initial   date   initial initial   date

e. **General.** The Fee is conditioned upon the Purchase of the Property or the acquisition by Buyer of property not in compliance with the requirements specified above but within the purview of this contract. This Fee is payable upon closing of the transaction, unless the seller fails to close through no fault of Buyer, in which event no Fee shall be due. In the event Buyer fails to close, the Fee shall be due and payable immediately. Broker shall not advance funds for Buyer. This Fee applies to Property contracted for during the original term of this contract or any extension(s) and shall also apply to Property contracted for within _____ days after this contract expires or is terminated if the Property was shown or specifically presented in writing to Buyer by Broker during the original term or any extension(s) of the term of this contract.

f. **Retainer.** Buyer shall pay Broker a non-refundable retainer Fee of $_____ upon the signing of this contract, which amount ☐ shall ☐ shall not be credited against the Fee indicated above.

8. **Disclosure of Broker's Role.** At the earliest reasonable opportunity, Broker shall inform all prospective sellers or their brokers with whom Broker negotiates pursuant to this contract that Broker is acting as an agent on behalf of Buyer.

9. **Disclosure of Buyer's Identity.** Broker ☐ does ☐ does not have Buyer's permission to disclose Buyer's identity to third parties without the subsequent prior written consent of Buyer.

10. **In-Company Sale.** An In-Company sale occurs when Buyer desires to view and/or purchase property listed with Broker where Broker is already acting as a limited agent on behalf of the seller. In such instances the attached "In- Company Sale Addendum" shall govern.

11. **Other Buyers.** Broker may show properties in which Buyer is interested to other prospective buyers without breaching any obligation, duty or responsibility to Buyer. In the event Broker is assisting multiple buyers all of whom are interested in the same property, Broker shall keep all information regarding each buyer and their proposed transaction confidential and shall not disclose any elements of any offer made by or to any buyer to any other buyer.

12. **Nondiscrimination.** The parties agree not to discriminate as provided by local, state and federal fair housing or laws, against any prospective seller. This includes discrimination based upon race, creed, color, sex, marital status, national origin, familial status, physical or mental handicap, religion or ancestry of such person.

13. **"Megan's Law".** If the presence of a registered sex offender is a matter of concern to Buyer, Buyer understands that Buyer must contact local law enforcement officials regarding obtaining such information.

14. **Recommendation of Legal Counsel.** By signing this document, Buyer acknowledges that Broker has advised that this document has important legal consequences and has recommended consultation with legal and tax or other counsel, before signing this contract.

15. **Attorney's Fees.** In case of arbitration or litigation between Buyer and Broker in their respective capacities, the parties agree that costs and reasonable attorney fees shall be awarded to the prevailing party. Any dispute shall be properly filed only in the State and County wherein Broker has its main offices.

16. **Assignment and Modification of this Contract.** No assignment of Buyer's rights or obligations under this contract and no assignment of rights or obligations in property obtained for Buyer under this contract shall operate to defeat any of Broker's rights. No subsequent modification of any of the terms of this contract shall be valid, binding upon the parties, or enforceable unless in writing and signed by the parties.

17. **Entire Agreement.** This contract constitutes the entire agreement between the parties and any prior agreements, whether oral or written, have been merged and integrated into this contract.

18. **Counterparts.** If more than one person is named as Buyer herein, this contract may be executed by each Buyer, individually, and when so executed, such copies taken together shall be deemed to be a full and complete contract between the parties.

19. **Copy of Contract.** Buyer acknowledges receipt of a copy of this contract signed by Broker.

20. **Price Determination.** Broker shall prepare a Competitive Market Analysis, for potential properties selected by Buyer, comprised of similar properties that have sold, are listed for sale or were rejected from the market, as reported to the MLS of which Broker is a member. This may not comprise all of the properties in the market area. Buyer is solely responsible for the determination of the contract price. Broker is not responsible for the determination of the contract price.

Buyer:

_____   _____
Buyer   date   Buyer   date

Broker: _____

_____
by   date

21. **Extension.** This contract is extended and shall continue until the earlier of _____, 20____, or completion of the acquisition of the Property.

_____   _____
Buyer   date   Buyer   date

Broker:

_____
by   date

Buyer: ____ ____ _____   Broker: ____ ____ _____   Page ____ of ____
    initial initial date   initial initial   date

Exclusive Right-to-Buy Contract
(Short Form)

_____, 20_____

_____ ("Buyer")

appoints _____ ("Broker")
as Buyer's exclusive limited agent for the purpose of representing Buyer to
acquire interests in real property ("Property") as indicated below under the
terms specified herein.

1. **Effect.** Broker is hereby engaged as Buyer's exclusive limited agent.
    Buyer shall conduct all negotiations for Property through Broker and
    refer to Broker all inquiries received from any source. Compensation is
    based upon the acquisition by Buyer of any interest in real property
    ("Purchase").

2. **Property.** Broker shall search the Multiple Listing Services of which
    Broker is a member ("MLS") and make submissions to Buyer describing
    and identifying properties contained therein appearing to Broker to
    substantially meet the requirements on the attached Property Preference
    Sheet.

3. **Duration.** Broker's authority as Buyer's exclusive agent shall
    commence _____, 20____, and shall continue
    until the earlier of _____, 20____, or completion
    of the acquisition of the Property unless extended as indicated below.

4. **Broker's Services.** Broker will exercise reasonable skill and care for
    Buyer, and make reasonable efforts to locate property. Broker has no
    duty to Buyer to conduct an independent inspection of Property for the
    benefit of Buyer and has no duty to independently verify the accuracy or
    completeness of statements made by the seller or independent
    inspectors.

5. **Compensation to Broker.** In the event no one else pays Broker at or
    before closing, Buyer shall, in consideration of the services to be
    performed by Broker, be obligated to pay Broker a "Fee" as follows:

Buyer: _____ _____ _____   Broker: _____ _____ _____   Page ___ of ____
    initial initial date   initial initial date

a. **Price of the Property ("Price").** Price as used in this paragraph shall mean: ☐ the price of the property indicated in the purchase and sale contract, or ☐ the price established by the seller on the first day the property is introduced to Buyer, or ☐ the lesser of the two, or ☐ the greater of the two.

b. **Property Listed in MLS.** In the event the Property is listed with the MLS, Broker's Fee shall be the greater of the amount actually paid by the Listing Broker or _____% of the Price.

c. **Property Not Listed in MLS.** In the event the Property is not listed with the MLS, Broker's Fee shall be _____% of the Price.

d. **Source of Funds.** Broker is authorized and instructed to request payment of Broker's Fee, on behalf of Buyer, from the following sources: ☐ Listing Broker ☐ Seller ☐ Other _____.

e. **General.** The Fee is conditioned upon the Purchase of the Property or the acquisition by Buyer of property not in compliance with the requirements specified in paragraph # 3 above but within the purview of this contract. This Fee is payable upon closing of the transaction, unless the seller fails to close through no fault of Buyer, in which event no Fee shall be due. In the event Buyer fails to close, the Fee shall be due and payable immediately. Broker shall not advance funds for Buyer. This Fee applies to Property contracted for during the original term of this contract or any extension(s) and shall also apply to Property contracted for within _____ days after this contract expires or is terminated if the Property was shown or specifically presented in writing to Buyer by Broker during the original term or any extension(s) of the term of this contract.

6. **In-Company Sale.** An In-Company sale occurs when Buyer desires to view and/or purchase property listed with Broker where Broker is already acting as a limited agent on behalf of the seller. In such instances the attached In-Company Sale Addendum shall govern.

7. **Other Buyers.** Broker may show properties in which Buyer is interested to other prospective buyers without breaching any obligation, duty or responsibility to Buyer. In the event Broker is assisting multiple buyers all of whom are interested in the same property, Broker shall keep all

---

Buyer: _____   Broker: _____   Page ____ of ____
   initial initial date   initial initial date

information regarding each buyer and their proposed transaction confidential and shall not disclose any elements of any offer made by or to any buyer to any other buyer.

8. **Recommendation of Legal Counsel.** By signing this document, Buyer acknowledges that Broker has advised that this document has important legal consequences and has recommended consultation with legal and tax or other counsel, before signing this contract.

9. **Attorney's Fees.** In case of arbitration or litigation between Buyer and Broker in their respective capacities, the parties agree that costs and reasonable attorney fees shall be awarded to the prevailing party. Any dispute shall be properly filed only in the State and County wherein Broker has its main offices.

10. **"Megan's Law".** If the presence of a registered sex offender is a matter of concern to Buyer, Buyer understands that Buyer must contact local law enforcement officials regarding obtaining such information.

11. **Entire Agreement.** This contract constitutes the entire agreement between the parties and any prior agreements, whether oral or written, have been merged and integrated into this contract.

_____   _____
Buyer   date   Buyer   date
Broker:

_____
by   date

12. **Extension.** This contract is extended and shall continue until the earlier of _____, 20___, or completion of the acquisition of the Property.

_____   _____
Buyer   date   Buyer   date

Broker/by:_____
                                    date

_____
Buyer: _____ _____ _____   Broker: _____ _____ _____   Page ___ of ____
      initial initial date   initial initial date

Exclusive Right-to-Buy Contract
(Plain Language – Office Representation)

Date:_____, 20_____

1. Definitions.

a. "I" or "Me" refers to the Salesperson or Associate Broker, "We", "Our" or "Us" refers to the entire real estate firm as a group, (Employing or Designated Broker, the Brokerage, Broker and all Salespeople and Associated Brokers). "You" and Your" refers to Buyer(s) or anyone acting directly or indirectly by or through You to purchase "Property." "Everyone" refers to both You and Us collectively. "Agreement" refers to this Exclusive Right-to-Buy Contract.

b. I shall search the Multiple Listing Services of which We are members ("MLS") and make submissions to You describing and identifying properties contained in the MLS, and Property actually known to Me, appearing to Me to substantially meet Your requirements indicated on the attached Property Preference Sheet, referred to as "Property".

c. Purchase means Your voluntary acquisition of any interest in Property or the voluntary creation of the right to acquire any interest in Property, including a contract, option, land contract, lease or otherwise, that is within the purview of this Agreement, including Property that You locate, Property that We locate or any other Property that You agree, during the term of this Agreement, to acquire.

d. The Term of this Agreement shall begin on the date of Your signature below and shall continue until the latter of; (i) completion of the Purchase of the Property or (ii)_____. We shall continue to assist You in the completion of any transaction for which a "Commission" is payable to Us. Should you select, or We introduce You to, a Property during the initial term of this Agreement, and You contract for it or close on it within _____ days after the time period indicated above, or any extension(s), You will owe Us the indicated Commission. This "holdover period" and is designed to protect Us when We have done the work but for some reason You did not contract for the Property during the initial term of Our Agreement.

2. Agreement.
You hereby irrevocably engage Us as Your exclusive agent to represent You in acquiring any real estate that You select. We are Your

limited agents and We will represent You, except when it is Our listing. You will conduct all negotiations for the purchase of any Property only through Us, and to refer to Us all communications received in any form from other real estate brokers, prospective sellers, or any other source during the term of this Agreement.

3.   Showing Properties. You are aware that there are various methods of showing Property; the seller can be present, the listing office can provide a key or there can be a lockbox on the Property, etc. There are no showing limitations associated with this Agreement.

4.   Services. We will exercise reasonable skill and care for You, and make reasonable efforts to locate the Property You indicated that You desire.

   a. We will promote Your interests with the utmost good faith, loyalty and fidelity, including, but not limited to:
   (1)   Seeking a price and terms which are acceptable to You, except that We shall not be obligated to seek other properties while You are a party to a contract to purchase a Property;
   (2)   Procuring acceptance of any offer to purchase the Property and to assist in the completion of the transaction;
   (3)   Presenting all offers to and from You in a timely manner, regardless of whether You are already a party to a contract to purchase a Property;
   (4)   Disclosing to You adverse material facts actually known to Me;
   (5)   Counseling You as to any material benefits or risks of the transaction which are actually known to Me;
   (6)   Advising You to obtain expert advice as to material matters about which I know but the specifics of which are beyond My expertise;
   (7)   Accounting in a timely manner for all money and Property received, and
   (8)   Informing You that You may be vicariously liable for Our acts when I am acting within the scope of this Agreement.

   b. We won't disclose to the seller or any other third party, without Your informed written consent:
   (1)   That You are willing to pay more than the purchase price for the Property;
   (2)   What Your motivating factor(s) are;
   (3)   That You will agree to financing terms other than those offered;

Exclusive Right-to-Buy Contract
Brokerage by:_____ dat____/____/____   Buyer_____ _____
Page ____ of ____
date___/___/___

(4)   Any material information about You unless disclosure is required by law or failure to disclose such information would constitute fraud or dishonest dealing; and

(5)   Any facts or suspicions regarding circumstances which would psychologically impact or stigmatize the Property.

c. We will disclose to any prospective seller all adverse material facts actually known by Me, including but not limited to adverse material facts concerning Your financial ability to perform the terms of the transaction and whether You intend to occupy the Property as Your principal residence.

d. When You desire to purchase a Property that is listed with Us, an In-Company transaction, We will assist both You and the seller in the capacity of either a ___ "dual agent" or a ___ "transaction broker", and:

(1)   We can not disclose to either You or the seller the motivating factors of the other party, nor

(2)   Can We disclose other confidential information about You or the seller, nor,

(3)   Can We disclose what You are willing to pay, nor,

(4)   Can We disclose, if We know, what the seller may have told Us the seller is willing to accept, nor

(5)   Can We disclose any financing terms either party may have told Us they will accept, nor

(6)   Can We disclose any material information about You or the seller unless disclosure is required by law or failure to disclose such information would constitute fraud or dishonest dealing, nor

(7)   Can We disclose any facts or suspicions regarding circumstances which would psychologically impact or stigmatize the Property.

5.   Costs of Services or Products Obtained from Outside Sources. We will not obtain or order products or services from outside sources unless You agree to pay for them promptly when due (examples: surveys, soil tests, radon tests, title reports, engineering studies, Property inspections). We are not be obligated to advance funds for You and You are not obligated to advance funds to Us. You agree to reimburse Us for payments made by Us for such other products or services authorized by You in advance in writing.

6.   Compensation. This is how We make Our living. It is our desire that You not be required to pay Us directly. We will seek compensation from any source You indicate, including but not limited to, the Listing Broker, Seller, Your home transfer company, and such other sources that You indicate. In most cases there will be a cooperative Commission offered by the listing broker, indicated in the MLS, that will serve to satisfy this compensation issue.

We encourage You, when the situation requires it, to direct Us to insert a clause in any contract, if You desire, that indicates *"buyer's obligation to buy is expressly conditional upon seller paying buyer's agent, simultaneous with closing, the sum of____% of the sales price as a Commission."* This will help to prevent You from paying Us a Commission on Property that is not listed or where the offered cooperative Commission is not sufficient to pay Us.

Our Commission is payable upon closing of the transaction unless the seller refuses to close and You are not in default, in which case no Commission will be due to Us. If it is Your default that prevents the closing, the Commission will be due and payable to Us immediately.

There is an instance where We will expect payment from You. In the event You contract for a Property and elect not to close or contract for a Property which closes, and no one else pays Our Commission, at or before closing, You shall, in consideration of the services to be performed by Us, be obligated to pay Us a Commission, based upon: ____ the price of the Property indicated in the purchase and sale contract, or ____ the price established by the seller on the first day the Property is introduced to You, or ____ the lesser of the two, or ____ the greater of the two, as follows:

   a. In the event the Property is listed with the MLS, Our Commission shall be the greater of the amount actually paid (including bonuses and other incentives) by the Listing Broker or _____% of the Price, or

   b. In the event the Property is not listed with the MLS, Our Commission shall be _____% of the Price.

   c. You ____ shall ____ shall not pay Us a non-refundable Commission retainer of $_____ now, and that amount ____ shall ____ shall not be credited against the total Commission due.

d. Other than as We have agreed in this Agreement, We will not accept compensation or "mark-ups" from any source without Your prior written consent.

7.   Disclosure of Your Identity. We ___ do ___ do not have Your permission to disclose Your identity to any third parties without Your prior written consent. At the earliest reasonable opportunity, We shall inform all prospective sellers or their brokers with whom We negotiate pursuant to this contract that We are acting as Your agent.

8.   Other Buyers. You understand that We and sometimes I represent or assist other buyers looking for Property. We may show properties You are interested in to other prospective buyers without breaching this Agreement or any obligation, duty or responsibility to You. In the event We are assisting or representing multiple buyers all of whom are interested in the same Property, We shall keep all information regarding each buyer and their proposed transaction confidential and shall not disclose any elements of any offer made by or to any buyer to any other buyer.

9.   Assignment. We can not assign this contract without Your consent and You can not assign it without Our consent.

10.   Nondiscrimination. Everyone agrees not to discriminate unlawfully against any prospective seller because of the race, creed, color, sex, national origin, familial status, physical or mental handicap, religion, marital status, or ancestry of such person.

11.   "Megan's Law". If the presence of a registered sex offender is a matter of concern to You, You must contact local law enforcement officials regarding obtaining such information. We can not obtain that information for You. We will provide you with the address and phone number of the appropriate agency that has the information.

12.   Recommendation of Legal and Tax Counsel. By signing this Agreement, You acknowledge that We have advised You that this Agreement has important legal consequences and have recommended consultation with legal, tax or other counsel, before signing it. We make the same recommendation regarding the signing of any contract to buy real estate.

13. Use of Professionals. You are advised to seek the advice of professionals, such as: attorneys, accountants, appraisers, surveyors, contractors, engineers, septic inspectors, well testers, water engineers, Property inspectors, environmental hazard and radon gas experts. We recommend that You obtain a written inspection report covering the Property and Inclusions, an improvement location certificate or survey to determine lot size, location of improvements, and any encroachments. You should verify all information using experts that You select. We will not conduct an inspection of the Property, the Inclusions, any Seller's Property Disclosure form, Title Documents (Abstract of Title, Title Commitment and related Documents) or other disclosure for You or for Your benefit.

14. Property Condition. Determining the condition of the Property is Your responsibility. Our presence at any viewing or inspection is not to be construed as an inspection. We will not verify the accuracy or completeness of statements made by any seller, seller's broker, independent inspectors, or other third parties, regarding anything to do with the Property, including but not limited to: the actual lot size, location and square footage of improvements, building, zoning and allowed use regulations, well (flow rate, capacity, depth, recovery rate, suitability for You needs, exempt status such as household, domestic, etc., water quality, potability, location on Property, etc.), septic (useful life of the system, capacity and suitability for size of house, pumping needs, location on Property, etc.), leach field (adequacy, location on Property, percolation, etc.), radiant heating systems (e.g. Entran II), electromagnetic fields (proximity to power lines), termites or other infestations, including mold, exterior insulation and finish systems (e.g. artificial stucco), polybutylene plumbing materials, roofing materials (e.g. Woodruf shingles), proximity to a flood plain or hazardous waste site and the quality of the schools, crime statistics and finally, the presence or any mold. You need to satisfy Yourself that any Property is in a condition that is acceptable to You.

15. Property Repairs/Improvements. You should obtain written cost quotations (bids) for all work You intend to have done to the Property to be fully aware of the costs of such repairs, maintenance, improvements and/or upgrades. We are not responsible for any recommendations as to professionals. Each professional should be able to provide You with a list of past customers or clients to assist You in making Your decision and selection. You are advised that all work done on the Property as part of any contract should be done by licensed contractors where possible, and inspected by the appropriate governmental authority.

16.   Homeowner's Warranty. You are aware of the existence of pre-owned home warranty programs which may be purchased and may cover the repair or replacement of some Inclusions. We are not liable for the financial integrity or subsequent performance or non-performance of such companies. You are encouraged to evaluate the terms of coverage and financial strength of any company offering to issue such a warranty.

17.   Possession, Lease and Insurance. If the Possession Date and **Time** are other than Closing Date, You, to protect Your real and personal Property interests, should consider obtaining casualty and liability insurance and a lease for the period between Possession Date and Time and the Closing Date.

18.   Price. I will prepare a Competitive Market Analysis (not an appraisal), for potential properties You select, comprised of similar properties that have sold, are listed for sale or were rejected from the market, as reported to the MLS's of which We are members. This may not comprise all of the properties in the market area. You are solely responsible for the determination of the contract price. We are not responsible for the determination of the contract price and advise you to have the Property appraised by a licensed appraiser.

19.   Mediation. We hope that We never have a dispute with You. However, should a dispute arise relating to this Agreement and is not resolved, then Everyone shall first proceed in good faith to submit the matter to mediation. Mediation is a process in which the Everyone meets with an impartial person ("mediator") who helps to resolve the dispute informally and confidentially. Mediators cannot impose binding decisions upon anyone. Everyone must agree before any settlement is binding. Everyone will jointly appoint an acceptable mediator and will share equally in the cost of such mediation. The mediation, unless otherwise agreed, shall terminate in the event the entire dispute is not resolved within thirty (30) calendar days from the date written notice requesting mediation is sent by You or Us to the other. Any lawsuit involving this contract can only be filed in the State and County where We have our principal offices.

20.   Attorney Fees. In case of arbitration or litigation between Everyone, Everyone agrees that costs and attorney fees shall be awarded to the side the wins.

21.   Our Purchases. We may, for our own account, purchase Property that is available for sale, including Property that may or may not have been shown to You.

22.   Facsimile and Electronic Signatures. Signatures ___ may ___ may not be evidenced by facsimile, and ___ may ___ may not be evidenced by electronic signatures. Documents with original signatures shall be provided upon request of any party.

23.   Modification of this Contract. No subsequent modification of any of the terms of this contract shall be valid, binding upon Everyone unless the modification is in writing and signed by Everyone.

24.   Counterparts. If You includes more that one person, this contract may be executed by each person individually, and when so executed, such copies taken together with one executed by Me shall be deemed to be a full and complete contract between everyone.

25.   Entire Agreement. This Listing Contract constitutes the entire agreement between Everyone and any prior agreements, whether oral or written, have been merged and integrated into this Listing Contract.

26.   Copies. You acknowledge receipt of a copy of this Agreement, including all attachments, if any, signed by Us.

27.   Attachments. The following items are a part of Our Agreement:
Exhibit _____, _____, consisting of _____ pages
Exhibit _____, _____, consisting of _____ pages
Exhibit _____, _____, consisting of _____ pages

28.   Additional Provisions.
_____
_____

Buyer: **Buyer:**

_____   _____
Print Your Name Here   Print Your Name Here

_____   _____
Sign Your Name Here and Date   Sign Your Name Here and Date

Exclusive Right-to-Buy Contract   Page _____ of _____
Brokerage by:_____ dat____/____/____   Buyer_____ _____ date___/___/___

Buyer's Address:_____

Buyer's Phone: _____ Fax: _____

Buyer's e-mail:_____

Brokerage Firm:

_____
Print Brokerage Firm Name Here

By: _____
Print Associate Broker/Salesperson Name Here

_____
Salesperson or Associate Broker Sign Here   Date

Broker's Address:_____

Broker's Phone: _____ Fax: _____

Broker's e-mail:_____

29. Extension.

We extend the date indicated in section 4d(ii) to _____,20___.

Brokerage Firm by: _____ _____   Buyer(s) _____ _____ _____
                          Initial and date   Initial and date

Exclusive Right-to-Buy Contract
(Plain Language – Designated Agent/Broker)

Date:_____, 20_____

1.   Definitions.

a. "I" or "Me" refers to the Salesperson or Associate Broker, "We", "Our" or "Us" refers to the entire real estate firm as a group, (Employing or Designated Broker, the Brokerage Firm, Broker and all Salespeople and Associated Brokers). "You" and Your" refers to Buyer(s) or anyone acting directly or indirectly by or through You to purchase "Property." "Everyone" refers to both You and Us collectively. "Agreement" refers to this Exclusive Right-to-Buy Contract.

b. I shall search the Multiple Listing Services of which We are members ("MLS") and make submissions to You describing and identifying properties contained in the MLS, and Property actually known to Me, appearing to Me to substantially meet Your requirements indicated on the attached Property Preference Sheet, referred to as "Property."

c. Purchase means Your voluntary acquisition of any interest in Property or the voluntary creation of the right to acquire any interest in Property, including a contract, option, land contract, lease or otherwise, that is within the purview of this Agreement, including Property that You locate, Property that We locate or any other Property that You agree, during the term of this Agreement, to acquire.

d. The Term of this Agreement shall begin on the date of Your signature below and shall continue until the latter of; (i) completion of the Purchase of the Property or (ii)_____. I shall continue to assist You in the completion of any transaction for which a "Commission" is payable to Us. Should you select, or I introduce You to, a Property during the initial term of this Agreement, and You contract for it or close on it within _____ days after the time period indicated above, or any extension(s), You will owe Us the indicated Commission. This "holdover period" and is designed to protect Us when I have done the work but for some reason You did not contract for the Property during the initial term of Our Agreement.

2. Agreement. I have been designated by the Brokerage Firm to act as, and You hereby irrevocably engage Me as, Your designated exclusive agent to represent You in acquiring any real estate that You select. I will be Your limited agent and I will represent You, even if the Property You select is listed with the Us, except when the Property You select is My personal listing. You will conduct all negotiations for the purchase of any Property only through Me, and to refer to Me all communications received in any form from other real estate brokers, prospective sellers, or any other source during the term of this Agreement.

3. Showing Properties. You are aware that there are various methods of showing Property; the seller can be present, the listing office can provide a key or there can be a lockbox on the Property, etc. There are no showing limitations associated with this Agreement.

4. Services. I will exercise reasonable skill and care for You, and make reasonable efforts to locate the Property You indicated that You desire.

   a. I will promote Your interests with the utmost good faith, loyalty and fidelity, including, but not limited to:

   (1)   Seeking a price and terms which are acceptable to You, except that I shall not be obligated to seek other properties while You are a party to a contract to purchase a Property;

   (2)   Procuring acceptance of any offer to purchase the Property and to assist in the completion of the transaction;

   (3)   Presenting all offers to and from You in a timely manner, regardless of whether You are already a party to a contract to purchase a Property;

   (4)   Disclosing to You adverse material facts actually known to Me;

   (5)   Counseling You as to any material benefits or risks of the transaction which are actually known to Me;

   (6)   Advising You to obtain expert advice as to material matters about which I know but the specifics of which are beyond My expertise;

   (7)   Accounting in a timely manner for all money and Property received, and

   (8)   Informing You that You may be vicariously liable for My acts when I am acting within the scope of this Agreement.

   b. I won't disclose to any seller or any other third party, without Your informed written consent:

Exclusive Right-to-Buy Contract
Brokerage by:_____ dat____/____/____   Buyer_____ _____

Page _____ of _____
date___/___/___

(1) That You are willing to pay more than the purchase price for the Property;

(2) What Your motivating factor(s) are;

(3) That You will agree to financing terms other than those offered;

(4) Any material information about You unless disclosure is required by law or failure to disclose such information would constitute fraud or dishonest dealing; and

(5) Any facts or suspicions regarding circumstances which would psychologically impact or stigmatize the Property.

c. I will disclose to any prospective seller all adverse material facts actually known by Me, including but not limited to adverse material facts concerning Your financial ability to perform the terms of the transaction and whether You intend to occupy the Property as Your principal residence.

d. When You desire to purchase a Property that is listed with Us, an In-Company transaction, I will continue to represent you as your agent. When you desire to purchase a Property that is listed by Me, I will assist both You and the seller in the capacity of either a ____dual agent or a ____ transaction broker, and:

(1) I will not disclose to either You or the seller the motivating factors of the other party, nor

(2) Will I disclose other confidential information about You or the seller, nor,

(3) Will I disclose what You are willing to pay, nor,

(4) Will I disclose, if I know, what the seller may have told Me the seller is willing to accept, nor

(5) Will I disclose any financing terms either party may have told Us they will accept, nor

(6) Will I disclose any material information about You or the seller unless disclosure is required by law or failure to disclose such information would constitute fraud or dishonest dealing, nor

(7) Will I disclose any facts or suspicions regarding circumstances which would psychologically impact or stigmatize the Property.

5.   Costs of Services or Products Obtained from Outside Sources. We will not obtain or order products or services from outside sources unless You agree to pay for them promptly when due (examples: surveys, soil tests, radon tests, title reports, engineering studies, Property inspections). We are not be obligated to advance funds for You and You are not obligated to advance funds to Us. You agree to reimburse Us for payments made by Us for such other products or services authorized by You in advance in writing.

6.   Compensation. This is how I make My living. It is Our desire that You not be required to pay Us directly. We will seek compensation from any source You indicate, including but not limited to, the Listing Broker, Seller, Your home transfer company, and such other sources that You indicate. In most cases there will be a cooperative Commission offered by the listing broker, indicated in the MLS, that will serve to satisfy this compensation issue.

We encourage You, when the situation requires it, to direct Me to insert a clause in any contract, if You desire, that indicates *"buyer's obligation to buy is expressly conditional upon seller paying buyer's agent, simultaneous with closing, the sum of ___ % of the sales price as a Commission."* This will help to prevent You from paying Us a Commission on Property that is not listed or where the offered cooperative Commission is not sufficient to pay Us.

Our Commission is payable upon closing of the transaction unless the seller refuses to close and You are not in default, in which case no Commission will be due to Us. If it is Your default that prevents the closing, the Commission will be due and payable to Us immediately.

There is an instance where We will expect payment from You. In the event You contract for a Property and elect not to close or contract for a Property which closes, and no one else pays Our Commission, at or before closing, You shall, in consideration of the services to be performed by Us, be obligated to pay Us a Commission, based upon: ___ the price of the Property indicated in the purchase and sale contract, or ___ the price established by the seller on the first day the Property is introduced to You, or ___ the lesser of the two, or ___ the greater of the two, as follows:

   a. In the event the Property is listed with the MLS, Our Commission shall be the greater of the amount actually paid (including bonuses and other incentives) by the Listing Broker or _____% of the Price, or

   b. In the event the Property is not listed with the MLS, Our Commission shall be _____% of the Price.

c. You ___ shall ___ shall not pay Us a non-refundable Commission retainer of $_____ now, and that amount ___ shall ___ shall not be credited against the total Commission due.

d. Other than as We have agreed in this Agreement, We will not accept compensation or "mark-ups" from any source without Your prior written consent.

7.   Disclosure of Your Identity. We ___ do ___ do not have Your permission to disclose Your identity to any third parties without Your prior written consent. At the earliest reasonable opportunity, We shall inform all prospective sellers or their brokers with whom We negotiate pursuant to this contract that We are acting as Your agent.

8.   Other Buyers. You understand that We and sometimes I represent or assist other buyers looking for Property. We may show properties You are interested in to other prospective buyers without breaching this Agreement or any obligation, duty or responsibility to You. In the event We are assisting or representing multiple buyers all of whom are interested in the same Property, We shall keep all information regarding each buyer and their proposed transaction confidential and shall not disclose any elements of any offer made by or to any buyer to any other buyer.

9.   Assignment. We can not assign this contract without Your consent and You can not assign it without Our consent.

10.   Nondiscrimination. Everyone agrees not to discriminate unlawfully against any prospective seller because of the race, creed, color, sex, national origin, familial status, physical or mental handicap, religion, marital status, or ancestry of such person.

11.   "Megan's Law". If the presence of a registered sex offender is a matter of concern to You, You must contact local law enforcement officials regarding obtaining such information. We can not obtain that information for You. We will provide you with the address and phone number of the appropriate agency that has the information.

12.   Recommendation of Legal and Tax Counsel. By signing this Agreement, You acknowledge that We have advised You that this Agreement has important legal consequences and have recommended consultation with legal, tax or other counsel, before signing it. We make the same recommendation regarding the signing of any contract to buy real estate.

13. Use of Professionals. You are advised to seek the advice of professionals, such as: attorneys, accountants, appraisers, surveyors, contractors, engineers, septic inspectors, well testers, water engineers, Property inspectors, environmental hazard and radon gas experts. We recommend that You obtain a written inspection report covering the Property and Inclusions, an improvement location certificate or survey to determine lot size, location of improvements and any encroachments. You should verify all information using experts that You select. We will not conduct an inspection of the Property, the Inclusions, any Seller's Property Disclosure form, Title Documents (Abstract of Title, Title Commitment and related Documents) or other disclosure for You or for Your benefit.

14. Property Condition. Determining the condition of the Property is Your responsibility. Our presence at any viewing or inspection is not to be construed as an inspection. We will not verify the accuracy or completeness of statements made by any seller, seller's broker, independent inspectors, or other third parties, regarding anything to do with the Property, including but not limited to: the actual lot size, location and square footage of improvements, building, zoning and allowed use regulations, well (flow rate, capacity, depth, recovery rate, suitability for You needs, exempt status such as household, domestic, etc., water quality, potability, location on Property, etc.), septic (useful life of the system, capacity and suitability for size of house, pumping needs, location on Property, etc.), leach field (adequacy, location on Property, percolation, etc.), radiant heating systems (e.g. Entran II), electromagnetic fields (proximity to power lines), termites or other infestations, including mold, exterior insulation and finish systems (e.g. artificial stucco), polybutylene plumbing materials, roofing materials (e.g. Woodruf shingles), proximity to a flood plain or hazardous waste site and the quality of the schools, crime statistics and finally, the presence or any mold. You need to satisfy Yourself that any Property is in a condition that is acceptable to You.

15. Property Repairs/Improvements. You should obtain written cost quotations (bids) for all work You intend to have done to the Property to be fully aware of the costs of such repairs, maintenance, improvements and/or upgrades. We are not responsible for any recommendations as to professionals. Each professional should be able to provide You with a list of past customers or clients to assist You in making Your decision and selection.

You are advised that all work done on the Property as part of any contract should be done by licensed contractors where possible, and inspected by the appropriate governmental authority.

16. **Homeowner's Warranty.** You are aware of the existence of pre-owned home warranty programs which may be purchased and may cover the repair or replacement of some Inclusions. We are not liable for the financial integrity or subsequent performance or non-performance of such companies. You are encouraged to evaluate the terms of coverage and financial strength of any company offering to issue such a warranty.

17. **Possession, Lease and Insurance.** If the Possession Date and Time are other than Closing Date, You, to protect Your real and personal Property interests, should consider obtaining casualty and liability insurance and a lease for the period between Possession Date and Time and the Closing Date.

18. **Price.** I will prepare a Competitive Market Analysis (not an appraisal), for potential properties You select, comprised of similar properties that have sold, are listed for sale or were rejected from the market, as reported to the MLS's of which We are members. This may not comprise all of the properties in the market area. You are solely responsible for the determination of the contract price. We are not responsible for the determination of the contract price and advise you to have the Property appraised by a licensed appraiser.

19. **Mediation.** We hope that We never have a dispute with You. However, should a dispute arise relating to this Agreement and is not resolved, then Everyone shall first proceed in good faith to submit the matter to mediation. Mediation is a process in which Everyone meets with an impartial person ("mediator") who helps to resolve the dispute informally and confidentially. Mediators cannot impose binding decisions upon anyone. Everyone must agree before any settlement is binding. Everyone will jointly appoint an acceptable mediator and will share equally in the cost of such mediation. The mediation, unless otherwise agreed, shall terminate in the event the entire dispute is not resolved within thirty (30) calendar days from the date written notice requesting mediation is sent by You or Us to the other. Lawsuits under this contract can only be filed in the location where We have our principal office.

20.   Attorney Fees. In case of arbitration or litigation between Everyone, Everyone agrees that costs and attorney fees shall be awarded to the side the wins.

21.   Our Purchases. We may, for our own account, purchase Property that is available for sale, including Property that may or may not have been shown to You.

22.   Facsimile and Electronic Signatures. Signatures ___ may ___ may not be evidenced by facsimile, and ___ may ___ may not be evidenced by electronic signatures. Documents with original signatures shall be provided upon request of any party.

23.   Modification of this Contract. No subsequent modification of any of the terms of this contract shall be valid, binding upon the Everyone unless the modification is in writing and signed everyone.

24.   Counterparts. If You includes more that one person, this contract may be executed by each person individually, and when so executed, such copies taken together with one executed by Me shall be deemed to be a full and complete contract between everyone.

25.   Entire Agreement. This Listing Contract constitutes the entire agreement between Everyone and any prior agreements, whether oral or written, have been merged and integrated into this Listing Contract.

26.   Copies. You acknowledge receipt of a copy of this Agreement, including all attachments, if any, signed by Us.

27.   Attachments. The following items are a part of Our Agreement:
Exhibit _____, _____, consisting of _____ pages
Exhibit _____, _____, consisting of _____ pages
Exhibit _____, _____, consisting of _____ pages

28. Additional Provisions.

_____

_____

_____

Buyer: **Buyer:**

_____   _____
Print Your Name Here   Print Your Name Here

_____   _____
Sign Your Name Here and Date   Sign Your Name Here and Date

Buyer's Address:_____

Buyer's Phone: _____   Fax: _____

Buyer's e-mail:_____

Brokerage Firm:

_____
Print Brokerage Firm Name Here

By: _____
     Print Associate Broker/Salesperson Name Here and   Sign here and   Date

Broker's Address:_____

Broker's Phone: _____   Fax: _____

Broker's e-mail:_____

Extension.

We extend the date indicated in section 4d(ii) to _____,20___.

Brokerage Firm by: _____ _____   Buyer(s) _____ _____ _____
                   Initial and date   Initial and date

Your Seller is Now a Buyer

When the seller, having listed his property with the broker, through the salesperson, now also wants to purchase a new or additional piece of property, the agent has the best of all real estate transactions. The agent and the seller already have established a rapport and are able to speak with candor. The agent has learned not only the likes and dislikes of his seller turned buyer but also his personal confidential secrets and motivations. The agent knows the amount of money the seller turned buyer probably has available, the relative financial worth of the various entities that his seller turned buyer may use to acquire property, the extent to which the seller turned buyer will go to attain his goals and the overall strategy of the seller turned buyer. In short, he knows how his seller turned buyer thinks.

In some parts of the country, some salespeople are still attempting to convert the former seller, their client, into a customer (someone that they do not represent) for the buying side of the transaction. This makes no sense. Most buyers feel that the agent with whom they are working is *"their"* agent. Imagine how the seller client feels after he has listed with the broker or agent, and is now going out to search for new acquisitions and is told that the former agent is now going to tell prospective sellers, strangers for the most part, the personal secrets and motivations of the seller turned buyer, the *former* client. We would guess that nearly one hundred percent of all sellers who are seeking to purchase real estate with their listing agents are convinced that the agent, *their agent*, is working for them.

The seller turned buyer thinks, and properly so, that he still has *his* REALTOR®. To argue any other way would be silly. Now we must deal with the eventuality that the seller turned buyer might want to see and buy another one of the salespersons listings or another listing in the office. There can be a real problem here. Yes, that is the "prime directive" – to get the seller's house sold.

This is the ever prevalent In-Company or "Same Salesperson"Sale. If you are in a designated brokerage state, the issue only arises when the seller turned buyer wants to buy one of your personal listings. Listings held by other salespeople in your office, other designated brokers, do not pose a conflict as you can continue to represent your seller turned buyer and the other salesperson can represent their seller. In a state that still uses the "whole office concept" the problem arises when the seller turned buyer wants to purchase any listing in your company.

Call your position dual agency, if you must, or refer to it as Transaction Broker if you want the title to fit the duties prescribed by the realities of the arrangement. Whatever the name, the role is that of a neutral party. Absent full disclosure, there is no doubt that the ultimate undisclosed dual agency arrangement has been created.

The agent becomes the agent of the buyer (former seller) and an agent of the new seller. Someone *should* have discussed this potential situation with every seller when the property was listed. Then when the seller turned buyer wanted to buy a company listing where there is a potential conflict, the new seller would be excited about the agent *advancing* to the neutral position. After all selling the property In-Company or yourself was the original plan. Think about how a court, or an uninitiated individual, might see things. It might be very confusing. It would appear that someone was trying to take advantage of someone else when, in fact, we know that is not the case at all.

Letter/e-mail – Seller is a Buyer – Buyer Agency/Dual Agency
(Whole Office Concept)

Mr. Sam Seller
Mrs. Sandy Seller
4750 Table Mesa Drive
Boulder, CO 80305

    Re: 4750 Table Mesa Drive

Dear Sam and Sandy:

I have been happy to assist you as your agent with the sale of your present home. Thank you for selecting me to help you with the new property that you are to purchase. I consider myself well qualified, not only since I have had the opportunity to get to know you and to determine what you desire in your new home, but also because I am very familiar with many of the properties available in this area. I enjoy helping a buyer select a new home. As members of the Multiple Listing Service, our office has access not only to our inventory of listings, but also to numerous properties available in this area that have been listed by other member brokers.

Unless you indicate otherwise, I will assist you as a buyer agent. That way I can continue to represent you instead of having to try to become a subagent of the various other sellers who have their homes on the market. I would have a hard time not being your agent and having to be the agent for a stranger. Our firm simply can not act as an agent for a seller who has listed his property with another office, while we are working with you.

We want you to be aware of the various relationships that are available for sellers who are interested in looking at houses. Not all of them are offered by this firm.

Our choice is to act as your agents. This is buyer agency. You may remember that I indicated to you that our firm pays buyer agents who assist me with the sale of your home. Well, the shoe is on the other foot now. Other firms will pay me to help them sell their seller's listings. In general almost all the other firms cooperate and compensate us, so there is no need for you to pay us separately.

I will do everything that I can to solicit the cooperation and fee split from the listing broker. In the event that is not feasible, such as in the case of a For Sale by Owner, then you can write a clause in the contract that will allow for the seller to pay me as a part of the transaction. However, in the event that I find the home that you select, and no one else will pay me, I need to know that you will pay me. Otherwise, I would be working for free. I am sure we both agree that I can not do that.

Some salespeople act as subagents of the other sellers on the market. Our office does not offer that selection. I can not be someone else's agent and be required to work for him when I am helping you find a home.

There is a possibility that you will be interested in one of the properties listed with our company. We have some very nice listings. In that instance, I will advance to being a dual agent. That means that I, and the other agents in my office, will be neutral throughout the transaction, acting simply as real estate brokers. This is really quite a simple solution. You may remember that I described dual agency to you when we discussed your listing. It is the same relationship that would have existed if I had sold your home myself to another one of my clients.

I have attached another copy of our In-Company Sale Addendum. Yes, it is the same one that was attached to your listing. Now that you are the buyer, we need to review it again. I will keep your personal secrets confidential and do the same for the personal secrets of the other sellers that we have listed. I will always indicate to you anything that I know about the physical condition of the property. I just can not tell the potential seller your motivation to buy, and I can not tell you the seller's motivation to sell.

Sincerely,
The Real Estate Company

by: Your Name Here,
REALTOR®, CRS, GRI

Letter/e-mail – Seller is a Buyer – Buyer Agency/Transaction Broker
(Whole Office Concept)

Mr. Sam Seller
Mrs. Sandy Seller
4750 Table Mesa Drive
Boulder, CO 80305

Re: 4750 Table Mesa Drive

Dear Sam and Sandy:

I have been happy to assist you as your agent with the sale of your present home. Thank you for selecting me to help you with the new property that you are to purchase. I consider myself well qualified, not only since I have had the opportunity to get to know you and to determine what you desire in your new home, but also because I am very familiar with many of the properties available in this area. I enjoy helping a buyer select a new home. As members of the Multiple Listing Service, our office has access not only to our inventory of listings, but also to numerous properties available in this area that have been listed by other member brokers.

Unless you indicate otherwise, I will assist you as a buyer agent. That way I can continue to represent you instead of having to try to become a subagent of the various other sellers who have their homes on the market. I would have a hard time not being your agent and having to be the agent for a stranger. Our firm simply can not act as an agent for a seller who has listed his property with another office, while we are working with you.

We want you to be aware of the various relationships that are available for sellers who are interested in looking at houses. Not all of them are offered by this firm.

Our choice is to act as your agents. This is buyer agency. You may remember that I indicated to you that our firm pays buyer agents who assist me with the sale of your home. Well, the shoe is on the other foot now. Other firms will pay me to help them sell their seller's listings. In general almost all the other firms cooperate and compensate us, so there is no need for you to pay us separately.

I will do everything that I can to solicit the cooperation and fee split from the listing broker. In the event that is not feasible, such as in the case of a For Sale by Owner, then you can write a clause in the contract that will allow for the seller to pay me as a part of the transaction. However, in the event that I find the home that you select, and no one else will pay me, I need to know that you will pay me. Otherwise, I would be working for free. I am sure we both agree that I can not do that.

Some salespeople act as subagents of the other sellers on the market. Our office does not offer that selection. I can not be someone else's agent and be required to work for him when I am helping you find a home.

There is a possibility that you will be interested in one of the properties listed with our company. We have some very nice listings. In that instance, I will advance to being a transaction broker. That means that I, and the other agents in my office, will be neutral throughout the transaction, acting simply as real estate brokers. This is really quite a simple solution. You may remember that I described transaction broker to you when we discussed your listing. It is the same relationship that would have existed if I had sold your home myself to another one of my clients.

I have attached another copy of our In-Company Sale Addendum. Yes, it is the same one that was attached to your listing. Now that you are the buyer, we need to review it again. I will keep your personal secrets confidential and do the same for the personal secrets of the other sellers that we have listed. I will always indicate to you anything that I know about the physical condition of the property. I just can not tell the potential seller your motivation to buy, and I can not tell you the seller's motivation to sell.

Sincerely,
The Real Estate Company

by: Your Name Here,
REALTOR®, CRS, GRI

Letter/e-mail – Seller is a Buyer – Designated Brokerage

Mr. Sam Seller
Mrs. Sandy Seller
4750 Table Mesa Drive
Boulder, CO 80305

Dear Sam and Sandy:

I have been happy to assist you as your agent with the sale of your present home. Thank you for selecting me to help you with the new property that you are to purchase. I consider myself well qualified, not only since I have had the opportunity to get to know you and to determine what you desire in your new home, but also because I am very familiar with many of the properties available in this area. I enjoy helping a buyer select a new home. As a member of the Multiple Listing Service, our office has access not only to our inventory of listings, but also to numerous properties available in this area that have been listed by other member brokers.

Unless you indicate otherwise, I will be assisting you as a buyer agent for all properties listed by this office and those listed by other offices. You may remember that I indicated to you that our firm paid the buyer agent who assisted me with the sale of your home. Well, the shoe is on the other foot now. Now, the listing broker will pay me to help sell a home another seller has listed with them. In general, almost all the other firms cooperate and compensate us, so there is no need for you to pay me separately.

I will do everything that I can to work with the listing broker, so that he will compensate me in what is called a cooperative commission split. Therefore, you will not need co compensate me. However, if that compensation is not paid by the listing broker, as in the case of a For Sale by Owner, I will ask you to write a clause in the contract which says, *"this contract is conditional upon the seller paying the buyer agent, simultaneous with closing, a fee equal to _____% of the final sales price,"* to insure that I get paid without your having to pay me. In the event that I find you a home that you just love and no one else will pay me, of course you will pay me. I need to know that someone will pay me. Otherwise, I would be working for free. I know that you do not expect that.

There is a possibility that you will be interested in one of the properties listed by me personally. I have some very nice listings. In that instance, I will advance to being a dual agent [transaction broker]. That means that I will be acting as a professional real estate broker and remain neutral throughout the transaction, while helping both you and my seller to contract for a purchase and sale. This is really quite a simple solution. You may remember that I described this situation to you when we discussed your listing. This is the relationship that would have existed if I had sold your home myself to another one of my personal clients, someone that I know like I know you.

I have attached another copy of my In-Company Sale Addendum. Yes, it is the same one that was attached to your listing. Now that you are the buyer, we need to review it again. I will keep your personal secrets confidential and do the same for the personal secrets of the other sellers whose homes I have listed. I will always indicate to you anything that I know about the physical condition of the property. I just can not tell your motivation to buy to any potential seller who is listed with me, nor can I tell you the seller's motivation to sell.

Sincerely,
The Real Estate Company

by: Your Name Here,
REALTOR®, CRS, GRI

Chapter 4

In-Company Sales

Selling Your Own Listing

Defining the Middle Ground

The In-Company Sale.   Sometimes referred to as "double ending," "getting both sides" or "double dipping," this is the sale that the seller anticipated when he hired you, and the sale that you want to make if you can.   The goal was to sell the home yourself from the start.

This is also the sale that the buyer envisioned when the buyer called on your advertisement or "For Sale" sign.   It is the sale that everyone hopes will happen.   Our job is to prepare for it and conduct it within the rules established by the law and our company policy.   The In-Company sale has a higher chance for litigation than an "out of company" sale.   You or your company are now liable to both sides.   Remember, once there is a breach of a fiduciary duty, the commission will be forfeited, regardless of loss.   The large awards often deal with In-Company cases.

Rule.   *Breach of a fiduciary duty forfeits the commission regardless of loss.*

In order not to breach your fiduciary duty to the seller, or the buyer, you must disclose to each in advance how you will handle the In-Company or "In-House" sale.   This is neutral ground.   Even if you get the house sold, we could lose the entire commission if you breach our fiduciary duty, namely the duty to tell the seller what you were doing on the seller's behalf.   If the buyer thought that you were his agent, you could lose as a result of a similar allegation from the buyer.

Tip.   *The seller wants "you to sell her house," so tell the seller how you do business, and let the seller determine if she wants to do business with you. You do not have to be all things to all people.*

Tip.   *The buyer wants "you to show and sell him your listing," so tell the buyer how you do business, and let the buyer determine if he wants to do business with you. You do not have to be all things to all people.*

Broker's Role. Establish an office agency policy, making certain that not only do you understand and believe in it, but that all your salespeople can easily understand the policy and can explain it.   Try having each person stand up at a sales meeting and give his/her presentation to the seller or the buyer for all to hear.   All salespeople in the office must be on the same team, playing by the same rules.   Allowing each salesperson to role play as the agent trying to list: a seller, a seller turned buyer, a buyer, or one of the principals (the seller or the buyer) will make the description of the services offered easier to explain. Soon people will understand the basic real estate services that your office offers to everyone. Those are the services that a neutral person provides in an In-Company sale.

Salesperson's Role. You must understand and be able to explain your office agency policy for the In-Company sale. In addition, you must understand your competitor's agency policy and why your policy is as good, or better. Never run down competitors. It will come back to haunt you when your policy changes. Emphasize the positive aspects of your office policy and not the negative aspects of the policies of other companies. Practice your role. This is real estate, not a courtroom.

Caution. *State laws vary here a lot. In addition, many states do not realize that there are options that may not involve agency since it "has been done that way for so long."* **Check with your local attorney.**

Rule. *The manner in which your office – yes the entire office – handles In-Company sales must be disclosed and agreed upon with either the buyer or the seller, at the time he signs the listing contract. It is not proper to try to get their consent once you have an offer.*

Choices for the In-Company Sale

There are essentially four choices for handling the In-Company sale.

1. **Seller Agency.** This is frequently referred to as "single agency." You inform the seller that you will represent the seller at all times. While this sounds great to everyone, it does not adequately address the prospect that you might actually sell the house to someone with whom you are now working as a buyer agent. In addition, when the seller's house sells, he will expect you to be "his agent" to help him buy a new property. Perish the thought that he should select another of your personal listings or one in your company's inventory. Now you need to explain your In-Company sale policy. Your policy will be one of the following, or you could refer the buyer to another broker outside of your company. Right!

2. **Dual Agency.** The agent attempts to represent two people, or two groups of people, with conflicting interests at the same time. You should check your state law. We need to define in advance what information will be passed along to the other party and what will be kept secret. This is a common term with a lot of

different interpretations. How can someone really be a "dual" agent, representing two people with conflicting interests at the same time? Of course, no one can. However, the term exists and will continue to exist. The practical application is that you provide a list of specific services to both the buyer and the seller.

3. **Transaction Broker.** The agent will assist two people, or two groups of people, with conflicting interests at the same time. The difference is that the term "dual agent," which confuses everyone, is replaced with "transaction broker," which is a more accurate term for the services performed and eliminates a lot of false expectations. This service is sometimes called intermediary, statutory broker, facilitator, transaction broker, or real estate broker – it is a non-agency relationship. A transaction broker accomplishes the same objective as a dual agent, the sale of a seller client's property to a buyer client. The real estate professional is neutral and provides a list of services to both buyer and seller. We need to define in advance what information will be passed along to the other party and what will be kept secret.

4. **Designated Agency (Designated Brokerage).** Sometimes this is referred to as "Split Agency." In general, it provides that in the event of an In-Company sale, the broker will designate two separate salespeople, one to assist the buyer and one to assist the seller, respectively. The broker will act as a broker for the transaction, a transaction broker or dual agent, and administer or supervise the transaction without taking sides. One salesperson, not the brokerage office, will represent the seller in the traditional agency sense of the word, and the other salesperson will represent the buyer in a similar manner.

The choice must be selected by the broker and utilized for all transactions in the office. You can not have the buyer or seller selecting methods on a case by case basis. A method of incorporating the selected policy into the buyer or seller listing agreement and the contract for sale is to make reference, in the respective contract, to the In-Company sale, which will be handled pursuant to the terms of the attached addendum. This allows the company to change or modify the addendum without having to reprint the entire listing form.

The following clauses address the different relationships potentially available with the buyer and/or seller. Read each to determine if it anticipates the buyer and seller initially having an *agency* or a *working* relationship with the broker. A "working relationship" is something very similar to a "customer" relationship.

Clauses and Addenda for In-Company Sales. We recommend an addendum in a form similar to the Dual Agency, Designated Agency, Designated Brokerage, Transaction Broker and In-Company sale addenda we have provided in this chapter. We hope these will assist those of you who do not have or currently use addenda, or such forms are not available through your state association or real estate commission. As always, you will need to modify the addenda to fit your company policy, as well as your state law. This is a serious area where caution is a password.

In the event you choose to use only a clause in the listing contract, following are some alternatives.

Clause: In-Company Sale – Dual Agency
1. A broker may not act as an agent for more than one party without prior written agreement between the broker, the buyer and the seller. When acting as a dual agent, the broker will retain the confidential information related to each party and disclose only the information related to the physical condition of the property, the buyer's ability to qualify for the proposed transaction and whether the buyer will occupy the property. The broker will not disclose to either party:
    (1) that either will accept any price other than as listed or as offered;
    (2) the motivation of the other party;
    (3) any other information a party specifically instructs the broker to keep confidential, unless the same is required by law, or the failure to disclose such information would constitute fraud or dishonest dealing.

We hereby agree that your firm, broker and salespeople, may act as dual agents in a transaction wherein your firm initially represents both the buyer and the seller.

Only one commission, the one indicated in the listing agreement, will be collected.

-or-

1. When acting as the agent for one party (either buyer or seller), the broker has duties and obligations which include utmost good faith, loyalty and fidelity to either the buyer or seller. If the principal (seller or buyer) consents, the broker may act as a dual agent when both the seller and buyer initially have an *agency* relationship with this real estate company (In-Company sale). A dual agent is a broker engaged as a limited agent for

both the seller and the buyer. Dual agency creates a conflict of interest because broker's duties and obligations of confidentiality, full disclosure and loyalty to one party (seller or buyer) conflict with those same duties to the other. The seller and the buyer may be vicariously liable for acts of a dual agent.

We hereby agree that your firm, broker and salespeople, may act as dual agents in a transaction wherein your firm initially represents both the buyer and the seller.

Only one commission, the one indicated in the listing agreement will be collected.

Clause: In-Company Sale – Transaction Broker

1. When acting as the agent for one party (either buyer or seller), the broker has duties and obligations which include utmost good faith, loyalty and fidelity to that one principal (buyer or seller). If the principal (seller or buyer) consents, however, the broker may act as a transaction broker (real estate broker), when both the seller and buyer initially have an *agency* relationship with the same real estate company (In-Company sale). A transaction broker is a broker engaged, not as a limited agent for both seller and buyer, but to assist both buyer and seller, without acting as the agent of either.

We hereby agree that your firm, broker and salespeople, may act as transaction brokers in a transaction wherein you initially represent both the buyer and the seller.

Only one commission, the one indicated in the listing agreement, will be collected.

-or-

1. When acting as the agent for one party (either buyer or seller), the broker has duties and obligations which include utmost good faith, loyalty and fidelity to that one principal (seller or buyer). If the principal (seller or buyer) consents, however, the broker may act as a transaction broker (real estate broker), when both the seller and buyer initially have either a *working* or *agency* relationship with the same real estate company (In-Company sale). A transaction broker is a broker engaged, not as a limited agent for both the

seller and buyer, but to assist both the buyer and seller, without acting as the agent of either.

We hereby agree that your firm, broker and salespeople, may act as transaction brokers in a transaction wherein you initially either represent, or are working with, the buyer and seller.

Only one commission, the one indicated in the listing agreement, will be collected.

Clause: In-Company Sale – Designated Brokerage – Transaction Broker

When an individual salesperson is acting as the agent for one party (either buyer or seller), that individual salesperson has duties and obligations which include utmost good faith, loyalty and fidelity to that one principal (buyer or seller). If the principal (seller or buyer) consents, however, the individual salesperson may act as a transaction broker (real estate broker), when both the seller and buyer initially have an _agency_ relationship with the same real estate company. A transaction broker is a broker engaged, not as a limited agent for both seller and buyer, but to assist both buyer and seller, without acting as the agent of either.

We hereby agree that the individual salesperson, designated by the broker, who previously represented both the buyer and seller may act as a transaction broker in a transaction when selling his/her own listing. Only one commission, the one indicated in the listing agreement, will be collected.

Clause: Miscellaneous In-Company

1. Seller hereby authorizes Broker to show the property to buyers with whom the broker has, or may have, an agency relationship, pursuant to the terms of the attached In-Company Sale Addendum.

-or-

1. Seller hereby authorizes Broker to show the property to buyers with whom Broker has, or may have, a "working relationship," pursuant to the terms of the attached In-Company Sale Addendum.

Clause: Designated Agency/Brokerage

In the event one salesperson in our firm is working with the buyer and another salesperson is working with the seller, each salesperson shall operate independently of the other, as they are distinct separate agents for the buyer and seller respectively. There shall be no imputation of any knowledge or information between the salespersons and the broker.

Only in the event that the buyer is procured by the same salesperson who listed the property will the In-Company Dual Agency provisions apply.

In the event the buyer and seller are represented by a single salesperson, either the buyer or seller may request the broker to assign a separate salesperson to each of the parties, buyer and seller, for the purposes of the transaction. In that event, the original salesperson shall not be able to assist either party.

In-Company Sale Addendum (Dual Agency)

1. **Amendment to Agency Contract.** This In-Company Sale Addendum is part of either an Exclusive Right to Buy Contract (Buyer Agency Contract) or a Listing Contract (Seller Agency Contract) between the broker named below and its sales agents ("Broker") and the undersigned Buyer or Seller, dated _____, 20_____ . This Addendum will control in the event of any conflict with the contract to which it is attached.

2. **Limitation of Broker's Agency Obligations.** When acting as the agent for one party (either Buyer or Seller), Broker has duties and obligations which include utmost good faith, loyalty and fidelity to that one principal. If the principal consents, however, Broker may act as a Dual Agent when both Seller and Buyer have an *agency* relationship with the same real estate company ("In-Company Sale"). A Dual Agent is a broker engaged as a limited agent for both Seller and Buyer. Dual agency creates a conflict of interest because Broker's duties and obligations of confidentiality, full disclosure and loyalty to one party conflict with those same duties to the other. Seller and Buyer may be vicariously liable for acts of a Dual Agent.
   a. If this addendum is signed by Seller, Broker will act only as the exclusive agent for Seller when the Property is shown to a prospective buyer who has a working relationship with another licensed real estate company, but will act as a Dual Agent only in an In-Company Sale.
   b. If this addendum is signed by Buyer, Broker will act only as the exclusive agent for Buyer when showing properties that are not listed with Broker, but will act as a Dual Agent only in an In-Company Sale.

The remaining provisions of this addendum describe significant changes to the obligations of Broker when acting as a Dual Agent in an In-Company Sale.

3. **Information that Must be Disclosed by a Dual Agent.**
   a. All adverse material facts actually known by Broker including but not limited to adverse material facts pertaining to the title to the Property which Seller indicates will not be remedied prior to the transfer of deed; and,
   b. All information actually known to Broker, now or during the pre-closing period, regarding the physical condition of the property; and,
   c. Any environmental hazards affecting the Property which are required by law to be disclosed.

| Buyer/Seller: ____ ____ ____ | Broker: ____ ____ ____ | Page____ of____ |
| initial initial date | initial initial date | |

4. **Matters that Cannot be Disclosed by a Dual Agent.** Broker, when acting as a Dual Agent, shall not disclose to either Seller or Buyer, without the prior written consent of the other party, any of the following information:
   a. That Buyer is willing to pay more than the purchase price offered for the property;
   b. That Seller is willing to accept less than the asking price for the property;
   c. The motivating factors for either party to buy or sell the property;
   d. That Seller or Buyer will agree to financing terms other than those offered;
   e. Any material information about the other party unless either:
      (1) the disclosure is required by law,
      (2) the disclosure pertains to material facts adverse to Buyer's financial ability to perform the terms of the transaction,
      (3) the disclosure pertains to Buyer's intent to occupy the property as a principal residence, or
      (4) failure to disclose such information would constitute fraud or dishonest dealing.

5. **No Duty for Dual Agent to Investigate**. Broker, when acting as a Dual Agent, has no duty to conduct an independent inspection of the property for the benefit of Buyer and has no duty to independently verify the accuracy or completeness of statements made by Seller or independent inspectors. Broker, when acting as a Dual Agent, has no duty to conduct an independent investigation of Buyer's financial condition or to verify the accuracy or completeness of any statement made by Buyer.

6. **Commission**. Only one commission shall be payable. Buyer and Seller acknowledge that the commission paid to Broker is reflected in the price of the property sold. Seller shall pay Broker the commission indicated in the Exclusive Right to Sell Listing Contract. Buyer shall not be obligated to pay any additional commission to Broker.

_____   _____
Buyer/Seller   date   Buyer/Seller   date

Broker: _____

_____
by   date

Buyer/Seller: ____ ____ ____   Broker: ____ ____ ____   Page___of___
           initial initial date   initial initial date

In-Company Sale Addendum Dual/Limited Agency

This Addendum is hereby made a part of either Seller Listing Contract, the Buyer Agency Contract or the Purchase and Sale Contract ("Contract"), between the undersigned real estate broker and its salespersons ("Broker") and the undersigned Seller and/or Buyer, ("Client"), collectively ("Parties"). In the event the terms of this Addendum conflict with, vary from, or modify the terms and provisions of the Contract, the terms of this Addendum shall control.

Fiduciary Duties. The Broker has fiduciary duties to the Client which include; *reasonable care* (to act in a reasonable manner), *undivided loyalty and confidentiality* (keeping the Client's confidences), *obedience and performance* (to comply with the Client's reasonable directions regarding the purchase and sale of real property), *accounting* (to disclose the status of all transactional money in broker's possession) and *full disclosure* (to transmit all relevant and material information known by Broker to the Client regarding the other party).

Seller-Broker Relationship. When real property is listed for sale or lease by Seller with Broker, Broker acts initially as the agent of, and owes fiduciary duties to, Seller ("Seller's Agent"). The Broker shall treat Buyer honestly and shall disclose to Buyer all defects of a material nature affecting the physical condition of the property actually known to Broker. The Broker shall have no obligation to inspect the Property. The Broker can not, without Seller's prior written consent, violate or modify Broker's duty of undivided loyalty and confidentiality and full disclosure.

Buyer-Broker Relationship. When a Buyer engages Broker to locate real property for purchase or lease, Broker shall act initially as the agent of, and owes fiduciary duties to, Buyer ("Buyer's Agent"). The Broker shall treat Seller honestly and shall not give Seller false information concerning the financial condition of the Buyer, nor disclose the financial affairs of the Buyer without Buyer's written consent. The Broker can not, without Buyer's prior written consent, violate or modify Broker's duty of undivided loyalty, confidentiality and full disclosure.

"Out of Company" or "Cooperative" Sales. When Broker represents Seller, and a buyer is procured through a brokerage office other than Broker's office, Broker shall transmit to Seller all information known to Broker regarding the transaction and the proposed buyer. When Broker represents Buyer, and the

| Buyer/Seller: _____ _____ _____ | Broker: _____ _____ _____ | Page___of___ |
| initial initial date | initial initial date | |

property is listed with a brokerage office other than Broker's office, Broker shall transmit to Buyer all information known to Broker regarding the transaction and the proposed seller.

In-Company Sales. The Buyer and Seller acknowledge that Buyer may seek to acquire a property listed with Broker, an "In-Company," "In-Office" or "In-House" sale. In such a transaction, Broker would owe conflicting fiduciary duties to both Buyer and Seller at the same time, an inherent conflict of interest. The Broker can not represent the interests of either party to the exclusion or detriment of the other party. In order for Broker to assist both Buyer and Seller in such transactions, the Parties must consent in writing to allow Broker to act as a "Dual (Limited) Agent," modifying the existing agency Contracts, Listing Contract and Buyer Agency Contract, between the Parties.

Dual (Limited) Agency Modification. The Parties agree that for all transactions wherein Broker may initially act as both a Buyer's Agent and a Seller's Agent, Buyer becoming interested in a property listed by Seller with Broker, Broker, except as herein indicated, shall provide *limited* representation to both Buyer or Seller in the same transaction. The Broker shall act as a Limited Dual Agent for both Buyer and Seller. The following shall be the duties, obligations and agreements between Broker and Buyer and Seller:

1. Broker shall exercise *reasonable care*, to act in a commercially reasonable manner, in the preparation of all documents and transmission of information. Broker shall answer all questions honestly, but shall properly refuse to answer questions that might violate a duty of confidentiality to either party.

2. Broker shall keep the former Client's confidences *confidential*, and not transmit any personal information known to Broker regarding either party.

3. Broker shall be *obedient and perform*, complying with the reasonable directions and requests of both parties to accomplish the drafting and fulfillment of the terms of the contract for sale. Broker shall assist both parties to comply with the terms and conditions precedent to the closing of the transaction and shall keep both Buyer and Seller fully informed regarding all aspects of the transaction.

4. Broker shall provide an *accounting* to all Parties, disclosing the status of all transaction money in broker's possession.

5. Broker shall *disclose*, and transmit to all Parties the information known by Broker regarding the physical condition of the property at all times prior to the transfer of deed.

6. Broker shall not give legal advice to anyone, including advice regarding the condition of the legal title to the property, nor as to the extent of the title insurance policy or exceptions.

7. Only one commission shall be payable. Buyer and Seller acknowledge that the commission paid to Broker is reflected in the price of the property sold. Seller shall pay Broker the commission indicated in the Exclusive Right to Sell Listing Contract. Buyer shall not be obligated to pay any additional commission to Broker.

8. A copy of this Addendum shall be a part of the final contract between Buyer and Seller.

The Parties acknowledge that this Addendum can not be entered into without the knowledge and written consent of all the Parties. Each has read this Addendum and sought the advice of an attorney, if they so desired.

_____   _____
Buyer/Seller   date   Buyer/Seller   date

Broker:_____

_____
by   date

In-Company Sale Addendum – Transaction Broker
(Initial Agency Relationship)

1. **Amendment to Agency Contract.** This In-Company Sale Addendum is part of either an Exclusive Right to Buy Contract (Buyer Agency Contract) or a Listing Contract (Seller Agency Contract), dated _____, 20_____, between the broker named below and its sales agents ("Broker") and the undersigned Buyer or Seller. This Addendum will control in the event of any conflict with the contract to which it is attached.

2. **Limitation of Broker's Agency Obligations.** When acting as the agent for one party (either Buyer or Seller), Broker has duties and obligations which include utmost good faith, loyalty and fidelity to that one principal. If the principal consents, however, Broker may act as a Transaction Broker (Non Agent) when both Seller and Buyer have an *agency* relationship with the same real estate company ("In-Company Sale"). A Transaction Broker is a broker engaged as a limited agent for both Seller and Buyer. Transaction Brokerage creates a conflict of interest because Broker's duties and obligations of confidentiality, full disclosure, and loyalty to one party conflict with those same duties to the other. Seller and Buyer are *not* vicariously liable for acts of a Transaction Broker.
   a. If this addendum is signed by Seller, Broker will act as the exclusive agent for Seller only when the Property is shown to a prospective buyer who has a working relationship with another licensed real estate company, but will act as a Transaction Broker only in an In-Company Sale.

   b. If this addendum is signed by Buyer, Broker will act only as the exclusive agent for Buyer when showing properties that are not listed with Broker, but will act as a Transaction Broker only in an In-Company Sale.

The remaining provisions of this addendum describe significant changes to the obligations of Broker when acting as a Transaction Broker in an In-Company Sale.

3. **Information that Must be Disclosed by a Transaction Broker.**
   a. All adverse material facts actually known by Broker, including but not limited to adverse material facts pertaining to the title to the Property

---

Buyer/Seller: ___ ___ ___   Broker: ___ ___ ___   Page___of___
     initial initial date   initial initial date

which Seller indicates will not be remedied prior to the transfer of deed; and,

b. All information actually known to Broker, now or during the pre-closing period, regarding the physical condition of the property; and,

c. Any environmental hazards affecting the Property which are required by law to be disclosed.

4. **Matters that Can Not be Disclosed by a Transaction Broker.** Broker, when acting as a Transaction Broker, shall not disclose the following information without the prior consent of the party concerned:

a. That Buyer is willing to pay more than the purchase price offered for the property;

b. That Seller is willing to accept less than the asking price for the property;

c. What the motivating factors are for any party buying or selling the property;

d. That Seller or Buyer will agree to financing terms other than those offered;

e. Any material information about the other party unless either:
   (1)   the disclosure is required by law,
   (2)   the disclosure pertains to adverse material facts about Buyer's financial ability to perform the terms of the transaction,
   (3)   the disclosure pertains to Buyer's intent to occupy the property as a principal residence, or
   (4)   failure to disclose such information would constitute fraud or dishonest dealing.

5. **No Duty for Transaction Broker to Investigate or Verify**. Broker, when acting as a Transaction Broker, has no duty to conduct an independent inspection of the property for the benefit of Buyer and has no duty to independently verify the accuracy or completeness of statements made by Seller or independent inspectors. Broker, when acting as a Transaction Broker, has no duty to conduct an independent investigation of Buyer's financial condition or to verify the accuracy or completeness of any statement made by Buyer.

6. **Commission.** Only one commission shall be payable. Buyer and Seller acknowledge that the commission paid to Broker is reflected in the price of the property sold. Seller shall pay Broker the commission indicated in the Exclusive Right to Sell Listing Contract. Buyer shall not be obligated to pay any additional commission to Broker.

_____ _____
Buyer/Seller   date   Buyer/Seller   date

Broker:_____

_____
by   date

In-Company Sale Addendum Transaction Broker
(Agency or Working Relationship)

1. **Amendment to Agency Contract.** This In-Company Sale Addendum is part of either an Exclusive Right to Buy Contract (Buyer Agency Contract) or a Listing Contract (Seller Agency Contract), dated _____, 20_____, between the broker named below and its sales agents ("Broker") and the undersigned Buyer or Seller. This Addendum will control in the event of any conflict with the contract to which it is attached.

2. **Limitation of Broker's Agency Obligations.** When acting as the agent for one party (either Buyer or Seller), Broker has duties and obligations which include utmost good faith, loyalty and fidelity to that one principal. If the principal consents, however, Broker may act as a Transaction Broker (Non Agent) when both Seller and Buyer have either an *agency* or a *working* relationship with the same real estate company ("In-Company Sale"). A Transaction Broker is a broker engaged as a limited agent for both Seller and Buyer. Transaction Brokerage creates a conflict of interest because Broker's duties and obligations of confidentiality, full disclosure and loyalty to one party conflict with those same duties to the other. Seller and Buyer are *not* vicariously liable for acts of a Transaction Broker.

   a. If this addendum is signed by Seller, Broker will act as the exclusive agent for Seller only when the Property is shown to a prospective buyer who has a working relationship with another licensed real estate company, but will act as a Transaction Broker only in an In-Company Sale.

   b. If this addendum is signed by Buyer, Broker will act only as the exclusive agent for Buyer when showing properties that are not listed with Broker, but will act as a Transaction Broker only in an In-Company Sale.

The remaining provisions of this addendum describe significant changes to the obligations of Broker when acting as a Transaction Broker in an In-Company Sale.

3. **Information that Must be Disclosed by a Transaction Broker.**
   a. All adverse material facts actually known by Broker, including but not limited to adverse material facts pertaining to the title to the Property

Buyer/Seller: _____ _____ _____   Broker: _____ _____ _____   Page___of___
      initial initial date   initial initial date

which Seller indicates will not be remedied prior to the transfer of deed; and,

b. All information actually known to Broker, now or during the pre-closing period, regarding the physical condition of the property; and,

c. Any environmental hazards affecting the Property which are required by law to be disclosed.

4. **Matters that Can Not be Disclosed by a Transaction Broker.** Broker, when acting as a Transaction Broker, shall not disclose the following information without the prior consent of the party concerned:
   a. That Buyer is willing to pay more than the purchase price offered for the property;

   b. That Seller is willing to accept less than the asking price for the property;

   c. What the motivating factors are for any party buying or selling the property;

   d. That Seller or Buyer will agree to financing terms other than those offered;

   e. Any material information about the other party unless either:
      (1)   the disclosure is required by law,
      (2)   the disclosure pertains to adverse material facts about Buyer's financial ability to perform the terms of the transaction,
      (3)   the disclosure pertains to Buyer's intent to occupy the property as a principal residence, or
      (4)   failure to disclose such information would constitute fraud or dishonest dealing.

5. **No Duty for Transaction Broker to Investigate or Verify.** Broker, when acting as a Transaction Broker, has no duty to conduct an independent inspection of the property for the benefit of Buyer and has no duty to independently verify the accuracy or completeness of statements made by Seller or independent inspectors. Broker, when acting as a Transaction Broker, has no duty to conduct an independent investigation of Buyer's financial condition or to verify the accuracy or completeness of any statement made by Buyer.

6. **Commission.** Only one commission shall be payable. Buyer and Seller acknowledge that the commission paid to Broker is reflected in the price of the property sold. Seller shall pay Broker the commission indicated in the Exclusive Right to Sell Listing Contract. Buyer shall not be obligated to pay any additional commission to Broker.

_____   _____
Buyer/Seller   date   Buyer/Seller   date

Broker:_____

_____
by   date

In-Company Sale Addendum
(Transaction Broker)

The following procedures for In-Company Sales are hereby made a part of the either Seller Listing Contract, Buyer Agency Contract or Purchase and Sale Contract, dated _____ 20_____, between the undersigned real estate broker and its sales agents ("Broker") and Seller and/or Buyer, collectively, ("Parties"), hereby acknowledge the following:

Understanding

1. Seller engaged Broker to market Seller's property to any prospective buyer, including buyers who have initially established an agency relationship with Broker. Buyer wants to see any property which meets Buyer's needs, including property listed by Broker. In the event Buyer becomes interested in a property listed with Broker, Seller and Buyer then desire to engage Broker to assist them both in the transaction.
2. The Broker, when acting as an agent, has fiduciary duties to only one principal, Seller or Buyer. These duties include: reasonable care, obedience, performance, accounting for funds received, undivided loyalty, confidentiality and full disclosure.
3. The Broker can not act as an agent for both Buyer and Seller in the same transaction at the same time without creating a potential conflict of interest since Broker's fiduciary duties of confidentiality, full disclosure and loyalty to one party would conflict with those same duties to the other party.
4. The Broker can, however, act as a licensed real estate broker ("Transaction Broker"), namely a broker who assists both Parties throughout the purchase and sale transaction and not as an agent for either Seller or Buyer. To so act requires the prior written consent of all Parties.

Agreement

The Parties agree that for all transactions in which Broker may initially act as a buyer's agent or a seller's agent, and Buyer becomes interested in viewing a property listed by Broker ("In-Company Sale"), the law of agency shall not apply, and in such event, Buyer and/or Seller and Broker hereby modify Broker's duties to allow Broker to act as a Transaction Broker. Buyer and Seller hereby consent to and waive any and all objections to Broker acting as a Transaction Broker. In such transactions the Parties agree that the duties,

Buyer/Seller: _____ _____ _____   Broker: _____ _____ _____   Page____of____
          initial initial date   initial initial date

obligations and agreements between Broker and Buyer and/or Seller are as follows:

1. Broker shall assist but not represent either or both Parties, independently or through attorney(s), with: the preparation of the purchase and sale contract ("Contract"); completion of and compliance with the terms and conditions of the Contract; and the closing and settlement of the transaction, keeping both Buyer and Seller fully informed regarding all aspects of the transaction.
2. Broker shall comply with all rules and regulations of the governmental licensing authority which governs the conduct of licensees in real estate transactions and with the laws of this state.
3. Broker shall have the following duties to both Parties: reasonable care, obedience and performance, accounting for funds received, disclosure of all material facts about the physical condition of property actually known to Broker, and to treat all Parties honestly.
4. Broker shall not disclose personal information about one party to the other party, unless the disclosure is required by law, or unless failure to disclose would constitute fraud or dishonest dealing.
5. Broker shall not disclose that Buyer will pay a price or agree to terms other than those contained in the offer, or that Seller will accept a price or terms other than those contained in the listing.
6. Broker shall not disclose the motivation of Buyer to buy or Seller to sell.
7. Only one commission shall be payable. Buyer and Seller acknowledge that the commission paid to Broker is reflected in the price of the property sold. Seller shall pay Broker the commission indicated in Seller Listing Contract. Buyer shall not be obligated to pay any additional commission to Broker.
8. This Addendum will control in the event of any conflict with the contract to which it is attached.

_____   _____
Seller/Buyer   date   Seller/Buyer   date

Broker:_____   by _____

                                                            date

_____
Buyer/Seller: ____ ____ ____   Broker: ____ ____ ____   Page___of___
             initial initial date   initial initial date

In-Company Sale Transaction Broker Addendum

This Addendum is hereby made a part of either the Exclusive Right to Sell Listing Contract or the Exclusive Buyer Agency Contract, as the case may be ("Contract"), between the undersigned real estate broker and its salespersons ("Broker") and the undersigned Seller or Buyer, ("Client"), collectively ("Parties"). In the event the terms of this Addendum conflict with, vary from, or modify the terms and provisions of the Contract, the terms of this Addendum shall control. Seller includes landlord. Buyer includes tenant. Sale and purchase includes lease.

Fiduciary Duties. The Broker has fiduciary duties to the Client which include: *reasonable care* (to act in a reasonable manner); *undivided loyalty and confidentiality* (keeping the Client's confidences); *obedience and performance* (to comply with the Client's reasonable directions regarding the purchase and sale of real property); *accounting* (to disclose the status of all transactional money in broker's possession); and *full disclosure* (to transmit all relevant and material information known by Broker to the Client regarding the other buyer or seller).

Seller-Broker Relationship. When real property is listed for sale or lease by Seller with Broker, Broker acts initially as the agent of, and owes fiduciary duties to, Seller ("Seller's Agent"). The Broker shall treat Buyer honestly and shall disclose to Buyer all defects of a material nature affecting the physical condition of the property actually known to Broker. The Broker shall have no obligation to inspect the Property. The Broker shall not, without Seller's prior written consent, violate or modify Broker's duty of undivided loyalty, confidentiality and full disclosure.

Buyer-Broker Relationship. When a Buyer engages Broker to locate real property for purchase or lease, Broker shall act initially as the agent of, and owes fiduciary duties to, Buyer ("Buyer's Agent"). The Broker shall treat Seller honestly and shall not give Seller false information concerning the financial condition of Buyer, nor disclose the financial affairs of Buyer without Buyer's written consent. The Broker shall not, without Buyer's prior written consent, violate or modify Broker's duty of undivided loyalty, confidentiality and full disclosure.

"Out of Company" Sales. When Broker represents Seller, and a buyer is procured through a brokerage office other than Broker's office, Broker shall transmit to Seller all information known to Broker regarding the transaction and the proposed buyer. When Broker represents Buyer and the property is listed with a brokerage office other than Broker's office, Broker shall transmit to Buyer all information known to Broker regarding the transaction and the proposed seller.

In-Company Sales. A buyer may seek to acquire a property listed by a seller with Broker, an "In-Office" or "In-House" sale. In such a transaction, Broker would owe conflicting fiduciary duties to both buyer and seller at the same time, an inherent conflict of interest. The Broker can not represent the interests of either a buyer or a seller to the exclusion or detriment of the other buyer or seller. In order for Broker to assist both a buyer and a seller in such transactions, both need to consent in writing to allow Broker to act as a "Transaction Broker" only, and thereby modify their original agency Contract.

Transaction Broker Modification. The Parties agree that for all transactions wherein Broker may initially act as both a Buyer's Agent and a Seller's Agent, and the buyer becomes interested in a property listed by Broker, the law of agency shall not apply. Broker, except as herein indicated, shall cease to represent either the buyer or the seller as an agent in the same transaction. The Broker shall act as a Transaction Broker, a licensed real estate broker, who is neither the agent of Buyer nor of Seller, but who is charged with assisting the buyer and seller in completing the transaction as contemplated by Buyer and Seller. The following shall be the duties, obligations and agreements between Broker and both the buyer and the seller:

1. Broker shall exercise reasonable care, to act in a commercially reasonable manner, in the preparation of all documents and transmission of information. Broker shall answer all questions honestly but shall properly refuse to answer questions that might violate a duty of confidentiality to either buyer or seller.

2. Broker shall keep all former Client's confidences confidential, and not transmit any personal information known to Broker regarding either buyer or seller.

3. Broker shall be obedient, following the lawful directions of both buyer and seller, in the drafting of, and the fulfillment of, the terms of the

Buyer/Seller: _____ _____ _____   Broker: _____ _____ _____   Page___of___
             initial initial date   initial initial date

contract for sale. Broker shall assist both buyer and seller in complying with the terms and conditions precedent to the closing of the transaction and shall keep both buyer and seller fully informed regarding all aspects of the transaction.

4. Broker shall provide an accounting to buyer and seller, disclosing the status of all earnest money in Broker's possession.

5. Broker shall disclose and transmit to buyer and seller the information known by Broker regarding the physical condition of the property and the ability of the buyer to qualify for the contract as written.

6. Broker shall comply with all the rules and regulations of the governmental licensing agency which governs the conduct of licensees in real estate transactions and with the laws of this state.

7. Broker shall not give legal advice to anyone, including advice regarding the condition of the legal title to the property or the extent of the title insurance policy or exceptions.

8. Only one commission shall be payable. Buyer or seller acknowledges that the commission paid to Broker is reflected in the price of the property sold. Buyer and seller understand that seller shall pay Broker the commission indicated in the Exclusive Right to Sell Listing Contract. Buyer shall not be obligated to pay any additional commission to Broker.

9. A copy of this Addendum shall be a part of the final contract between the buyer and seller for the purchase, sale or lease of a property that comes within the purview of this Addendum.

The Parties acknowledge that this Addendum can not be entered into without the knowledge and written consent of all Parties. Each has read this Addendum and sought the advice of an attorney, if so desired.

_____   _____
Buyer/Seller   date   Buyer/Seller   date

Broker:_____   by _____
                                                                    date

_____
Buyer/Seller: ____ ____ ____   Broker: ____ ____ ____   Page___of___
              initial initial date   initial initial date

Dual (*Limited*) Agency Addendum

This Addendum is hereby made a part of either Seller Listing Contract, the Buyer Agency Contract and/or the Purchase and Sale Contract ("Contract"), between the undersigned real estate broker and its salespersons ("Broker") and the undersigned Seller and/or Buyer, ("Client"), collectively ("Parties"). In the event the terms of this Addendum conflict with, vary from, or modify the terms and provisions of the Contract, the terms of this Addendum shall control. Seller includes landlord. Buyer includes tenant. Sale and purchase includes lease.

Fiduciary Duties. The Broker has fiduciary duties to the Client which include: *reasonable care* (to act in a reasonable manner); *undivided loyalty and confidentiality* (keeping the Client's confidences); *obedience and performance* (to comply with the Client's reasonable directions regarding the purchase and sale of real property); *accounting* (to disclose the status of all transactional money in broker's possession) and *full disclosure* (to transmit all relevant and material information known by Broker to the Client regarding the other buyer or seller).

Seller-Broker Relationship. When real property is listed for sale or lease by Seller with Broker, Broker acts initially as the agent of, and owes fiduciary duties to, Seller ("Seller's Agent"). The Broker shall treat Buyer honestly and shall disclose to Buyer all defects of a material nature affecting the physical condition of the property actually known to Broker. The Broker shall have no obligation to inspect the Property. The Broker shall not, without Seller's prior written consent, violate or modify Broker's duty of undivided loyalty, confidentiality and full disclosure.

Buyer-Broker Relationship. When a Buyer engages Broker to locate real property for purchase or lease, Broker shall act initially as the agent of, and owes fiduciary duties to, Buyer ("Buyer's Agent"). The Broker shall treat Seller honestly and shall not give Seller false information concerning the financial condition of Buyer, nor disclose the financial affairs of Buyer without Buyer's written consent. The Broker shall not, without Buyer's prior written consent, violate or modify Broker's duty of undivided loyalty, confidentiality and full disclosure.

Buyer/Seller: _____ _____ _____   Broker: _____ _____ _____   Page___of___
             initial initial date   initial initial date

"Out of Company" or "Cooperative" Sales. When Broker represents the seller, and a buyer is procured through a brokerage office other than Broker's office, Broker shall transmit to seller all information known to Broker regarding the transaction and the proposed buyer. When Broker represents Buyer, and the property is listed with a brokerage office other than Broker's office, Broker shall transmit to Buyer all information known to Broker regarding the transaction and the proposed seller.

In-Company Sales. A buyer may seek to acquire a property listed by a seller with Broker, an "In-Company," "In-Office" or "In-House" sale. In such a transaction, Broker would owe conflicting fiduciary duties to both buyer and seller at the same time, an inherent conflict of interest. The Broker can not represent the interests of either a buyer or a seller to the exclusion or detriment of the other buyer or seller. In order for Broker to assist both a buyer and a seller in such transactions, both need to consent in writing to allow Broker to act as a "Dual (Limited) Agent," modifying their original agency Contract.

Dual (Limited) Agency Modification. The Parties agree that for all transactions wherein Broker may initially act as both a Buyer's Agent and a Seller's Agent, and the buyer becoming interested in a property listed by Broker, Broker, except as herein indicated, shall provide *limited* representation to both Buyer or Seller in the same transaction. The Broker shall act as a Limited Dual Agent for both Buyer and Seller. The following shall be the duties, obligations and agreements between Broker and both the buyer and the seller:

1. Broker shall exercise *reasonable care*, to act in a commercially reasonable manner, in the preparation of all documents and transmission of information. Broker shall answer all questions honestly, but properly shall refuse to answer questions that might violate a duty of confidentiality to either buyer or seller.

2. Broker shall keep the former Client's confidences *confidential*, and not transmit any personal information known to Broker regarding either the buyer or the seller.

3. Broker shall be *obedient*, following the lawful directions of both buyer and seller, in the drafting of, and fulfillment of, the terms of the contract for sale. Broker shall assist both buyer and seller in complying with the

terms and conditions precedent to the closing of the transaction and shall keep both buyer and seller fully informed regarding all aspects of the transaction.

4. Broker shall provide an *accounting* to everyone, disclosing the status of all earnest money in Broker's possession.

5. Broker shall *disclose*, and transmit to buyer and seller the information known by Broker regarding the physical condition of the property and the ability of the buyer to qualify for the contract as written.

6. Broker shall comply with all the rules and regulations of the governmental regulatory agency which governs the conduct of licensees in real estate transactions and with the laws of this state.

7. Broker shall not give legal advice to anyone, including advice regarding the condition of the legal title to the property or the extent of the title insurance policy or exceptions.

8. Only one commission shall be payable. Buyer or seller acknowledge that the commission paid to Broker is reflected in the price of the property sold. Buyer and seller understand that seller shall pay Broker the commission indicated in the Exclusive Right to Sell Listing Contract. Buyer shall not be obligated to pay any additional commission to Broker.

9. A copy of this Addendum shall be a part of the final contract between the buyer and seller for the purchase, sale or lease of property.

The Parties acknowledge that this Addendum can not be entered into without the knowledge and written consent of all of the Parties. Each has read this Addendum and sought the advice of an attorney, if they so desired.

_____   _____
Seller/Buyer   date   Seller/Buyer   date

Broker:_____

_____
by   date

Buyer/Seller: ___ ___ ___   Broker: ___ ___ ___   Page___of___
    initial initial date   initial initial date

Dual (*Limited*) Agency Addendum
(For use with In-Company Sales Only)

This Dual (*Limited*) Agency Addendum is hereby made part of either an Exclusive Right to Sell Listing Contract or an Exclusive Buyer Agency Contract between the broker named below and its sales agents ("Broker") and the undersigned buyer or seller ("Principal"), or a Purchase and Sale Contract between a seller and a buyer.

The undersigned Principal(s) acknowledge that:

1. Principal is a buyer interested in viewing any property which buyer feels might suit buyer's needs, including property listed by a seller with Broker.

2. Principal is a seller interested in marketing a property to any prospective buyer, including buyers who have an agency relationship with Broker.

3. The Broker acting for a single Principal, seller or buyer, owes that Principal a duty of undivided loyalty, confidentiality and full disclosure.

4. Dual (*Limited*) Agency, when Broker owes duties of undivided loyalty, confidentiality and full disclosure to both a buyer and a seller, creates a conflict of interest.

5. The Broker can act as a Dual (*Limited*) Agent of both Principals, a seller and a buyer, in the same transaction, only upon the prior written consent of Broker, buyer and seller.

Principal(s) and Broker hereby agree:

1. Principal(s) hereby consents or ratifies Principal's previous consent (re-affirm by signing again when made an exhibit to the sale contract) to this modification to provide that Broker's duties are modified, so that Broker may act as a Dual (*Limited*) Agent and hereby waives all objections to Broker acting as a Dual (*Limited*) Agent for a transaction for the sale of seller's property to buyer, wherein Broker initially represented seller and buyer.

Buyer/Seller: ___ ___ ___   Broker: ___ ___ ___   Page___of___
           initial initial date   initial initial date

2. Once Broker becomes a Dual (*Limited*) Agent, and so informs both Principals, Broker shall not disclose to either seller or buyer, without the prior written consent of the other, any of the following information:

   a. Material information regarding the other party, unless disclosure is required by law, or unless failure to disclose would constitute fraud or dishonest dealing.

   b. That the buyer will pay a price or agree to terms other than those contained in the proposed offer to purchase, or that seller will accept a price or terms other than those contained in the listing agreement.

   c. The motivation of the buyer to buy or the seller to sell.

   d. Information protected by any applicable "Fair Housing" laws and regulations and information which "psychologically impacts" the property.

3. The Broker shall disclose all information regarding the physical condition of the property actually known to Broker and information indicating if the buyer can qualify for the contract as written. Broker is not obligated to inspect the property.

4. Broker shall be entitled to one commission, which the Parties agree is reflected in the purchase price, indicated in the Exclusive Right To Sell Listing Agreement.

5. This Addendum shall control in the event of any conflict with the contract to which it is attached.

_____   _____
Seller/Buyer   date   Seller/Buyer   date

Broker:_____

_____
by   date

Buyer/Seller: _____ _____ _____   Broker: _____ _____ _____   Page___of___
             initial initial date   initial initial date

Designated Agency Addendum

This Addendum is hereby made part of either the Seller Listing Contract, the Buyer Agency Contract or the Purchase and Sale Contract between the below indicated Parties, dated _____20____.

[Check only one box and initial]

☐ ____ ____ ____ ____**Designated "Split" Agency.** In the event Buyer and Seller are working with or represented by Broker through *separate* Salespersons, for the sale of a listed property the parties hereby agree that:

 1. The selling Salesperson represents the buyer exclusively; and,

 2. The listing Salesperson represents the seller exclusively; and,

 3. The Broker shall be a Dual Agent, defined below; and,

 4. Seller shall pay the commission indicated in the listing agreement; and,

 5. Buyer shall not pay an additional commission; and,

 6. Broker and Salespersons shall share in the commission; and,

 7. No knowledge shall be imputed to Broker.

☐ ____ ____ ____ ____**Dual Agency.** In the event Buyer and Seller are working with or represented by Broker through *the same* Salesperson, for the sale of a listed property, the Parties hereby agree that:

 1. A conflict of interest exists because the parties' interests may be different; and,

 2. Broker and Salesperson shall act as Dual Agents of both Seller and Buyer; and,

 3. Dual Agents *shall not*:
    a. Disclose any price or terms other than those indicated by Buyer or Seller;
    b. Disclose the motivating factors of either Buyer or Seller; nor the price that Seller is willing to accept;

Buyer/Seller: ____ ____ ____   Broker: ____ ____ ____   Page___of___
           initial initial date   initial initial date

c. Disclose any confidential information about a party;

d. Advocate or promote the interests of a party;

e. Give advice to any party to the detriment of the other party;

f. Disclose any material information about a party unless:

    i) the disclosure is required by law; or,

    ii) the disclosure pertains to adverse material facts about Buyer's ability to perform the terms of the transaction or occupy the property; or,

    iii) failure to disclose would constitute fraud or dishonest dealing.

g. Impute knowledge to Broker.

4. Dual Agents shall:

    a. Disclose all material facts actually known to Broker or Salesperson pertaining to the physical condition, including environmental hazards, of the property; and,

    b. Assist the parties with the preparation of the contract; and,

    c. Assist the parties with financing and closing of the transaction.

☐ _____ _____ _____ _____**No Agency/Transaction Broker.** In the event Buyer and/or Seller is working with, or is represented by Broker through *any* Salesperson, for the sale of a property *listed with or not listed with* Broker and both parties elect not to have an agency relationship, the Parties hereby agree that:

1. A conflict of interest may exist because the Parties' interests may be different; and,

2. Broker and Salesperson shall *not act as agents of either* Seller or Buyer; and,

3. Broker and Salesperson (Non Agents) *shall not:*

    a. Disclose any price or terms other than those indicated by Buyer or Seller; or,

    b. Disclose the motivating factors of either Buyer or Seller; nor the price that Seller is willing to accept or Buyer willing to offer; or,

    c. Disclose any confidential information about a party; or,

    d. Advocate or promote the interests of a party; or,

    e. Give advice to any party to the detriment of the other party;, or

    f. Disclose any material information about a party unless:

        i) the disclosure is required by law; or,

    ii) the disclosure pertains to adverse material facts about the buyer's ability to perform the terms of the transaction or occupy the property; or,

    iii) failure to disclose would constitute fraud or dishonest dealing.

    g. Impute knowledge to Broker.

4. Broker and Salesperson (Non Agent) *shall*:

    a. Disclose all material facts actually known to Broker or Salesperson pertaining to the physical condition, including environmental hazards, of the property; and,

    b. Assist the parties with the preparation of the contract; and,

    c. Assist the parties with financing and closing of the transaction.

_____   _____
Buyer   date   Seller   date

_____   _____
Buyer   date   Seller   date

Broker:

_____

_____   _____
by Salesperson   date   by Salesperson   date

Designated "Split" Agency Contract Addendum

This Addendum is hereby made part of either the Seller Listing Contract, the Buyer Agency Contract or the Purchase and Sale Contract between the below indicated Parties.

[Check only one box and initial]

☐ _____ _____ _____ _____**Designated "Split" Agency.** In the event Buyer and Seller are working with or represented by Broker through *separate* Salespersons, for the sale of a listed property, the Parties hereby agree that:
1. The selling Salesperson represents the buyer exclusively; and,

2. The listing Salesperson represents the seller exclusively; and,

3. The Broker shall be a Dual Agent, defined below; and,

4. Seller shall pay the commission indicated in the listing agreement; and,

5. Buyer shall not pay an additional commission; and,

6. Broker and Salespersons shall share in the commission; and,

7. No knowledge shall be imputed to Broker.

☐ _____ _____ _____ _____**Dual Agency.** In the event Buyer and Seller are working with or are represented by Broker through *the same* Salesperson, for the sale of a listed property, the Parties hereby agree that:
1. A conflict of interest exists because the parties' interests may be different; and,

2. Broker and Salesperson shall act as Dual Agents of both Seller and Buyer; and,

3. Dual Agents *shall not*:
   a. Disclose any price or terms other than those indicated by Buyer or Seller; or,
   b. Disclose the motivating factors of either Buyer or Seller, nor the price that Seller is willing to accept; or,

---

Buyer/Seller: _____ _____ _____   Broker: _____ _____ _____   Page___of___
             initial initial date   initial initial date

     c. Disclose any confidential information about a party; or,

     d. Advocate or promote the interests of a party; or,

     e. Give advice to any party to the detriment of the other party; or,

     f. Disclose any material information about a party unless:

        i) the disclosure is required by law; or,

        ii) the disclosure pertains to adverse material facts about Buyer's ability to perform the terms of the transaction or occupy the property; or,

        iii) failure to disclose would constitute fraud or dishonest dealing,

     g. Impute knowledge to Broker.

4. Dual Agents shall:

     a. Disclose all material facts actually known to Broker or Salesperson pertaining to the physical condition, including environmental hazards, of the property; and,

     b. Assist the parties with the preparation of the contract; and,

     c. Assist the parties with financing and closing of the transaction.

☐ ____ ____ ____ ____**No Agency/Transaction Broker.** In the event Buyer and/or Seller is working with or is represented by Broker through *any* Salesperson, for the sale of a property *listed with or not listed with* Broker, and both parties elect not to have an agency relationship, the parties hereby agree that:

1. A conflict of interest may exist because the parties' interests may be different; and,

2. Broker and Salesperson shall *not act as agents of either* Seller or Buyer; and,

3. Broker and Salesperson (Non Agents) *shall not*:

     a. Disclose any price or terms other than those indicated by Buyer or Seller; or,

     b. Disclose the motivating factors of either Buyer or Seller, nor the price that Seller is willing to accept; or,

     c. Disclose any confidential information about a party; or,

     d. Advocate or promote the interests of a party; or,

     e. Give advice to any party to the detriment of the other party; or,

     f. Disclose any material information about a party unless:

        i) the disclosure is required by law; or,

ii) the disclosure pertains to adverse material facts about Buyer's ability to perform the terms of the transaction or occupy the property; or,

iii) failure to disclose would constitute fraud or dishonest dealing.

g. Impute knowledge to Broker.

4. Broker and Salesperson (Non Agents) *shall*:

a. Disclose all material facts actually known to Broker or Salesperson pertaining to the physical condition, including environmental hazards, of the property; and,

b. Assist the parties with the preparation of the contract; and,

c. Assist the parties with financing and closing of the transaction.

No Duty for Dual Agent or Transaction Broker to Investigate. Broker and Salesperson(s) have no duty to: 1) conduct an independent inspection of the property for the benefit of Buyer; or 2) independently verify the accuracy or completeness of statements made by Seller or independent inspectors; or 3) conduct an independent investigation of Buyer's financial condition; or, 4) verify the accuracy or completeness of any statement made by Buyer.

_____   _____
Buyer   date   Seller   date

_____   _____
Buyer   date   Seller   date

Broker:_____

_____
by Salesperson   date

_____
by Salesperson   date

Chapter 5

The Contract

Drafting the Offer and Counteroffer

General Contract Drafting Tips

The contract will govern the entire transaction. Use care in drafting it. Filling in the blanks is one thing, but drafting extensive "additional provisions" is quite another. Some say that the drafting or use of lots of additional provisions is the unauthorized practice of law.

After the contract is signed, the terms are fixed. From this point forward the agreement is set in stone. The agreement should never be modified orally. Always use an amend/extend form or other contract amendment form executed by both the buyers and the sellers – all of them. Amendments or extensions can only be accomplished via written mutual consent of all parties to the contract.

Agency is no longer an issue in the transaction. The real estate professional is charged with making certain that the terms of the contract are carried out. It is your job to not interfere with the contract throughout the closing process. On the contrary, you are to expedite that process no matter whom you think you represent. To interfere is considered to be "tortuous interference with contract." It would be wise for home transfer and home guarantee companies to understand this concept.

Although this is not a complete forms manual for completing a sales contract, the authors have included multiple clauses that pertain to items discussed in this book. As always, check with your local attorney and/or broker on usage in your area. Think of these clauses as a place to start, make you think and get the creative juices running. Caution, not all states allow you to draft your own clauses. Many consider even using forms like these as the unauthorized practice of law. You should know the law in your state.

Timing. You will often need to condition a contract term on a certain date. Try hard to set the contract to run in 4-5 phases in order to make compliance with performance deadlines easy to understand and accomplish. This way many of the events will come due on the same day and make it easier to track.

Phase 1. The document delivery, loan application phase. We like to specify that the documents that need to be delivered, whether from buyer to seller or the reverse, are all accomplished in the first week. Some people prefer a period of five to twelve days after acceptance of the contract. It is your decision. Either select to have the dates tied to "acceptance," or use specific dates. The following items are not all inclusive. The entire document delivery process would be facilitated if the listing broker routinely left the documents to be delivered to the buyer on the property in a package, so that they all could be attached to the contract when written.

Items to be delivered to the buyer include:
- Title commitment or abstract and the supporting documents
- Long legal description
- Copies of surveys
- Seller's Property Disclosure Form
- Lead Based Paint Form
- Disclosure of "off record matters" (unrecorded easements, etc.)
- Condominium and home owners association documents and financial statements

These may be in the form of actual paper documentation, but with more frequency, they can be obtained on a CD or DVD from a secure website for the transaction. [Hint: Always obtain for the buyer the actual paperwork that supports any exceptions to title.] These documents are for the *buyer* to review, not you. Do not fall into the trap of interpreting the content. Assist the buyer with any questions by guiding them to the expert in the field. For instance, direct title questions to a real estate attorney or the title officer and property disclosure discrepancies to an inspector or engineer. Do not assume the role of defendant.

Other things that the buyer should be doing in this time period:
- Make a loan application
- Verify the availability of hazard insurance
- Make a determination a to whether a survey or improvement location certificate will be needed
- Order the survey or improvement location certificate
- Order the appraisal
- Order inspection(s)

Items is to be delivered to the seller include:
- In the event of an owner carry finance, the buyer's financial information (financial statement, income tax returns, etc.)
- Loan commitment letter if the buyer had a pre-approval

Phase 2. The Objection ("Fuss") Phase. We like to specify that the buyer elect to object to the property or other items and then nullify the contract or attempt to resolve the issues (amend/extend) in the second week. This would be one week following the document delivery and loan application (Phase 1). Within this period as many issues as possible are addressed and resolved, so that everyone knows if the buyer is in or out of contract.

Items to be addressed in this phase are:
- Inspection of the property and resolution of issues
- Inspection of the title and resolution of issues
- Inspection of the matters that are "off-record," not recorded (easements, etc)
- Selection of loan terms, if one is warranted

Phase 3. The Loan Approval. We like to specify that this is the third week after contract drafting, and a week after all inspection objections are addressed and resolved. As with all of these time periods, adjust to suit your area or the particular transaction. By the end of this time period, the buyer is definitely in contract or not, as a result of the loan condition and the appraisal.

Items to be addressed may include:
- Loan approval
- Appraisal
- Receipt and review of the survey if ordered (While it would have been preferable to have this in Phase 2, the survey often is not ordered until after the property inspection is finished in order to save money.)

Phase 4. Final Approvals. This phase is optional and is generally one week after Phase 3. Just think of it as a time period to address items that are not going to be resolved in the earlier time periods. This is the time to get everything set and obtain agreement on all amendments. Sometimes this phase is necessary for late loan approval or a late appraisal that you want to occur after the survey period. We are in the final stages of preparation for closing.

Phase 5. Closing. There needs to be at least a week after the end of Phase 3 or 4, as the case may be. We like to allow the buyer, and especially the seller, sufficient time to prepare for the move, knowing that the conditions are all met. At this stage they can be assured that closing is a very real probability.

Attempt to have as few dates as possible on which contingencies or conditions must be completed rather than continuously creating additional date expirations. If at all possible link things to the property inspection date, Phase 2.

Keep the language simple. If you can not understand it, how will a judge ever understand the intent? Only draft terms or clauses you are capable of drafting and legal for you to draft. Do not place yourself in the position of defendant in order to save your client or customer money. The buyer and seller want to *use* you and then *sue* you when you fail. Know when to call the attorney and then call one.

Closing Date. "Date of Delivery of Deed" The actual closing date, recordation date or date that the property is conveyed or the deed is delivered to buyer, should be a date that is realistic for all parties. It is preferable to have closing and delivery of the deed occur on the same date and on a weekday if possible. Allow time for mailing closing documents and mortgage documents if the entities are in different geographical locations. Unfortunately, you can not always rely upon the postal service to deliver in a timely manner. Also, ascertain early in the transaction if either the buyer or seller will require a power of attorney. Again, the title company, mortgage lender and attorney must have the correct information in order to prepare documents properly for final closing.

Contingencies or Conditions. Remember the difference between promises and contingencies. Terms must be written to reflect the intent of the party who will benefit, provide a time limit for the term to be satisfied and a provision for the consequences in the event of non-compliance. By writing "Buyer to make loan application," the seller may have no recourse in the event of non-performance. "The obligation of the seller to sell is contingent upon the buyer making loan application within five days of acceptance" provides both an avenue for declaring the contract null and void as well as setting a deadline for satisfaction of the contingency.

Do not neglect to provide for the return of the buyer's deposits with deductions, if any, in the event a contingency is not met by a specific deadline. When a contingency depends upon an approval by either the buyer, seller, or third party, it is best to indicate that written disapproval must be provided within a specific time frame in order to declare the contract null and void, or that approval will be deemed to be granted and the contingency thereby removed.

Creative Financing. More than any other aspect of a transaction, except possibly an undetectable defect in the condition of the property which was not discoverable and which does not show its ugly head until well after the closing, financing has become the hotbed of potential liability and loss. Much like latent defects, problems with financing can exist in a dormant state well into the future. The advent of complex arrangements and extensive television coverage of what some might consider "creative" methods of acquisition and financing that are not normally utilized, has only partially educated the public and left them often worse off than before the process began.   The misconceptions about financing that prevail among all segments of society, and even in the ranks of attorneys and some real estate professionals, never cease to amaze us.

The disclosure and explanation of the seller's involvement in the financing is best given at the time the listing contract is completed. Because the subject of financing alternatives may be lost in the multitude of other concerns during the initial marketing process, it may be appropriate to repeat the seller's financing involvement again at the time of the presentation of a contract. In any event, before the seller or buyer signs a contract that indicates seller involvement in the existing financing, a disclosure must be made.

The existing responsibility of the seller and/or the new obligation of the buyer to repay the existing loan can be altered dramatically in a transfer of property.   With an assumption – the promise to pay the debt of another – the buyer is added to the list of obligors on the promissory note. If the transfer is subject to the existing promissory note, the seller remains solely responsible for the loan payment, and the buyer is not personally liable to pay. With a novation, the seller is released of any future obligation to repay the loan, and the buyer is responsible for the loan's repayment. In addition, any of the foregoing alternatives can be coupled with a seller carry-back or owner-carry second mortgage.

Assumable financing may be the very factor that induces a buyer to purchase a particular house.   However, the agent often fails to explain adequately the ramifications of the different alternatives until after the contract has been accepted or even after the closing. Even though assumable, the seller often remains liable for the payment of the debt. Assumable does not mean that the seller is released from liability.

Caution. *The "free living" effect. As a result of the slow economic conditions existing in some areas, the time-consuming and previously obscure foreclosure laws, the rules preventing or delaying the entry of deficiency judgments in some states, and the delay imposed as a result of the modern Bankruptcy Code, some owners are realizing that they can stop making payments on the existing loan – whether they assumed it or took the property subject to the loan – and live in the residence from six to eighteen months rent free. The longest term Oliver knows was forty-two months – that's right, forty-two months – without the owner making a single payment.*

A family with any income can amass a good deal of money in that time period. Therefore, they have the down payment for the next home when they are finally removed from their current residence. You got it. This person now has the cash to assume another non-qualifying assumption (VA and FHA, subject to some restrictions, and some private and conventional financing) and could be looking at your current listing. Buyers with that kind of cash are rarely the subject of scrutiny, almost never trigger the request for a credit report, are hard to recognize and even harder for some brokers and sellers and other desperate people to turn down.

Default. Draft the contract carefully, so that you clearly indicate the responsibilities of each party. In the event of a default, as the drafter of the contract, you will immediately be on the hot seat to explain the term and the element of default. Write clearly. Use simple sentences. Avoid complex punctuation. For one thought, use one sentence.

Either the buyer or seller may be in default. Before you get carried away, remember that in almost all circumstances, it is difficult to demand specific performance from either party. Rarely is the seller forced to sell or the buyer compelled to purchase. Damages and/or attorney's fees may be the most realistic recourse for either party. In most circumstances the seller will not compel performance and will be relegated to retention of the earnest money. If the earnest money is substantial, litigation is almost assured.

Fraud and the Government Loan. With the tendency of the federal government agencies, especially the FHA and the VA, to be apparently unresponsive and unaware of what is happening in the world, some people have decided that the regulations that govern such loans are like the fifty-five mile speed limit. They believe that the regulations are ineffective, unrealistic, often unenforced and carrying only a inconsequential penalty when adjudicated. You can be assured that although these giants appear to have a hard time getting anything accomplished and appear oblivious to the transgressions that are occurring, they have enlisted, in addition to their own in-house staff of overworked investigators, a cadre of FBI agents and the offices of the U.S. Attorney to assist in their search for, and prosecution of, those that are defrauding the government.

Some real estate licensees still are trying to have someone obtain an "owner occupant" loan, when in fact the prospective borrower never intends to live in the property. Others have determined that a new FHA loan enhances the marketability of the property and are encouraging sellers to refinance and then sell the property. Yet another group is encouraging people to refinance and immediately sell to a buyer procured prior to the refinance.

The professional broker and agent, while never engaging in such activities, may be caught in the ever-expanding net thrown to capture the true offenders. Care needs to be taken in even the most routine transaction involving government loans to ensure that everything is properly completed. When the pressure starts, the buyer and seller point to the broker as being responsible.

The following case in point, while not exactly indicative of the foregoing, exemplifies the ramifications of what appears to be a normal transaction for a hectic agent.

Case in Point.

The hurried, experienced agent (ten years plus in the business) answers a call on an advertisement for the sale of a friend's property. A smooth showing results in a contract indicating a new VA loan. The agent takes the buyer to the lender who "does all my business." The loan goes through the normal process and is approved and ready to close. A delay in funding forces the lender to re-verify the employment of the purchaser. The call to the employer results in the reply: "He has never worked for my husband."

The lender contacts the agent who talks with the buyer who assures the agent that all is well; he just does not get along with the spouse of the boss. Believing the buyer he barely knows, the agent suggests to the lender that it is all a mistake. The lender calls the VA who comes to see the agent. Believing that the truth is a good defense and easily noticed by trained investigators, the real estate agent talks to the investigating agents, who include an FBI agent, and explains all he knows.

The result is that the agent is involved in a grand jury investigation which almost leads to his being indicted on several felony counts. The buyer, who never was employed by anyone, had sent the verification to himself. When confronted by the investigators, the buyer replied, "The agent thought up the entire scam."

Fortunately, the investigators also later talked with the friend-employer. Poorer now from attorney's fees but still married, sane and alive, the agent pleads guilty to a misdemeanor and bargains for two years probation, not because he is guilty, but because he can not win. During that time the agent will not be allowed to be involved in any VA loans.

The good news for this case is that the prohibition against being involved in VA loans is reduced to only those transactions involving the agent. Formerly, it had been anyone associated with the agent. How could an office list property in good faith if VA financing was not an alternative for any buyer or seller?

The result was that a very good real estate professional almost lost it all. The lessons are clear and simple. Know at least a little about your buyer; maybe make a call to the place of work. Realize that due to the efforts of a terrible few, government loans are under attack and your reputation, which was made one deal at a time over a long period of time, may be the only thing that can save you when the going gets tough. In this case, a good reputation was one of the deciding factors.

Fraud in the Price. Some unsuspecting brokers find that they wrote the contract for a high price, so that the buyer could get an 80% loan based upon that price. The "actual" price is far less than indicated in the contract. The penalty for that conduct is time in the penitentiary. Seriously, such schemes are really conspiracies to defraud a local lender, or a federally insured lender. If you are at a loss for housing needs and want the state or federal government to make housing available to you on a long term basis, this is the course of action to take. Remember that your choice of roommates will be made for you and that these are not patio homes, but more of the dormitory system.

Names. When working with multiple parties as buyers or sellers, use the entire name for each entity. Married couples should be addressed as Sandy Reece and Kim Reece, instead of Sandy and Kim Reece. Use the "and" and "or" as applicable and not "and/or." And/or implies differing connotations to different people. Does it mean either? Does it mean both? It is best just to say "and" if you mean a group and "or" if you mean either.

Party Designation. Use the same designation for the players throughout the contract and all addenda. Once you refer to the buyers as "Buyers," do not alter the designation to "Purchasers." Use the same terminology throughout the contract. We find the easiest way to avoid the single party or multiple party designations is to use Buyer(s).

Power of Attorney. These should not be prepared by a licensee. To do so is the unauthorized practice of law in almost every state, not to mention the fact that the chance of an error is large. In addition, the power of attorney must fulfill the requirements of those who will accept them in lieu of the signature of the grantor. Make sure that the proposed power of attorney is approved by the lender and title company. One option is to have the title company or lender initial the approved form in the lower left hand corner. Finally, everyone wants an original, so when the power of attorney is drafted, make six copies prior to signing. Then have all of them signed, and you now have duplicate originals for each person who requests one, as well as one for your file.

Price and Loan Adjustments. Discount points and loan origination fees also need complete, timely and adequate presentation prior to the seller or buyer becoming obligated to a contract. Does the seller have to pay the agreed-upon discount even if the buyer uses the money to obtain a lower interest rate? Is a discount point different from a loan origination fee? The payment of large sums to induce a lender to make a loan is being viewed by some regulators as a reduction in the effective purchase price and, consequently, a reduction of the amount upon which the commission is calculated. The use of zero coupon bonds, gems or questionable paper to offset the purchase price is receiving close scrutiny. Sometimes it can be very embarrassing when the broker can not explain the ramifications of using such items.

Case in Point.

*At the direction and suggestion of the purchaser, a broker provides in the contract that a seller accept a zero coupon bond as partial payment of the listed price in order to obtain the full listed price, which both purchaser and seller have verbally agreed is in excess of the fair market value of the property. The bond had a current market value of about $2,000 and a future value, upon redemption in twenty years, of about $12,000. The seller is to give the purchaser a credit equal to the **future** value of the bond. It was easy for the licensee to just go along with the transaction. However, this was not equitable for the seller.*

The transaction closes pursuant to the terms of the contract, and the bond is purchased and delivered to the seller. The seller, now out of state and looking for a method to extract funds from the broker, files a complaint with the Real Estate Commission. They determine that there should have been no commission charged on the amount of the purchase price represented by the future value of the bond and "suggest" that the broker make an appropriate refund. It was nice that they did not try to get the broker to buy the bond today at tomorrow's price.

How lucky the broker was. In this particular case he did nothing wrong. However, with a little change in circumstances, he could have had a securities problem. He could have had a problem with the side agreement that was not available to the new lender who made the new loan. The lender thought that there really was a credit of $12,000.00, not the present value of the bond. He *could have gone to jail. Do not worry, he is still out there waiting to be your subagent.*

Rough Draft. The ease or "dis-ease" with which any transaction reaches final closing is primarily dependent upon how well the contract is written in the first place. Whether you represent the buyer submitting an offer, represent the seller in preparation of a counteroffer, or simply are a real estate broker in a neutral position, draft the first contract in pencil. Yes, write the entire proposal in pencil, or on the computer with "draft" written over the page, to force you to review and rethink the terms. It is rare to be able to include all that is important on a first draft that will, in fact, be in the final copy. Try not only to determine the conditions that must be addressed and the time periods within which these conditions must be satisfied, but also the default or waiver of rights in the event a particular action is not taken.

Of course, there are those times when you are writing the proposal on the hood of the car, in the airport before the buyer or seller catches the next flight and in the fast food booth with ketchup dripping on the papers. *Expediency should never become more important than accuracy.* In instances such as these, using a manual of clauses as a guideline is critical. It is much simpler to pick and choose the exact phraseology than rely on composing a complete clause when you may be too tired to think. Resist the temptation to "wing it" without prior approval from your broker. An incomplete or "open ended" condition will only lead to misconceptions and misunderstandings during the closing process. The key to a smooth transaction is to foresee any possible problems that may arise during the course of the escrow or closing process and address them in the proposal.

Whether representing the client in an agency capacity or assisting the customer when you have no agency status, you must be certain to present all the options to the buyer and/or seller. It is the salesperson's duty to provide information on all of the options that are available, so that the buyer or seller may make their own decisions.

Side Agreements – "Suicide" Agreements. The use of the term alone should trigger the conscience of most real estate professionals. Why is there an agreement that can not be a part of the contract? There can be no answer other than that the facts expressed in the side agreement are to be concealed from someone who, had they known all of the facts of the proposed transaction, would have reacted in a fashion different from what was intended– also often referred to as "Criminal Fraud on a Federally Chartered or Insured Lender."

With the exception of such obvious motivations such as keeping a relative or mother-in-law from knowing where you are moving or the purchasing of commercial property as an undisclosed agent, there are very few times when any side agreement is appropriate. This is a good area to avoid. The "If I do not see it, it does not exist" ostrich theory offers no safe haven. Once you know of an irregularity, you are under several, often conflicting, duties to report to the lender, the government, the seller, the buyer, your board and, always, your broker. Do not be a co-conspirator.

Case in Point.

The listing agent, who is a friend of the wife of a client-couple involved in a divorce, agrees to list the property for one commission and rebate a portion of the commission to the wife. The other seller, the husband, has no knowledge of this "side agreement." Is that not fraud? Are not both the sellers your clients? Could your breach of fiduciary duty to one client result in your refunding the entire commission? Yes.

The final straw is the agent's remark when questioned. He said, "I just wanted to help the wife. You know we have been friends for a long time."

Remember that the fiduciary duty is owed by an agent to all the principals.

Standard Forms.   Always use the standard forms proffered by your board or association, real estate commission and/or by your real estate office. There is no excuse for not starting with these forms. Expediency in preparation is not a good defense. The judge will want to know why you did something different from the standard practice for this particular buyer or seller, especially if some protection is lost.

Standard Builder Contract.   Many builders, feeling for whatever reason that the forms offered by whatever agency of the government, a board or the bar association, are not as they would wish them, have developed a specific form for the use of all agents working through their listing broker. Although there is no prohibition indicating that a prospective buyer can not utilize any form that strikes his fancy, these sellers are so heavily regulated and concerned about litigation that they will generally insist that all offers be on their form. Only the pressure of the market can alter this firm stance. The broker needs to make his agents and subagents aware of the seller's requirements. At the same time s/he must indicate to all concerned that the broker is not responsible for the contents of, or omissions in, this or any other form.

Non-Standard Builder Contracts. The tendency for some licensees to use the regular re-sale contract for a new home is fraught with peril. The resale contract anticipates a house that is already constructed. Use of this form with some sort of addenda is never as wise as using a proper form for a new home currently under construction, or soon to be so. Yes, that might necessitate an attorney. If there were ever a time when you needed to refer someone to an attorney, this is the time. Attempting to "draft" and include all the contingencies that might occur are the areas where the licensee gets into trouble,

Transfers Without Prior Lender Consent, Silent Assumptions. With rates being as low as they have been lately, this form of financing is less prevalent than it was a few years ago. Still, many people decide to run the risk of a transfer without the prior consent of the lender, sometimes known as a "silent assumption." Since the advent of new FHA rules, this may become a more prevalent situation if notification of FHA is not desired by one or both of the parties. Such an assumption requires, as a minimum, an absolute disclaimer prior to contract acceptance. This is one instance where, no matter how firm the disclaimer, the parties will go ahead and do as they please anyway. Make your disclaimer very clear. When the trouble starts, everyone is going to try to point to the broker.

Water and Ditch Rights. Make sure that the property description includes all other rights, such as water and ditch rights. Check to ensure that these water or ditch rights are not separately encumbered. The water is often more valuable than the land. Some contracts specify that the water is "all owned by seller." It would be best to specifically indicate what water is being transferred, and by what instrument (deed, bill of sale or stock certificate). Make sure that you know what you are talking about. Water attorneys are a special breed that only deal with water issues. Water is so different across the country, state by state and federally. Use caution!

Clause:

The Property shall include _____ shares of the _____ _____ ditch, which shall be transferred as personal property to the buyer by bargain and sale deed.

Letter/e-mail – Contract Form

Mr. Lawrence S. Schreder, President
Central Colorado Construction Company, Inc.
4th and Main Street
Colorado Springs, CO 80903

    Re: Standard Form Contracts

Dear Larry:

I am happy to have the listing on the existing and "to-be-built" homes in your subdivision. I know that you understand that I need to write this letter to confirm what we have discussed in the past regarding your instructions for the use of your standard form contract that you have provided to our office.

Let me congratulate you on your efforts to select and draft a contract, specifically for your sales, to be utilized instead of using the standard real estate commission approved form. As you know, I am a real estate broker and not an attorney. Therefore, I could not help with the drafting effort. It is nice to have legal counsel to write contracts, so that all we have to do is fill in the blanks.

Neither this company nor any of its agents can possibly be responsible for the content of the contract. However, we will complete it according to your direction. In addition, as you have indicated, we have been telling, and continue to tell, all potential buyers that all offers must be on your form. This may not stop someone from trying another form of an offer, but it should discourage all but a few. Whatever form is utilized by a buyer, we will present it to you for your consideration.

                                           Sincerely,
                                           The Real Estate Company

                                         by: Your Name Here,
                                       REALTOR®, CRS, GRI

Letter/e-mail – Use of Special Contract Form

Ms. Jo Patel, Broker
Patel and Company Properties, Ltd.
789 West Haven Drive
Maui, HI 96813

    Re: Central Hawaii Construction Company Homes

Dear Jo:

    This will confirm that our office, as the listing agent for the above builder, has been instructed to utilize the contract form provided by our principal for the sales of properties in this development. I have enclosed copies of the desired form, so that you will have them available for any sales you may make in this area.

    Understand that this office is not responsible for the content of this contract. Should you need assistance in its completion, please do not hesitate to ask for a sample of a completed contract. I think that the seller has obtained this contract from his attorney and will not consider the use of other forms. However, I will be happy to present any offer that may be requested by one of your customers.

    Finally, regardless of any other arrangement that we may have with respect to co-op fees on other properties, your office will receive a co-op fee equal to ____% of the total sales price, including extras, upon the actual closing and receipt of the purchase price by the seller. The only reservation is that you can not attempt to act as a subagent of the seller/builder.

    I look forward to your selling one of these fine homes. Let me know if there is anything that I can do to help. We welcome your cooperation.

                    Sincerely,
                    The Real Estate Company

                    by: Your Name Here

Financing Options, Clauses and Terminology

Cash. While a cash offer often sounds like the best financing alternative to the seller, that perception can crumble rapidly when it is determined that the cash is not available. The transaction may progress through to closing, only for the seller to discover that there was no cash, or that it was not available at the time of closing. When the contract indicates cash, a verification of the availability of the cash, as well as its location and accessibility, must be made. Specify the bank or financial institution when you can.

Clause:

Buyer shall, within _____ days of contract acceptance, provide listing broker with a verification from a state or federally chartered bank located within _____ miles of the property, indicating that the cash indicated in the contract is in fact on deposit and available for immediate withdrawal without restriction or limitation, and shall remain so until the date of closing. Buyer's failure to provide this verification shall be considered as a default on the part of the buyer.

New Financial Institution Loan. This is the easiest way to go for a qualified buyer. Keep the time periods reasonable but short. There are many terms to consider.

Clause:

1. $_____ as the net proceeds of a new first loan.

-or-

1. $_____ as the net proceeds of a new first loan to be obtained from a financial institution authorized to do business in this location.

-or-

1. $_____ as the net proceeds of a new first loan to be obtained from _____.

2. $_____ as a result of Buyer seeking and obtaining a new first loan from _____, amortized over a period of _____, years at approximately $_____ per month,

including principal and interest, not to exceed _____% per annum, plus, if required by Buyer's lender, a monthly deposit of 1/12 of the estimated annual real estate taxes, property insurance premium and mortgage insurance premium.   If the loan is an adjustable interest rate or graduated payment loan, the monthly payments and interest rate for the initial term of the loan shall not exceed the figures herein set forth.

3.   Said loan shall be obtained at an interest rate of not less than _____ per cent per annum, nor more than _____ percent per annum, and for a term of not less than ____ years, nor more than ____ years, acceptable to Buyer.

-or-

3.   Said loan shall be obtained at an interest rate of not less than _____ per cent per annum, nor more than _____ percent per annum, and for a term of not less than ____ years, nor more than ____ years, acceptable to Buyer.   Provided however, Buyer shall notify the listing broker in writing within ____ days of the acceptance of this Contract of the exact loan terms.   Failure to so notify the listing broker shall terminate this Contract, and all earnest money shall immediately be returned to Buyer.

-or-

3.   The loan shall be amortized over a period of _____ years, at approximately $_____ per month, including principal and interest not to exceed _____% per annum, plus, if required by Buyer's lender, a monthly deposit of 1/12 of the estimated annual real estate taxes, property insurance premium and mortgage insurance premium.

4. $_____ by Buyer obtaining a new first loan. The loan shall be of the following type: (Check applicable boxes.)
☐ Conventional   ☐ Fixed interest rate
☐ FHA   ☐ Adjustable interest rate
☐ VA   ☐ Graduated payment
☐ Other _____

5.   The loan may be increased by an amount equal to the cost of mortgage insurance, a VA funding fee, if any and any other items, for a total loan amount not in excess of $ _____.

6.   Loan discount points, if any, shall be paid to lender at closing and shall not exceed _____% of the total loan amount. Notwithstanding the loan's interest rate, the first _____ loan discount points shall be paid by _____, and the balance, if any, shall be paid by _____.

7.   Buyer shall timely pay to the lender a loan origination fee not to exceed _____% of the loan amount and Buyer's loan costs.

8.   Buyer reserves the right to designate an alternate loan, on such other terms and conditions as are acceptable to Buyer, for the indicated amount only, provided the lender issues an irrevocable commitment to provide said loan within the time period herein provided for loan approval.

9.   Buyer shall promptly make application within _____ days of Contract acceptance for, and diligently comply with all requests made by lender to obtain, loan approval.

-or-

9.   Within _____ days of Contract acceptance, Buyer shall promptly make loan application, cooperate with lender to obtain loan approval, diligently and timely pursue the same in good faith, execute all documents and furnish all information and documents required by the lender and timely pay the costs of obtaining such loan or lender consent.

-or-

9.   Buyer shall promptly apply for, and comply with all the requirements indicated by the lender to obtain, a loan commitment.   Buyer's obligations hereunder shall be conditional upon the loan actually funding.

-or-

9.   If Buyer obtains the indicated written loan commitment and complies with the requirements indicated, and the loan is not available at closing, through no fault of Buyer, this Contract shall terminate.

-or-

9. If Buyer is to pay all or part of the purchase price by obtaining a new loan, this contract is conditional upon lender's approval of the new loan on or before _____, 20___. If not so approved by said date, this contract shall terminate.

10. If Buyer does not obtain the loan indicated herein, or if the loan is not funded, on or before the Closing Date, this Contract shall terminate.

11. Buyer cannot waive the condition of obtaining a written loan commitment. If Buyer fails to deliver a copy of the written loan commitment to Seller on or before the Loan Commitment Deadline, this Contract shall terminate.

Assumption. "The promise to pay the debt of another" is the definition of an assumption. You will note that the definition makes no mention of consent being sought or obtained by the lender. That issue is addressed later. Assumption agreements are two-party agreements between the person who is going to accept responsibility for the payment of the obligation and the individual to whom the promise is made. The recipient of the promise may or may not already have an obligation to discharge the debt. An example of the latter might be an astute broker who previously accepted the property as part of a guaranteed sale and wisely took the property subject to the loan. Therefore, the broker is not personally obligated to repay the loan. The broker then requires the new purchaser to assume the obligation to pay the loan.

Assumption imposes a personal obligation and liability upon the individual making the promise to repay the debt according to its terms. It is important to note that there is no mention of a release of liability for the prior obligor, or borrower. A common misconception, even among some attorneys, is that an assumption releases the original obligor, usually the seller, from any ongoing personal obligation to repay the debt. The easy rule to remember is that no one is released from any obligation to pay unless the lender does so in writing. Therefore, the assumption of a debt merely adds another obligor for the lender to pursue. In some states, there are laws that prohibit some lenders from obtaining personal deficiency judgments against borrowers, thereby reducing this effect of an assumption.

If all or part of the purchase price is to be paid by an assumption, the contract needs to reflect the amount to be assumed and the extent to which the seller will remain liable for payment in the event of default. Remember that a release of liability requires a well qualified buyer – one that is most probably qualified to obtain a new loan.

Check your state law to ensure that you understand any continuing seller liability for loans that are assumed.

Clause:

1. $_____ as a result of Buyer's assuming and agreeing to pay an existing _____ loan of record in this approximate amount, presently payable at $_____ per month including principal, interest presently at _____% per annum and an escrow for the following: ☐ real estate taxes, ☐ property hazard insurance premium, ☐ mortgage insurance premium.

2. Buyer agrees to pay a loan transfer fee not to exceed $_____. At the time of assumption, the new interest rate shall not exceed _____% per annum, and the new monthly payment shall not exceed $_____ principal and interest, plus escrow, if any.

3. Buyer shall apply for assumption with lender within _____ days of contract acceptance and shall cooperate with lender to obtain loan assumption approval, diligently and timely pursue the same in good faith, execute all documents, furnish all information and documents required by the lender and timely pay the costs of obtaining such loan or lender consent.

4. It shall be a condition precedent to performance by Seller that Seller ☐ shall ☐ shall not be released from liability on said loan.

5. It shall be a condition precedent to performance by Seller that Seller shall be released from liability on said loan. In the event lender approves the assumption without a release of liability for Seller, Seller may, at Seller's election, waive the requirement for release of liability.

6. Buyer and Seller understand that the broker has not done any independent investigation of Buyer's ability to pay the indicated loan. Broker shall not be responsible to anyone in the event Buyer does not pay the same according to its terms.

7. Seller understands that in the event of an assumption without release of liability, Seller remains liable for payment of the loan and the lender may enforce the note and mortgage against Seller as well as Buyer.

8. Seller shall provide copies of the loan documents (including note, mortgage and all modifications) to Buyer within _____ calendar days from acceptance of this Contract. This Contract is conditional upon Buyer's review and approval of the provisions of such loan documents. Buyer consents to the provisions of such loan documents if no written objection is received by Seller from Buyer within _____ calendar days from Buyer's receipt of such documents.

9. If the lender's approval of a transfer of the Property is required, this Contract is conditional upon Buyer's obtaining such approval without change in the terms of such loan, except as indicated herein. In the event lender's approval is not obtained on or before _____, 20____, this contract shall be terminated on such date.

Subject To. The key distinction in a "subject to" transaction is the lack of any personal obligation on the part of the buyer to retire the obligation. That is, there is no personal liability to pay the loan. In either an assumption or "subject to" financing, the property is transferred with the existing loan intact. In either instance, the buyer pays the lender because if s/he does not, the lender will foreclose on the property and the buyer's equity will probably be lost. The larger the down payment, the less the risk to the seller of eventual foreclosure because the buyer will have more potential loss. A broker, doing a guaranteed sale, would want to take property subject to the existing financing, so that he will not be personally liable for repayment indefinitely. In addition to disclosing to his client, the seller, that he would not be obligated on the loan and thus not responsible for its ultimate repayment, such a broker would want to ensure that his transferee assumed the loan.

Tip.   *When the broker or salesperson guarantees that "if it does not sell, we will buy it" the seller is thinking about an assumption. Maybe the broker wants to take the property subject to the existing loan and require an assumption on resale.*

Clause:

Broker is buying the Property pursuant to a guaranteed sale. Broker shall not assume, nor agree to pay, the loan for the remainder of its term. Broker shall assume, and agree to pay, the loan for the period of time title is in the broker's name. Broker shall require the subsequent buyer to assume the loan as condition of the subsequent sale. Broker shall not be obligated to "qualify" the subsequent buyer.

Novation. Novation is often confused and merged in some people's minds with the idea of an "approved" assumption. Be careful. When the lender accepts the new purchaser and qualifies that purchaser for the assumption, the lender may or may not grant a release of the old borrower. When the lender releases the old borrower, a novation has occurred. This is often referred to as "assumption with release of liability." The lender may, however, retain all parties on the debt in which event there is no novation. This is often referred to as "a qualifying assumption." A common misconception is that an assumption with a change in the rate or other terms becomes a novation, and the original borrower, the seller, is automatically released. A written clarification of everyone's rights, duties and obligations after an approved assumption is very important.

Clause:

1. Buyer shall immediately make application for an approved assumption of the existing loan and comply with all the reasonable requirements imposed by the existing lender. Approval of said assumption shall include a release of liability for Seller.

2. Buyer shall apply for a novation wherein Buyer becomes a borrower and Seller is released from liability on the existing loan.

Case in Point.

The sellers, one of whom was a tax attorney and the other a chemical engineer, filed a complaint with a real estate licensing board requesting that the board revoke the license of a broker who failed to explain the difference between an assumption and a novation prior to listing the property and prior to the contract for sale being executed. Once the contract was executed the tax attorney did not want an assumption, he wanted a novation, so that he would not remain liable for the continued payment of the loan. The attorney for the broker argued that the difference was surely in the knowledge bank of the tax attorney. The attorney general, representing the state, replied that "just being an attorney, even a tax attorney who did not deal with real estate on a regular basis, was not enough to let the broker off the hook for not explaining the difference."

Seller Financing – Purchase Money Mortgage. This is probably the most dangerous area of the real estate transaction, and yet an absolute necessity in many of today's transactions. Unfortunately for many sellers and buyers, all the ramifications of a particular seller-financed transaction are simply never explained, let alone understood. Care should be taken to explain the entire transaction, not only orally, but also in writing and to indicate in advance all of the alternatives to, and ramifications of, the proposed financing. It is imperative to realize that the broker and salesperson are, for all practical purposes, practicing law in this area. Therefore, their actions will be held to the standard of an attorney. Danger lurks because the documents written or completed by the broker will last longer than the memory of even the most conscientious agent or other parties in the transaction.

There is no "standard" set of new loan documents upon which to rely. Whatever you write will be a condition of the owner carry back financing. If you have a standard form, use it. Do not modify the mortgage. That is work for an attorney. The note terms are something that you can put in the contract. Some people, especially commercial brokers, attach a fully filled out note and mortgage to the contract as an addendum and dispense with describing the terms and conditions in the contract.

As one regulator expressed, the perils of suggesting, drafting, structuring, or even allowing a seller to consider accepting some form of creative financing demand a similar detailed explanation and disclosure prior to placing such terms in a listing agreement or sales contract. Whenever the seller is going to remain involved with the financing of the real estate, that seller is going to have a tendency to look to the broker to "guarantee" the performance of the buyer.

Seller Financing – Terms and Conditions. The checklist may seem endless, but you should recognize that several items are imperative.

1. **Interest.** Double-check the normal ("face") interest rate and default interest rate that will accrue. Are the rates fixed or variable, and if variable, to which index are they tied? Do you understand that index?

2. **Late Charges.** Explain the existence, amount of, and effective date for a late charge. Remember, a late charge can be collected only once on each payment, as opposed to once for each month the payment remains unpaid.

3. **Dates, Amount, Application.** Cover all the dates and how the payment will be applied. Spell out the dates on which the payments will become due, and the amount of each of the payment, the date and amount of non-periodic payments and the application or allocation between principal and interest of each of the payments.

4. **Escrow.** Note the inclusion of an additional amount for an escrow for taxes and insurance. Note also the extent of the services and responsibilities of the escrow agent. Never become, or allow yourself to be coerced into becoming, an escrow

agent. There is always a greater fool – a title company, a bank, a neighbor, or someone else for the job. Explain the rate of interest, if any, that will accrue upon the funds in escrow or the allocation of any escrow charges with regard to the escrow account. If no one is designated as being responsible for the monthly fee, we know who will get to pay it: the real estate broker. So share the fun and designate some other deserving party.

5. **Prepayment.** Detail the ability to prepay, the minimum amount of any prepayment and the timing of a prepayment. Some sellers may not be able to accept a prepayment for tax reasons. Unless specified in the note to the contrary, there is no right to prepay.

6. **Assumption.** Specify whether or not the loan is assumable and, if so, under what conditions. Unless specified otherwise, all loans are assumable. The word "assumability" is a misnomer. What one really means is: Does the loan contain a due-on-sale clause? Confusion here is to be avoided. Any method of qualifying a new borrower that calls for the subjective approval of the seller is to be avoided. Idea: Make the loan due-on-sale until the principal balance is reduced to a certain figure; thereafter, allow a transfer so long as the loan is assumed. Consider the inclusion of a clause providing for the increase in the interest rate upon each transfer.

7. **Common Sense.** Can the seller really do without the money? Is this a good investment for the seller, especially given the current rates available in certificates of deposit? Although it is not your job to do financial planning for a seller, a thirty-year fixed rate loan comprising all of the assets of an elderly seller might cause one to pause and encourage the intervention of a trusted accountant, priest, or an attorney.

8. **Foreclosure.** Clearly explain the effect upon the seller if the buyer stops making the payments. Does the seller understand the foreclosure alternatives, the cost, the time delay and the possible outcome? Many older sellers think that the buyer does not own the house until the debt is paid. They confuse a transaction which transfers legal title by deed with one where the seller retains title to secure the repayment in the form of a mortgage. Retaining title to secure payment is often also known as an installment land contract. (The law concerning Installment Land Contracts or Contracts for Deed vary so much from state to state that you need to seek local counsel before trying to explain this option.)

9. **Form Selection and Terms.** The best solution to avoid future misunderstandings is to annex the owner carry-back note and mortgage or other financing documents, completed in as much detail as possible, as an exhibit to the sales contract. That way there is no confusion about what was actually intended or which form will be utilized.

There are many clauses that you can use. Here are some options that you might consider. Remember the seller might not be able to take the money in a particular tax year without substantial hardship.

Clause:

1. $_____ as a result of Buyer executing a promissory note payable to Seller, or his order, with the following terms and conditions:

   a. The promissory note shall be amortized on the basis of _____ years, payable at $_____ per month, including principal and interest at the rate of _____% per annum. Payments shall commence _____, 20____ and shall be due on the _____ day of each succeeding month.

   b. If not sooner paid, the balance of principal and accrued interest shall be due and payable _____.

   c. If any payment is not received within _____ calendar days after its due date, a late charge of _____% of such monthly payment, but in no event less than $_____, shall be due.

   d. In the event of default, the interest rate shall increase to _____% per annum.

   e. Prepayments shall not relieve the maker of the obligation to make the agreed successive monthly payments.

   f. All prepayments shall be in the minimum amount of $_____, or multiples thereof.

   g. Buyer may prepay at any time, and from time to time, without a penalty or premium, except _____.

h. The note shall be secured by a second mortgage, junior to the existing first loan, or the loan indicated herein to be in the first position.

All-Inclusive Financing. The All-Inclusive Note and Mortgage, or Deed of Trust in some areas, allows the seller to carry back a note and mortgage that "wraps around," or includes, another senior note and mortgage. In essence, there is an existing first loan of record. The seller desires to carry back a loan without regard for the existing loan or record. **Use caution here!**

Example: The property sells for $100,000.00. There is an existing loan for $60,000.00. The buyer will put $20,000.00 cash down and owe the seller a balance of $80,000.00 on the purchase price. The seller will carry the entire $80,000.00 evidenced by an All-Inclusive Note and Mortgage. There will be no assumption. The buyer takes the property "subject to" the existing note and mortgage, which the seller shall discharge according to its terms. In short, the buyer owes the seller the full $80,000.00 and the seller is charged with paying the existing $60,000.00 first loan.

Clause:
1. The attached All-Inclusive Promissory Note and Mortgage, consisting of _____ pages, are hereby made a part of this contract as Exhibits ____ and _____ respectively.

- or -

2. $_____ to be evidenced by Buyer executing an all-inclusive note secured by an all-inclusive mortgage substantially in the form attached hereto as `Exhibit A - All Inclusive Note and Mortgage' consisting of ____ pages.

Buyer's Ability to Pay. In the event of an assumption or an owner carried loan, the ability of the buyer becomes paramount. You do not want to become liable for the buyer's financial ability to pay. Add a clause that puts the obligation on the buyer and seller to make these determinations. The seller can not run a credit report on a buyer without his social security number and authorization. Anyone who runs a credit report without the express authorization of the buyer is in big trouble.

Clause:
1. Buyer hereby grants Seller the right to obtain a credit report upon Buyer. Buyer's social security number is _____.

- or -

2. Should Buyer be paying all or part of the purchase price by executing a promissory note in favor of Seller, or if an existing loan is not to be released at closing, this Contract is conditional upon Seller's approval of Buyer's financial ability and credit worthiness, which approval shall be at Seller's sole and absolute discretion.

- or -

3. Buyer shall supply to Seller, on or before _____, 20___, at Buyer's expense, information and documents concerning Buyer's financial, employment and credit condition, a current financial statement and a current credit report.

-or-

4. Information and documents received by Seller shall be held by Seller in confidence, and not released to others, except to protect Seller's interest in this transaction.

-or-

5. In the event Seller does not provide written notice of Seller's disapproval to Buyer on or before _____, 20___, then Seller waives the condition providing for approval of Buyer's ability to pay. In the event Seller does provide written notice of disapproval to Buyer on or before said date, this contract shall terminate.

Letter/e-mail – Assumption, Subject To, and Novation

Mr. Sam Seller
Mrs. Sandy Seller
4750 Table Mesa Drive
Boulder, CO 80305

Dear Sam and Sandy:

With the market in its current condition, and the attractive terms already in place in the loan that you currently have on your property, there is a good possibility that we will receive an offer which requests that you allow the assumption of your existing loan. You indicated in your Listing Agreement that this was an acceptable alternative.

Because of the long-term nature of this arrangement, I would like to review the differences between the "Assumption" of the existing debt, the taking of the property "Subject To" the existing debt and a "Novation." Please review it now, so that you will be familiar with the differences prior to receiving an offer that poses one of these alternatives. As the law is constantly changing in this area, you may wish to seek legal advice. This is a good topic to discuss with your real estate attorney.

First, let's review the process of "Assumption." Our attorney has advised us that when someone such as you allows your loan to be assumed, the buyer promises you that he will pay the lender, thereby promising to discharge the loan according to its terms. At this point, the buyer is personally liable to the lender and to you to complete that obligation. You remain liable for the repayment personally. Should the buyer not perform, you remain liable for the repayment of the obligation.

Should the lender commence a foreclosure, it could prove detrimental to your credit. This is a strange area since some lenders do not adversely reflect upon the credit of the original and intermediate borrowers, concentrating instead on the last person in line to formally, properly, assume the loan. Other lenders, however, do look to the original borrower. There seems to be no standard procedure. In the event of a foreclosure sale that is insufficient to fully retire the loan, some states allow the lender to commence a suit against all who are obligated on the note for the deficiency, while other states expressly prohibit such deficiency judgment actions. Colorado allows deficiency judgments and all lenders, with the notable current exception of FHA, are currently reviewing their loans to determine if such an action is justified.

When you allow your property to be transferred "Subject To" the loan, there is no personal obligation on the part of the buyer to pay the loan. The mortgage payments are made because the buyer knows that if they are not made, the lender will probably foreclose and take the property away from the buyer. You remain liable personally for the ultimate repayment, just as indicated in the assumption option. The buyer simply agrees to take title to the property with your existing loan in place.

A "Novation" occurs when the lender releases you from your personal obligation of, and liability for, the repayment of the loan and substitutes the new buyer. The original loan remains in place, just like the other alternatives. However, the lender, usually after qualifying the buyer, agrees that in the future the lender will look only to the new buyer, and not to you for repayment. This may sound like the best solution, but it is not often a reality. The lender wants all the borrowers it can get to remain personally liable for the repayment of your loan. To require a novation will eliminate your liability in much the same manner as if the buyer had obtained a new loan. It will also greatly reduce your ability to sell your home since, one of the attractive features of your existing financing is the fact that the loan can be assumed without any qualification or with the limited approval of the lender. The decision is a hard one, and only you can make it.

In either event, your loan could go into foreclosure and you would be powerless, as a practical matter, to stop the foreclosure and recover the property from your buyer or from a subsequent purchaser. While you always have the opportunity to pay the lender, the ability to recover the property might involve a lawsuit and all the requisite delays and expenses associated therewith. This is simply a function of today's real estate market and the legal system. There is not an easy answer to this dilemma. Legal advice may help you understand everything a little better.

If you would like to discuss this matter further with either Kathy or me, please feel free to give one of us a call at any time. Financing is one of the more complicated aspects of modern real estate transactions and needs to be given careful consideration. We want to ensure that all our clients and customers have an ample opportunity to learn about, understand and explore all the available options.

Letter/e-mail to Seller – Offer Proposes Owner Financing

Mr. Sam Seller
Mrs. Sandy Seller
4750 Table Mesa Drive
Boulder, CO 80305

Re: 4750 Table Mesa Drive

Dear Sam and Sandy:

As you know by now, we are happy to have an offer on your home for your consideration. This particular offer, like all others, needs to be carefully reviewed to determine if it suits your needs. It is important that you fully understand the implications of the transaction as it is proposed, so feel free to contact me at any time to further explain the ramifications of the transaction as proposed by the buyer.

Please note that this offer proposes that you will lend the buyer some money, in the form of a second note and mortgage, as part of the purchase price. Your position will be junior to that of the existing first mortgage lender. Therefore, your rights will be subject to the senior lender's rights. A failure to make the payments on the senior mortgage may make it difficult for you to reclaim the property fast enough to realize on your security.

As I am sure you can understand, we are professionals in obtaining buyers but do not have the expertise to determine their current financial qualifications. Nor can we determine whether they will meet their obligations now or in the future. We simply can not be responsible for the credit-worthiness or the present or future performance of the buyer. I am amazed at the complex nature of the credit reporting system. Although we encourage you to obtain a financial statement and credit report, we must direct you to other professionals to interpret these documents. I have found that the use of your local banker or a trip to the credit bureau with the buyer will provide you with some insight into the qualifications of the buyer, as well as which additional documents might be necessary to help determine the credit-worthy nature of the buyer.

Note that the proposed instruments to evidence the debt and secure its repayment have been attached and are included in the contract, should you decide to accept the buyer's offer and provide the requested financing. This is the time to review and understand these documents. I would be willing to explain them in general to you and also encourage you, if you so desire, to seek the advice of a real estate lawyer to assist you with the final decision. If you would like me to go along, I would be happy to help explain the transaction.

No home is ever sold until it closes. We realize that you are going to make some tentative commitments based on the contract as accepted. Therefore, we want to remind you that there are a lot of circumstances that must occur before the closing transpires. Be careful not to over commit your resources until we actually close.

We are on the way to closing, and I want to thank you for always having your home in such nice condition. I know the neat, clean appearance took some extra time and effort, but I am sure it was a factor in attracting this buyer.

Sincerely,
The Real Estate Company

by: Your Name Here,
REALTOR®, CRS, GRI

Letter/e-mail to Seller – Offer Proposes an Assumption

Mr. Sam Seller
Mrs. Sandy Seller
4750 Table Mesa Drive
Boulder, CO 80305

    Re: 4750 Table Mesa Drive

Dear Sam and Sandy:

As you know by now, we are happy to have an offer on your home for your consideration. This particular offer, like all others, needs to be carefully reviewed to determine if it will suit your needs. Even though this offer is not exactly what you had requested, it deserves careful consideration. In a market such as this one, no reasonable offer should be dismissed. It is important that you fully understand the implications of the transaction as it is proposed. Please do not hesitate to call on me at any time to explain the ramifications of the proposal.

Please note that this offer proposes that your existing loan be assumed by the buyer. Assumption is a promise by the buyer to pay your note and mortgage according to its terms. Two items need your review:

First, the note and mortgage require that the buyer apply for, and be approved for, the assumption of the loan and the transfer of the property as proposed in the contract. This procedure keeps the lender from exercising its right to call the loan due and payable in full, or due-on-sale. Do not place too great a significance upon the lender's approval of the buyer for the assumption. Although we will request a novation or release of your personal obligation to repay the note, it is not currently a condition of the contract. Pressing too hard for one could undermine the transaction as proposed and is rarely given by this lender.

Second, since this is an assumption, both you and the buyer will be jointly and severally liable for the repayment of the loan unless the lender agrees to the contrary. In the event the buyer or his successor in interest does not make the payments, the lender has the option to seek payment in full from you. We do not know the effect that this might have on your credit. You will probably not be able to obtain a voluntary reconveyance of the property from the buyer or his successor in interest.

As we discussed when you listed your property, an assumption makes this property easier for a buyer to buy. Consider the offer carefully. I have asked the other salesperson to provide us with a financial statement and credit report, so that you can better evaluate the offer. We do not review credit reports. We recommend that you contact your local banker and have him go over it with you. I will be glad to set up that appointment and go with you if it will help you evaluate this offer.

Sincerely,
The Real Estate Company

by: Your Name Here,
REALTOR®, CRS, GRI

Letter/e-mail to Seller – Offer Proposes "Silent" Assumption
Not VA or FHA

Mr. Sam Seller
Mrs. Sandy Seller
4750 Table Mesa Drive
Boulder, CO 80305

    Re: 4750 Table Mesa Drive

Dear Sam and Sandy:

As you know by now, we are happy to have an offer on your home for your consideration. This particular offer, like all others, needs to be carefully reviewed to determine if it will suit your needs. Even though this offer is not exactly what you had requested, it deserves careful consideration. In a market such as this one, no reasonable offer needs to be summarily dismissed. It is important that you fully understand the implications of the transaction as it is proposed. Please do not hesitate to call on me at any time to explain the ramifications of the proposal.

Please note that this offer proposes that your existing loan be assumed by the buyer. Assumption is a promise by the buyer to pay your note and mortgage according to its terms. Two items need your review:

First, the note and mortgage require that the buyer apply for, and be approved for, the assumption of the loan and the transfer of the property as proposed in the contract. This procedure keeps the lender from exercising its right to call the loan due and payable in full, or due-on-sale. Do not place too great a significance upon the lender's approval of the buyer for the assumption. Although we will request a novation or release of your personal obligation to repay the note, it is not currently a condition of the contract. Pressing too hard for one could undermine the transaction as proposed and is rarely given by this lender.

Second, since this is an assumption, both you and the buyer will be jointly and severally liable for the repayment of the loan unless the lender agrees to the contrary. In the event the buyer or his successor in interest does not make the payments, the lender has the option to seek payment in full from you. We do not know the effect that this might have on your credit. You will probably not be able to obtain a voluntary reconveyance of the property from the buyer or his successor in interest.

As we discussed when you listed your property, an assumption makes this property easier for a buyer to buy. Consider the offer carefully. I have asked the other salesperson to provide us with a financial statement and credit report, so that you can better evaluate the offer. We do not review credit reports. We recommend that you contact your local banker and have him go over it with you. I will be glad to set up that appointment and go with you if it will help you evaluate this offer.

You may be thinking about selling the property and not having the lender approve of the credit of the buyer. I certainly understand your feelings. This is your decision, not mine. There is a substantial risk that the buyer may not perform and that the lender may not take the transfer lightly. In fact, the existing lender can call the entire loan due and payable in full should the lender discover the transfer to the buyer. We strongly advise you to consult with your attorney prior to deciding to complete such a transaction. Should you decide to proceed with such a transfer, you will get a letter from my broker that indicates:

You and the buyer have agreed, in spite of our advice to the contrary, that neither of you will seek the approval of the holder of the loan. That is, of course, your decision. Please understand that neither this office nor anyone associated with it, including but not limited to Katherine Reece and myself as broker, can be responsible or liable for any action taken by the holder of the loan or anyone else, or for any other ramifications of this transaction that may arise as a result of your following this course of action. These ramifications could include a foreclosure action and/or your being named in a lawsuit upon the note. You are advised to seek the advice of an attorney before embarking on such a course of action.

So long as your loan is not a VA or FHA loan and the title company or an attorney of your choosing will close the transaction, we will happily accept our fee for finding the buyer. Again, we strongly advise you to get legal assistance.

Most sincerely,
The Real Estate Company

by: Your Broker, Broker

Letter/e-mail to Seller – Offer Proposes FHA/VA Assumption

Mr. Sam Seller
Mrs. Sandy Seller
4750 Table Mesa Drive
Boulder, CO 80305

    Re: 4750 Table Mesa Drive

Dear Sam and Sandy:

As you know by now, we are happy to have an offer on your home for your consideration. This particular offer, like all others, needs to be carefully reviewed to determine if it will suit your needs. Even though this offer is not exactly what you had requested, it deserves careful consideration. In a market such as this one, no reasonable offer needs to be summarily dismissed. It is important that you fully understand the implications of the transaction as it is proposed. Please do not hesitate to call on me at any time to explain the ramifications of the proposal.

Please note that this offer proposes that your existing FHA or VA loan be assumed by the buyer. Assumption is a promise by the buyer to pay your note and mortgage according to its terms. Two items need your review:

First, the note and mortgage require that the buyer apply for, and be approved for, the assumption of the loan and the transfer of the property as proposed in the contract. This procedure keeps the lender from exercising its right to call the loan due and payable in full, or due-on-sale. The consent of the government through the lender is required for the transfer of FHA and VA loans lender, period. To do otherwise might cause a violation of the law.

Do not place too great a significance upon the lender's approval of the buyer for the assumption. Although we will request a novation or release of your personal obligation to repay the note, it is not currently a condition of the contract. Pressing too hard for one could undermine the transaction as proposed and is rarely given by this lender.

Second, since this is an assumption, both you and the buyer will be jointly and severally liable for the repayment of the loan unless the lender agrees to the contrary. In the event the buyer or his successor in interest does not make the payments, the lender has the option to seek payment in full from you. We do not know the effect that this might have on your credit. You will probably not be able to obtain a voluntary reconveyance of the property from the buyer or his successor in interest.

As we discussed when you listed your property, an assumption makes this property easier for a buyer to buy. Consider the offer carefully. I have asked the other salesperson to provide us with a financial statement and credit report, so that you can better evaluate the offer. We do not review credit reports. We recommend that you contact your local banker and have him go over it with you. I will be glad to set up that appointment and go with you if it will help you evaluate this offer.

You may be thinking about selling the property and not having the lender approve of the credit of the buyer. **Forget it. It violates the law, period. This brokerage company can not participate in such a transaction as we all might go to prison. This is serious business.** I certainly understand your feelings. However, in the event that you decide to transfer title to the buyer, we will not close the transaction. We strongly advise you to consult with your attorney prior to deciding to complete such a transaction.

Sincerely,
The Real Estate Company

by: Your Name Here,
REALTOR®, CRS, GRI

Letter/e-mail to Seller – All-Inclusive Financing

Mr. Sam Seller
Mrs. Sandy Seller
4750 Table Mesa Drive
Boulder, CO 80305

    Re: 4750 Table Mesa Drive

Dear Sam and Sandy:

As you know by now, we are happy to have an offer on your home for your consideration. This particular offer, like all others, needs to be carefully reviewed to determine if it will suit your needs. Even though this offer is not exactly what you had requested, it deserves careful consideration. In a market such as this one no reasonable offer needs to be dismissed. It is important that you fully understand the implications of the transaction as it is proposed. Please do not hesitate to call on me at any time to explain the ramifications of the proposal.

Please note that this offer proposes that you carry an All-Inclusive Note and Mortgage. Let me explain how such a note and mortgage works. First, your existing first loan stays of record. The buyer does not assume it nor agree to pay it. You remain totally responsible for payment of that loan.

The buyer executes a large note that includes the balances due on the existing first loan. This large or "All-Inclusive" note is payable to you in monthly installments as indicated in the proposal. It is secured by an All-Inclusive Mortgage showing you as the beneficiary. From each such installment you make the payments on the existing first note and mortgage.

This All-Inclusive Note and Mortgage allows you to reserve the right at your option to foreclose upon your All-Inclusive Mortgage and obtain the return to you of the property without disturbing the underlying loan. If this is interesting to you, we can explore it in more detail. It is an effective tool when the underlying financing does not have a due-on-sale clause such as your current first loan.

Should you elect to consider this option seriously, we will need to have you talk with your attorney to make sure that you understand the risks associated with the proposed transfer. We are real estate brokers and not attorneys.

A copy of the proposed All Inclusive Mortgage is attached for your review. Since it is not a standard form we can not review it for you nor assist you with revisions that you might desire to make. Please take it to your attorney and have her review it. This offer contains a five day attorney review clause, so that each side can seek legal counsel on this transaction.

I am happy that we found a buyer that meets your criteria for a transaction that is this sophisticated. I admire your understanding and willingness to venture out on this course of action. I look forward to receiving a copy of the attorney review.

Sincerely,
The Real Estate Company

by: Your Name Here,
REALTOR®, CRS, GRI

Letter/e-mail to Seller – Offer Proposing New Financing

Mr. Sam Seller
Mrs. Sandy Seller
4750 Table Mesa Drive
Boulder, CO 80305

    Re: 4750 Table Mesa Drive

Dear Sam and Sandy:

The news we have all been waiting for has arrived. This letter contains an offer from Jon and Mimi Goodman. They are both attorneys, but that is no cause for alarm. The terms are not exactly what you wanted, but they are very close. Review the offer as quickly as possible because it expires tomorrow at midnight. While it is always possible for a buyer to withdraw an offer before it is accepted, I think the Goodmans want you to consider their offer very seriously. They have already met with a lender, and a letter indicating their pre-qualification for the proposed financing has been submitted with the offer.

This offer indicates that the buyers' obligations are conditional upon their being able to obtain a new first loan in the amount of $256,000.00, which represents a 77% loan-to-value ratio of their proposed contract price. While there is a risk that they cannot qualify for the financing, there are very few buyers who can either pay cash or enter into a contract without such a loan condition. You will note that the application must be made by Tuesday of next week and the loan approved on or before fifteen days prior to closing. Thereafter, the earnest money could be in jeopardy.

It is impossible for us to determine if any buyer will qualify for the proposed loan. For purposes of this offer, I have asked that the buyer present a financial statement and work history with the offer to assist you in determining if they are a good risk.

Your home will be effectively off the market while the loan application is in process. Although we can continue to solicit backup offers, the news that a house is under contract discourages other potential buyers from trying to purchase it.

                Sincerely,

Letter/e-mail to Seller – Offer Proposing New Financing

Mr. Sam Seller
Mrs. Sandy Seller
4750 Table Mesa Drive
Boulder, CO 80305

    Re: 4750 Table Mesa Drive

Dear Sam and Sandy:

    The news we have all been waiting for has arrived. This letter contains an offer from Jon and Mimi Goodman. They are both attorneys, but that is no cause for alarm. The terms are not exactly what you wanted, but they are very close. Review the offer as quickly as possible because it expires tomorrow at midnight. While it is always possible for a buyer to withdraw an offer before it is accepted, I think the Goodmans want you to consider their offer very seriously. They have already met with a lender, and a letter indicating their pre-qualification for the proposed financing has been submitted with the offer.

    This offer indicates that the buyers' obligations are conditional upon their being able to obtain a new first loan in the amount of $256,000.00, which represents a 77% loan-to-value ratio of their proposed contract price. While there is a risk that they can not qualify for the financing, there are very few buyers who can either pay cash or enter into a contract without such a loan condition. You will note that the application must be made by Tuesday of next week and the loan approved on or before fifteen days prior to closing. Thereafter, the earnest money could be in jeopardy.

    It is impossible for us to determine if any buyer will qualify for the proposed loan. For purposes of this offer, I have asked that the buyer present a financial statement and work history with the offer to assist you in determining if they are a good risk.

    Your home will be effectively off the market while the loan application is in process. Although we can continue to solicit backup offers, the news that a house is under contract discourages other potential buyers from trying to purchase it.

A new loan will cause your old loan to be paid off in full, which may trigger the payoff penalty that we discussed earlier. One good aspect of such a payoff is the termination of your personal liability for the repayment of that loan. If you wish to require that the buyer first try to get a loan from the holder of your mortgage in order to possibly avoid that penalty, a provision will need to be inserted in a counter proposal before the contract can become a firm and final deal. The buyer then has the following options: accepting the counter proposal, rejecting the entire transaction, or making another offer.

Since the offer is within the limits that you initially set when we first listed your house, I think that you should seriously consider accepting it as written. I will try to encourage the buyer to use your existing lender. However, it would seem that you would hate to lose this buyer who looks quite qualified and is paying a reasonable price over the payoff penalty. Please advise me.

Sincerely,
The Real Estate Company

by: Your Name Here,
REALTOR®, CRS, GRI

Contract – Special Terms

Acceptance. Contracts and offers are accepted only in written form signed by the party to be charged. This is often referred to as "the statute of frauds." When working with multiple parties in different geographical locations, people may suggest that "the contract be accepted orally." Do not become involved in oral acceptances or counter proposals. Use either the overnight mail or provide for use of a facsimile.

Clause:
1. Acceptance may be evidenced by facsimile.

-or-

1. Acceptance may be evidenced by facsimile. In the event of acceptance by facsimile, an original shall be sent by overnight mail on the same date as the transmission of the facsimile.

-or-

1. Acceptance may be by either returning an executed duplicate original, fax or by e-mail, with a copy also simultaneously sent to broker@myoffice.com

Acreage. In the event the acreage has a material significance, its accuracy should be addressed. This is not applicable for a "lot" of approximately 20 acres where 20 acres to 21 acres has no significance. It is for a parcel where the exact acreage is critical. For example, to have horses you must have 1.5 acres per horse. The buyer wants to keep two horses. The acreage is critical. The price is reflective of the acreage. The buyer wants to buy the acreage for $1,000,000.00 only if there are 100 acres, otherwise the price is to be adjusted.

Clause:
1. Seller represents that the Property consists of _____ acres. In the event that the Property is discovered to contain less than that amount of acreage, as the result of an ALTA survey performed by a registered land surveyor within 3 months before or after the transfer of deed, Buyer shall be entitled to an immediate credit equal to: the result of, the Total Purchase Price, divided by the above indicated acreage (determines the the Per Acre Price)

multiplied by the number of acres, to the hundredths decimal place, that are missing.

In the event that the determination is made prior to the transfer of deed, the price shall be so adjusted. This Contract shall survive the transfer of deed for this section and all remedies provided in this Contract shall apply to recovery of the amount due, plus reasonable attorneys fees and interest at the statutory rate from the date of the survey.

-or-

1. Seller represents that the Property consists of _____ acres. In the event that the Property is discovered to contain less than that amount of acreage, as the result of an ALTA survey performed by a registered land surveyor within 3 months before the date of transfer of deed, Buyer shall be entitled to an immediate credit equal to: the result of, the Total Purchase Price, divided by the above indicated acreage (determines the the Per Acre Price) multiplied by the number of acres, to the hundredths decimal place, that are missing, or in the alternative, to terminate the Contract and all earnest money shall be returned to buyer immediately.

-or-

1. Seller represents that the Property consists of _____ acres. In the event that the Property is discovered to contain more or less acreage the purchase price shall be adjusted proportionately to reflect the actual acreage.

-or-

1. Seller represents that the Property consists of _____ acres. In the event that the Property is discovered to contain more or less acreage, Buyer may, at Buyer's election, either terminate this Contract and all earnest money shall be returned to Buyer immediately, or continue with the Contract and the purchase price shall be adjusted proportionately to reflect the actual acreage.

Appraisal Condition. Even though there is a new loan condition, an appraisal condition can be very important. Generally, the new loan condition is thought to cover the appraisal. You will hear salespeople say, "Do not worry, if the lender does not appraise it high enough, the lender will not make the loan." This is very true if the loan is 80% loan-to-value or greater. If the loan to value is less than 80% or the buyer is paying all or a large portion of the selling price in cash down, the lender may not be as interested in the appraisal. Now the buyer needs some protection.

Clause:

1. Buyer shall have the right to have the Property appraised by an appraiser engaged by either Buyer, or Buyer's lender, at Buyer's election and expense. In the event the Property does not appraise for an amount at least equal to the purchase price, and written notice indicating that fact, signed by Buyer, is not delivered to Seller or listing agent, with a copy of such appraisal, on or before _____, 20 ____ (Appraisal Deadline), the Property's valuation shall be deemed to be satisfactory to Buyer. In the event said notice is received by Seller, and Buyer and Seller have not agreed, in writing, to a settlement thereof on or before _____, 20 ____ (Resolution Deadline), this contract shall terminate one calendar day following the Resolution Deadline unless, within that one calendar day, Seller receives written notice from Buyer waiving any objection to the Property's valuation.

-or-

1. Buyer shall have the right to have the Property appraised by an appraiser engaged by Buyer or lender, at Buyer's election and expense. If the Property does not appraise for an amount at least equal to the purchase price and:
   a. written notice, signed by or on behalf of Buyer; and
   b. a copy of such appraisal or a written notice from the person or entity who engaged the appraiser which confirms the Property's valuation as less than the purchase price, is not received by Seller on or before _____, 20 ____ (Appraisal Deadline), the Property's valuation shall be deemed to be satisfactory to Buyer.

If such notice is received by Seller and if Buyer and Seller have not agreed, in writing, to a settlement thereof on or before _____, 20 _____ (Resolution Deadline), this contract shall terminate unless, on or before the Resolution Deadline, Seller receives written notice from Buyer waiving any objection to the Property's valuation.

Buyer's Agency Fees. Prior to discussing fees with anyone, you must have your fee arrangement in place with your client, the buyer. If it is an oral agreement, a confirming cover letter is a good idea. That letter should restate your fee basis and the other critical aspects of your relationship with the buyer. Once you start to write the letter you will realize that it is the Buyer Agency Agreement in a letter format.

Caution. *You can not ask the other side – the seller, REALTOR®, or listing broker – for a fee until it is agreed upon in advance with your client. To attempt to negotiate your fee with the other side prior to making a fee agreement with your client is a violation of your fiduciary duties and the Code of Ethics.*

The First Effort. If possible, obtain your buyer agency fee through the REALTOR® family. Work through the Multiple Listing Service, Board or Association of REALTORS®. Real estate is a team sport. After making the fee agreement with your client, call the other side and determine how much of your agreed fee they will pay. In most circumstances, the listing broker recognizes that they are paying you to find the buyer and help on the buyer's side of the transaction. The listing broker sees you as the "cooperating broker" more than as the buyer agent. In that event, all that is needed in the sale contract is a recital of the fee structure for disclosure purposes to everyone. If you are comfortable with your arrangement with your client and the other broker, you may not even need a clause in the contract. Some states prohibit such clauses in the contract unless requested by the buyer. You could confirm your fee agreement by facsimile or letter. Consider using the *Agency and Compensation Card/Fax* discussed earlier.

Caution. *Do not become what you abhor in an attorney. Do not make the decisions for your client. Inform the client and let them make the decisions. This is especially true when it comes to the source of your fee.*

Second Line of Defense. If you have been unable to confirm with the seller (for sale by owner) or listing broker a satisfactory fee arrangement pursuant to your buyer's instructions, you must insert a clause into the contract that reflects your buyer's desires. The buyer may want to make sure that the listing broker is going to pay you. That can not be accomplished in the sale contract. The listing broker is not a party to the sale contract. Only the buyer and seller are parties to the sale contract. In this event, you will need to have the seller agree to pay you. In essence, the seller is agreeing to pay a buyer expense, your fee. This is similar to the payment of discount points.

Multiple Sources of Payment. Multiple sources of payment for a single broker, either a buyer's broker or a selling broker, are not frequent but are very possible. It is perfectly all right for a buyer to hire a broker to assist the buyer with the selection of a property and offer to pay that broker, in addition to the cooperative commission received from the other office, an additional fee. This could be in the form or a retainer or a success fee.

What disclosure needs to be made to the buyer or seller? The buyer already knows what is going on as it is part of the letter of confirmation or the buyer listing agreement. The seller needs only to know that the buyer is paying the selling broker an additional fee. Check your state to see if the amount of that fee must be disclosed. The listing broker's fee is between the listing broker and the seller. The same should be true for the selling broker's fee. Our favorite is number 4 below.

Clause:
1. The parties acknowledge that the listing broker is paying the buyer broker, upon closing of the transaction, a fee equal to _____% of the final sales price.

-or-

1. The parties acknowledge that the listing broker is paying the buyer broker, upon closing of the transaction, a fee equal to $_____.

-or-

1. The parties acknowledge that the listing broker is paying the buyer broker, upon closing of the transaction, a fee equal to _____% of the final sales price. In addition, the buyer agent is collecting a separate fee from Buyer.

2. Buyer's obligation to buy is expressly conditional upon Seller paying the buyer agent (_____), simultaneously with the closing of this transaction, a fee equal to _____% of the final sales price.

-or-

2. Buyer's obligation to buy is expressly conditional upon Seller paying the buyer agent (_____), simultaneously with the closing of this transaction, a fee equal to _____% of the final sales price. Said fee is the sole compensation received by the buyer agent.

3. Seller shall pay, or cause to be paid to the buyer agent (_____), at the closing of this transaction, a fee equal to _____% of the final sales price.

-or-

3. Seller recognizes that the buyer agent procured Buyer and assisted Buyer with the purchase of the Property. Buyer agent has sought a fee from the listing broker without satisfaction. In order for Buyer to buy, the buyer agent must be paid a fee. Therefore, the parties agree that Seller shall pay or cause to be paid to the buyer agent (_____), a fee equal to ____% of the final sales price upon the closing of the transaction. The purchase price offered by Buyer takes this fee into account.

Transaction Broker Fees.
Clause:
1. The parties acknowledge that the listing broker is paying the selling broker, upon closing of the transaction, a fee equal to _____% of the final sales price.

-or-

1. The parties acknowledge that the listing broker is paying the selling broker, upon closing of the transaction, a fee equal to $_____.

-or-

1. The parties acknowledge that the listing broker is paying the selling broker, upon closing of the transaction, a fee equal to _____% of the final sales price. In addition, the selling broker is collecting a separate fee from the buyer.

2. Buyer's obligation to buy is expressly conditional upon Seller paying the selling broker, simultaneously with the closing of this transaction, a fee equal to _____% of the final sales price.

-or-

2. Buyer's obligation to buy is expressly conditional upon Seller paying the selling broker, simultaneously with the closing of this transaction, a fee

equal to _____% of the final sales price. Said fee is the sole compensation received by the selling broker.

3. Seller shall pay or cause to be paid to the selling broker, at the closing of this transaction, a fee equal to _____% of the final sales price.

-or-

3. Seller recognizes that the selling broker procured Buyer and assisted Buyer with the purchase of the Property. Selling broker has sought a fee from the listing broker without satisfaction. In order for Buyer to buy, the selling broker must be paid a fee. Therefore, the Parties agree that Seller shall pay or cause to be paid to the buyer broker (_____) a fee equal to _____% of the final sales price upon the closing of the transaction. The price offered by Buyer takes this fee into account.

4. The selling broker is not acting as an agent for either Buyer or Seller. The selling broker is a broker licensed to sell real estate in this state.

Cash at Closing. Designate what form of money will be acceptable at the final closing. If you use escrow agents, sometimes this is part of the instructions. Many escrow agents will not accept cash and will require a cashier's check to be drawn on a local clearing house bank. If in fact the "cash at closing" means real cash, remember that the Internal Revenue Service wants to know about cash transfers in excess of $10,000.00. Do not become involved in "laundering" the cash for your buyer or seller. Do not let them give you some cash in return for your check. The effect is to obviate the reporting requirement.

Clause:
$_____, plus Buyer's customary closing costs, to be paid by Buyer at closing by cash, electronic transfer funds, certified check, savings and loan teller's check, or cashier's check drawn on a _____ clearing house bank.

Backup Offer. In times when the market is really hot and inventory is moving rapidly, it is possible to have multiple offers on one property. The seller may also decide to take backup offers when the initial accepted contract has some "shaky" contingencies, either planned or just developing.

Offering, presenting, and negotiating on a backup offer follows all the same rules as if it were being considered for first position. Most of the time the buyer will want to have the option to continue to search for other available homes and reserve the option to purchase another instead. You will need to provide an avenue to extract that buyer from the backup position. The key elements are the triggering method that allows the backup contract to assume first position. Use caution so as not to put the seller in jeopardy. Note 6 below. We want to keep the seller in a position that will enable him to continue working with the original offer if that is his desire.

Clause:
1. Buyer is aware that Seller has an accepted previous offer on the Property ("Senior Contract"). This Contract shall be junior to the Senior Contract.

-or-

1. This contract shall become the Senior Contract only in the event that the existing Senior Contract is terminated. In no event shall Seller or Buyer be obligated to close, or otherwise perform under this Contract, so long as the Senior Contract is in existence.

2. In the event the Senior Contract does not close on or before _____, this Contract shall become the Senior Contract.

-or-

2. In the event the Senior Contract shall terminate for any reason, this shall become the Senior Contract.

-or-

2. In the event the previous Senior Contract is the subject of litigation or threatened litigation, Seller shall not be obligated to perform hereunder.

3. Seller reserves the right to extend, renegotiate or modify the Senior Contract.

4. Buyer reserves the right to terminate this Contract, at Buyer's election, at any time prior to this Contract becoming the Senior Contract. Such termination shall be effective upon receipt of written notification of the same being given to Seller or listing broker.

5. All performance dates shall be extended once by a number of days equal to the difference between the date of acceptance of the contract and the date this Contract becomes the Senior Contract.

Contingency Sale. Buyer has to sell an existing home to qualify for the new home. This is a tough area. Use caution when drafting clauses that contemplate the parties being subject to another contract beyond the reach of the seller. Many buyers need to sell a current home in order to purchase the next. Depending on the market activity in the area, the buyer may lose negotiating power when needing to disclose this as a contingency. Now the seller not only worries about his property closing, but also the underlying contract and escrow. However, in a slow seller's market the seller may welcome this type of an offer when the alternative choice is no offer at all.

Assuming you have a buyer and seller willing to negotiate under these terms, there are some critical issues related to the contingency sale. Will there be an early or late occupancy and possession to allow the two properties to close simultaneously? Keep in mind that you can close on two properties simultaneously on paper, but it is impossible to move furniture out, clean and move in on the same day! You have not lived until you have the buyer's moving van sitting in the seller's driveway waiting to unload as the seller's movers are packing. There are better ways to be entertained in life.

Always compose your contract to allow for a review of any contract on the buyer's home. If possible, the seller most likely would prefer not to have a domino effect of that contract with a "contingency to sell" also. Consider if the seller wishes either to take his home off the market until the buyer's home sells, or if the seller will continue to market with a "bump" clause if another acceptable offer is received.

Remember that the removal of this "loan condition" will not solve the problem. As a practical matter, the buyer will not be able to qualify for the new loan. Therefore, the buyer is still protected. Meanwhile, the seller, thinking that there is no contingency, believes he has a firm unconditional sale. Nothing could be further from the truth. Remind the seller that the buyer can not qualify for a new house until the old one is sold, no matter what the contract says. If the contingency to sell is removed from the contract, the seller will need to verify that the funds to close are on deposit ready for immediate withdrawal without restriction.

Clause:
1. Seller is aware that Buyer must sell an existing home to be able to buy the Property. A portion of the down payment, and the ability to qualify for a new

loan, are conditional upon the sale and closing of Buyer's existing home located at _____. In the event Buyer does not enter into a firm contract to sell his existing house and deliver a copy of the same to seller within _____ days of acceptance of this offer, Seller may declare this Contract null and void, and all deposits shall be returned to Buyer.

-or-

1. Seller is aware that a portion of the down payment will come from the proceeds of the sale of Buyer's home located at _____
_____.
In the event Buyer does not enter into a firm contract to sell the above referenced property and deliver the contract to Seller within _____ days of acceptance of this offer, Seller may declare this Contract null and void, and all deposits shall be returned to Buyer.

2. In addition, Seller shall have ____ days from receipt of said Contract for the sale of Buyer's property to approve the same in the sole discretion of Seller and deliver evidence of approval to Buyer or the salesperson assisting Buyer.

3. In the event Buyer's property is unable to close pursuant to the terms of this Contract within the time period provided, Buyer may once extend the closing date specified in this Contract for a period not to exceed _____ calendar days.

Jurisdiction. In the event that you are sued, you want the case to be heard in your location, so you do not have to travel halfway across the country to bring your case or to defend it. The location where a lawsuit is heard by a court is known as the "jurisdiction" or "venue". With the advent of interstate and global contracts, think about including a clause dealing with the venue or appropriate jurisdiction for your dispute resolution activities – mediation, arbitration or litigation.

Clause:
Governing Law. This Agreement shall be governed by and construed and enforced in accordance with the laws of the State of _____.
Jurisdiction for any dispute shall be the District Court in and for the County of _____, State of _____, or such district Court wherein Broker brings an action.

Jurisdiction shall be proper only in the State and County where Seller's Broker has its primary offices.

First Right of Refusal. The buyer cannot fully commit to the purchase the property because the buyer has a house to sell. Maybe the buyer is not a buyer at all. This usually comes to a head with a seller who is a little desperate to get "any" offer. The desire to "have it sold" overcomes the problems that will follow when the buyer's house does not sell. First rights of refusal are attempts to get the best of both worlds. They generally fail at both.

Should your buyer be tempted to write, or the seller be tempted to accept, a contingency sale offer, read the following form. It anticipates that once the right is executed and a second buyer comes along, the original buyer will need to remove the conditions and become "real," so that failure to close by buyer number one is not a possibility. The buyer will need to be "locked in," so that the seller can rest assured his home is really "sold." Use the form with care. Remember that regardless of what the contract says, if there is no loan there almost always is no closing. When people lose earnest money, they have a tendency to sue other people. The deadline for the buyer to remove the conditions must always be hours, never days, from the time of notification. At least then you can only be off by sixty minutes.

Fill in the section indicating the amount of additional earnest money when the addendum is first prepared and attach to the original contract or the counter proposal. Do not save that task until it is in the Notice and Decision Period. The amount of additional earnest money has to have been agreed upon in advance when the addendum is signed. This puts the buyer in the position, once Notice is received, of being able to walk away and get all the buyer's earnest money back if the buyer decides not to proceed. In the alternative, once Notice is given and the Removal of Conditions is signed, the buyer is on the hook for the increased earnest money. Some say that it makes the earnest money "hard" or non-refundable. That is not true. Remember, that the seller could also default by not being able to provide clear title as agreed or by not being able to close on the specified date. In that event, the earnest money would be refunded to the buyer.

First Right of Refusal Addendum

Re: Contract, dated _____, between _____
_____, as "Seller,"
and _____, as "Buyer,"
regarding the "Property" commonly known as _____
_____. This "Addendum" is hereby
made a part of this Contract. In the event of a conflict between this Addendum
and the Contract, this Addendum shall prevail.

Removal of Conditions. Seller may continue to market the Property for sale.
Upon Seller providing written "Notice" below, to Buyer, indicating either Seller's
intent to accept an alternative offer on the Property or Seller's conditional
acceptance of an alternative offer on the Property, Buyer shall have _____
hours from receipt of the Notice ("Decision Period"), in which to execute and
deliver the Removal of Conditions Agreement indicated below. Failure of
Buyer to deliver the executed Removal of Conditions Agreement shall cause
the Contract to terminate on the expiration of the Decision Period. **IF BUYER
EXECUTES THE REMOVAL OF CONDITIONS AGREEMENT, WAIVING
THE CONDITIONS, AND DOES NOT CLOSE, BUYER SHALL BE IN
DEFAULT.** Notices shall be effective when received by a party or that party's
broker, as specified in the Contract.

NOTICE

Seller hereby provides the Notice, indicated above, to Buyer, and the Decision
Period has commenced, effective upon receipt by Buyer or Buyer's agent. I
have delivered this Notice to Buyer or Buyer's agent, on _____
at _____ (__).m. by delivery to the address of _____
_____.
_____

Seller or Seller's Agent:

_____
Sign and Print name above

REMOVAL OF CONDITIONS AGREEMENT

1. Additional Earnest Money. Buyer hereby deposits with Broker, accompanied by this Removal of Conditions Agreement, an additional earnest money deposit in the amount of $_____; and,

2. Removal of Conditions. The following conditions (contingencies) precedent are eliminated from the contract.
   a. All financing conditions; and,
   b. All appraisal conditions; and,
   c. All conditions allowing for objections to title; and,
   d. All conditions allowing objection to "off-record matters"; and,
   e. All conditions relating to the inspection of the Property,

All other terms and conditions of said contract shall remain the same. Buyer understands that in the event that Buyer does not close the transaction as provided in the contract, Buyer will be in default.

Delivered to Seller or Seller's agent, on _____ at _____ (__).m. by delivery to the address of _____.

Buyer or Buyer's Agent:

_____
Sign and Print name above

The Seller Finance Alternative. Rather than going the route of a contingency sale, with the associated risks of a seller losing the sale of his home to a "real buyer" as he waits for the buyer under contract to sell that home, think about this option. This type of creative financing not only sounds good, it works. The exact order and explanation follows. Go over it slowly for the first time. Hints that will make this successful are at the end.

Problem:
1. Seller has a house [House #1] to sell for $300,000.00.
2. Buyer also has a house [House #2] to sell valued at $200,000.00
3. Buyer's house [#2] has a loan of $100,000.00.
4. Buyer wants to buy Seller's house [#1] before someone else does.
5. Seller wants the house [#1] sold, not just "maybe sold." He is not willing to wait for the sale of Buyer's house [#2].
6. Finally, Seller wants cash.

Hints/Rules of Thumb:
1. Seller's house financing is irrelevant; it could be 100% financed, as in the case of a builder in trouble.
2. Buyer needs to move up by an order of 50% from the $200,000.00 house to the $300,000.00 house. Much less than this 50% and the transaction will not work.
3. Buyer needs to have 50% equity, real equity, in Buyer's house.
4. Buyer needs 10% cash to put down on Seller's house. This will pay for the agents' commissions.

Solution:
1. Buyer buys house #1 and closes in 21 days.
2. Buyer puts down 10%.
3. The Seller carries a loan for the balance of $270,000 [$300,000.00 sales price, less the 10%, $30,000.00 down payment]
4. The security for that loan is a first on the Seller's house, house #1, and a second on the Buyer's house, house #2. Seller is well secured.
5. Loan calls for 1% loan origination fee paid by Buyer. [You will see why later.]
6. The rate of interest should be what is generally charged by local banks for bridge loans [that is all this really is] plus one percent.
7. No payments for 6 months.
8. Default rate is six percent over the face rate.

Result:

1. Buyer goes to the listing broker for the Buyer's house and indicates that the Buyer is ready to lower the price to fair market value. If it sells fast, the Buyer saves the 1% loan origination fee, as the Buyer will not need the Seller's financing. They will get a new loan [1% motivates].
2. Seller goes to his bank and sells the bank the note that the Seller is taking back.
3. The bank loves it. They charge 1% [see there it is again] and are happy to earn an extra point on the loan principal.
4. They give the Seller cash, $270,000.00, less the payoff on his house, if any, so the Seller has all cash.
5. The bank is out $270,000.00, but has a first on a $300,000.00 house and a second on another $100,000.00 of equity. That is total equity of $400,000.00 on a $270,000.00 loan.

Hints:

1. Banks like loans less than one year and prefer 6 months.
2. Banks like to make a "point" when they originate a loan.
3. If the bank buys the loan, it is often not as picky as if the bank originates it.
4. There must be 50% equity in the Buyer's house.
5. Six months to pay makes it easy for the Buyer, as they do not have two monthly payments to make. This is a definite advantage over a "bridge loan" that has monthly payments.

Clause:

Buyer shall execute a promissory note in favor of Seller, in the amount of $270,000.00, bearing interest at _____% per annum with a default rate six percent greater than the face rate, secured by a first deed of trust (mortgage) upon [new house address] and a second deed of trust (mortgage) upon [buyer's existing house address], which property is currently subject only to an existing first loan of $_____. The note shall not require monthly payments, shall be pre-payable at will without penalty, and in the event it is not sooner paid, shall be due in full six months from execution. Buyer shall pay Seller a loan origination fee of _____ % of the principal amount of the loan.

Seller's obligation is conditional upon Seller determining, in Seller's sole discretion, that the existing first loan on [buyer's existing house address] is in fact current and represents not more than 50% of the fair market value of the property, on or before _____.

Earnest Money.   Although there is no substitute for a well drafted contract, it is earnest money and the fear of its loss, that motivates the buyer.   Try to obtain an earnest money deposit that represents a significant amount of money for both the buyer and seller.   For some contracts $500.00 is sufficient, while other more expensive properties may require $25,000.00.   Court systems have lower courts (example $0.00 to $15,000.00 for county court) and higher courts (cases over $15,000.00).   Nothing is more frustrating than having a contract where the earnest money is on the cusp, $16,000.00.   Oliver would advise the buyer or seller to stay in the lower court and let the additional $1,000.00 go.   Of course the buyer or seller will look to you for that difference.

Designate whether the earnest money was paid in cash, check (personal or corporate) or a promissory note.   Should the listing contract provide that in the event of default the broker may be entitled to a portion of the earnest money, think about using your portion to help settle the case.

To further show good faith on the buyer's behalf, an additional deposit may be made within a specified time after acceptance or when additional contingencies are satisfied. Do not let the earnest money come in on a monthly basis, as some might claim the contract to purchase was in fact an installment sale.

Whoever holds the earnest money will be named in a suit to determine who gets it. To avoid being involved, you might not want to hold it.   Think about letting someone else hold the earnest money.   We recommend a reputable title company.

In addition, the question of interest on earnest money must be addressed.   Think about how much interest will actually accrue before you decide that the earnest money should earn interest.   The total interest is reflected by the amount held and the time it will be on deposit.   If the amount of interest is anticipated to be less than $100.00, the time, effort and cost of setting up, and maintaining, an interest bearing account may not be warranted.   Many companies raise that threshold to $500.00.

The first clause designates that the interest will be additional earnest money.   This makes the rest of the decisions simple.   If the contract closes, the buyer gets the interest, pays tax on it and uses it towards the purchase.   In the event that the transaction does not close, and the earnest money is forfeited to the seller, the seller receives the entire amount including the interest, but the buyer still pays tax on the interest.   Other alternatives become a problem as the social security number for the account needs to be given to the bank when the account is set up.   Changing the account number after interest is paid can be difficult. It is a nightmare if the interest is later credited to a different party.

Clause:

1. The earnest money shall be deposited in _____ financial institution in the name of the entity designated herein as the holder of the earnest money. Interest shall be reported in the name of the buyer. Interest on the earnest money shall become additional earnest money.

2. The earnest money is in the form of _____.

3. Broker is authorized to deliver the earnest money deposit to the closing or escrow agent, if any, at or before closing.

4. Notwithstanding any termination of this contract, Buyer and Seller agree that, in the event of any controversy regarding the earnest money, unless mutual written instructions are received by the holder of the earnest money, the party holding the earnest money shall not be required to take any action, but may await any legal proceeding, or at their option and sole discretion, may interplead all parties, deposit any monies into a court of competent jurisdiction and shall recover court costs and reasonable attorney fees.

5. The parties authorize delivery of the earnest money deposit, by endorsement of the original earnest money check or otherwise, to the Closing Company, if any, at or before closing.

6. Parties acknowledge that the earnest money is being paid by electronic transfer (Visa or MasterCard debit card) and that the merchant fee for use of a credit or debit card actually incurred by the holder of the earnest money shall not be considered as earnest money but shall be a buyer's non-refundable expense.

Hazard Insurance. The buyer needs to know that s/he can obtain a new policy on the acquired property at a rate that the buyer can afford. With the advent of C.L.U.E. Reports, the buyer needs some time to verify that adequate insurance is obtainable.

Clause:

If Buyer is unable to obtain or verify the availability of property insurance for the Property on terms acceptable to Buyer (including, but not limited to, coverage and premium), Buyer shall have the right to terminate this Contract by giving written notice of termination to Seller on or before the Inspection Objection Deadline. If Seller does not receive such written notice of termination by the Inspection Objection Deadline, Buyer waives any right to terminate under this provision.

Home Warranty. The buyer or seller has the property inspected by a home warranty company. That company, for a relatively small fee, issues a policy that guarantees those items that have a measured useful life. These include items such as the appliances, the furnace, the roof, etc. Each policy is a little different. There is a difference of opinion as to whether this is a "warranty" or an "insurance policy." Make sure that you are aware of the determination in your state. An error could be expensive. Insurance salespersons need a license. One of the main distinctions is the amount of the earned premium that is saved in reserve, reserve requirements, for claims. Insurance companies are heavily regulated in this area, other ventures are not.

Read the Policy. There is no substitute for reading the policy. Know what the policy that you sell or endorse covers. This is not a structural warranty. The public is often confused about the extent of coverage which needs to be carefully investigated. Someone other than the licensee needs to make sure that the policy actually provides the coverage that the buyer thinks it does. Just as important, save all the promotional material that was provided to induce the purchase of the policy.

Having said all that, we still feel that the good home warranty companies and "policies" are well worth consideration and should be mentioned to a prospective seller or buyer. In the situation where the home is older, the appliances are not in good condition or the buyers have limited resources to replace a defective item, the warranty can present a possible solution.

Tip. *It is the role of the salesperson to make sure that the buyer understands whether a home warranty is or is not available. If it is not available, the buyer needs to know why it is not available. Sometimes the salesperson will receive a commission as a result of the issuance of a home warranty. That fact needs to be clearly stated to everyone and may have Federal Government regulatory problems (RESPA).*

Getting Part of the Premium. Buyer agents should be careful not to recommend a firm without an adequate disclosure of their interest in that firm, if any. In many states, if one sells or collects the premium or shares in the premium, they become an insurance salesperson. Caution is urged in this regard. Finally, the federal government takes a dim view of a licensee getting a fee for a referral only. Getting a referral fee on an insurance policy or warranty policy may be more trouble than it is worth. If that is a significant portion of your revenue, you are in the wrong business.

Agency.   Remember, if you are a seller's agent, absent an agreement to the contrary, you owe any referral fee paid to you by the home warranty company to the seller, your client. If you are a buyer's agent, absent an agreement to the contrary, you owe any referral fee paid to you by the home warranty company, to your client, the buyer. Agency means there is an absolute fiduciary duty to a client, above the duty to self.

Caution. *Home warranty companies have had a tendency to go out of business. It is very possible that the warranty company may not be around to pay the claim in the future. Many well meaning warranty companies are no longer in business. That leaves the individual or company that "recommended the policy to us," or "told us it would cover us if there was a problem," in the position of being able to pay claims, without the benefit of collecting premiums. Make sure that you are aware of your role.*

Caution. *Some real estate companies have rules that say that you can not make a profit or fee from referring people to a home warranty company. These real estate companies are using good judgment. The federal government through the Real Estate Settlement Procedures Act (RESPA), takes a dim view of referrals for the sake of collecting a fee only with no work being performed.*

Clause:

1. Buyer has been informed that a home warranty ❑ is ❑ is not available for this property. Buyers have elected ❑ to ❑ not to obtain a home warranty. The home warranty, if selected, shall be paid as a ❑ Buyer's ❑ Seller's expense. If Seller's expense is selected, Seller's expense shall be limited to $_____, and the balance shall be paid by Buyer.

2. The parties are aware that there are many home warranty insurers in the marketplace. In the event that [name of company] is selected as the home warranty company, [name of your company] shall receive a commission of $_____ on the sale of the warranty.

-or-

2. The parties are aware that there are many home warranty insurers in the marketplace. In the event [name of warranty company] is selected as the home warranty company, [name of your company] shall receive a commission of $_____ on the sale of the warranty which shall be credited to Buyer.

-and-

3. Seller and Broker are not responsible for the financial integrity of the home warranty company. In the event that the home warranty company fails to perform, there shall be no cause of action against Seller or Broker.

4. Buyer may obtain a home warranty from [name of warranty company]. The first $_____ shall be paid by Seller and the balance, if any, shall be paid by Buyer.

5. If Buyer is unable to obtain or verify the availability of a home warranty on terms acceptable to Buyer (including, but not limited to, coverage and premium), Buyer shall have the right to terminate this Contract by giving written notice of termination to Seller on or before the Inspection Objection Deadline. If Seller does not receive such written notice of termination by the Inspection Objection Deadline, Buyer waives any right to terminate under this provision.

Standard Broker Sold Home Warranty
Election or Waiver Form

Property:_____

Home Warranty Company:_____

We want all buyers and sellers to be aware of the availability of a home warranty program for this property. We are authorized representatives of the indicated home warranty company. As such, we will receive a fee in the event you select a home warranty from that company. A copy of the policy is attached for your review. There are other home warranty companies in the marketplace. We will be happy to locate one that suits your needs.

We encourage all buyers and sellers to consider a home warranty program. Brokers and salespeople are not obligated to discover defects, only to disclose defects known to us. This warranty is issued by a third party company, not the real estate firm. You need to review the policy carefully to make sure that it covers what you intend it to cover. *This is not a structural policy.*

- A home warranty ❑ *is* ❑ *is not* available for this property.
- Buyers have elected ❑ *to* ❑ *not to* obtain a home warranty.
- The home warranty shall be paid as a ❑ *Buyer's* ❑ *Seller's* expense.
- If Seller's expense is selected, Seller's expense shall be limited to $_____, and the balance shall be paid by Buyer(s).
- Broker ❑ *will* ❑ *will not* credit Buyer(s) with the fee received by Broker as a result of the selection of a home warranty policy sold through this company.
- Commission to Real Estate Broker: $_____

Buyer   **Buyer**

_____   _____
                date   date

Standard Third Party Home Warranty
Notification, Election and/or Waiver Form

Property:_____
This property may qualify for a home warranty. Not all properties qualify, and you need to read the policy carefully. We are not authorized representatives of any home warranty company. Some companies pay us a fee as a result of the buyer or seller obtaining a home warranty. We refund that fee to the party that paid it.

We encourage all buyers and sellers to consider a home warranty program and investigate the company and the coverage. Brokers and salespeople are not obligated to discover defects, only to disclose defects known to us.

Warranties are issued by third party companies, not this real estate firm. You need to review the policy carefully to make sure that the coverage includes what you intend it to cover. These home warranties generally do not provide any coverage for structural defects. That is why we strongly recommended a home inspection, and if you so desire, an inspection by a structural engineer.

Home Warranty Companies:
_____
_____

- A home warranty ❑ *is* ❑ *is not* available for this property.
- Buyers have elected ❑ *to* ❑ *not to* obtain a home warranty.
- The home warranty premium shall be paid as a ❑ *Buyer's* ❑ *Seller's* expense at closing.

If Seller's expense is selected, Seller's expense shall be limited to $_____, and the balance shall be paid by Buyer(s). Once signed by all parties, this agreement shall become a part of the Buy/Sell Contract between the parties.

Buyer

_____   _____
                date   date
Seller

_____   _____
                date   date

Inclusions and Exclusions.   When reviewing the proposal for final revisions, be certain you have adequately identified any personal property to be included in the contract.   This includes appliances, light fixtures or chandeliers, window coverings, air conditioners, pool or spa equipment or furnishings designated on an inventory.   It is just as important to note any specific exclusions.   By specifically listing and deleting any item to be excluded, any misunderstandings will be eliminated about what actually is conveyed with the home.   Hopefully, this will prevent the salesperson from being obligated to purchase a replacement appliance.   It takes buying only one appliance to learn this lesson!

If an item is being conveyed, but its continuing operation is questionable, explain the exact status of that particular item.   Explain not only the condition of the item, but also if it is to be repaired, replaced or accepted in its condition with no warranties expressed or implied.

In general, if an item is attached to the property, such that tools would be required to remove it, that item is considered real property.   Conversely, if the item is not so attached, it is not real property, but personal property.   Classic examples include a free standing range that is not hard wired and does not have tile in front of it.   That is personal property.   Once the range is hard wired or tile is placed in front of it, it becomes real property.   Care should be taken to check satellite dishes, *and the controls*, to ascertain if they are real or personal property.   Natural gas cylinders and burglar alarm systems may be leased by the seller and therefore are not owned by the seller.

Watch for expensive drapes and wall hangings.   Carpet that "looks" wall to wall might be an area rug.   The real estate salesperson needs to pay attention when viewing the property.   Make a checklist for each room in order to prepare a contract that accurately reflects the buyer's desires or is a true reflection of what the seller intends to convey.   Do not indicate "all" or "any" for remote controls.   That means that when they are not located, the REALTOR® gets to buy "all" or "any" that the buyer thought they needed.   Try to use a specific number in that slot. Always have the buyer or seller personally read, and verify that the items checked are accurate.

Remember, what is missing is the problem of the REALTOR®.   It is always that way. Here is a hint that works well. As you show the house, take out an old fashioned steno pad, and on the left indicate "Stays" [included and stays with the house as part of the price] and on the right "Goes" [goes with the seller]. Now as you tour each house say "If you like this house, do you want the bookshelves?" Cover all the items in the house that you do not want to buy, attached or not. Then when you write the contract, specify in the inclusions, and/or exclusions, the results of your notes. The steno pad makes a great buying sign, also. When the buyer is ready to buy, he will say "Have you got that pad?"

With the advent of Home Owner's Associations, shared parking, assigned parking, owned parking and other living arrangements, the parking and storage need to be addressed as either included or excluded. Sometimes the parking is not owned by the seller. Sometimes the parking space is worth a lot of money.

Clause:
1. The Purchase Price includes the following items:
   a. If attached to the Property on the date of this Contract: lighting, heating, plumbing, ventilating and air conditioning fixtures; TV antennas; inside telephone wiring and connecting blocks/jacks; plants; mirrors; floor coverings; intercom systems; built-in kitchen appliances; sprinkler systems and controls; built-in vacuum systems (including accessories); garage door openers, including _____ remote controls; and _____

   _____

   _____.

   b. If on the Property, whether attached or not, on the date of this Contract: storm windows, storm doors, window and porch shades, awnings, blinds, screens, window coverings, curtain rods, drapery rods, fireplace inserts, fireplace screens, fireplace grates, heating stoves, storage sheds and all keys. Check applicable box(es) if included: ☐ Water Softeners, ☐ Smoke /Fire Detectors, ☐ Security System(s), ☐ Satellite System (including satellite dishes and any accessories); and _____

   _____.

   c. Seller is the owner of parking spaces identified as _____
   _____, which are part of the Property.

   - or -

   c. Seller is not the owner of any parking spaces. Parking spaces are assigned by the Homeowners Association ("HOA"). Currently, Seller is assigned spaces _____. These spaces may be reassigned at the discretion of the HOA, pursuant to the covenants and by-laws of the HOA.

d. The following legally described water rights (personal property) are included as part of the Property:_____

e. The above-described included items (Inclusions) are to be conveyed to Buyer, by Seller, by bill of sale at the closing, free and clear of all taxes, liens and encumbrances, except as provided herein.

2. The following items, attached or not, are excluded from this sale:_____
_____.

3. Seller will remove the excluded items, prior to closing, without damaging the Property.

4. The sum of $_____ shall be escrowed with the closing agent to insure that Seller removes the excluded property within _____ days after closing.

Inspection.   Make sure that the buyer knows that not only are they entitled to an inspection, you recommend one. The largest single claim by buyers relates to the physical condition of the property. An inspection is a must. Do not select the inspector. We need a system to allow the parties to rectify the situation, agree on a closing and modification of the contract to correct defects on terms agreeable to both parties.

Clause:
1. Seller agrees to provide Buyer on or before _____, 20___, a Seller's Property Disclosure Statement completed by Seller to the best of Seller's current actual knowledge.

2. Buyer, or any designee, shall have the right to enter upon the property at reasonable hours, with _____ hours prior notice, and have one or more inspections of the physical condition of the Property and Inclusions, at Buyer's expense. In the event written notice of any unsatisfactory condition, signed by Buyer, is not received by Seller on or before _____, 20_____ ("Objection Deadline"), the physical condition of the Property and Inclusions shall be deemed to be satisfactory to Buyer. In the event such notice is received by Seller as set forth above, and Buyer and Seller have not agreed, in writing, to a settlement thereof on or before _____, 20_____ ("Resolution Deadline"), this contract shall terminate one calendar days following the Resolution

Deadline; unless, within the one calendar day, Seller receives written notice from Buyer waiving objection to any unsatisfactory condition. Buyer is responsible for, and shall pay for, any damage which occurs to the Property and Inclusions as a result of such inspection.

Legal Description.   Many contracts have a space for the insertion of the legal description. If the information will fit, that is the place for the legal description. If however, the space provided on the standard form is inadequate, then you must attach an addendum. Finally, there are times when you do not have the legal description and must provide that it be attached at a later date.

Clause:
1. The Legal Description on the attached addendum, "Legal Description", consisting of _____ pages, is hereby made a part of this Contract.

-or-

1. Exhibit A, Legal Description, consisting of _____ pages, is hereby made a part of this contract.

-or-

1. The Legal Description shall be provided to Buyer and attached to this offer by Seller within ____ days of contract acceptance. Thereafter, Buyer shall have ten calendar days to review and approve the Legal Description by signing and dating the bottom of the same. Failure of Seller to provide the Legal Description, or failure of Buyer to sign it, shall make this Contract void.

2. The Legal Description shall be attached by the Title Company on or before the _____ date.

-or-

2. The Legal Description shall be delivered with the Title Documents and reviewed in accordance with the review of those documents.

-or-

3. The legal description shall be provided to Buyer and attached to this Contract by Seller within _____ days of contract acceptance. Thereafter, Buyer shall have ten calendar days to review and approve the Legal Description by signing and dating it at the bottom. In the event that Seller does not provide the Legal Description within the specified time period, Buyer may, at Buyer's option, terminate the Contract and Buyer shall be entitled to the immediate return of all earnest money. In the event that Buyer does not sign the Legal Description within the specified time period, this Contract shall terminate, and Buyer shall be entitled to the immediate return of all earnest money.

Possession, Insurance and a Lease. Two things need to occur to the broker. First, the insurable interest of the parties must be determined. If the seller owns the property and the buyer occupies the property prior to closing, the buyer is a tenant. If the buyer closes and the seller occupies the property, the seller is a tenant. Most homeowners policies do not cover tenants. The tenant needs a renter's policy.

Caution. *Do not let people move in early or stay after closing, if at all possible. Do not draft their occupancy agreements (leases).*

Second, while everyone thinks things will go as planned, the buyer who moved in early may not close, but still remain in the property. The buyer moved in because, "they had no where to live." That condition still exists.

The seller may close, agreeing to late occupancy or, "seller to remain for five days after closing," and never vacate the property. The parties need a lease and not a "move in early or seller to stay after closing" clause or side agreement. A comprehensive standard form lease can and should be attached to the contract. It will provide for eviction, attorney's fees, deposit and other items that should be part of any comprehensive rental agreement.

Clause:
1. Possession of the Property shall be delivered to Buyer as follows:_____
_____
subject to the following lease(s) or tenancy(s):_____
_____.

2. In the event Seller, after closing, fails to deliver possession on the date herein specified, Seller shall be subject to eviction, and shall be additionally

liable to Buyer for payment of $_____ per day, from the date of agreed possession until possession is delivered.

3. Seller shall occupy the property for a period of ____ days after closing, pursuant to the terms and conditions of the lease attached hereto as exhibit _____.

-or-

3. Buyer shall be permitted to occupy the property prior to closing for a period of ____ days, pursuant to the terms and conditions of the lease attached hereto as exhibit _____.

4. Broker has advised both Buyer and Seller to consult with their respective insurance agents to determine the extent to which either needs additional insurance. Broker is not responsible for any loss sustained to the Property at any time.

Price (Consideration). Many standard contracts have ample space here for clauses. However, there are often some different possibilities that arise. Care needs to be taken to ensure that the total numbers are, in fact, equal to the total price.

Clause:
1. The price shall be payable in U.S. Dollars.

2. The Purchase Price indicated was determined after making a careful inspection of the property. Buyer has not relied upon any information contained in the Multiple Listing Service, websites or on any listing information sheets, which may contain errors, such as the total amount of square footage, the size of the lot, the school district, the availability of water, etc.

Property Condition. Standard in some contracts, this clause needs to be exact. Over 65% of all claims to the malpractice carrier are related to the condition of the property. Be specific about what is included and excluded, so that there are no misunderstandings.

Clause:

1. Except as otherwise provided in this contract, Property and Inclusions shall be delivered in the condition existing as of the date of this Contract, ordinary wear and tear excepted.

   a. Casualty; Insurance. In the event the Property or Inclusions shall be damaged by fire or other casualty prior to Closing, in an amount of not more than ten percent of the total Purchase Price, Seller shall be obligated to repair the same before the Closing Date. In the event such damage is not repaired within said time or if the damages exceed such sum, this Contract may be terminated at the option of Buyer by delivering to Seller written notice of termination. Should Buyer elect to carry out this contract despite such damage, Buyer shall be entitled to a credit, at Closing, for all the insurance proceeds resulting from such damage to the Property and Inclusions payable to Seller but not the owners' association, if any, plus the amount of any deductible provided for in such insurance policy, such credit not to exceed the total Purchase Price.

   b. Damage; Inclusions; Services. Should any Inclusion(s) or service(s) (including systems and components of the Property, e.g. heating, plumbing, etc.) fail or be damaged between the date of this contract and Closing or the Possession Date and Time, whichever shall be earlier, then Seller shall be liable for the repair or replacement of such Inclusion(s) or service(s) with a new unit of similar size and capacity, or an equivalent credit, but only to the extent that the maintenance or replacement of such Inclusion(s), service(s) or fixture(s) is not the responsibility of the owners' association, if any, less any insurance proceeds received by Buyer covering such repair or replacement. Seller and Buyer are aware of the existence of pre-owned home warranty programs which may be purchased and may cover the repair or replacement of some Inclusion(s).

   c. Walk-through; Verification of Condition. Buyer, upon reasonable notice, shall have the right to walk through the Property prior to Closing to verify the physical condition of the Property and Inclusions.

2. Neither Seller, the listing or selling broker, nor any of their agents or employees are responsible for the condition of the Property, the representations of Seller, as outlined on the Property Disclosure Statement, attached hereto as Exhibit _____, consisting of _____ pages, or for other

representations made directly to Buyer, or for the items outlined in the foregoing paragraph.

3. Buyer acknowledges that, prior to completing this offer, he has received a copy of the Property Condition Report and Soils Report completed by Seller which describes the condition of the property.

4. Neither Seller, Buyer, nor any of their agents are relying on any representation, or omission of or by, any real estate broker or salesperson associated with this transaction for any decision as to the value of the Property, the condition of the Property, the decision to purchase the Property, or by the terms and conditions of sale that are incorporated in this Contract.

5. The parties acknowledge that none of the brokers or salespeople associated with this transaction have made an inspection of the Property, and none are responsible for any defect that such an inspection might have revealed.

6. Buyer understands that there is a home warranty currently covering the Property. Buyer has made an independent investigation as to the term remaining, the extent of coverage, and the extent to which the available coverage has been utilized. Buyer realizes that the brokers and salespersons are not warranting the condition of the Property and are not responsible for physical defects that might come to light after the sale.

7. Buyer is purchasing the Property in AS IS condition, without any warranty from Seller or from any broker or salesperson working with Seller or Buyer. There is no warranty that the Property is fit for any particular purpose. Buyer understands, and has been encouraged to have the Property inspected by experts of Buyer's selection. Buyer realizes that the brokers and salespeople are not engineers, and that they are not warranting the structural condition of the Property, nor the condition of any appliances or systems, or otherwise.

-or-

8. Buyer understands and hereby agrees Buyer is purchasing the Property in "AS IS" condition. Without limiting the foregoing, Buyer understands that there are existing structural problems with the Property, the extent of which

Seller is unaware. Buyer acknowledges that the Purchase Price under this Contract reflects the uncertainty surrounding the condition of the Property. Seller makes no warranties, representations, or guarantees, either express or implied, of any kind, nature, or type whatsoever. Except as provided in the immediately preceding sentence, and without in any way limiting the generality of the immediately preceding sentence, Buyer further acknowledges and agrees that in entering into this Contract and purchasing all or any part of the Property:

a. Neither Seller nor anyone acting for or on behalf of Seller has made, and does not and will not make, any statements, promises, warranties or representations, either express or implied, with respect to the Property; the appurtenances, facilities and improvements thereon; the grading, the soil condition, the geologic condition and other physical aspects and conditions thereof; the value, profitability, marketability, feasibility, desirability, or adaptability thereof; or the projected income and expenses thereof. The engineering reports which may have been given to Buyer are not intended to be relied upon by Buyer.

b. Neither Seller nor anyone acting for or on behalf of Seller has made, and does not and will not make, any warranties or representations, either EXPRESS OR IMPLIED, with respect to the Property's MERCHANTABILITY, TENANTABILITY, HABITABILITY, SUITABILITY, or FITNESS FOR A PARTICULAR PURPOSE or USE.

c. Buyer has *not* relied upon any statement, promise, warranty or representation of Seller, or anyone acting for or on behalf of Seller, nor on any particular skill, knowledge or expertise of Seller, or anyone acting for or on behalf of Seller.

d. Buyer has made all legal, factual and other inquiries and investigations as Buyer deems necessary, desirable, or appropriate with respect to the Property, its value, suitability and marketability thereof, and the appurtenances, facilities and improvements thereon, and Buyer is purchasing the Property based on Buyer's own inspection and examination thereof. Such inquiries and investigations made by Buyer shall be deemed to include, without limiting the generality thereof, (i) the availability of water, sewer, gas, electricity, telephone service and all other public utility services necessary or desirable for any development of the Property contemplated by Buyer, (ii) the existence of mold, or other materials that may pose a health hazard, (iii) the grading, the soil and geologic conditions of the Property, (iv) such state of facts as an accurate improvement survey plat prepared in accordance with state law would show, and (v) the present and future subdivision and zoning ordinances, resolutions and regulations of the city, county and state where the Property is located and of any other governmental agency having jurisdiction over the Property.

e. Buyer shall acquire the Property in an "AS IS" and "WITH ALL FAULTS" condition and state of repair.

f. BUYER DOES HEREBY WAIVE, and SELLER DOES HEREBY DISCLAIM, ALL REPRESENTATIONS and WARRANTIES, EXPRESS OR IMPLIED, of any kind, nature, or type whatsoever with respect to the Property (except as expressly contained in the deed contemplated hereby and the warranties provided herein), including, by way of description, but not limitation, those of CONDITION, MERCHANTABILITY, TENANTABILITY, HABITABILITY, SUITABILITY, and FITNESS FOR A PARTICULAR PURPOSE or USE. In addition, Seller hereby specifically disclaims any representations or warranties regarding the accuracy of any materials delivered or to be delivered to Buyer by Seller, or contained in the files of Seller, or prepared by agents of Seller, it being Buyer's intent to purchase the Property without reliance on any materials prepared by Seller or its agents.

g. Notwithstanding the foregoing, nothing herein shall relieve Seller from responsibility for any misrepresentations or omission of material facts known by Seller. Buyer acknowledges that Seller has provided to him copies of preliminary soils reports and alerted Buyer to potential soils problems with the Property. Seller shall not be liable or responsible for, and Buyer assumes all risks related to, soils conditions.

h. The acknowledgments, agreements, and disclaimers contained herein shall be binding on Buyer and his/her successors and assigns and shall run with the Property.

9. Release of Seller and Agents. Without in any way limiting the generality of the preceding Paragraph, Buyer hereby specifically acknowledges and agrees that Buyer waives, releases, and discharges all claims Buyer now has, might have had, or may hereafter have against Seller and Seller's

Agents with respect to the condition of the Property, either patent or latent; Buyer's ability or inability to obtain preliminary approval or final approval of any zoning, subdivision plat, P.U.D., or any other development plan for the Property; Buyer's ability or inability to obtain or maintain building permits, temporary or final certificates of occupancy, or other licenses for the development, use, or operation of the Property or any other improvements thereto, or certificates of compliance for the Property or any improvements thereto; the actual or potential income or profits to be derived from the Property; the real estate taxes now or hereafter payable thereon; and any other state of facts which exists with respect to the Property, provided.

Short Payoff. This guidelines for a short payoff vary from state to state. In some states the lender is prohibited from suing for a deficiency, the amount that remains due after the foreclosure sale is held. Others, called "deficiency states," allow lenders to sue on the note for the deficiency or shortfall. In the event that the existing loan exceeds the market value, the salesperson may try to assist the seller in obtaining a "short payoff." The lender consents to accepting the net proceeds in full satisfaction of the existing debt. In an area where troubled real estate is the watchword, this can be the difference between the end of the nightmare and the second chapter.

Clause:

Seller's obligations under this contract are expressly conditional upon the lender holding the note secured by the first mortgage upon the Property, agreeing in written form, on or before _____, 20__, to accept the net proceeds (sales price less commission, new loan points, tax prorations, other contract obligations and customary closing costs) in full satisfaction of the indicated indebtedness.

Tenancy. *This is a very important part of the contract, and yet it is the most often overlooked. Think before you give advice on how an individual or individuals should assume tenancy. The tax implications, potential creditor remedies, flexibility of any future sale, and any other future ramifications of this selection can be very extreme.* The rules for holding title vary from state to state.

Tenancy in Common. The definition of tenancy in common varies from state to state. You will need to know the rules for your state. In general, tenancy in common means that each owns an undivided portion of the property. Each could transfer his/her portion to whomever he/she desired without the consent of the other. There is no right of survivorship, meaning that when one party dies, his/her portion does not automatically go to the remaining tenant. The grantee, buyer, can designate how much of the property he wants each tenant to own. For example: "Jonathan A. Goodman and Mimi Goodman as tenants in common," would indicate that they own equal portions of the property. "Jonathan A. Goodman (75%) and Mimi Goodman (25%) as tenants in common," would indicate that they own their respective percentages. In most states, tenants in common can designate the percentages that they desire.

Joint Tenants. The definition of joint tenancy varies from state to state. You will need to know the rules for your state. In general, joint tenancy means that each owns an *equal* undivided portion of the property. Generally, each party *can* transfer or encumber their portion without the consent or joinder of the other joint tenant. The grantee, buyer, *can not* designate how much of the property he wants each joint tenant to own. For example: "Thomas R. Reece and Hazel Reece as joint tenants," indicates that they own equal portions of the property as joint tenants. "Thomas R. Reece (75%) and "Hazel Reece (25%) as joint tenants," would not be proper. Joint tenancy has a right of survivorship. If either tenant dies, the portion of the property titled in the dead tenant's name *automatically and immediately* transfers to the surviving tenants. *It does not pass through probate, ie., a will.*

There are a lot of people who think that joint tenancy is the best option. Keep in mind that people with two sets of kids from previous marriages might not have considered the disposition of their house in the event of their deaths. Maybe an attorney should help. If in doubt, we prefer tenants in common. Then the portions can be designated in the will of each party.

Case in Point.
The buyers are a happily remarried couple. Mr. Buyer has two sons and Mrs. Buyer has two daughters. The children are young, and everyone loves everyone else. The Buyers are putting all the money that they have into the new home since they need lots of space and a low payment. The real estate professional tells them that joint tenants is the best option for them. After the closing, on the way to the airport there is a terrible traffic accident. Mrs. Buyer is killed instantly. Three days later, after a rough time in intensive care Mr. Buyer dies. When Mrs. Buyer died her property automatically went to Mr. Buyer. Now, the property all goes to Mr. Buyer's children. The daughters of Mrs. Buyer receive nothing.

Tenancy by the Entirety. This is a form of tenancy that is available for legally married people in some states. It has certain creditor protection aspects and is available only for the couple. Neither spouse can sell without the consent of the other. If additional parties are in title, they would hold title as tenants in common or joint tenants with the married couple, who hold their portion of title as tenants by the entirety.

While it is best to designate the manner in which the buyers intend to take title "_____ *Buyer(s), (as joint tenants, tenants in common, tenants by the entirety),* " you can leave it to a later designation, when you are under less stress to get the contract signed, and the buyers have had an opportunity to consult legal counsel.

Clause:

> The buyers reserve the right to designate the tenancy at any time prior to the delivery of deed. In the event that they do not designate any tenancy, then the title will reflect equal portions as tenants in common.

Use of Professionals.   Encourage the use of professionals for areas outside the expertise of the broker. Stay in the real estate business, and let the other professionals run their own risks.   You may save the buyer or seller money by taking on the additional responsibility associated with a professional opinion, but the personal liability you assume in doing so is simply not worth it. After reading these clauses, we hope that you see the need for professionals.

Clause:

1. Buyer is advised to seek, select and retain the professionals s/he desires to investigate the following: the presence and extent of radon gas or other hazardous materials or substances (mold); the physical condition of the Property, including its structural integrity; the condition of appliances, heating, plumbing, air conditioning, electrical and other mechanical and structural devices and systems; the condition of the soils and surrounding soils; the existence of, proximity to, adequacy and expense of utilizing or obtaining the services for water, sewer, natural gas, electrical, television and other services and utilities; the terms and conditions of all covenants and restrictions that affect the Property; the condition and extent of the title, the rights, duties and obligations that may exist as a result of existing documents of record; the obligations, duties, rights and privileges this transaction may impose or create, including the terms conditions and provisions of financing arrangements; and the character of allowed uses, zoning or other public or private regulations, codes, ordinances or the like that may affect the property.

-or-

1. This Contract contemplates the purchase and sale of real property. All parties are hereby advised, and have been advised, to seek competent legal, accounting and such other advice as they, in their own discretion, determine to be advisable. All the brokers and salespeople do not, and have not, offered any legal, tax or accounting advice with regard to this, or any other transaction, involving these parties or otherwise.

-or-

1. The brokers and salespeople licensed in this state are not licensed as attorneys, inspectors nor accountants. This is a legal contract. Seek competent legal or accounting assistance. Do not accept any statements made by any broker or salesperson as legal advice.

1031 Exchanges. Once a difficult transaction, 1031 Exchanges are now quite easy to complete. There is no need to locate the replacement property prior to sale of the relinquished property. The ability to defer some or all of the gain on a property makes understanding an exchange a must for the modern real estate salesperson. "Like-kind" property essentially means that the property is not owner occupied. You will need access to a good CPA to make sure that you are up to date on any tax code changes. While no clause is required, the following two clauses will help if you need to insert a clause into a contract.

The fact that one party needs an exchange may well be confidential information that the other party should not know. The use of the first clause listed below, as a standard clause in all contracts, will ensure the confidentiality of either party's participation in a 1031 Exchange. It becomes just window dressing on the routine contract; yet, it ensures the cooperation and consent when an exchange is applicable.

Clause – 1031 Exchange:
   Each party shall cooperate with the other to effectuate an I.R.C. §1031 Tax Deferred Exchange, including consenting to and acknowledging assignments of this Contract to a Qualified Intermediary, so long as such cooperation is not to the financial detriment of the other party.

Clause – Relinquished Property Contract:
   Buyer shall cooperate in structuring this transaction as a like-kind exchange for the benefit of Seller; provided, however, that Buyer shall incur no additional cost or expense in connection therewith. Notwithstanding anything to the contrary contained herein, Seller shall have the right to

assign Seller's rights and obligations hereunder to Frascona and Joiner Financial Services Corporation as Qualified Intermediary, for purposes of initiating the contemplated exchange; however, no such assignment shall have the effect of releasing Seller from continuing liability for performance of any of Seller's obligations. In the interest of convenience, however, Seller shall convey title to the Property directly to Buyer on behalf of the Qualified Intermediary. In no event shall Seller's structuring Seller's disposition of the Property as a like-kind exchange delay the closing of this transaction without Buyer's prior written consent.

Clause – Replacement Property Contract:

Seller shall cooperate in structuring this transaction as a like-kind exchange under Section 1031 of the Internal Revenue Code as to Buyer; provided, however, that Seller shall incur no additional cost or expense in connection therewith. Notwithstanding anything herein contained to the contrary, Buyer shall have the right to assign Buyer's rights and obligations to Frascona and Joiner Financial Services Corporation as Qualified Intermediary, for the purpose of completing the contemplated exchange; however, no such assignment shall have the effect of releasing Buyer from continuing liability for performance. Seller shall convey title to the Property to a grantee specified by Buyer. In no event shall Buyer's structuring of Buyer's acquisition of the Property as a like-kind exchange delay the closing of this transaction, without Seller's prior written consent.

General "Boiler Plate" Clauses. These are samples of various clauses. They can be used as a template for other clauses. If you get to a point where you may have forgotten what you said earlier and want to be sure that the clause that you are about to write will override other clauses, use *"notwithstanding anything herein contained to the contrary,"* which will put the new clause in a priority position.

Clause:

1.   Cost of any appraisal to be obtained after the date of this Contract shall be timely paid to the appraiser by _____.

2.   This Contract shall not be assignable by Buyer without Seller's prior written consent, which consent may be withheld for any reason.

3.   Except as so restricted, this Contract shall inure to the benefit of, and be binding upon, the heirs, personal representatives, successors and assigns of the parties.

4. Time is of the essence hereof. If any note or check received as earnest money hereunder, or any other payment due hereunder, is not paid, honored or tendered when due, or if any other obligation hereunder is not performed or waived as herein provided, there shall be the following remedies:

    a. In the event Buyer is in default, Seller may elect to treat this Contract as cancelled, in which case all payments and things of value received hereunder shall be forfeited and retained on behalf of Seller, and Seller may recover such damages as may be proper, or Seller may elect to treat this Contract as being in full force and effect, and Seller shall have the right to specific performance or damages, or both.

    b. In the event Seller is in default Buyer may elect to treat this Contract as cancelled, in which case all payments and things of value received hereunder shall be returned. Buyer may recover such damages as may be proper, or Buyer may elect to treat this Contract as being in full force and effect. Buyer shall have the right to specific performance or damages, or both.

    - or -

4. Time is of the essence hereof. If any note or check received as earnest money hereunder or any other payment due hereunder is not paid, honored or tendered when due, or if any other obligation hereunder is not performed or waived as herein provided, there shall be the following remedies:

    a. In the event Buyer is in default, all payments and things of value received hereunder shall be forfeited by Buyer and retained on behalf of Seller, and both parties shall thereafter be released from all obligations hereunder. It is agreed that such payments and things of value are liquidated damages and are Seller's sole and only remedy for Buyer's failure to perform the obligations of this Contract. Seller expressly waives the remedies of specific performance and additional damages.

    b. In the event Seller is in default, Buyer may elect to treat this Contract as cancelled, in which case all payments and things of value received hereunder shall be returned. Buyer may recover such damages as may be proper, or Buyer may elect to treat this Contract as being in full force and effect. Buyer shall have the right to specific performance or damages, or both.

5. Anything to the contrary herein notwithstanding, in the event of any arbitration or litigation arising out of this Contract, the arbitrator or court shall award to the prevailing party all reasonable costs and expenses, including attorney fees.

6. By signing this document, Buyer and Seller acknowledge that the Selling Company or the Listing Company has advised that this document has important legal consequences and has recommended the examination of title and consultation with legal, tax or other counsel before signing this Contract.

7. In the event this Contract is terminated, all payments and things of value received hereunder shall be returned, and the parties shall be relieved of all obligations hereunder.

8. The listing broker, _____, and its salespersons have been engaged as _____.

9. The selling broker, _____, and its salespersons have been engaged as _____.

10. Any notice to Buyer shall be effective when received by either Buyer or the party indicated in paragraph _____ herein.

11. Any notice to Buyer shall be effective when received by either Buyer or the party indicated in paragraph _____ herein, or three days after the same is deposited in the United States Mail, properly addressed to Buyer at the address herein provided for notice.

12. Any notice to Seller shall be effective when received by either Seller or the party indicated in paragraph _____ herein.

13. Any notice to Seller shall be effective when received by either Seller or the party indicated in paragraph _____ herein, or three days after the same is deposited in the United States Mail, properly addressed to Seller at the address herein provided for notice.

14. Any notices required under this Contract shall be personally delivered, or sent by regular or certified mail, postage prepaid, and addressed as follows:

If to Sellers: _____
_____
_____

copy to: _____
_____
_____

If to Buyer: _____
_____
_____

copy to: _____
_____
_____

Notice shall be deemed given when delivered, if personally delivered, or two business days after mailing, if mailed. Either party may change the address or addresses to which subsequent notices shall be sent, by notice given in accordance with this paragraph.

15. No subsequent modification of any of the terms of this Contract shall be valid, binding upon the parties, or enforceable, unless made in writing and signed by the parties.

16. This Contract constitutes the entire contract between the parties relating to the subject hereof, and any prior agreements pertaining thereto, whether oral or written, have been merged and integrated into this contract.

17. A copy of this document may be executed by each party, separately, and when each party has executed a copy thereof, such copies taken together shall be deemed to be a full and complete contract between the parties.

19.   This Contract incorporates all the terms and conditions of all agreements between the parties.   There are no promises, agreements, or representations, except as outlined herein.   Neither the broker nor the sales agent has made any promises or representations to induce any party to enter into this Contract.

Once the Offer is Signed

Contract Cover Letter.   Whether preparing the offer for the buyer or the counter offer for the seller, it is wise to provide the cooperating agent with a cover letter for the contract.   This is useful especially when you will not be presenting your client's offer to the other party.   The letter may certainly be the difference between an acceptance and/or counter proposal, or an outright rejection.   Do not rely upon the cooperating salesperson to favorably present all the terms.   In addition, personal notes about the person made in the offer or complimentary phrases about the home itself will personalize the offer.

Introduce the buyer to the seller by giving some background information.   Be careful before indicating whether both spouses work, the buyers have children or are excited about any special amenities of the neighborhood.   Such statements might give the seller information about the buyer's desire to buy.   This information is confidential and should not be disclosed without the buyer's prior approval.

Discuss the financing and any pre-qualification assurances from the lender.   Continue with an explanation for the terms incorporated in the proposed contract. Disclosing the rationale behind specific terms will soften what may initially be perceived as an unreasonable request.   Be careful that you do not compromise the buyer's or seller's negotiating position by overstating or making commitments not outlined in the actual proposal.   Finish the letter on a complimentary note about the home, the terms, or the other party.

Tip.   *Address the proposal cover letter to the cooperating salesperson with s/he knowledge that they must share it with the seller client.*

Contract Letter to Seller.   This form of cover letter is used when sending an initial offer and when sending a counter proposal through another agent to the other party. During the frenzy and excitement of receiving an offer, the seller may not absorb all the details of the transaction, regardless of how explicitly you review the terms.   With the length of the standard contract in many states, just covering all the disclaimers would exhaust any seller. Primarily the seller is interested in two items: the purchase price and the bottom line net proceeds. It is the responsibility of the salesperson to explain, in a form that will hopefully reach the other party, the interrelationships between the remaining terms and the impact each may have on the final closing date. Stating the buyer's qualifications, the reasons for some of the terms included and the desire of the buyer to make this a hassle free transaction can make the difference. A letter serves to explain the offer and to make the buyer a real person.

Explain just enough about the buyer's finances to let the seller know that these buyers are qualified and also to intimate that it is the maximum amount that they can pay. Having a buyer that is "pre-qualified" is great. Remember that the pre-qualification letter should only be for the purchase price, or loan amount of the offer. Yes, for a different offer you will have to get another letter.

If the contract calls for cash, the seller will wonder where it is coming from. A copy of a letter from the bank indicating that the money is on deposit helps a lot in this instance. Never give a copy of the bank statement, as it contains other confidential information that your buyer will not want disclosed.

The same procedure can be used for counteroffers, which should always be in written form. Write a cover letter explaining the counter offer, so that the intentions of the seller are clear and personalized for the buyer.

Letter/e-mail – Offer Cover Letter

Diane Koontz
K & D Properties, Limited
14 Your Street
Honolulu, HI 99999

Dear Diane:

Please extend my appreciation to your sellers for allowing us to view their home on such short notice today. It is easy to see that the Sellers maintain their home in "show condition" as a routine matter.

Bill and Betty Buyer have relocated to Hawaii from Boulder. Bill is a physician with Physician's Hospital and Betty has her degree in Business Administration with a concentration in finance. Betty is currently interviewing with several banks for employment opportunities. She already has offers for employment in a position in bank administration, similar to the one she held in the Peoples Republic of Boulder.

Bill and Betty will have no difficulty qualifying for the loan amount in the financing terms on Bill's income alone. They have no outstanding debt. [They have already met with the loan officer at _____ Mortgage Company and will do their formal loan application immediately upon acceptance of their offer.] [They have already been "pre-qualified" by the Mortgage Company. A copy of that letter is attached.] This should help the seller realize that these people are able to buy the home.

The buyers are aware of comparable sales in the neighborhood and are offering an exceptionally good price for the home. Their offer of $450,000.00 maximizes their available cash for down payment and closing costs. Certainly a benefit to the sellers would be to sell their home in today's market with no contingencies.

The Buyers are aware that the roof will most likely require replacement within the year, as indicated in the Sellers' Property Disclosure and that the carpet will need to be replaced. They understand the seller wanted to leave these types of replacement items to the discretion and personal tastes of the new owner.

From their first drive through the neighborhood, Bill and Betty indicated they were attracted to the overall sense of community. They liked the open floor plan of your home, as well as the yard size for their two children. A pool was not a requirement in their search for a home and actually somewhat of a concern with the two small children, but it is acceptable.

Diane, I look forward to working together toward a mutually beneficial transaction for both the buyer and seller. Please call me directly if you or your clients have any particular questions. My cellular telephone is 999-226-0896, and my digital pager is 999-578-2649. You also contact me via email at me@myemail.com.

Sincerely,
The Real Estate Company

by Your loyal Agent

Letter/e-mail – Counter Offer Cover

Mary Begier
The Begier Real Estate Connection
P. O. Box 3113
Boulder, Colorado 80307

Dear Mary:

Thank you for your time and effort in showing the sellers' home and in preparing an offer on the home. It is obvious your buyers placed a great deal of thought in making their decision.

The sellers are in agreement with most of the terms and conditions of the offer. Only minor changes have been made, and these are incorporated into the counter offer proposal.

The adjustment in selling price reflects the price the sellers feel is reasonable. They, too, are aware of the comparable sales in the neighborhood and feel that the addition of the pool and kitchen upgrades justify a higher price than the recent sold comparables without similar improvements. They do not anticipate any difficulty with a full price appraisal.

The sellers do recognize the benefit of a "clean" offer with no contingencies. Therefore, they are prepared to vacate the home earlier than planned in order to accommodate the buyers' proposed closing date.

The sellers were impressed with the thorough approach of the buyers in already meeting with their lender. It is always a pleasure to cooperate with such a professional. I look forward to hearing from you on the seller's counter proposal soon.

Sincerely,
The Real Estate Company, Inc.

By

Letter/e-mail – Obligation to Present All Offers

Mr. Sam Seller
Mrs. Sandy Seller
4750 Table Mesa Drive
Boulder, CO 80305

    Re: 4750 Table Mesa Drive

Dear Sam and Sandy:

Please understand that we are obligated by law to present directly to you for consideration any and all offers that are delivered to us. Although it would be nice to empower us to make the initial determination, that is simply not the law, nor is it the policy of this office. You, and you alone, are the decision maker. Regardless of how far-fetched or unworkable the offer may seem at first, it is still a written indication that someone wants to find out if there is a possible avenue for the acquisition of your property.

Some of the offers will not be what you want to see. You may even ask us to tell you about them over the telephone. Unfortunately, we do not make telephone presentations unless you are out of the area. In that event, we first fax the proposed contract to you and then review it when we both have a copy.

Attempted telephone acceptance violates the statute of frauds. That means that a telephone agreement is not an enforceable agreement if the subject matter is the sale of real estate. In addition, when someone accepts a proposal over the telephone, we have found that their willingness to sign that proposal changes rapidly. We present contracts only in person and request that salespeople from other offices do the same.

Thank you for your understanding. Now, when one party signs the proposal, we know that we will eventually have a firm enforceable contract.

            Sincerely,
            The Real Estate Company

Letter/e-mail – Counter Proposals

Mr. Sam Seller
Mrs. Sandy Seller
4750 Table Mesa Drive
Boulder, CO 80305

Re: 4750 Table Mesa Drive

Dear Sam and Sandy:

Thank you for talking with me on the telephone today. I want to be sure that you understand the effect of a counter proposal. This offer is capable of acceptance in its present condition. Any changes that are made, either by crossing out a term and initialing it or by executing a counter proposal, give the other party the opportunity to walk away from the transaction with impunity.

A counter proposal is a rejection of the initial offer and a return offer by you to the buyer. By definition, the initial offer is no longer capable of acceptance. Should you later change your mind and wish to accept the initial offer that will not be possible. You will have to wait for the buyer to make another offer or you will have to initiate such an offer.

With that in mind, let me encourage you to review each proposed change to determine if it is critical to the transaction before making any change to the offer. I know that we both want a sale that is as proper and correct as possible. However, I do not want to see you counter the offer for details that might give the buyer the ability to walk away. Thank you for your consideration.

As always, the advice of an attorney is recommended. If I can be of assistance in explaining the alternatives to you and/or your attorney, accountant, priest or other advisor, please do not hesitate to call. This is an important point in the sale, and you need to feel comfortable in your understanding of the alternatives and in your ultimate decision.

It is a pleasure to be your listing agent for the sale of your property. If there is anything that I can do to assist you please do not hesitate to let me know.

Sincerely,

Letter/e-mail – Offer Proposing Questionable Deal

Mr. Albert A. Desperate
Mrs. Martha B. Desperate
6990 Hopeless Avenue
Madison, MN 90303

Mr. Wilber C. Hungry
Mrs. Freda D. Hungry
Apartment 210 A
West End Apartments
999 Last Avenue
Madison, MN 80305

     Re: 6990 Hopeless Avenue
          Desperation City, XX

Dear Mr. and Mrs. Desperate and Mr. and Mrs. Hungry:

     I know that all of you are anticipating this letter, and I am sorry that I have to write it. I simply have no other option than to formally clarify my position, and that of this office, with regard to the transaction that you are proposing. Please understand our position and review this letter carefully.

     As I indicated to all of you over the phone today, and in person over the last two days, your joint decision to allow the sellers to apply, for and utilize their credit to obtain, a new FHA loan as owner occupants, with the intention of immediately upon closing of said loan transferring the property to the buyers via assumption of the new FHA loan, is a violation of the rules and regulations promulgated by the Department of Housing and Urban Development. Neither I nor this office can be a party to such a transaction.

     We understand your respective desperate needs to sell and buy the home in question. We are not passing on the validity of the transaction, but only stating that it violates the regulations as we understand them. You are, of course, free to take whatever action you desire. We would advise you to seek the closing services of a title company, or other suitable closing agent, to ensure that the transaction's financial calculations are properly calculated. In addition, we again advise you to seek the services of a real estate attorney, or to contact the FHA directly, to fully understand the ramifications of the transaction you propose.

There is no doubt that the buyer was procured by the efforts of this office. Should the transaction close, we will be entitled to receive our commission, as indicated in the listing agreement. There is no requirement that we draft the contract or conduct the closing. We must only provide you with a buyer acceptable to you, or that you transfer the property to a buyer that was procured by us.

I know that you understand our position, and we appreciate your respecting the fact that we can not be a part of the transaction as you propose it. Nevertheless, congratulations on the pending purchase and sale of this property.

As with any assumption, there is a potential for damage to be inflicted to the credit of both parties in the event that the loan payments are not timely made. Reference should be made to the pamphlet we have given you, "Assumption, Subject To and Novation; Your Liabilities and Rights."

Sincerely,
The Real Estate Company

by: Your Name Here,
REALTOR®, CRS, GRI

Letter/e-mail – Offer Matching the Listing

Mr. Sam Seller
Mrs. Sandy Seller
4750 Table Mesa Drive
Boulder, CO 80305

    Re: 4750 Table Mesa Drive

Dear Sam and Sandy:

With this letter, we are happy to include an offer that exactly meets the terms and conditions you requested in your Listing Agreement. It is always a pleasure to present this kind of offer. It is important that you fully understand the implications of the transaction as proposed by the offer, so feel free to contact me immediately to explain to you the ramifications of the proposed transaction. As always, should you feel you need it, the advice of an attorney is recommended.

Few people are capable of paying all cash, so I have insisted that the earnest money be equal to five percent of the total sales price. It is rare to obtain such a substantial amount of earnest money. Although all indications are that it will be a quick closing within the next few weeks, I never consider a property sold until the actual closing, the funds having been paid and having cleared the bank. [Contrary to popular opinion, even certified funds must clear and are subject to stop payment orders.] I would advise you not to obligate yourselves irrevocably based upon this contract until it actually closes.

                Sincerely,
                The Real Estate Company

                by: Your Name Here,
                REALTOR®, CRS, GRI

Letter/e-mail – Offer Conditional Upon Sale of Current Home

Mr. Sam Seller
Mrs. Sandy Seller
4750 Table Mesa Drive
Boulder, CO 80305

    Re: 4750 Table Mesa Drive

Dear Sam and Sandy:

    As you are aware by now, we are happy to have an offer on your home for your consideration. It has been a difficult job to market your home due to the large inventory of other homes on the market in your price range. There are just too many from which to choose. We really appreciate your efforts to have the home always ready to show even on a few moments notice. I believe the buyer selected your home because of the superb condition of the property, and you deserve credit for your efforts.

    This offer indicates that the buyer will have to sell and close upon his/her present home before s/he can be obligated to purchase your home. This imposes some degree of risk because the contract for the sale of the buyer's current home has its own potential problems. I have insisted that a copy of the buyer's contract for the sale of the buyer's home be attached to this offer, so that you can review it in detail.

    In addition, I have contacted the agent who is assisting the ultimate buyer in the purchase of your buyer's house and indicated that you will probably be calling to discuss the status of that transaction. The agent for the ultimate buyer has indicated that you are more than welcome to speak to him if it will help you decide to accept this offer. The ultimate buyer's agent's office and home telephone numbers follow:

    Agent for the ultimate buyer of the buyer's house:
    James E. Rodenbeek
    The Rodenbeek Agency
    Scott City, Kansas (316) 872-5134

Most people who will be able to afford your home are the owners of an existing house. The sale of their current residence, although sometimes not indicated in the contract, is going to be the deciding factor in the approval process of the new lender. The lender will probably make the closing of the current home a condition of loan approval.

As with any offer, even ones that have no indicated conditions, there is a degree of uncertainty until the deal actually closes. It is with this in mind that we caution you not to rely too heavily on this particular sale until it is final. We can not be responsible for actions or inactions that are not within our control, and the abilities and intentions of a buyer are definitely outside of our control. Although we will try hard to keep ourselves abreast of the events as they unfold, we can not make the decisions for any of the parties.

This particular offer, like any other legally binding contract, needs to be carefully reviewed to determine if it suits your needs. It is important that you fully understand the implications of the transaction as it is proposed, so please feel free to ask me at any time to explain further the ramifications of the proposed transaction. We can not give legal advice, and, therefore, you may wish to use an attorney for that purpose. However, we can explain the contract in detail, so you can make an informed decision.

I know I speak for the entire staff when I say that we have enjoyed having your home in our inventory. I think the buyers are excited to be buying your house and that good feeling is certainly a nice help in keeping them interested through the rigorous loan application, qualification, and closing processes.

Sincerely,
The Real Estate Company

by: Your Name Here,
REALTOR®, CRS, GRI

Letter/e-mail – Practice of Law – *Just for Fun*

Sam and Sandy Seller
4750 Table Mesa Drive
Boulder, CO 80305

Re: 4750 Table Mesa Drive

Dear Sam and Sandy:

As you are aware by now, we are happy to have an offer on your home for your consideration. It has been a difficult job to market your home due to the large inventory of other homes on the market in your price range. There are just too many from which to choose. We really appreciate your efforts to have the home always ready to show, even on a few moments notice. I believe the purchasers selected your home because of the superb condition of the property, and you deserve the credit for your efforts.

We would be happy to accompany you to your attorney's office to help review the contract if you wish. If you decide not to select an attorney, we will just do his job without compensation. In the event we do not meet your expectations, you can feel free to sue us. Our contracts are so poorly drafted that we are nervous about having you take them to an attorney.

In addition, since you never really agreed to anything in the contract and are so unsure of the transaction, we are very suspect of your taking the contract to anyone to review it. If you are such a simple-minded fool to let some lawyer talk you out of the deal, there is really no need to go see one. I can just take care of the details he would normally do, such as reviewing the title commitment, only to find that you do not really own the property, and only finding that out now because I was too lazy to order a commitment before I listed your property. Plus, I can also give you erroneous financial and tax advice.

I know I speak for the entire staff when I say that we have enjoyed having your home in our inventory. I think the buyers are excited to be buying your house, and that good feeling is certainly a nice help in keeping them interested through the rigorous loan application, qualification, and closing processes.

Sincerely,

Chapter 6

After the Contract is Signed

The Road to a Successful Closing

Contract Progress

The Oral Counter. There are kitchen counters, but no oral counters. There is no contract until it is in writing and signed by all parties. Each party to the contract must have a copy of the document, fully executed by the other party, electronically or otherwise.

Contract is Signed. At some point, whether after the initial offer or after one or more counteroffers, the final document is signed, and the real estate professional feels that there is a contract. Communicating the fact that the final document has been signed, rather than that there is a contract, is necessary to the transaction. *Presenting the facts and allowing the parties to draw their own conclusions is the best way to be professional.*

Agency after the Contract is Signed. Remember that once signed, it is the duty of the real estate professional to effectuate the contract. That means to try to schedule the events that are conditions precedent to closing, so the closing will actually take place.

Backup Contract Issues. When there are two contracts on the same property, the licensee needs to be especially careful not to "tortuously interfere" with one or the other. For example, the first contract is for $245,000.00, and the backup contract is for $265,000.00. The seller wants number one (the senior contract) to go away and number two (the junior position contract) to become the operative contract. It would be a mistake for the seller's agent to drag his/her feet on the appraisal, scheduling termite people or other necessary events, in the hopes that the first buyer would tire, or worse yet, not meet a deadline and bail out. Such actions have been viewed by the courts as improper and damages are awarded. Do not be mislead or fooled by your seller's instructions. Following such instruction is not an agency issue. Such conduct is "tortuous interference with contract."

Performance Deadlines for Conditions. The complexity of today's real estate transaction necessitates that many contingencies are often incorporated into the contract with specific deadlines for performance, or removal, by either the seller or the buyer. Failure to do so may render the contract null and void or waive the benefitting party's right to make the specific item a contract issue at any future date. It becomes imperative that all parties to the contract – buyer, seller, real estate brokers, lenders, escrow officers and attorneys – be in full agreement on the performance deadlines for all contingencies in the accepted contract. For this reason, a form that itemizes these dates in chronological sequence, circulated and signed by all parties, will facilitate timely compliance as well as eliminate any misunderstandings in the future.

The performance deadline form can be used both in the beginning for the initial concurrence of specific performance deadlines required, as well as for periodic updates as each deadline is met. It is a simple matter then to fill in the date completed, highlight the item addressed, perhaps write a short confirming note and mail it. Copies to your clients, the cooperating broker, the lender, the escrow or title company or other third parties keeps everyone aware of the progress being made.

Notification of Failure to Perform or Pending Deadline Expiration. Keeping all parties to the transaction informed about the status of impending performance deadlines encourages each one to track the events more carefully and take responsibility for their own actions or inactions. Consider programming e-mails to arrive when required, so that you do not need to send them each day. Set up a rule or program to automatically send the e-mail on particular dates.

Remember how effective it is to copy the other parties, so the lender or appraiser is nudged along. Since everyone got a copy, they know that we know that they are not yet performing. If a performance deadline needs to be modified or extended, all parties know well in advance, and a solution can be negotiated between all parties before tempers flare over last minute changes.

Other Realty. Generally, it is not permissible to communicate directly with any party to the transaction other than your client, but you can direct your correspondence to the other party in care of the other agent. Do not be afraid to include all agent duties for both the seller and buyer agents, so everyone is aware of the duties expected of them. Your organizational skills will be recognized and well rewarded.

Lenders. We all know how difficult it is to get some lenders to play on the team. They talk the talk, but do not get things on time. By adding them to the list of recipients for the performance deadline checklist and requesting their sign off, they are placed in a position of accountability, as well. They can more readily see how the loan process deadlines affect and are influenced by the other conditions in the contract. Bring them in to the whole picture.

Letter/e-mail – Assignment of Tasks

Mr. Sam Seller
Mrs. Sandy Seller
4750 Table Mesa Drive
Boulder, CO 80305

Mr. Ben Buyer
Mrs. Beverly Buyer
Unit 6, Hotel Alley
My Town, CO, 80305

c/o Other Realty
1234 Prospect Lane
Property, CO 80305

    Re: 4750 Table Mesa Drive

Dear Sam, Sandy, Ben and Beverly:

    If you are represented or assisted by a real estate licensee in this transaction, this letter has been forwarded to you through your real estate agent. That is the proper method of communication with you. In the event you do not have the assistance or representation through a real estate professional, we have communicated with you directly and will continue to do so for future updates. It is our desire that all parties to this transaction and affiliates be informed as the contract progresses toward closing.

    Now that we have a contract, a copy of which is attached, there are a number of tasks that must be accomplished to ensure a prompt and proper closing. Some tasks we accept responsibility for; some are the buyer's obligation; some are the seller's obligation; and some are the obligation of the other salesperson and many third parties.

    To assist everyone in determining who has the responsibility for each item, I have enclosed a list showing the tasks, the party that needs to complete each item, and, in parentheses, the completion date for each item. Please consult the list and advise me if you need additional help with any of your responsibilities. Although we can not guarantee the performance of the other parties, we will endeavor to assist them, in every reasonable way possible, to complete their tasks in a timely fashion. Anything that you can to do to assist those entities such as lenders, appraisers, home inspectors, or other affiliates is greatly appreciated.

The names, phone numbers and e-mail addresses are indicated to expedite communication. You will note that I have arranged the tasks once by deadline for everyone and then for each party in date sequence.

To be sure that we are all in agreement and that the delegation of duties works for everyone, please sign and fax back to me as soon as you can.

Sincerely,
The Real Estate Company

by: Your Name Here,
REALTOR®, CRS, GRI

cc:Lender
    Appraiser
    Home Inspector
    Title Company
    New Insurance Company

Contract Deadlines Form

PROPERTY ADDRESS: _____

CONTRACT DATED _____

SELLER _____   **BUYER** _____

Phone: _____   Phone: _____

Fax: _____   Fax: _____

E-mail: _____   E-mail: _____

LENDER _____   **TITLE COMPANY** _____

Phone: _____   Phone:_____

Fax: _____   Fax:_____

E-mail: _____   E-mail: _____

HOME INSPECTOR_____   **ESCROW COMPANY** _____

Phone: _____   Phone_____

Fax: _____   Fax:_____

E-mail: _____   E-mail: _____

NEW INSURANCE COMPANY_____

Phone: _____

Fax: _____   E-mail: _____

GENERAL

Event:	Deadline:	Completed:	Notes:

BUYER

Event:	Deadline:	Completed:	Notes:

SELLER

Event:	Deadline:	Completed:	Notes:

This is to confirm all the dates necessary to achieve a smooth closing. Please verify the dates with either the buyer or seller, sign the form, keep a copy, mail a copy to either the buyer or seller and return a copy to me.

REALTOR® assisting Buyer:_____ Date:_____

REALTOR® assisting Seller:_____ Date:_____

SELLER: _____ Date:_____

BUYER: _____ Date:_____

LENDER: _____ Date:_____

Letter/e-mail – Broker to Buyer After Offer Accepted

Mr. and Mrs. Beverly Buyer
Apartment 610 A
12th and Main Street
Denver, CO 80305

  Re: 909 East First Street

Dear Mr. and Mrs. Buyer:

  Congratulations on the purchase of your new home! As you have probably heard, your offer on 909 East First Street was accepted and signed by the seller this Tuesday at 10:00 P.M.   There are many things that need to be done to get ready for the closing and possession of the home. In order to let everyone know who has what responsibility, let me outline the various assignments for all concerned.

  First, you will need to apply for a loan fitting the minimum parameters of the contract – loan amount of $245,000.00 with an interest rate of 10% per annum, amortized over thirty years – within the next five days. I have provided you with a partial list of lenders who have elected to have their rates and other information included in the list and who are currently doing business in this area. Although not exhaustive, it should give you a good place to start. As always, the ultimate selection of a lender is yours. We recommend that you call a few lenders for rate quotations and then select one or two for your initial application. Each has its own programs and alternatives in addition to the standard government (VA and FHA) loans.

Deadline for loan application is _____.

  It has been our experience that purchasers like to discuss their finances with a loan officer of their choice and let that lender assist them in making the personal determination of the exact type, terms and amount of loan that will suit their needs. For this reason, we do not attempt to counsel anyone concerning the best loan for his needs. When you have selected a lender and made a loan appointment, please let us know, so we can assist you and that lender in gathering the information and documentation that the lender requires. To assist you in preparing for the initial interview, I have enclosed a partial list of information often requested, so you can gather as much of it as possible in advance and expedite the application process.

Second, you will need to select a home inspection service and termite inspection service. While many home inspection and termite inspection services are available, we have included a list of services used by previous customers for your review. Each should be happy to provide you with a list of past customers to assist you in making your decision.

Inspection Objection Deadline is _____.

Third, you will need to decide on the educational alternatives available. A list of the public and private schools within a reasonable distance from your new home is included. It has been so long since any of the salespeople in the office attended school that an opinion on the quality or availability of various educational services would not be reliable. Each person evaluates the needs of their children and the various offerings of each school system differently. It is a personal choice. Please note the phone number of the school board. Its members are available to assist you and can provide answers to your questions in the future.

Remember, the closing date is set for Friday, the 15th of March, and you will need to have your funds available. To expedite obtaining the balance of the down payment for the closing, I would suggest opening a local bank account at your earliest convenience. I am sure that whomever you initially select will be able to get you started with an account and provide you with certified funds for closing. I have included the names and numbers of bankers in the area with whom I enjoy working.

Thank you for allowing me to serve you in viewing and selecting the home of your choice. It has been fun helping you to locate your new home. I am confident you will be very happy with your selection.

Sincerely,
The Real Estate Company

by: Your Name Here,
REALTOR®, CRS, GRI

enclosures:

Letter/e-mail – Home Warranty Program

Mr. and Mrs. Beverly Buyer
c/o Martha Douglas
Douglas and Company Real Estate
12th and Main Street
Longmont, CO 80000

    Re: 909 First Street

Dear Mr. and Mrs. Buyer:

    In response to your recent inquiry about the availability of a Home Owners Warranty on the property, I contacted _____ at _____ and s/he indicated that there is a policy, #_____, currently in effect. I would suggest that you talk with her directly, so she can answer your questions. That way there will be nothing lost in the transmission, and you can ask follow-up questions without having to contact me.

    Since our firm has a policy that prohibits us from making any guarantees with regard to any property, I always encourage interested buyers to talk directly with the insurance agency to avoid confusion. I would encourage you to inquire about the extent of the coverage, the term remaining, the balance of the unexpired limits which remains available. Thank you for your understanding. If you reach an impasse, please do not hesitate to let me know and I will try to find the person over there who can assist you.

                              Sincerely,
                              The Real Estate Company

                              by: Your Name Here,
                              REALTOR®, CRS, GRI

Escrow Instructions.   Every area of the country calls them something different. Some states do not have escrow instructions and simply use the contract as the basis for the closing entity to prepare for closing.   Many brokers do the closing themselves as a service to both buyer and seller.

Some states utilize a third party escrow service to receive and distribute the funds and ensure that all conveyance documents are properly prepared, executed and recorded in a timely fashion. Sometimes this party is an attorney.

Delivering a clear set of instructions, accompanied by the earnest money, a copy of the contract and all the necessary additional disclosures and documents, to the escrow company will facilitate the process.   In the event the earnest money is held by other than the escrow agent, a copy of the receipt showing the depository of the earnest money will suffice. By sending copies to all entities at the same time, you will ensure that each of the entities starts with an identical set of copies. If you use an electronic fax, simply coping these entities on your e-mail works well. Memos, an e-mail or a letter with the deadlines delineated and delivered to the escrow agent with a copy to the cooperating salesperson and the proposed lender will keep all the parties to the transaction well informed of the progress.

One salesperson sends a letter or an e-mail with a copy of the documents along with instructions to inform him immediately if any corrections are necessary. He also attaches a blue backing sheet, similar to the ones that attorneys use for wills, so the package will remain intact. Yes, the backing sheet does have his company name, address and telephone number.

Escrow Checklist.   A checklist of activities necessary to close your transaction is invaluable when attempting to track multiple escrows. With one quick glance at the checklist, you can ascertain what has been accomplished and what yet needs to be done. If you are working with an assistant, the checklist can eliminate duplicate efforts and keep you both informed about what has been done. Your communication with your buyer or seller will be both concise and precise.

Letter/e-mail – Contract Review and Assignment of Tasks

Mr. Sam Seller
Mrs. Sandy Seller
4750 Table Mesa Drive
Boulder, CO 80305

    Re: 4750 Table Mesa Drive

Dear Sam and Sandy:

Enclosed you will find an exact copy of the contract as it was finally signed and initialed. Please review it immediately to verify that in fact it represents the transaction as you think it should be. You will note that I have sent an identical copy to your designated lender, the title insurance company (closing or escrow agent), the Buyer and all REALTORS® involved.

Now that we have a contract there are a number of tasks that must be accomplished to ensure a prompt and proper closing. Some tasks we accept responsibility for; some are the buyer's obligation; some are the seller's obligation; and some are the obligation of the cooperating salesperson.

To assist everyone in determining who has the responsibility for each item, I have enclosed a list showing the tasks, the party that needs to complete each item and, in parentheses, the completion date for each item. Please consult the list and advise me if you need additional help with any of your responsibilities. Although we cannot guarantee the performance of the other parties, we will endeavor to assist them in every reasonable way possible to complete their tasks in a timely fashion.

                        Sincerely,
                        The Real Estate Company

                        by: Your Name Here,
                        REALTOR®, CRS, GRI

cc:Everyone

Escrow Instructions Form

TO:_____ Escrow Officer:_____

_____ Escrow Phone:_____

_____ Escrow Fax:_____

E-Mail:

_____

Contract Date:_____ Escrow No:_____

Acceptance date:_____ Escrow Opened:_____

Please open escrow for the following:
Property Address:

Closing Date:_____ Early Occupancy:_____
Initial Deposit: $_____ Lease Form: _____
Add'l Deposit: $_____ Loan Type: _____
Down Payment: $_____ Loan amount: $_____
Purchase price: $_____

Sellers:_____ **Buyers:**_____
Address: Address:

Home: _____   _____
Work: _____   _____
Cell: _____   _____
e-mail: _____   _____

Broker Information

Seller's S'person:_____   Buyer's S'person:_____
Address: Address:

Home: _____   _____
Work: _____   _____
Cell: _____   _____
e-mail: _____   _____

Existing Lender:_____   **New Lender:**_____
Loan Amount: $_____   Loan Officer:_____
Address: Address:

Loan Type:(FHA)(VA)(CONV)
Processor:_____
Phone:(o)_____(f)_____(c)_____ (e) _____

Attorney for legal
documents:_____
Phone:(o)_____(f)_____ (e-mail) _____

Commission Division from Escrow:

Company:_____   Amount: $_____
Company:_____   Amount: $_____

Enclosures

_____Original contract dated:_____
_____Check in the amount of $_____ Dated:_____
_____Counter proposal dated:_____
_____Other_____
_____Other_____

Escrow Checklist Form

Client Name:_____

Property Address:_____

Sales Price:_____Contract Date:_____Accept Date:_____
Loan Amount:_____Loan Company:_____

Loan Officer:_____ Phone:_____Fax:_____
   E-Mail: _____Cell: _____

Cooperating Office
Broker:_____Salesperson:_____
Office Phone:_____Direct Line: _____
Office Fax:_____Direct Fax: _____
                                 Home:_____
                                 Cell: _____
                                 E-Mail: _____

Escrow Company:_____
Officer:_____
Phone: _____ Fax: _____ File No: _____
E-Mail: _____ Cell: _____

Money
____Earnest money deposited
____Add'l Earnest money deposited
____Tasks letter sent

Appraisal
____Ordered on_____
____Company_____
____Comps prepared
____Appraiser met
____Appraisal in

Documents
____Preparer_____
____Deed ordered
____Lease ordered
____Mortgage ordered

Existing loan
____Lender_____
____Payoff ordered
____Payoff received

Property disclosure
____Received from seller
____Delivered to buyer
____Accepted

Condo/Association documents
____Ordered
____Delivered to buyer
____Accepted by buyer
____Objections
____Turned over to_____

Loan

_____Application made with_____

_____Commitment date_____

_____Interest lock in date_____

_____Rate locked in by_____

_____Points locked in by_____

_____Appraisal ordered

_____Appraisal in

_____Property appraised

_____Loan amount fixed

_____Loan confirm letter sent

Inspections

_____Pool Ordered from_____

_____Done

_____Accepted

_____Appliances w/buyer

_____Done

_____Accepted

_____Home Warranty _____

_____Policy commitment received

_____Repair items noted

_____Repairs ordered

_____Termite inspection ordered

_____Company_____

_____Key to company

_____Lockbox combo to company

_____Completed

_____Inspection letter sent

Insurance

_____New policy ordered from_____

_____Old policy proration ordered

_____Buyer advised

_____Escrow notified

Early occupancy

_____Lease to buyer

_____Lease to seller

_____Insurance notification

_____Buyer policy issued

_____Seller policy issued

_____Utilities switched over

Closing

_____Date scheduled

_____Informed buyer

_____Informed seller

_____Power of atty for _____

_____Lender appv Power of Attorney

_____Escrow/Title co approved POA

_____Confirmed w/other S'person

_____Obtained amount for buyer

_____Gave amount to buyer

_____Confirmed buyer has money

_____It closed

Keys for buyer

_____Received from seller

_____Delivered to buyer

_____Letter sent

Gifts

_____Arranged

_____Delivered

Marketing letters

_____Prepared

_____Sent

Telephone Log.   The importance of maintaining a telephone log and continuous written correspondence during the contract closing process can not be overstated. Adopt a system that works for you. Just do it. Indicate in the log if the calls made are incoming or outgoing, the party with whom you actually speak (name), the context of the conversation and even the time of day.   Indicate when calls are made, but not answered, or when a message is left on a recording machine.   Follow either with a memo that states *"sorry I missed you by telephone, but I would like to discuss..."*   Be as detailed as you possibly can.   At times when memories are failing, your telephone log will prod even the most confused mind to recall explicit events clearly.   The person with the telephone log is the credible witness.   The consistency of a standard of practice employed on all transactions is the best defense in time of trouble.

DATE	IN/OUT	PARTY	COMMENTS:

Removal of Conditions Precedent.   As each of the conditions listed in the contract is satisfied, it is important to notify the parties of this progress.   Notification of the fact that an item has been removed or satisfied is better than drawing a conclusion as to the effect of the removal.   This is a good stage at which to send copies of a letter addressed to one party to the other parties.   Careful structure here can be an adroit way to accomplish your objectives.

Title Insurance Commitment Arrival.   In most contracts, it is important to ensure that the buyer receives and receipts for the title insurance commitment prior to the date specified in the contract.   Once this has occurred, everyone needs to be notified.   There have been successful attempts by supreme courts to make the selling agent, even if a subagent, an agent of the buyer for the purposes of receipt of the title commitment. In those cases the buyer can not claim he did not receive the title commitment if it was delivered to a subagent assisting him in the purchase.

Notification serves two purposes.   First, it confirms that the commitment was actually delivered.   Second, it puts the recipient on notice that in the event the notification is defective, he must speak up or there or will arise a presumption that the notification was correct as delivered.   In other words, notification gives the recipient notice that he must address any discrepancy or waive any future right to do so.

Letter/e-mail – Title Insurance Commitment
Need for Copies of Exceptions

Ms. Sharon Reichman
Reichman Title and Abstract Company
1600 Fairview Lane
Boulder, CO 80305

Re: Commitment Number 56-89234-890

Dear Sharon:

Thank you for moving fast to obtain the title insurance commitment for this transaction. I appreciate your delivering a copy of it to the buyers at their address in the contract, as well as the copy that you left at this office. As usual I have told the buyers that you are the person to contact if they have any questions about the specifics of the commitment.

As you know, I like copies of all documents that relate to any exceptions, covenants and restrictions that affect the property attached to each copy of the commitment. The copy of the commitment I received did not contain all of the covenants and restrictions, and I am concerned that the buyer's copy may also have been short. If you would deliver a full set of the indicated copies, I would appreciate it.

Please excuse my nagging. I am a detail oriented person who must know that the parties have all the information they require to arrive at their own decisions. I know that we both want a perfect closing and an informed buyer. I have indicated to the buyers that as long as we close in your office, you will update the commitment to the latest possible date and provide gap protection for any items that do not appear on the commitment or the update, which go of record prior to the recording of the deed. Although I am sure that the buyers desire this coverage, I am ordering it in my own right if necessary to ensure that it is in effect. I have assured the buyers that you will take care of obtaining the endorsement and gap protection.

You have my standard closing instruction sheet, and I would appreciate your delivering a set of the closing papers to both attorneys indicated thereon for their review at least three days prior to the closing. Again, it is a delight to do business with such a professional title company. I am aware that it is your efforts that make the transaction close properly. I am proud to be able to send you this additional business. If there is anything that I can do to expedite this transaction, please let me know right away.

The Real Estate Company

by: Your Name Here,
REALTOR®, CRS, GRI

Loan Application and Commitment. Communicate the information firmly to the other party when the buyer has commenced a loan application, or when s/he has been approved for the loan. Often this is first done by telephone. However, a follow-up letter will avoid potential problems with the timing and content of the telephone conversation.

Cover letters to lenders are an integral part of any transaction. The market changes quickly. There is intense competition in the mortgage lending business. The pressure on the loan officers to make deals and attract business, while at the same time ensuring that the business is profitable, is extreme. The memories of all parties in a transaction are taxed to the maximum. A simple cover letter with the appropriate copies can help to redefine the deal, keep good business friends happy, and protect yourself, as well as informing the other parties of the exact contents of the quotation or commitment. Think for a minute: Who can lock in the rate? Is it the buyer, the seller or someone's agent? It is generally accepted that the lender is in the buyer's camp. Federal statutes prevent the lender from disclosing the buyer's financial status, or information about the buyer's financial ability to pay, except in communications with the borrower (buyer) or upon the instructions of the buyer.

It is always a good idea to ask for the specific terms of any loan commitment notice when you represent the seller. Do not rely on the mortgage knowledge of the cooperating broker when he informs you verbally that his client has a final loan commitment. Many times the lender will give "conditional approval," and you may learn that the "condition" is the buyer securing a new job! There are no "conditional approvals" – only loan approvals which are unconditional. These are almost impossible to obtain.

By nature, all loans are conditional upon such things as the continued employment, not buying a new car or incurring any installment debt, no change in financial circumstances, etc. However, these are the only conditions that are acceptable.

Finally, you may think that the contract is conditional upon loan approval, but loan approval is very different from loan commitment or loan funding. Check the contract to see what sort of loan condition your contract contains.

Case in Point.
   Katherine represented a seller who had already moved out of state prior to closing and was anxiously awaiting recordation on the vacant home. Two weeks prior to closing, loan commitment was obtained and the buyer requested an early occupancy. Further inquiries to the loan officer revealed that the loan commitment

was conditional upon the buyer securing a new job similar to his previous one in the military. The lender had processed the loan as if the buyer would be maintaining his active duty status when in fact his verification of employment actually indicated he would be separating from the military service within a month. (This was a new lender who was unfamiliar with his own forms, but the buyer liked his "bargain" rates.)

What appeared to be a "dead deal" to the buyer, lender, and buyer's broker was successfully closed with a delayed closing, an early occupancy with non-refundable deposit sufficient to cover re-marketing the home if necessary, a seller who had funds to continue making mortgage payments, and Katherine working directly with the buyer and lender to acquire the new job position that met all the requirements, within the new deadlines accepted by all.

Caution. *When you tackle early occupancy, make sure that you have a lease, not just an "early occupancy agreement." In addition, consult with a local attorney to make sure that "non-refundable deposits" are not possibly characterized as down payment on an installment sale instead of a lease.*

Letter/e-mail – Lender – Confirming Quotation

Ms. Valerie Simpson, Senior Loan Officer
CBB Mortgage, Inc.
1900 West Chambers Drive
Denver, CO 80007

     Re: Loan Quotation

Dear Val:

    Thank you for taking the time to give me an oral quotation yesterday.   With the market as hectic as it appears, I know you have a lot to do, and I appreciate your stopping to help me. I have passed the information you gave me to my buyers. I just wanted to make a little note, so I will remember the specifics of the quotation.

    I understand that any quotation presupposes that the buyers/borrowers can qualify. This is to confirm that the quotation is as follows:

    Purchase price:_____   Loan amount:_____
    Loan type:_____   Discount points:_____
    Quotation firm until:_____   Loan origination fees:_____

    This quotation is open for the period indicated. You will honor it, regardless of the market conditions at the time of application, so long as the application is within the above time period. I have explained to the buyers that the loan origination fee will be payable when the rate is locked and is a non-refundable fee.

    Since this is a conventional loan, I understand that, depending on the loan-to-value ratio, you may require private mortgage insurance (PMI). If this is the case, the loan will have to be approved not only by your loan committee, but also by your PMI underwriter, which you think usually takes an extra three days.

    If I have made an error, please call me at the above telephone number and follow that call with a letter. I hope the buyers' contract is accepted, and they select you for the new loan. I know you can get the processing done on time in a professional manner and will get the loan closed on the scheduled date. You know

I enjoy working with you and your company, and I look forward to another successful contract, loan and closing.

Sincerely,
The Real Estate Company

by: Your Name Here,
REALTOR®, CRS, GRI

Letter/e-mail – Loan Approval – Other Broker

Mrs. Sandy Miller
SanVern Realty and Investment
Boulder, CO. 80305

     Re: 4750 Table Mesa Drive

Dear Sandy:

     Thank you for the news that the loan requested by the buyers was approved by Howard Mortgage yesterday. I knew Val Simpson would be able to help them determine the best financing and process the application to a commitment. I know you have conveyed the news to the buyers. I have told the seller the good news. It is also nice to have the commitment before the deadline in the contract. Thank you for your efforts.

     There are still a few items to be completed. I wanted to outline them here, so we may each know the extent of our tasks.

_____

_____

_____

_____

     I look forward to another smooth closing. It has been nice to have you as the buyers' agent on this particular transaction. I enjoy working with you. Please let me know if there is anything that either I or the seller can do to assist you in your transaction.

                    Sincerely,
                    The Real Estate Company

                    by: Your Name Here,
                    REALTOR®, CRS, GRI

cc: Sam and Sandy Seller
       CBB Howard Mortgage

Letter/e-mail – Loan Approval – Lender

Ms. Frankly Amazing, Loan Officer
Amazing Mortgage
4444 Salt Lake City Boulevard
Your Town, CO 00000

      Re: Loan Commitment/Bob and Betty Buyer

Dear Ms. Amazing:

     I was so happy to get your call today, indicating that the loan you helped these borrowers select for their new home has been approved. I know how much you like to help buyers select the loan best suited for their needs. Thank you for helping them and taking the time to call.

     I have told the buyers that you indicated that their loan approval was on the terms listed below. Please take a minute to check my understanding and let me know by telephone and certified mail if this is not the case.

1. Loan Amount:$ _____
2. Fixed interest rate of: _____% per annum.
3. Thirty-year term.
4. Loan origination fee of: ____%
5. Loan discount fees of: _____%
6. The loan is "locked" through: _____.

     I knew you could get this loan approved, and I appreciate the opportunity to be involved with a loan that you are handling. I know that you were of great assistance in helping the buyers review their personal finances and in selecting this particular loan as the best one for their needs. Good loan counselors such as you are hard to find. I look forward to seeing you at closing.

                         Sincerely,
                         The Real Estate Company
                         REALTOR®, CRS, GRI

cc: Sam and Sandy Seller
       The Listing Office
       Bob and Betty Buyer

Letter/e-mail – Loan Approval – Buyer

Mr. James R. Rodenbeek
Room 24 Lookout Motel and Casino
Grand Forks, WA 99876

     Re: 4750 Table Mesa Drive

Dear Jim:

This letter has good news, and I am glad to bring it to you. Enclosed is a copy of the letter I just sent to the mortgage officer confirming my conversation with him today, wherein he indicated that your loan has been approved on the terms you requested.

You should be receiving a written letter from them any day now. When you get it, please let me know immediately. We can review your letter from the lender to make sure that it complies with your expectations and my confirming letter to the lender.

I am only convinced of loan approval when the mortgage company actually writes the check, but I have scheduled the closing for the date indicated in the contract. I will be contacting you as soon as I have the exact figures, so we can arrange for the actual closing time. I can provide you with directions at that time.

Just a last reminder, please review the title insurance commitment that I dropped off yesterday. Just call the title company if you have questions. They are ready to answer any questions that you may have. I noted on the commitment the name of the in house examiner with whom you can talk. If I do not hear to the contrary, I will assume that the document meets with your approval.

There are only a few items left on the checklist to be completed. Remember, you need to:

1. Contact Public Service to arrange for the power to be turned on.

2. Contact the telephone company to ensure that you will get phone service in this century. Remember to think about high speed data options at this time.

3. Make your final inspection on _____. I will be picking you both up at the motel at 2:45 p.m. I have asked the home inspector who did the initial inspection to meet us at the house accompany you through the home. After all, he is the one that knows about house condition.

4. Confirm with the movers that all is set for the big day.

5. Verify once again that the hazard insurance is ready to go on the closing date. We do not want any time to pass between closing and issuance of the insurance policy.

If there is anything else that I can do, please do not hesitate to call me immediately. Looks like you are on the way to owning your new home. Congratulations!

Sincerely,
The Real Estate Company

by: Your Name Here,
REALTOR®, CRS, GRI

Letter/e-mail – Document Delivery to Lender

Ms. Frankly Amazing, Loan Officer
Organized Crime Lending
4510 Salt Lake Boulevard
San Quentin, CA 00000

    Re: Charles A. Reasoner's Application

Dear Ms. Amazing:

    I hope all is going well with this loan application. The approval deadline is coming up fast. The seller's agent reminds me that there are other contracts just waiting for this one to collapse, so please let me know if there is anything else that I can do to help you. The proper, timely completion of this loan application and the closing of the contract are the most important things to me.

    Here is the copy of the Planned Unit Development that you asked me to pick up for you. I just asked for the documents that you indicated. If it is not what you need, please let me know today.

    Again, I want to thank you for working with the buyers and helping them with their selection of their loan program. I know how to sell real estate, but I like leaving the selection of the proper and adequate financing to you and the buyers privately. I know they value your professional assistance.

               Sincerely,
               The Real Estate Company

               by: Your Name Here,
               REALTOR®, CRS, GRI

cc: Charles E. Reasoner, Buyer

Letter/e-mail – Broker to Buyer FHA Appraisal Low

Mr. and Mrs. Scott Plum
12th and Main Street
Denver, CO 80305

Re: 909 East First Street

Dear Mr. and Mrs. Plum:

The time is fast approaching when you will make the final walk-through of your new home. Keep in mind that while it is new to you, the home has been around for some time. For you review, I have included a list that I provide to sellers when I am assisting them.

The lender has ordered and completed the appraisal that the lender requires to determine whether he will make the loan you have requested. The FHA appraisal has come back a few thousand dollars lower than anticipated. Therefore, you are in a position to either proceed with the purchase as proposed, making up the loan proceeds shortage with additional down payment, or consider the contract as void, and allow someone else to purchase the home. Please let me know of your decision, so I can advise the seller immediately and prepare the necessary addendum or release form.

The survey required by the lender is not really a survey at all, it is an Improvement Location Certificate. It merely indicates that the house is on the lot and roughly in the proper position. It is not intended to be relied upon for any other uses, such as the exact location of any of the improvements or easements in reference to other items. There is no substitute for a boundary survey if you are going to build additions to your property or want an accurate determination of the exact physical location of the property. As we discussed, that is not a requirement for the loan and is not included in the expenses of the seller as outlined in the contract.

I am sure you are happy and excited to be getting close to moving day. Completing all the closing conditions has been a real project, but we are almost finished. Soon you will be settled in your nice new home. We are glad you selected us to assist you. Please let me know if there is anything I can do to help with the move or in further preparing for the closing.

Final Inspection.   Prior to final closing and recordation of the deed, most contracts allow a final walk through, not an inspection, of the premises by the buyer to ensure that the home is in the same condition and working order as it was at the date of contract acceptance.   An item in the contract that indicates, "the buyer will be entitled to a walk-through prior to closing," can put you in a tough position.   There is often no mention of what will happen if the buyer disapproves of anything, major or minor, regarding the condition of the house.   You may have created a monster.   Use precise wording about any walk-through procedure.   Do not let your deal walk through the door.   A well written contract would have already addressed any special conditions in "as-is" clauses or specific items to be repaired or replaced at the seller's expense, prior to recordation.

Sellers are held more and more accountable for the condition of their homes, especially in a resale.   Keep in the mind that the seller expects to convey the home just as he is currently living in it, and the buyer most often is expecting a "resale" in "new" condition.   It is difficult to explain to the seller that contractual expectations of the consumer have changed dramatically since the time he purchased the home and that new guidelines may exist that depict the common standard of practice for the area as well as compliance with state and federal law.   At the same time, it is important to help the buyer understand that a resale will be conveyed in working order "consistent with its age."

It is best to "pave the way" with potential objections and expectations of both the buyer and the seller in order that frustrations can be avoided later.   It is silly to lose a transaction over a minor item such as a leaking faucet at the end of the transaction, but deals have been lost over even less significant issues.   Disclosure to the seller early in the listing period of potential problems that may be identified during a final inspection can facilitate a smooth conveyance.

A "standard" pre-closing walk-through inspection sheet with "standard" wording printed at the bottom can be a useful tool.   This is a good opportunity to avoid responsibility for items that were never your responsibility in the first place.   Have the seller and buyer check off the condition of the house as they go through it together.

Appliance and Features Checklist

_____ Range/Oven

_____ Refrigerator (ice maker)

_____ Disposals

_____ Washer and Dryer (properly hooked up and operational)

_____ Garage door openers

_____ Fireplace

_____ Hot tub

_____ Sprinkler system

_____ Exterior lighting

_____ Gas BBQ (grill)

_____ Boundary markers checked

_____ Other:

Discrepancies:_____
_____
_____
_____

We have conducted a walk-through inspection of the property, and it is in the condition indicated on the contract, except as noted on this form. We understand that, excluding any attempt to conceal a defect known only to the broker, the broker and his agents are not responsible for the condition of the property. We accept the property in the condition indicated on this form on this date.

_____   _____
Buyer   date   Buyer   date

Problems Frequently Identified
During a Final Walk Through

The purpose of this list is to identify problems that often arise during a buyer's final walk-through. It is normally much easier and far less costly to fix problems prior to the walk-through than during the frequently hectic days immediately prior to closing. This is not a second inspection.

1. **General Comments.**
   a. It is important to operate all equipment on all cycles or setting prior to the walk-through. Frequent offenders are dishwashers, washing machines and dryers.

   b. All equipment features are expected to operate unless identified otherwise in the contract. For example, a refrigerator with an ice maker is expected to keep food cold and make ice.

   c. A condition that existed when you bought the home does not relieve you from the responsibility of correcting the problem when it is your turn to sell. "It has always been that way," is usually not an acceptable reason not to fix a problem. Common offenders are missing keys for locks, sliding glass doors that are locked by way of a wooden rod in the track and electric outlets/switches that are inoperable.

   d. Older, non-digital, built-in clocks and oven timing devices are frequently a problem. Over a period of time the heat from the oven will dry out the lubricating oil causing a built-in clock to malfunction.

   e. Expect the buyer to operate window cranks for all windows including those that may have been untouched for years. Prior to the inspection operate them all yourself. Ensure that there are no broken or chipped panes. Also ensure that all sliding glass doors and screen doors operate and lock properly.

   f. Expect a buyer to try the heating and air conditioning systems to ensure that they not only blow air, but that the air is hot or cool.

2. **Water Problems.**
   a. When a dishwasher is seldom used, grease will frequently build-up in the drainage line, causing water to come out of the anti-syphon device.

b. Check under all sinks (bathroom and kitchen) with a flashlight while the water is running for leaks and drips.

c. Ensure that all water cutoff valves are fully operational. Some of them are seldom operated and will tend to freeze in the open position over a period of time. Common offenders are sink and toilet cutoff valves.

d. All tub, shower and sink faucets and diverters need to be operated to ensure that there are no leaks or drips.

e. Tub and sink stoppers need to be operational and able to hold water.

f. Toilets need to operate properly and flush without leaking.

g. If you have a sprinkler system for your lawn, ensure that it is operating properly. Expect buyers to test the system and inspect each outlet for proper spray and flow.

h. Know where your main water shut-off is.

3. **Electrical Problems.**
    a. Know what each switch operates. Expect the buyer to test each one. Expect a buyer to test the sockets to ensure that electricity reaches each outlet.

    b. All three prong outlets must be grounded.

    c. Prior to the walk-through, replace any burned out light bulbs. Pay particular attention to outside garage lights.

    d. Inoperable doorbells are a frequent problem.

    e. Test your smoke detectors and fire alarms to ensure proper operation. Replace batteries if necessary.

    f. Expect the buyer to operate all exhaust fans. They should operate without any excessive noise. The range exhaust fan should attract and hold a piece of paper.

Letter/e-mail – Broker to Buyer – Checklist for Closing

Mr. Scott Plum
12th and Main Street
Denver, CO 80305

     Re: 909 East First Street

Dear Mr. Plum:

The time is fast approaching when you will make the final walk-through of your new home. Keep in mind that while it is new to you, the home has been around for some time. For your review, I have included a list that I provide to sellers when I am assisting them.

In addition, the contract calls for you to review the title insurance commitment. I have enclosed your copy. The contract provides that unless you register some objection to the title commitment by _____, it will be deemed accepted. You have only a few days, so please give this your prompt attention.

Questions about the commitment? Contact the title officer indicated at the top of the commitment. In the event that it is not satisfactory let me know, and I will deliver a copy to the attorney of your choice. Of course we do not review title commitment as that would be the unauthorized practice of law.

The lender will also probably review it for his own purposes to assure that he is happy with the condition of title. You should not allow the lender's acceptance of the commitment to influence your determination of its sufficiency since the lender has no obligation to you with regard to their determination of the adequacy of the commitment.

              Sincerely,
              The Real Estate Company

              by: Your Name Here,
              REALTOR®, CRS, GRI

Letter/e-mail – Broker to Buyer – Checklist for Closing

Mr. and Mrs. Scott Plum
12th and Main Street
Denver, CO 80305

    Re: 909 East First Street

Dear Mr. and Mrs. Plum:

    The time is fast approaching when you will make the final walk-through of your new home. Keep in mind that while it is new to you, the home has been around for some time. For your review, I have included a list that I provide to sellers when I am assisting them.

    The lender has ordered and completed the appraisal that the lender requires to determine whether he will make the loan you have requested. Although you pay for the appraisal, it is the property of the lender. However, they will indicate the amount of the appraisal since we made that a condition of the contract.

    The survey required by the lender is not really a survey at all, it is an Improvement Location Certificate. It merely indicates that the house is on the lot and roughly in the proper position. It is not intended to be relied upon for any other uses, such as the exact location of any of the improvements or easements in reference to other items. There is no substitute for a boundary survey if you are going to build additions to your property in the future or want an accurate determination of the physical location of the property. As we discussed, that is not a requirement for the loan and is not included in the expenses of the seller as outlined in the contract.

    This would be a good time to verify that your mover has the correct date and time of your anticipated move and that your bank has the balance of the funds needed to complete the transaction on deposit, ready and available for closing. The title company will require that the funds be in the form of a certified check to the order of the title company. I have requested that the title insurance company provide us with the exact amount as soon as possible to facilitate this process.

I am sure you are happy and excited to be getting close to moving day. Completing all the closing conditions has been a real project, but we are almost finished. Soon you will be settled in your nice new home. Do not forget to verify that your new hazard insurance carrier is ready to deliver the required binder to the closing company.

We are glad you selected us to assist you. Please let me know if there is anything I can do to help with the move or in further preparing for the closing.

Sincerely,
The Real Estate Company

by: Your Name Here,
REALTOR®, CRS, GRI

Letter/e-mail – Removal of Conditions

Mr. Sam Seller
Mrs. Sandy Seller
4750 Table Mesa Drive
Boulder, CO 80305

   Re: 4750 Table Mesa Drive

Dear Sam and Sandy:

I am happy to be able to tell you that the purchaser and his engineer went through the property yesterday for their second inspection. As of this date, I have not heard any complaints. The contract provided the following:

"Purchaser, accompanied by such professionals as he alone shall select, shall have the right to inspect the property at the purchaser's expense to determine if the property, in the opinion of the purchaser, is structurally sound. In the event that the purchaser does not indicate to the contrary, the property shall be deemed to be of sound character acceptable to the purchaser. Notice to the contrary must be written, specify the exact details of the deficiency and be delivered to the listing broker prior to the 28th of June, 2010."

At this time I am assuming that this condition is no longer a factor. It looks as though we are one step closer to the closing. The property shows so nicely, and I know it is the result of your efforts. I appreciate being selected to help you sell your house.

                        Sincerely,
                        The Real Estate Company

                        by: Your Name Here,
                        REALTOR®, CRS, GRI

cc: Buyer

The Contract Changes

Consideration, The Key. Somewhere along the line, the original contractual agreement as proposed by the buyer and accepted by the seller may change. Consideration is the key to unlocking this puzzle. Always ensure that each side has altered its obligation in some manner.

Case in Point.

The classic case is the one where the builder and owner sign a contract for the construction of a building. Halfway through the construction, the builder announces that there is not enough money to finish the project and that he will quit if the contract can not be renegotiated. The parties then agree to a new contract for more money. The builder goes back to work and completes the building. When asked to pay the additional amount, the owner refuses and the case goes to court.

The decision: There was no consideration for the revision. The owner was entitled to exactly what he received as outlined in the first contract, and the builder provided nothing new in return for the increased price. Lacking additional consideration, the new contract was not enforceable.

Extension and Modification Agreements. Great care should be exercised to recite the additional consideration, if it exists, for the modification or extension of the contract. Generally, if the obligations of both sides are altered, that is enough. The use of the words "this contract supersedes and replaces all previous contracts between the parties for this property" should be used only when that is the intent of the parties. Be careful that all the desired clauses from the first contract make it into the subsequent modified contract. Often it is better to draft a modification agreement, keeping all unchanged parts of the contract intact and only changing some of the terms.

Use of a Contract Modification and Mutual Release Agreement. When the modifications are negotiated in return for some performance or when the parties have made concessions, whether through threat of nonperformance or to settle claims, it is very nice to obtain a final settlement agreement. This is a good place to try to limit the recourse against the broker.

Never Record your Listing Agreement. If the transaction is not going to close, or will close but you are not going to get paid at closing, be careful not to breach your fiduciary duty to your client by recording your listing contract. In most states, the real estate broker does ***not*** have any lien rights in the property as a result of the listing contract. Recording that listing contract will probably subject you to discipline by your real estate commission, and additionally cause the client to have a great case for not paying you at all. You went from being the procuring cause of the sale to breaching your fiduciary duty and losing the entire commission. You may be furious, but obtain good legal advice prior to taking any action. If your attorney makes a mistake, your case against the attorney may be your best source of final payment.

Release Agreements and Instructions – General Comments and Format. The title to the document is not important, so it could be called "Release," "Instructions," "Agreement" or "Amend/Extend" (our favorite). Feel free to eliminate the lawyer words such as "Witnesseth," "Whereas," "Now, Therefore," etc.

The agreements that follow contain many provisions that are not needed in the average simple agreement. In addition, there are several appropriate clauses for general contract preparation that could be taken from this agreement. Please note the difference between a "Release" and "Instructions." Did you really mean it to be a release, or was it just instructions for the distribution of money? Care should be used to make sure that the licensee is not extracting a release of any liability on the part of the licensee from the seller, the buyer or both as a condition for the release or distribution of the earnest money.

"WHEREAS" paragraphs report what has occurred. These are descriptive paragraphs to orient the reader with regard to which transaction is the subject of the release, the things that led up to the settlement, and a little about the dispute. Be concise. Use as many as you need to use.

Quotation marks (" ") around a word are a way to label or identify a specific word. From then on, the identified word can be used with an initial capital letter. For example, John and Mary Buyer may be first written as John and Mary Buyer, "Buyers." Henceforth, the use of Buyers will identify those people, specifically, and the use of the word buyers (in lower case) will identify anyone who might be a buyer.

Dating and initialing each page is always a good idea. You can also photo copy the first page to the reverse of the second page, and then all you need to do is sign the bottom of the second page. However, we always recommend that all pages be initialed and dated, no matter what. Someone will inevitably try to allege that they did not know what s/he was signing and that the document entered as evidence is not what s/he signed.

Release Agreement

THIS AGREEMENT, made and entered into this_____ day of _____, 20___, by and between _____, "Seller," and _____, "Buyer," collectively the "Parties;"

WITNESSETH:

WHEREAS, the Parties entered into a contract for the purchase and sale of the property known as:_____, the "Property;"

NOW, THEREFORE, each of the parties, in consideration of the promises and agreements herein contained, hereby agrees with the other, understanding that the other party is relying upon the representations and agreements herein contained, as follows:

1. _____
   _____
2. _____
   _____
   _____

IN WITNESS WHEREOF, we have executed this Release Agreement on the day and date immediately following our respective signatures and hereby receipt for a copy of the same.

Seller:

_____   _____
date   date

Buyer:

_____   _____
date   date

Contract Modification and Mutual Release Agreement
(Standard – Includes Brokers)

THIS AGREEMENT, entered into this _____ day of _____, 20 ___, by and between the undersigned; "Seller", "Buyer", "Seller's Broker" and "Buyer's Broker," collectively the "Parties;"

WITNESSETH:

WHEREAS, Seller and Buyer entered into a certain Contract for the Purchase and Sale of Real Estate ("Contract") regarding the "Property" commonly known as: _____; and,

WHEREAS, Seller entered into a Listing Contract with Seller's Broker obligating Seller to pay a commission; and,

WHEREAS, Seller's Broker and Buyer's Broker, collectively "Brokers", have a commission sharing agreement; and,

WHEREAS, the Parties wish to resolve their disputes as they relate to the Contract and the commissions due as a result of the Contract, and to forever fully release and discharge each other from any and all liability of any nature which may have arisen as a result of the indicated Contract and the events that followed, and provide for the closing and transfer of a proper deed as contemplated in the Contract;

NOW, THEREFORE, each of the Parties hereby irrevocably covenants, promises and agrees as follows, with the knowledge and intent that the other parties rely on these promises, covenants, agreements and representations:

1. The Sales Price shall be $_____; and,

2. That _____ hereby credits _____ in the amount of $_____; and,

3. That Brokers shall be paid as follows: _____
   _____
   _____.

---

4. _____
_____ ; and,

5. Possession shall be _____ ; and,

6. The items contained in the Bill of Sale are the only items that are being transferred as a part of the Contract, that they have a relative value of $_____, and are hereby receipted for by Buyer in their present condition; and,

7. That Buyer has had ample time and opportunity to inspect the Property, and hereby accepts the Property in its present condition, AS IS, WITHOUT ANY WARRANTY, EXPRESS OR IMPLIED, INCLUDING ANY WARRANTY OF FITNESS FOR A PARTICULAR PURPOSE; and,

Except with respect to the enforcement of this Mutual Release, the Parties, for themselves, their heirs, successors and assigns, do hereby remise, release and forever discharge each other, their representatives and agents, servants, officers, directors, heirs, successors and assigns, of and from any and all claims, actions, causes of action, demands, agreements, damages, costs, promises, expenses and compensation, in law or in equity, known or unknown, which the undersigned Parties, their respective, heirs, successors or assigns, or any of them, may have against one another or which may hereafter accrue or occur, in connection with, on account of, or in any way stemming from any transaction, matter, thing or occurrence the source of which is the Contract, including but not limited to, any and all claims of breach of any contract or agreement whether written or oral, any claims for money had and received, fraud, misrepresentation, negligence, breach of a fiduciary duty, specific performance and any other claims based on any and all legal or equitable theories upon which a claim for relief or recovery can or could be based; and,

That the Parties have each had an opportunity to seek legal counsel and have done so or elected not to do so as their sole and independent act and have not relied in any fashion on any representation made by any party or any agent or employee of any party, for any advice or direction as to the advisability of entering into this Mutual Release; and,

That all Parties understand that after this Release is executed, there will be no opportunity to reevaluate or reopen the matters herein indicated. It is the express purpose of this Mutual Release for everyone to forever completely release the other from any and all claims arising out of the Contract; and,

That in the event any party commences any legal action as a result of this release, whether to enforce it, defend an action based on it or otherwise, the non-defaulting party shall be entitled to a judgment in addition to all other sums, equal to the non-defaulting party's actual reasonable attorney's fees.

This agreement contains the full and complete agreements of the Parties. There are no promises, agreements or representations between any of the Parties except as set forth in this Agreement.

This agreement shall be construed under the laws of the State of _____ and agree the venue shall be proper in the _____ Court located in _____.

This Agreement may be executed in counterparts and, in that event, the counterparts, taken together, shall constitute a single instrument.

IN WITNESS WHEREOF, we, the undersigned, after having fully read this agreement, hereby execute the same and acknowledge receipt of a duplicate original of the same on the day and date first above indicated.

Print names below signatures.

Seller: **Buyer:**

Print: _____ Print: _____
            date   date

Print: _____ Print: _____
            date   date

Seller's Broker: **Buyer's Broker:**
Print: _____ Print: _____

By:_____ By:_____
            date   date

Release of Earnest Money

When earnest money has been deposited with the broker, and a dispute arises as to the application of the funds, the only way to ensure that the broker will be able to distribute the money, without the possibility of a future suit, is to call for the mutual release by all parties and specify the directions to be followed for the disbursement of the funds.

There is no doubt that the pressure will be increasing from either or both parties, as well as from the cooperating broker, to have the broker make a determination regarding who is entitled to the money, based on a subjective look at the actions or inactions of either or both parties. To allow yourself to get caught here, no matter what you believe is correct, is an error in judgment and a good time to fall back on "company policy," that is, a mutual release.

Do not let the threat of litigation or the assurance that "everything will be all right" or the promise, no matter how tempting, that one party, usually the seller, will "indemnify you against loss" lull you into a false sense of security. Sure, everybody is going to sue you because you have the money. Get the case settled now while you have the money. When you have had enough, you can ask the court to take the money and decide who gets how much of it – interpleader action. In addition, you may still reserve your claim to a portion of the money. To be effective, any release form should indicate that the court "shall," not "may," award attorney's fees to the prevailing party. Courts are wary of having to determine attorney's fees, and they avoid the imposition of an award for fees unless the contract is specific.

The Mutual Release that follows contains very comprehensive release language, but you should be able to pare your own form down a bit. For a legal appearance it is good to give it a format similar to the one presented; however, a letter format is just as binding. The "Whereas" clauses simply state facts already agreed to and lay the foundation for the solution. You can do this in a letter in any fashion you wish. The "Now, Therefore" clause sets forth the action agreed to and to be taken. Note some of the boilerplate language about reliance. This is nice to have in a release letter.

A form like this can be set up for any mix of parties and agents and is best in a format that is printed and appears to be "standard." Even if the form is designed for a specific case, title it with a "standard" label, right margin justified, and then copy it, so that it does not appear to be special. People sign "standard" forms much more easily than ragged-right, double-spaced letters because there is a sense of correctness about a "standard" form. Use this to your advantage.

Release vs. Instructions.   Remember that you are not a party to the contract. Therefore, a "release" which has to do with earnest money should not include the broker. The earnest money release and distribution is a matter between the buyer and seller. If you, the broker, are holding the earnest money, "directions" or "instructions" from the buyer and seller are all that you should request. If one party instructs you in writing to deliver the earnest money to the other party, you need to do it. It would be improper to wait for approval of some sort of release agreement if one was not made a condition of the delivery of the money.

Note that the first form is a Mutual Release and Distribution Agreement – Standard Form, contemplating that the transaction will not close, and the earnest money will be release and divided. This form looks the same as the Contract Modification and Mutual Release Agreement form, a few pages back. They are different. Our current favorite earnest money distribution form is the last one, titled Agreement to Amend/Extend Contract.

Mutual Release and Distribution Agreement
Standard Form
(Includes Brokers)

THIS AGREEMENT, entered into this _____ day of _____, 20 ___, by and between _____ ("Seller"); and _____ ("Buyer"); and _____ ("Seller's Broker"), and _____ ("Buyer's Broker"), all of whom shall constitute the parties ("Parties");

WITNESSETH:

WHEREAS, Seller and Buyer did on _____, enter into a Contract for the Purchase Real Estate ("Contract") for the purchase and sale of the property located at _____, ("Property"); and,

WHEREAS, pursuant to said Contract, Buyer deposited with Seller's Broker as Earnest Money ("Earnest Money") the amount of $_____ in the form of a personal check; and,

WHEREAS, there is a dispute between the Parties and they wish to resolve their disputes as they relate to this Contract and to forever fully release and discharge each other from any and all liability which may have arisen as a result of the indicated Contract and the events that followed and provide for the disbursement of the Earnest Money;

NOW, THEREFORE, each of the Parties hereby irrevocably covenants, promises and agrees as follows, with the knowledge and intent that the other Parties rely on these promises, covenants, agreements and representations:

1. That the Earnest Money, as soon as the funds are considered collected funds, are available for withdrawal without limitation, and have cleared the banking system, be distributed as follows:

Mutual Release and Distribution Agreement
Buyer:_____ _____ _____
Buyer's Broker: _____ _____

Page ___ of ___
Seller:_____ _____ _____
Seller's Broker _____ _____

Seller: $_____ Buyer: $_____
Seller's Agent: $_____ Buyer's Agent: $_____
Other:_____

2. Except with respect to the enforcement of this Mutual Release, the Parties, for themselves, their heirs, successors and assigns, do hereby remise, release and forever discharge each other, their representatives and agents, servants, officers, directors, heirs, successors and assigns, of and from any and all claims, actions, causes of action, demands, agreements, damages, costs, promises, expenses and compensation, in law or in equity, known or unknown, which the undersigned Parties, their respective heirs, successors or assigns, or any of them, may have against one another or which may hereafter accrue or occur, in connection with, on account of, or in any way stemming from any transaction, matter, thing or occurrence the source of which is the Contract, including but not limited to, any and all claims of breach of any contract or agreement whether written or oral, any claims for money had and received, fraud, misrepresentation, negligence, breach of a fiduciary duty, specific performance and any other claims based on any and all legal or equitable theories upon which a claim for relief or recovery can or could be based; and,

3. That the Parties have each had an opportunity to seek legal counsel and have done so or elected not to do so as their sole and independent act and have not relied in any fashion on any representation made by any party or any agent or employee of any party for any advice or direction as to the advisability of entering into this Mutual Release; and,

4. That all Parties understand that after this release is executed there will be no opportunity to reevaluate or reopen the matters herein indicated. It is the express purpose of this Mutual Release for everyone to forever completely release the other from any and all claims arising out of the Contract; and,

5. That in the event any party commences any legal action as a result of this release, whether to enforce it, defend an action based on it or otherwise, the non-defaulting party shall be entitled to a judgment in addition to all other sums, equal to the non-defaulting party's actual reasonable attorney's fees. Jurisdiction shall be proper only in the State and County where Seller's Broker has its primary offices.

Mutual Release and Distribution Agreement   Page ___ of ___
Buyer:_____ _____ _____   Seller:_____ _____ _____
Buyer's Broker: _____ _____   Seller's Broker _____ _____

6. This Agreement may be executed in counterparts and, in that event, the counterparts, taken together, shall constitute a single instrument.

7. Other terms: _____

_____

_____

_____

_____

_____

_____

_____

_____

_____

IN WITNESS WHEREOF, after having fully read this agreement, I hereby execute the same and acknowledge receipt of a duplicate original and of my respective checks in the amount indicated, on the day and date first above indicated.

_____   _____
Seller   date   Seller   date

_____   _____
Buyer   date   Buyer   date

Seller's Broker: Buyer's Broker:

_____   _____

by: _____   by: _____
                    date   date

Mutual Release and Distribution Agreement   Page ___ of ___
Buyer:_____ _____ _____   Seller:_____ _____ _____
Buyer's Broker: _____ _____   Seller's Broker _____ _____

THIS FORM HAS IMPORTANT LEGAL CONSEQUENCES AND THE PARTIES SHOULD CONSULT LEGAL AND TAX OR OTHER COUNSEL BEFORE SIGNING.

Agreement to Amend/Extend Contract
(Contract Termination and Earnest Money Distribution Instructions)

Date:_____

Re: Contract, dated _____, between _____
("Buyer") and _____ ("Seller"), relating to the sale and purchase of the following described real estate:

known as No._____ ("Property").

Buyer and Seller hereby agree to amend the aforesaid contract as follows:
1. The Contract is hereby terminated by mutual agreement.

2. The parties hereby direct the holder of the earnest money to disburse as follows:

       Buyer shall be paid $_____
       Seller shall be paid $_____

       _____

       _____

3. The parties release each other, without limitation, from any and all claims arising out of the Contract.

A copy of this document may be executed by each party, separately, and when each party has executed a copy thereof, such copies taken together shall be deemed to be a full and complete contract between the parties.

_____   _____
Seller   date   Seller   date

_____   _____
Buyer   date   Buyer   date

Notice and Agreement to Amend/Extend Contract
(Notice and Earnest Money Distribution Instructions)

Date:_____

Re: Contract dated _____ between _____
("Buyer") and _____ ("Seller"), relating to
the sale and purchase of the following described real estate:

known as No. _____ ("Property").

This is Formal Notice of:_____
_____
_____
_____

Buyer and Seller hereby agree to amend the aforesaid contract as follows:
1. The Contract is hereby terminated by mutual agreement.

2. The parties hereby direct the holder of the earnest money to disburse as follows:

_____
_____
_____

3. The parties release each other, without limitation, from any and all claims arising out of the Contract.

A copy of this document may be executed by each party, separately, and when each party has executed a copy thereof, such copies taken together shall be deemed to be a full and complete contract between the parties.

_____   _____
Seller   date   Seller   date

_____   _____
Buyer   date   Buyer   date

Letter/e-mail – Earnest Money Dispute

Mr. Sam Seller
Mrs. Sandy Seller
4750 Table Mesa Drive
Boulder, CO 80305

Mr. Bob Buyer
Mrs. Betty Buyer
25 Temporary Housing Square
Boulder, CO 80305

    Re: 4750 Table Mesa Drive

Dear Sam, Sandy, Bob and Betty:

    It is unfortunate that there has been an impasse as to the disposition and distribution of the earnest money deposit held by this company. There is currently on deposit in our trust account the sum of $_____. We are prohibited from assessing the merits of competing claims to the earnest money or whether there is or is not a contract or a breach of contract. That is the job assigned to the court system. We, as real estate professionals, are simply not licensed by this state to make that determination.

    We will continue to hold the earnest money in our trust or escrow account, segregated from our general operating funds, as provided by law. Funds will be distributed when the court directs us as to how much and to whom to distribute the funds or we receive either the enclosed Instructions for Release of Escrow or the Agreement to Amend/Extend Contract agreement signed by one of you directing us to release the money to the other or in the alternative an Agreement to Amend/Extend Contract agreement signed by all of you directing us to disburse some money to each party.

    In the event that this does not transpire on or before _____, we will interplead the money into the court, name each of you as having an interest in the funds, and ask the court to make a determination. You will note that your contract provides that we are entitled to recover our attorney's fees out of the earnest money in the event we are involved in any action dealing with the disposition of the earnest money. For that reason, we will endeavor to wait for what we feel is a reasonable time before taking any legal action to resolve the dispute.

I encourage you to seek competent legal counsel and decide amongst yourselves how you want the money to be distributed. I am sorry that I can not make this determination for us all. It is simply illegal for me to attempt a determination on the merits. I am a real estate broker and have no desire to be an attorney or a judge in this matter.

Thank you for your cooperation, understanding, and assistance in this matter. Please let me know if there is anything that I can do to assist either of you or your attorneys. Since we also have an attorney, we are sure that you will understand that we would like all communication to go through this office before our attorney is contacted. It is our desire to prevent our collective attorneys' fees from exceeding the earnest money.

I await your response.

Sincerely,
The Real Estate Company

by: B. Sieged, Broker

cc: ORIGINALS SENT CERTIFIED
      Copies sent Regular Mail
      Other parties

Letter/e-mail – Earnest Money Dispute/Title Company

Mr. Sam Seller
Mrs. Sandy Seller
4750 Table Mesa Drive
Boulder, CO 80305

Mr. Bob Buyer
Mrs. Betty Buyer
25 Temporary Housing Square
Boulder, CO 80305

    Re: 4750 Table Mesa Drive

Dear Sam, Sandy, Bob and Betty:

It is unfortunate that everyone can not agree on the distribution of the earnest money deposit, currently in the amount of $_____, held by the title or escrow company _____ in its trust account. This firm and the title company are prohibited from determining the merits of competing claims to the earnest money or whether or not there is a valid contract dealing with the Property or the earnest money or whether that contract has been breached. That is the job assigned to the court system. We, as real estate professionals, are simply not licensed by this state to make that determination.

My conversations with the title company's representative indicate that a Release Agreement executed by everyone will be required before any action will be taken to disburse the earnest money. A sample of the title company's standard agreement is attached for your review. The title company has the option of interpleading the money into the court, naming each of us as someone it feels may have an interest in the funds, and asking the court to make a determination.

I encourage you to seek competent legal counsel and decide amongst yourselves how you want the money to be distributed. I am sorry that I can not make this determination for us all. It is simply illegal for me to attempt a determination on the merits. I am a real estate broker and have no desire to be an attorney or a judge in this matter. Do not expect the title company or escrow company to make a determination either.

Thank you for your cooperation, understanding, and assistance in this matter. Please let me know if there is anything that I can do to assist either of you or your attorneys. Since we also have an attorney, we are sure that you will understand that we would like all communication to go through this office before our attorney is contacted, so that we too can keep our attorney's fees from exceeding the earnest money.

I await your response.

Sincerely,
The Real Estate Company

by: Jim Real Estate, Broker

cc: ORIGINALS SENT CERTIFIED
Copies sent Regular Mail
Other parties

enclosure:

Returning Earnest Money to a Trusted Client

Basic Guidelines. There are those occasions when, for whatever reasons, you decide to deliver either all or part of the earnest money to one of the parties. Sometimes it is apparent that one party does not intend to take any action or employ an attorney but is simply stalling and refusing to execute a release. Other times, for whatever reason, the amount in question simply does not lend itself to litigation.

General Rule. As a general rule, it is best never to transfer the money to anyone other than your client. Cooperation, testimony, interest and pressure are easier to control if you keep the money.

Broker Portion. You may be entitled to a portion of forfeited earnest money. Retention of your portion may help to offset your potential loss and make the matter less risky. Care should be exercised prior to distributing any money to a subagent, as its recovery may be more difficult when the action starts. As a general rule, never pay anyone, especially subagents, buyers' brokers, or independent contractors until the matter is resolved. Obtaining a return of the money delivered, no matter what agreement has been reached, will never be cost effective.

Notice. Prior to distribution of the earnest money, it might be a good idea to put everyone on notice that you intend to distribute it and to specify the basis for your determination. The longer you have had the money, the greater the need to notify people. The failure to receive any formal or timely requests for its delivery does not eliminate the need to provide everyone with some form of notice. Certified Mail, Return Receipt Requested, Addressee Only, is obviously the best of the options.

Indemnification. There is no need to give anyone any money without an Indemnification Agreement holding the broker, agent, subagent, or other parties, harmless against any and all loss that the broker may sustain, including attorney's fees, in the defense or ultimate payment of a claim to the money. The broker should reserve the right to settle any claim by paying the claim in full and receiving recovery from the seller.

Collected Funds. Many brokers have written checks on uncollected funds in their hurry to resolve an earnest money problem. Be sure that the check that you received for the earnest money has cleared both your bank and the bank it was drawn on before you hand over the money. A good general rule is ten days, but make two simple phone calls and confirm it.

Tip. *The seller has 37 properties listed with you for sale. You collect $500.00 earnest money on a particular contract. When the contract does not close, and the seller wants the earnest money, what do you do? This is not legal advice, but here is a suggestion. Some states' listing contracts indicate broker and seller split 50/50 the earnest money. That will certainly help.*

Pay the seller the seller's share of the earnest money from your operating account, not your trust account, and obtain an assignment to the seller's rights to the earnest money. Now you own any rights to the earnest money in a later dispute resolution situation. Then settle with the buyer the best that you can from the earnest money account. In event the buyer will settle for $250.00, you get the balance. This is accounted for as "marketing." The money that you lose, if any, is a small price for retaining the 36 remaining listings.

Attorney Fees. Remember that if the contract calls for attorneys fees to the winner, the earnest money action takes on a completely different appearance.

Letter/e-mail – Aggressive Position – Earnest Money

Certified Mail

Mr. Sam Seller
Mrs. Sandy Seller
4750 Table Mesa Drive
Boulder, CO 80305

Mr. Bob Buyer
Mrs. Betty Buyer
25 Temporary Housing Square
Boulder, CO 80305

     Re: 4750 Table Mesa Drive

Dear Sam, Sandy, Bob and Betty:

     This firm has been holding the earnest money on this contract, in the amount of $_____, for over a year since the transaction was scheduled to close. This is a small amount of money, and it does not seem appropriate for us to retain it indefinitely. Although we have the right to pay the money into the registry of the court and give you both the ability to enter your appearances and fight over the money, we have decided to take an alternate action.

     After careful consideration and review of the matter with our attorneys, our feelings are as follows: The purchaser will never willingly allow the earnest money to be distributed under any terms to anyone; there is not enough money for anyone to hire an attorney and fight the matter; there has been no claim for the money in the form of litigation; the purchaser has never presented us with a substantiated claim to the money. Therefore, feeling confident as we do in our relationship with the seller, and after receiving from the seller an assurance of indemnification in a form acceptable to us, we are going to distribute the money to the seller.

     If, however, the buyers can, prior to noon on _____, present and substantiate their claim to the earnest money, specifically itemizing the facts that support the buyers' position in a manner that, in our opinion, is sufficient to warrant continued retention of the monies, we will continue to retain the money.

We realize that this decision is not the wisest, but we are ready to get this money out of our account. Your options, as the buyer and seller are to either sue each other or deal with our decision.

Sincerely,
The Real Estate Company

by: Sue Happy, Broker

cc: Copies sent Regular Mail

Chapter 7

Closing Matters

The End of the Road

Professional Details

As closing approaches and passes, there are a lot of little items that will need your attention. This is a good time to mend strained relationships, confirm forever the strong ones, and have a last attempt at protecting yourself from the potential problems that lurk out there after closing. This is the time to reconfirm oral representations, attempt to bootstrap disclaimers that should have been made but were not, and to try to make everyone feel that they will never have a claim against you in the future. Most litigation, with the exception of earnest money actions, comes after closing.

The Late Disclaimer. Closing is upon you, and there are a few problems you would like to put to bed. Disclaimers, to be effective, must have taken place before the decision to purchase or sell was made. The theory is that the party had all the information, including the disclaimers, before he obligated himself on the contract. Once a party has changed his position, he will claim that if he had known the facts you revealed in the disclaimer, he would not have changed his position. In other words, he relied upon your silence or what he thought you indicated, and you are now prevented from making an effective disclaimer since he can not reverse the transaction, absent rescission. Do not let that deter you. "Better late than never" definitely applies here. It is how the parties feel that is most important. If they feel that they have released you, that may be enough to remove from their minds an action against you.

Memorandum of Previous Oral Disclaimer. If you are placed in the above position, you should structure all disclaimers and other attempts to limit your liability in the form of memoranda of what was previously, timely and orally indicated to the proper party. Just start the statement with, "This is a memorandum of our previous oral understanding," and then state whatever you feel you need.

Protective Language Placement at Closing. The best place to add the necessary statements is directly on the closing statement. The front page is appropriate but the back will suffice. Statements in your handwriting are not as good as typed ones and can raise some questions, but they are better than none at all. If you can get the person from whom you are trying to protect yourself to write it in his/her handwriting, you are doing very well indeed.

Hazard and Fire Insurance. This is an area very few people spend much time considering. It is a place in the transaction where a disaster can strike. It is something for which you will probably be held responsible. You will only have to have one fire while you are at closing, or one fire in the post closing pre-occupancy period, to become a devout insurance fanatic. Regardless of the form of financing, always check for the existence of insurance.

For an assumption, the insurance premium is often prorated, and the policy is transferred to the new buyer. Care needs to be exercised to ensure that there is in fact a policy in force and that, effective with the closing date, the buyer will be a named insured. There is no substitute for a written letter or endorsement from the insurance company or the insurance agent. The principal, the insurance company, is bound to uphold what the insurance agent writes.

For a new loan you need to verify, in addition to the verification done by the new lender, that the insurance premium is paid and the insurance is in force as of the date of the transfer of deed. The buyer will elect to buy a homeowner's policy or a fire and extended insurance policy. The first is for owner occupants and the latter for a rental house. Do not give advice on the type of policy that is selected. Never give advice regarding the company to select nor the extent of coverage.

Nothing takes the place of a paid policy. Everything else is open for interpretation. Insurance companies make money by collecting premiums, not by paying claims. They know that.

Homeowner vs. Rental Policy. Different coverage exists for owner-occupied and rental, or nonowner-occupied, property. If there is a change in the character of occupancy, even for a few days, make sure the insurance reflects the actual use of the property. This loss is so rare that we tend to ignore the potential problem, yet the insurance to cover a potential disaster is so easy to obtain.

If the seller remains in possession of the property after the closing, he most probably has either canceled or transferred his policy to the buyer. Therefore, he is not covered since he is now a tenant. He is not insured and neither is his property. He needs a tenant's policy for this limited period.

Likewise, the buyer, not yet the occupant, may have obtained, either by assignment from the seller or independently, a homeowner's policy, although he technically is not an owner-occupant. His new insurance will not cover the loss of the possessions of the old owner occupant. He needs coverage similar to that of a landlord for this short period.

Case in Point.

Oliver will never forget sitting at the closing table with the buyer and seller. The property had just transferred, when the call came in that his buyer's, his customer's, new home was on fire. He was in his rookie year and knew nothing about insurance. The seller's policy was not in effect, and the buyer's policy covered an owner- occupied home. The seller had forgotten to turn off a burner on the stove, and the buyer had put down a newspaper. Fortunately the loss was a little less than Oliver's commission. A hard lesson to learn.

Title Insurance. Some companies never issue the Title Insurance Policy. Without the actual policy, no one can make a claim. A tickler for follow-up in about two weeks after closing can avoid latent problems. This also gives you the chance for additional contact with the purchaser, and an opportunity to show how professional and detail oriented you are.

Security. There is no excuse for failing to give a new buyer a written suggestion to get the property re-keyed immediately. Do not suggest anyone to perform this task, nor take this as a job that you will be responsible for arranging. It is simply a task for the buyer. So simply remind him.

Payment History. In the event that there is owner financing, the chances are good that no one will ever keep an accurate record of the payments made, the dates, the amounts, etc. Even new lenders make mistakes on occasion. The recommendation of a ledger system for each party to track the payments serves two purposes. First, it gives them both the same form on which to make their entries. This alone will help simplify any potential problem should one arise. Second, for the life of the loan your name will be printed on the sample ledger card!

These items should be included as a minimum:

Date Paid	Check No.	Total Paid	Interest	Principal	Balance Due

Document Retention. Few people have a grasp on the nature and value of important documents. Most people have not suffered a major casualty or loss by fire or theft. Advise the use of a safe deposit box for the Deed, the Title Insurance Policy and especially for the owner-carry Note and Mortgage. If none is available, maybe you, under the right circumstances, could offer that service. It might be a nice way to keep in contact with the parties. Make sure you retain documents under a specific agreement.

Homeowner's Exemption. In order to qualify for the homeowner's property tax exemption available in some states, it is necessary to complete a form prior to the end of the year that the home was purchased. The buyer who occupies his home is then eligible for a reduction in his property taxes for the next tax year and each year thereafter. Most buyers forget to do this after all the documentation is signed, and they are busy with their move and transition into the new neighborhood. A reminder to complete this task is another useful method of keeping in contact with the new buyer.

Tip.   *Research the tax department to ascertain if homeowners in your farm area are entitled to, or are already registered for their tax exemption. Send out a friendly reminder to do so with the appropriate tax information attached. This is always guaranteed to generate calls.*

Renewal of Insurance and Payment of Taxes. In the event that the transaction involved "owner carry" financing, there is the possibility that the taxes and insurance will not be paid on time. You may wish to utilize the letter on page 526 to attempt to limit your loss and still retain their future business.

Formal Notice of Contract Closing and Settlement. The following form is designed to be copied front to back, so that the final document is one, two sided page. It is designed to be prepared and served by the Sherif of your county. In our state people show up at closing. I have had great luck with this form when the buyer or seller decides that they are not going to attend. Serve it the day before the scheduled closing in the afternoon. If you are in an escrow state, you will have to modify it a little to compel delivery of documents rather than attendance. It is the service by the Sherif that is the key. The impact is fantastic. Check with a local attorney to see that it does not violate some local or state law, but i doubt it. There is nothing illegal or inappropriate about asking someone, even if it is the Sherif, to deliver some documents to another party.

FORMAL NOTICE
of
Contract Closing and Settlement

YOU ARE HEREBY FORMALLY INFORMED THAT on the day and date below indicated, the indicated closing agent will, after preparing all the required legal documents and calculating the amounts due and payable, be present, pursuant to the terms of the contract for the purchase and sale of real property dated _____, 20____, to conduct the closing of that certain contract entered into by and between _____
_____, as "Buyers," and _____
_____, as "Sellers," for the purchase and sale of the following described real property, to-wit:

CLOSING AGENT/LOCATION:_____
_____

CLOSING DATE/TIME:_____, 20_____. _____:_____ (a.m.)(p.m.)

WHEN AND WHERE YOU MAY APPEAR prepared to close according to the terms of said contract.

FAILURE TO APPEAR may subject you, the defaulting party, to the following legal action indicated in the contract:

FUNDS REQUIRED: The Buyer and/or Seller must present a cashier's or certified check drawn on a local clearing house bank, payable to the order of the indicated closing agent, or cash in the final settlement amount herein below indicated. The basis for, and the calculation of, said amount shall be made available to all parties for inspection at the date, place and time of closing.

Seller:$_____ Buyer:$_____

IN WITNESS WHEREOF, AFTER BEING DULY SWORN UPON OATH, the undersigned has executed this Formal Notice of Contract Closing and Settlement this _____ day of _____, 20_____. FOR _____ Seller or _____ Buyer

by:_____, as authorized agent.

WITNESS MY HAND AND OFFICIAL SEAL this _____ day of _____, 20_____.

(Notary Seal/Court Clerk) _____

My commission expires:_____

CERTIFICATE OF SERVICE

I, the undersigned Sheriff, in and for this county, hereby certify that on the date indicated I delivered the original of this Notice to the indicated individuals.

Date: _____   Time: _____

Individuals Served: _____

Served at (Location): _____

Details of Service: _____
_____
_____

Sheriff:

_____

Letter/e-mail – Document Retention

Mr. Sam Seller and Mrs. Sandy Seller
25 Temporary Housing Square
Boulder, CO 80305

Mr. Bob Buyer and Mrs. Betty Buyer
4750 Table Mesa Drive
Boulder, CO 80305

    Re: 4750 Table Mesa Drive/Document Retention

Dear Mr. and Mrs. Seller and Mr. and Mrs. Buyer:

    Congratulations on the successful conveyance of this exceptional property. All of us at The Real Estate Company are glad to have been able to assist all of you with this transaction. After closing there are a few administrative details that remain. Although we indicated them to each of you at the closing, we like to follow-up with a letter to confirm what is yet to be done for your records. As you have surely surmised by now, we are detail oriented letter writers.

    The transaction provided for a loan to be carried by the seller for the buyer. Since neither of you is in the lending business, we would suggest a simple record-keeping procedure for you. Of course, this is just our idea, and your accountant, or tax adviser, may require different standards and records to be kept. Our suggestions are for the practical and not the legal or accounting record-keeping rules.

Date Paid	Check No.	Total Paid	Interest	Principal	Balance Due

    In addition, save all checks and receipts that relate to the expenses related to the loan, the insurance, any improvements that you might make or the taxes and assessments. The holders of the note and mortgage need to keep these in a very safe place since they will be required to present them for the release of the mortgage and receipt of the final payment.

    If we can assist you in any way, please do not hesitate to call.

Payment History

Date Paid	Check No.	Total Paid	Interest	Principal	Balance Due

Letter/e-mail – Owner Carry Update

Mr. Bob Buyer and
Mrs. Betty Buyer
4750 Table Mesa Drive
Boulder, CO 80305

Mr. Sam Seller and
Mrs. Sally Seller
3459 New Point Boulevard
Madrid, Spain

    Re: Taxes and Insurance Payments

Dear Everyone,

It was great to be able to help with this transaction. As you both know from the previous letter that I sent with the amortization schedule, there are payments to be made over a long period of time. A portion of those payments are escrows that are collected by Sam and Sally for the payment of taxes and insurance premiums as they become due in the future.

Please understand that I can not be responsible for the verification that future tax and insurance payments are made. This is a critical aspect of an owner mortgage. If the taxes are not paid, there is some time to redeem or remedy the situation although it may prove short. However, in the event of an uninsured loss, as the result of a failure to pay insurance premiums, the result can be catastrophic.

It is for that reason that we are strongly recommending that you confirm directly with the recipient the payment of all taxes and insurance premiums on a regular and timely basis. I am not responsible for that verification.

        Sincerely,
        The Real Estate Company

        by: Your Name Here,
        REALTOR®, CRS, GRI

Letter/e-mail – Tax/Insurance Reminder

Mr. Bob Buyer and
Mrs. Betty Buyer
4750 Table Mesa Drive
Boulder, CO 80305

    Re: Taxes and Insurance Payments

Dear Bob and Betty,

    You may recall that, after the closing, I sent you a letter indicating that you need to confirm with the collecting entity that the taxes and insurance payments were properly paid. I also advised you that it was not my responsibility to ascertain that this was done.

    Well, a year has passed, and you might want to take a moment to verify that the insurance premium was paid and that the taxes are current. I am not going to take on that responsibility. In addition, since the loss in the event of a failure to keep the insurance and taxes current is so great, *I can not be responsible and am not obligated to send you another reminder*. Sorry about that. I just do not want you to rely on me for this.

                        Sincerely,
                        The Real Estate Company

                        by: Your Name Here,
                        REALTOR®, CRS, GRI

Letter/e-mail – Buyer Broker to Buyer – Title Policy and Deed

Mr. Bob Buyer and
Mrs. Betty Buyer
4750 Table Mesa Drive
Boulder, CO 80305

    Re: 4750 Table Mesa Drive

Dear Bob and Betty:

I am so glad that we could help you with the purchase of your new house. Nothing is as rewarding as knowing that I have been able to help a nice family like yours acquire this home. I know you will enjoy the home, and I am glad that we have become friends. You made a good selection.

There are a couple of items to which you need to be alert in the near future. First, after the deed has been recorded, it will be returned to your current address. If you do not get it in three weeks, please let me know. When it arrives, you should be prepared to put it in a safe place. The act of recording the deed evidences your acceptance of it and puts the world on notice that you own the property. A deed is not transferred by endorsement. Therefore, no one could obtain the physical deed and endorse it over to another purchaser in the way one might endorse a check. Still, I like to recommend that the deed be retained in a safe place.

Similarly, the title insurance policy will arrive in the mail in about four weeks. This is a different matter. The actual title insurance policy needs to be retained in a safe place since it will have to be surrendered in the event of a problem or in the event that you want a reissue rate on a subsequent sale. If you do not receive this in the allotted time, contact me or the title company directly. It is very important that you obtain the policy and that it be reviewed to ensure that it reflects exactly the terms of the commitment.

If you need someone to assist you in obtaining these documents, please let me know. There is no charge for this service, and I want to make sure the transaction is completed properly. I look forward to seeing you both as soon as you are settled.

           Sincerely,

JUST A REMINDER!

Mr. Bob Buyer and
Mrs. Betty Buyer
4750 Table Mesa Drive
Boulder, CO 80305

        Re: 4750 Table Mesa Drive

Dear Bob and Betty:

        Do you have your receipt for having filed the Homeowners Tax Exemption
Form? In order to qualify for the homeowners exemption for next year as the new
owner for your home, you must file with the Tax Office no later than the last day of
this year. You may recall we discussed the form just prior to the closing of your
new home.

        If you are uncertain whether or not you are registered at the Tax Office or
need information for filing now, please call me at my home or office number
immediately. I can not file this for you. You must do it yourself. I want to make
sure that you obtain all the tax relief to which you are entitled.

                        Sincerely,
                        The Real Estate Company

                        by: Your Name Here,
                        REALTOR®, CRS, GRI

Letter/e-mail – Buyer – New Keys

Mr. Bob Buyer and
Mrs. Betty Buyer
4750 Table Mesa Drive
Boulder, CO 80305

    Re: 4750 Table Mesa Drive

Dear Bob and Betty:

    Congratulations on your new home! I know you are excited to have completed what may have seemed like an ordeal at times. It took work and lots of decisions on your part to find it, contract for it, finance it and close the transaction. Although we were the agents for the seller, we enjoyed assisting you in the transaction.

    I know I mentioned this at closing, but I want to remind you again that the key to your home has passed through many hands during the showing and sale process. While we do not know of any unaccounted-for keys, we always recommend that new owners have the property re-keyed as soon as possible. We can not possibly be responsible for the security of the home or represent that you are the only people with keys.

    If I can help you with a locksmith, just let me know. I look forward to seeing the house after you finish all that you indicated you were going to do to it. A new house is a lot of work and a lot of fun. Thank you again.

               Sincerely,
               The Real Estate Company

               by: Your Name Here,
               REALTOR®, CRS, GRI

Letter/e-mail – Buyer – New Keys #2

Mr. Bob Buyer and
Mrs. Betty Buyer
4750 Table Mesa Drive
Boulder, CO 80305

Re: 4750 Table Mesa Drive

Dear Bob and Betty:

Congratulations on your new home! I know you are excited to have completed what may have seemed like an ordeal at times. It took work and lots of decisions on your part to find it, contract for it, finance it and close the transaction. Although we were the agents for the seller, we enjoyed assisting you in the transaction.

I know I mentioned this at closing, but I want to remind you again that the key to your home has passed through many hands during the showing and sale process. While we do not know of any keys that are unaccounted for, we always recommend that new owners have the property re-keyed as soon as possible. We can not be responsible for the security of the home or represent that you are the only people with keys. We have made arrangements with the locksmith indicated below to re-key your home at our expense. All you need to do is call them.

Thank you for selecting a property listed with this office. I am glad that we have met. I hope your son is enjoying the swing set and the tree house. I will look forward to seeing you at the pool this summer.

Sincerely,
The Real Estate Company

by: Your Name Here,
REALTOR®, CRS, GRI

cc: Fast Action Locksmiths
        Phone:

Letter/e-mail – Cooperating Salesperson

Thomas A. Gill
The Other Real Estate Company
400 Way
AcrossTown, CO 00001

    Re: Property located at 4750 Table Mesa Drive

Dear Tom:

    Congratulations on your successful sale. I do not know about you, but closings are the best part of this business to me. Any delays or exasperation experienced by either or both of our clients are now mostly forgotten by all, and we finally can measure the value of our work by the paycheck we receive.

    It has truly been a pleasure to work with you in the successful closing of this property. Your dedication and professionalism in the negotiations both before and during the escrow process certainly helped to reduce potential tension and stress. I look forward to many more transactions together in the months ahead.

    Let's do it again soon!

                Sincerely,
                The Real Estate Company

                by: Your Name Here,
                REALTOR®, CRS, GRI

Goodbye and Good Luck!

We have had a good time compiling and writing this book. This is our second effort together in book writing. Thanks for all the helpful messages and words of advice. We have tried to incorporate all your requests for additional information in this book. Please keep the cards, letters and e-mails coming with suggestions or comments for future updates. You may send those directly to oliver@frascona.com. We want to continue making this guide as useful a tool as we possibly can, and we value your thoughts as you modify and apply these ideas and methods in the course of your own work.

We wish to acknowledge Andy Dudley, GRI, a practicing Broker in Colorado, for his assistance in the editing of this edition. We have great admiration for the work of Dr. Kenneth W. Edwards, GRI. Dr. Edwards is a practicing broker in Corvallis, Oregon, Book and Video Review Editor for The Real Estate Professional Magazine, Professor at Oregon Community College and author of Your Successful Real Estate Career, published by American Management Association Books, NY. He can be reached at: e-mail: DoctorKenisin@aol.com , telephone: 541-757-1379 or fax: 541-754-2945.

We hope that this book will help you attract and retain buyers and sellers. We wish you the best of prosperity, clarity and the resulting happiness that comes from the inner knowledge that you are doing a professional job of assisting people with their most basic of needs, shelter.

It has been our desire to create a comprehensive manual for all real estate professionals, both the inexperienced and seasoned, salespeople and brokers. Not all the letters and forms will work for you. Take the ones that do and ignore the others. Modify the terms and conditions as you need to reflect the particularities of your marketplace.

The way the consumer views you as a professional is determined by the way you conduct yourself. They see you first and last in your written communication. Consumers today expect the latest in technology to help them acquire or convey real estate. However, you can not ignore the most important expectation of the customer or client – that s/he will receive service. That service includes not only the personal rapport necessary to identify individual needs, but also the clarity and business acumen to negotiate successfully and close the transaction on the consumer's behalf.

Appendix

INDEPENDENT CONTRACTOR AGREEMENT

THIS AGREEMENT, made this _____ day of _____, 2____, is by and between _____ a, brokerage company currently having office(s) located within the state of _____ ("Broker" or "Company"), and:_____,
whose address is: _____,
("Independent Contractor," "Contractor" or "Agent"), collectively, the "Parties".

WHEREAS:

1. Broker is a real estate brokerage, operating one or more _____ Franchises issued by _____, engaging the services of real estate licensees as independent contractors. Independent Contractor wishes to enter into this Agreement to provide such services to Broker for compensation as set forth herein.

2. Independent Contractor has been issued a real estate license by the _____ Real Estate Commission and desires to work as a _____ real estate licensee under the license of Broker. Independent Contractor does not have an active license in any other state unless provided in additional provisions.

3. Independent Contractor desires both to work with Broker and to receive the benefits of association with Broker; Independent Contractor also desires to benefit from the other unique and valuable opportunities, financial and otherwise, which Broker has developed over time and which Broker provides as a benefit to its Independent Contractors.

NOW, THEREFORE, in consideration of the promises, mutual covenants, and agreements herein contained, and for other good and valuable consideration, the receipt and sufficiency of which are hereby acknowledged, it is hereby agreed as follows:

2. **RECITALS.** The Parties agree that the above-recitals are true and correct and are incorporated herein by reference.

3. **CONTRACT FOR INDEPENDENT SERVICES.**
   a. **Independent Contractor.** Independent Contractor shall, as an independent contractor engaged in the real estate brokerage business, perform such services as are specified to be performed by the; Laws of the State of _____, the Laws of the United States, the _____ Real Estate Commission ("REC"), the Code of Ethics of the National Association of REALTORS® ("Code"), the _Office Policy Handbook_ (a copy of which is hereby receipted for), and such policies and procedures disseminated from time to time. Independent Contractor shall be free to devote such portion of Independent Contractor's time, energy, efforts, and skills, as Independent Contractor sees fit. The Real Estate Brokerage includes: soliciting, seeking and obtaining listings from sellers of property for sale; assisting buyers with the acquisition of property; marketing and selling real estate; managing, drafting and obtaining signatures upon and facilitating the closing of sales contracts and the closing of transactions and attending closings; comply with all continuing education and training requirements of the REC and Broker and all membership requirements of the local, state and national associations of REALTORS®. Independent Contractor may be required to keep definite office hours for "floor duty" and shall be required to attend general sales meetings or general training sessions and be available as may be necessary for adequate supervision, and to adhere to sales quotas. Nothing contained in this paragraph shall be regarded as creating a relationship between the Parties of employer/employee, joint venture, partnership, shareholder, or other than Independent Contractor as herein set forth. Broker may, from time to time, in order to properly supervise under the requirements of the _____ Real Estate Commission, may hold training or other office meetings at which Contractor's attendance shall be required.

   b. **No Workman's Compensation.** Independent Contractor has received notice that Broker has subscribed to the worker's compensation statutes of this State. In the event a court or arbitrator should find that Independent Contractor has entered into an employer/employee relationship with Broker, (which relationship Broker and Independent Contractor expressly deny), Independent Contractor hereby gives Broker notice that Independent

Contractor elects not to be covered by the worker's compensation policy to which Broker has subscribed and Independent Contractor does hereby waive claim to Independent Contractor's right of action in common law or under any statute or other law to recover damages for any injuries sustained in the course of Independent Contractor's independent contractual relationship. Independent Contractor rejects the coverage provided by the worker's compensation act of this State.

c. **Independent Contractor not Employee.** Independent Contractor shall not be treated as an employee with respect to the services performed hereunder for purposes of federal income tax, (I.R.C. § 3508 et sec) accounting, insurance, pension, or profit sharing, or for any other purpose.

d. **Duration.** Except as otherwise provided herein, this Agreement shall be for a period of one (1) year from the effective date written above, and may be renewed for additional one (1) year periods by mutual agreement, utilizing the then current Independent Contractor Agreement of Broker, and upon the timely payment by Independent Contractor of any agreed-upon fees. If Contractor does not wish to renew the independent contractor relationship, s/he must so notify Broker, in writing, at least fourteen (14) days prior to expiration of this Agreement as the same may have previously been renewed. In the event no renewal agreement is executed and Independent Contractor continues to work as an Independent Contractor for Broker with the consent of Broker, evidenced by Contractor's real estate license "hanging" under Broker's license, this Agreement shall be deemed to be extended for a consecutive one (1) year term. Subsequent renewals shall occur until terminated as provided herein.

4. BROKER'S RESPONSIBILITIES.

a. **Payment of Commissions.** In addition to any obligations imposed by law, Broker's sole financial obligation to Independent Contractor shall be to distribute to Independent Contractor sums earned by Independent Contractor and received by Broker at the rates and in the amounts provided for on Exhibit A "Fees and Costs" attached hereto and incorporated herein. All of these sums shall be "Net Commissions" on closed sales and not an hourly wage. As used in this Agreement, the term "commission" shall include all charges and payments of every nature made or received for any service performed by Independent Contractor in connection with a real estate transaction in accordance with the terms of this Agreement. Broker shall determine the amount of commission to be charged. Remuneration to which Independent Contractor is entitled by virtue of Independent Contractor's work on any real estate transaction will be promptly paid to Independent Contractor, but only after the commission has been paid to, received, deposited and cleared by Broker's bank. Said commission checks will be available from Broker's central accounting office to be picked up by Independent Contractor. Broker will make every effort to distribute all commission checks as quickly as possible. Any payment of commission by check or note that is not paid on presentation shall not be deemed a payment to Broker that would entitle Independent Contractor to payment of compensation only when the same becomes a Net Commission, ie. good funds. Commission payments made by note are collected by Broker in its sole discretion. In the event of collection expenses by Broker upon a note or check, those expenses shall be deducted to calculate the Net Commission for distribution. Broker however, shall also have the option to enforce said note, at Broker's expense, if desired.

b. **"Net Commissions"** as that term is used in this Agreement, shall be the total commissions ("Gross Commission") actually received by Broker in good funds less any sums due from or payable by Broker to anyone, including, without limitation, cooperating commissions due to selling brokers, franchise fees, collection expenses or referral or other broker associate commission sharing arrangements. If Independent Contractor owes a referral, or owes a share of a commission to a cooperating sales associate, such amount shall be deducted by Broker and paid to such individual or entity prior to the final Net Commission calculation. Independent Contractor may make any arrangement with other sales associates associated with Independent Contractor concerning division of commissions so long as: (a) such division is within Broker's established guidelines, (b) such division is consistent with the direction of Broker's principal, and (c) Broker receives Broker's share of commission received by cooperating sales associates in accordance with its independent contractor agreement with that sales associate. In no case shall Broker's portion be reduced by any commission splitting arrangement. Any dispute shall be resolved by Broker or Broker's Manager, whose decision in such matters shall be final.

c. Facilities Provided. Broker agrees that in consideration of the fees paid and commissions shared by Independent Contractor, Broker shall make available to Independent Contractor an office or desk space and reception area, together with available listings, forms, advertising, telephone and other communications equipment shared by all Contractors (other agents). Independent Contractor shall be given the nonexclusive use of all of such facilities and equipment, together with other contractors and employees of Broker located in the same premises as Independent Contractor shall be assigned by Broker.   Broker shall submit to Independent Contractor a monthly statement reflecting Independent Contractor's pro rata share of the shared expenses, fees, and financial obligations set forth herein.

d. Leads/Referrals. Broker may, but shall have no obligation or responsibility to, provide leads or referrals to Independent Contractor. Although Broker may provide leads and referrals to Independent Contractor, Independent Contractor shall not rely upon any history of providing leads and referrals. Broker may provide such leads and referrals to other Independent Contractors as Broker determines in such order and quantity as Broker alone determines. The commission schedule for Leads/Referrals is as set forth on Exhibit A "Fees & Costs."

e. Office Leads. Broker may, at Broker's sole discretion, establish a system for distributing referrals, listings, and buyer inquiries that come into any place of business ("Office"). A referral, listing, or buyer inquiry that comes into the Office, or is generated by the Office, shall constitute an "Office Lead." A referral, listing, or buyer inquiry that comes directly to Licensee or is generated by Licensee's own marketing activities shall constitute an "Agent Lead." Licensee shall not at any time refer to, or treat, any valid Office Lead as an Agent Lead for Licensee. Referring to, or treating, any valid Office Lead as an agent lead shall be deemed theft of Broker's property and a violation of professional ethics, and as such, will result in the immediate termination of this Agreement and Licensee's association with Broker.

5. INDEPENDENT CONTRACTOR'S RESPONSIBILITIES.

a. Best Efforts. Independent Contractor agrees the Independent Contractor shall use Independent Contractor's best efforts as an independent real estate licensee in selling and/or leasing real estate listed with Broker or with other brokers and in obtaining listings for all types of interests in and to real estate. Independent Contractor shall strictly adhere to Broker's Company Agency Policy, communicated to Independent Contractor orally and evidenced as part of the _Office Policy Handbook_. Independent Contractor agrees that any and all listings of real estate or any interest therein and all employments in connection with the purchase, sale, rental, or management of real estate or any interest therein shall be taken in the name of Broker, as required by the rules and regulations of the _____ Real Estate Commission, and of any other governmental licensing authority of this State; and such listings and employment agreements shall be filed with Broker within one (1) business day after they have been accepted by Independent Contractor. Said listings and employment agreements shall become and remain the exclusive property of Broker. All listings shall be shared with all other independent contractors of Broker, and Independent Contractor shall have the right to utilize the listings and all other facilities similarly given to Broker by other contractors.

b. **Advertisement.** All advertisements shall be approved in advance of being run or disseminated outside of the office, by Broker and shall indicate Broker's company name, and comply with all applicable local, state and federal laws, rules and regulations and all Real Estate Commission, Multiple Listing Service ("MLS"), REALTOR® or Franchise regulations, including, but not limited to, areas of Fair Housing, ADA, Federal Trade Commission, Truth in Lending.

c. **Payment of Expenses; Financial Obligations.**
    i. Personal Expenses. Independent Contractor shall be responsible for and shall pay for all Independent Contractor's long distance (toll charge) phone calls and for all personal expenses, including, but not limited to, automobile, travel, insurance, entertainment, food, lodging, license fees and dues, training and continuing education programs, income taxes, withholding taxes and the like which may result from Independent Contractor being licensed and associated with Broker.
    ii. Shared Expenses. Broker may, at its option, from time to time include within a separate category called "shared expenses," additional expenses requested by a majority of the independent contractors then under contract with Broker (i.e., common advertising, extra ordinary supplies with quantity discounts, etc). Broker will give Independent Contractor

an additional bill for Independent Contractor's pro rata share of such miscellaneous shared expenses, which Independent Contractor hereby promises to pay and which shall be due and payable on date of presentation by Broker.

iii. <u>Additional or Optional Expenses</u>. Independent Contractor may avail him/herself of certain additional services, which may or may not be made available by Broker, all of which are at Independent Contractor's sole expense, such as, without limitation, all: automobile; advertising unless otherwise agreed; telephone line and long distance and other charges for home, cell, pager, etc.; clothing (required or optional); Errors and Omissions Insurance; professional photographs, including those of Independent Contractor and properties listed for sale; all payments, bonuses, "referral fees," incentives and the like of any nature, payable to third parties (clients, customers or otherwise) all of which shall comply with the above indicated laws, rules and regulations, including RESPA; signs, exclusive of "yard signs which are provided by Broker, tags and sign name riders; MLS fees of all sorts (books, initial and ongoing dues fees and other expenses); business cards, personal office and desk supplies, advertising and promotional brochures, personalized stationery including stationary and envelopes, postage; calculating, accounting, bookkeeping, copying, reproduction equipment and services; insurance premiums, including such accident, sickness health, disability, liability and life insurance benefits and programs as may be made available by Broker to Independent Contractor on an optional basis, at such rates and on such terms as Broker shall establish. Broker will give Independent Contractor an additional bill for such additional or optional services, which Independent Contractor hereby promises to pay and which shall be due and payable on date of presentation to Independent Contractor by Broker. Independent Contractor shall be solely responsible for, and shall promptly pay when due, all of Independent Contractor's real estate license fees, professional association fees, multiple listing service fees and similar costs, charges, and expenses.

iv. <u>Authorization for Payment of Fees.</u> Should Contractor fail to pay when due any bills presented, Contractor, by signing this Agreement, Independent Contractor hereby irrevocably authorizes Broker to charge the same on Independent Contractor's Master Card or Visa credit card. Independent Contractor shall, from time to time, keep Broker advised of new card numbers and expiration dates to facilitate charges.

d. Ethics; Appearance; Attitude and Conduct. Independent Contractor shall abide by laws, rules and regulations of those entities indicated herein above. Independent Contractor agrees that Independent Contractor will do everything possible and reasonably required to protect and maintain a high ethical standard in the conduct of Independent Contractor's real estate business. Independent Contractor shall maintain Independent Contractor's personal appearance and the appearance of Independent Contractor's office and vehicle (if any) in a clean and orderly manner. Independent Contractor shall provide dependable, efficient, courteous, high quality and professional real estate services to the public, of the same high quality and integrity as other Broker contractors in order to create and maintain goodwill among the public for Broker. In this regard, Independent Contractor agrees to strictly observe the most current operating procedures established by Broker. Independent Contractor acknowledges that adherence to such procedures is a material consideration for the execution of the Agreement. At all times, Independent Contractor shall maintain a proper, professional and courteous attitude toward the public, Broker and Independent Contractor's fellow Broker contractors and shall not engage in acts or activities that disrupt Broker's business or any of its offices. At all times Independent Contractor has a fiduciary duty to Broker, including without limitation, a duty of utmost loyalty, absolute fidelity and confidentiality and shall be loyal to and support _____ organization and shall maintain a proper professional attitude toward the public, Broker and fellow Independent Contractor's, and licensees in other real estate offices. Independent Contractor shall not engage in any acts or activities that disrupt the office or are likely to adversely affect the image of _____, other _____ offices, _____ Regional or International, Inc., or that may detract from or tend to undermine the growth of the _____ organization including, without limitation, any acts in furtherance of any non-_____ real estate business or the establishment of, or acquiring an investment or ownership interest in, any non-_____ real estate business or the recruiting of any _____ Sales Associates for any existing or future non-_____ real estate business which does or may compete with the _____ Organization.

e. Internal Office Regulations. Independent Contractor agrees to adhere to and abide by all rules, regulations and operating procedures, including those outlined in the *Office Policy Handbook*, established by Broker from time to time.

f. No Sub-Agency and No Dual Agency. Independent Contractor shall not hire, employ, contract with or for, retain, license, or sponsor for license any "subagent(s)." Independent Contractor shall not license, sponsor for license, or hold the license of any real estate licensee who is not under direct contract with Broker. Independent Contractor shall not engage in dual agency.

g. Agreement Binding. Independent Contractor shall honor all of Independent Contractor's obligations under this Independent Contractor Agreement which shall be construed under the laws of the state of _____.

h. Automobile Insurance. Independent Contractor shall maintain in full force and effect, subject no limitations, at Independent Contractor's sole and exclusive expense, fully paid in advance, general liability insurance (which coverage may, at Independent Contractor's election, be added to existing automobile insurance policies) in the face amount of not less than Three Hundred Thousand Dollars ($300,000.00), combined single limit of liability, or One Hundred Thousand Dollars ($100,000.00) for any one person, Three Hundred Thousand Dollars ($300,000.00) for more than one person arising out of a single accident or transaction and One Hundred Thousand Dollars ($100,000.00) for property damage. Said insurance shall protect the Independent Contractor against any liability that may arise in connection with the operation of his business as a real estate licensee. All policies of insurance to be maintained by Independent Contractor shall contain a separate endorsement naming Broker as additional insured and shall not be subject to cancellation, except upon ten (10) days prior written notice to Broker as provided herein for notice. Independent Contractor shall cause a Certificate of Insurance with a copy of the original policy attached, showing compliance with the above requirements, to be deposited with Broker on or before the effective date and each renewal date of this Agreement. If such insurance is not obtained, or if it lapses or is canceled, Broker shall have the right to suspend Independent Contractor and place Independent Contractor in inactive status.

i. Errors and Omissions Insurance. Independent Contractor obtain, as and when available, (on next renewal date) and shall maintain, at Independent

Contractor's expense, the mandatory errors and omissions insurance required of all real estate licensees pursuant to state law (as it may be amended from time-to-time) available through the carrier designated by Broker, currently the State of _____ designated carrier, together with the excess limits coverage for a total of $250,000.00, offered under the _____ group plan. Additionally, Broker may, in Broker's sole and absolute discretion, obtain additional supplemental errors and omissions insurance. If Broker does obtain such supplemental insurance, it will assess the pro rata share of the cost of such supplemental insurance to Independent Contractor as a general operating cost as set forth herein.

j. Property Management. Independent Contractor shall not agree, orally or in written form, to manage, manage or accept, any payment for managing, any real property in _____ without Brokers prior written consent which may be withheld for any reason. This includes property owned by anyone, even Independent Contractor.

k. Liability and Indemnification. Broker shall not be liable to Independent Contractor for any expenses incurred by Independent Contractor, nor shall Independent Contractor have authority to bind Broker by any promise, representation, or contract, oral or written, unless specifically authorized in advance and in writing by Broker. From time to time, claims, complaints, or litigation involving Broker may arise directly from the activities of Independent Contractor. Independent Contractor agrees to pay all damages, costs and expenses, including, but not limited to, the full amount of any errors and omissions insurance deductible assessed against or incurred by Broker in defending or satisfying any claim or judgment imposed against Broker because of Independent Contractor's activity, even if such claim or judgment is brought or filed subsequent to the expiration or termination of this Agreement or any renewals or extensions hereof. Further, Independent Contractor agrees to pay all reasonable legal fees and other out of pocket expenses incurred by Broker that may arise from Independent Contractor's activities. Broker agrees to work closely with Independent Contractor to keep such expenses at a minimum, but Broker reserves the right to select the attorney(s) and reserves the right to defend any such complaint, claim or litigation as Broker, in Broker's sole discretion, sees fit. Independent Contractor shall indemnify Broker and hold Broker harmless from all damages, fines, levies, suits, proceedings, claims, actions, or causes of action of any kind and of whatsoever nature, including, but not limited to, all costs, court costs, litigation expenses and reasonable attorneys' fees arising from, growing out of, in connection with, or incidental to Independent Contractor's activities and operation of a real estate business. Maintenance of any insurance required by this Agreement shall not relieve Independent Contractor of liability under this paragraph.

6. COMMISSION DISPUTES.

a. Commission dispute with another Broker, Real Estate Company. Independent Contractor agrees that if any dispute regarding commissions or any other matter should arise between Independent Contractor and any other independent contractor or broker associated with other than Broker, i.e., a sales office not associated with Broker acting as listing office, i.e., competitive real estate company, such dispute will be referred immediately to Broker, by giving Broker's manager a written request for resolution setting forth the essence of any dispute or potential dispute. Contractor shall give the manager his/her full cooperation in the manager's and/or Broker's efforts to settle the dispute in as simple and amicable a manner as possible on behalf of Broker and Contractor. If, after all reasonable efforts, Broker is unable to effect a settlement acceptable to Broker in Broker's sold discretion, and Broker feels that the dispute is capable of being arbitrated at the Board/Association of REALTORS®, the same shall be referred to the appropriate Board/Association of REALTORS® for resolution in accordance with the Code of Ethics and Arbitration Manual adopted by that Board or Association. The expenses of such resolution shall be shared in the same proportion as the proceeds would be shared and should Broker elect, each party, Broker and Contractor shall contribute to legal and other expenses in advance.

b. Commission dispute with another Independent Contractor associated with Broker. Independent Contractor agrees that if any dispute regarding commissions or any other matter should arise between Independent Contractor and any other Independent Contractor associated with Broker, Broker shall, in Broker's sole and absolute discretion, decide the matter on such criteria as Broker alone shall determine is proper. No previous decision of Broker shall be a factor in a subsequent decision.

7. TERMINATION.

a. Termination. In the event Independent Contractor violates this Agreement or otherwise fails to conduct his/her business in accordance with the terms of this Agreement, Broker may in Broker's absolute discretion, terminate this Agreement immediately without notice "Termination."

b. Effect on Compensation. Upon termination, including failure to renew in the time allotted herein, other than for a breach of a fiduciary duty or a violation of the terms indicated herein, for which there will be no compensation paid to Contractor, the compensation for any transaction that is "in process," meaning that there is a valid contract in force, shall be, to the extent money is actually received by Broker, divided upon receipt by Broker of the compensation and after deductions otherwise attributable to the transaction, as provided for herein, as follows:

    i. In the event that the contract "Closes," meaning that the sale is consummated such that Broker is paid the indicated commission, within 30 days of Termination, Independent Contractor shall be paid a sum equal to 75% of the previously indicated amount, absent Termination, as set forth on Exhibit A "Fees & Costs."

    ii. In the event that the contract "Closes,"within 60 days of Termination, Independent Contractor shall be paid a sum equal to 50% of the previously indicated amount, absent Termination, as set forth on Exhibit A "Fees & Costs."

    iii. In the event that the contract "Closes,"within 90 days of Termination, Independent Contractor shall be paid a sum equal to 25% of the previously indicated amount, absent Termination, as set forth on Exhibit A "Fees & Costs."

    iv. In the event that the contract "Closes," in excess of 90 days of Termination, Independent Contractor shall not due be any compensation.

    v. In the event, after Contractor has been under this Agreement for a period of one year or more and has closed at least $10,000.00 of Gross Commissions to the Company, that there is not at least $2,500.00 of Net Commissions "in process," due on the date of Termination, Contractor shall pay to Broker as fee equal to the greater of ten (10) percent of the previous annual commissions actually paid to Contractor or $1,000.00 as a Termination fee.

Extensions of time, Amend/Extend Agreements, indicating substantially the same contract for sale and between the same buyer and seller, including entities controlled in whole or in part by individuals (changing entities) shall not extend the indicated time periods. Independent Contractor shall not be entitled to any compensation in the event that the property needs to be "re-sold" or the contract is terminated and then "re-written." In the event of such an event the decision of Broker shall be absolute.

c. **Effect on Listings** In the event that this Agreement is Terminated, all valid, current listings as of the date of termination, shall remain the property of Broker. The preceding sentence notwithstanding, if, and only if: (a) Broker's principal (Seller) gives informed written consent on terms acceptable to Broker and Seller, and after meeting between Seller and Broker; and (b) there are no uncured defaults under this Agreement, including all amounts due or to become due, and subject to the laws of this State, Independent Contractor may "transfer" (Broker will cancel Broker's listing to allow Independent Contractor to list in the name of the subsequent Broker) any listing agreements and employment agreements procured by Independent Contractor to Independent Contractor's new Employing Broker. Such "transfers" shall be accomplished by the execution of an Amend/Extend Contract with Broker executed by Seller and Broker, not Seller and Independent Contractor on Broker's behalf.

d. **Payment in General.** Independent Contractor shall be entitled to any Net Commission earned by Independent Contractor and received by Broker (regardless of whether said compensation is received after Termination of this Agreement) if and only if such transaction was under contract prior to the Termination of this Agreement, and only upon the closing and funding of any such transaction and only upon the complete compliance by Independent Contractor of all obligations under this Agreement upon termination.

8. **Subsequent Business Activity**
   a. **Use of Broker's Materials.** Contractor shall not, after termination or expiration of this Agreement, for any reason, use or permit, suffer or tolerate the use, to his/her own advantage or the advantages of any other person or entity, any information gained from the files or business of Broker, and Contractor further agrees that the sales plans, programs, materials, manuals,

rosters, forms, contracts, agreements, brochures and other training, listing and sales materials including signs, "Broker's Property," provided hereunder by Broker are the exclusive property of Broker and shall not be utilized in connection with any business hereafter carried on by Contractor, whether alone or in conjunction with other individuals or entities, or otherwise in any way divulged by Contractor to any third parties. All such supplies shall be returned, without demand, to Broker upon Termination.

b. **Broker Programs**. Broker has developed unique programs, knowledge and techniques for its own benefit and for the benefit of independent contractors, real estate agents and brokers. Broker has invested time and money developing particular and special relationships with natural persons, legal entities, and state and federal entities and agencies. Such programs, knowledge, techniques and relationships are singularly designed to increase the effectiveness of Broker's personnel, including Contractors, in the _____ real estate market. These also present independent contractors working with Broker with significant opportunities. Broker and Independent Contractor agree that the value of access to Broker's programs and opportunities is valuable and sufficient consideration for all covenants contained herein.

c. **Confidential Matters**. Contractor acknowledges that he/she has obtained knowledge of confidential matters, trade secrets, techniques, accounting procedures and other methods developed by Broker, which are owned by Broker and without which Contractor could not effectively and profitably conduct his/her business. Contractor further acknowledges that this confidential information was not known to him/her prior to execution of this Agreement and are unique and necessary to Broker's business. Contractor agrees that he/she will take all steps necessary, at his/her own expense, to protect such confidential information and the he/she will not divulge the same, either during the term of this Agreement or upon Termination of this Agreement, without the prior written consent of Broker. Contractor acknowledges Broker's exclusive right to its real estate system, its method of operation, its distinguishing characteristics, including but not limited to, service marks, trademarks, trade names, copyrights, certification marks, designs, slogans, logos, names or other advertising copy now or hereafter displayed, used or becoming a part of Broker's business. Contractor shall not discuss the terms and conditions, including compensation plans, with other Contractors.

9. **Miscellaneous.**

    a. **Notice.** Any notice required to be given pursuant to this Agreement shall be given in writing and delivered in person or by certified or registered mail, return receipt requested, postage prepaid, to the Party entitled to receive notice. To Independent Contractor at the address given above and to Broker at:

Attention: _____

_____

_____

Copy to: _____

_____

_____

Notices, so mailed, shall be deemed given three days after time of deposit with the United States mail. Changes of address may be given in the same manner as other notices.

    b. **Remedies.** The Independent Contractor acknowledges and agrees that the covenants and restrictions contained in the provisions of this Agreement are necessary to prevent irreparable harm to Broker, and that in the event of any breach or threatened breach by the Independent Contractor of this Agreement, Broker shall be entitled, if Broker so elects, (in addition to any other remedies it may have, including a claim for money damages caused by breaches to this Agreement) to institute and prosecute proceedings in any court of competent jurisdiction to enjoin such breach or threatened breach, to enforce specific performance of such covenant or restriction, or to obtain any other relief available to Broker for such breach or threatened breach. None of the provisions of this Paragraph shall be construed to limit Broker's rights or remedies for any breaches of this Agreement.

    c. **Survival and Independence**. The covenants and restrictions contained in this Agreement shall be construed as independent of any other agreements between the Parties and shall survive the Termination of this Agreement. The existence of any claim or cause of action by the Independent Contractor against Broker, whether predicated on this Agreement or otherwise, shall not constitute a defense to the enforcement by Broker of the covenants and restrictions contained in the foregoing provisions of this Agreement

d. Attorneys' Fees. In the event of any dispute between the Parties arising out of or in any way related to this Agreement, or in any litigation to enforce the terms of this Agreement, the prevailing party shall be entitled, in addition to any other remedies, to recover its costs and reasonable attorneys' fees actually incurred in connection with such dispute or litigation. The same to be made a part of any Judgment rendered by a court of competent jurisdiction.

e. No Waiver. The waiver by Broker of a breach of any provision of this Agreement by the Independent Contractor shall not operate or be construed as a waiver of any subsequent breach by the Independent Contractor. No delay on the part of Broker in enforcing its rights under this Agreement shall operate or be construed as a waiver thereof.

f. Modification. No change or modification of this Agreement shall be valid unless the same shall be in writing and signed by all of the Parties hereto. The Parties acknowledge that this is the complete and final expression of their Agreement.

g. Severability. The invalidity or unenforceability of any provision of this Agreement shall not impair or affect in any manner the validity, enforceability or effect of the remainder of this Agreement, and in the event that any court should construe the geographical limitation, the scope or the time period contained in any of the foregoing restrictive covenants to be too broad, it is the intention of Broker and the Independent Contractor that the court should construe the limitation to be the maximum limitation, within the limits herein set forth, which a court would find reasonable.

h. Binding Upon Successors in Interest. This Agreement, while not assignable by Contractor, shall become binding upon and inure to the benefit of the Parties hereto, their heirs, executors, administrators, successors and assigns. Broker reserves the right to assign, pledge, hypothecate, or transfer this Agreement, or its interest herein, provided that Independent Contractor's rights and privileges granted herein shall not be affected.

i.   **Governing Law.** This Agreement shall be governed by and construed and enforced in accordance with the laws of the State of _____. In addition to any obligations imposed by this Agreement, Independent Contractor and Broker shall at all times abide by _____ law. Jurisdiction for any dispute shall be the District Court in and for the County of Boulder, State of _____ or such district Court wherein Broker brings an action.

j.   **Broker Set-Off Rights.** Notwithstanding anything to the contrary contained herein, Broker may set off any obligations Independent Contractor has to Broker against any Broker obligation to pay compensation to Independent Contractor.

k. **Other States.** Independent Contractor does not have any current licenses in other jurisdictions, outside of _____, and will not obtain additional licenses in other jurisdictions nor participate, negotiate or assist any party with real estate, within or without the state of _____ except as provided in this Agreement, without the prior written consent of Broker which consent may be withheld for any reason. This section is designed to prohibit Independent Contractor from practicing or attempting to practice real estate in any other state.

DISCLAIMER

The success of independent contractor in a broker real estate service business is speculative and will depend on many factors including, to a large extent: independent contractor's business acumen and ability. Independent contractor has not relied on any warranty or representation, written, printed, or oral, express or implied, as to independent contractor's potential success in the business venture contemplated hereby.

IN WITNESS WHEREOF, this Agreement is executed on the day and year first set forth above. Signatures of Contractor and Broker (two signatures required, Manager and _____, Broker of Record) are required.

AUTHORIZATION TO CHARGE CREDIT CARD

If the card information (number and expiration date) is completed, Contractor hereby authorizes Broker to charge Contractor's card for all amounts due hereunder.

Name as it appears on card: _____

Card No. _____-_____-_____-_____, exp date ____/____.

INDEPENDENT CONTRACTOR: BROKER:

_____   By: _____
(signature)   date   Manager (signature)   date

By: _____
date

Index

Forms

Real Law Books, Inc.

Order Form

| Post Office Box 3113 | Boulder, Colorado 80307-3113 |

The Digital Paper Trail

in Real Estate Transactions
Forms, Letters, Clauses and E-mails
by Oliver E. Frascona, Esq. and Katherine E. Reece

_____ Books, The Digital Paper Trail **79.95** $_____

_____ Book and CD Sets, **159.90** $_____
The Digital Paper Trail

CD contains: all the *Forms, Letters, Clauses and
E-mails in* **Adobe®, Word®, WordPerfect®**
and **ASCII** *plus Creative Financing in Power Point®*

Colorado residents add 7.51% sales tax $_____

Postage and handling   10.00

Please print or attach business card   **Total Order** $_____

Name: _____

Company: _____

Address: _____

City: _____ State:_____ Zip:_____
Charge my credit card:

_____-_____-_____-_____ Exp Date:_____/_____

Signature: _____

Phone: (_____) _____-_____

For faster service **Call: 303-494-3000** or **Fax: 720-294-0077**
Thank You!
Real Help for **Real** People in **Real** Estate®

The Digital Paper Trail Companion CD

This disk contains a series of "saved files" – data files – that are ready to be opened in the appropriate program and modified by you. This disk does not contain a "program."

Clauses: Clauses are listed by page number in Word, WordPerfect, ASCI text and Rich Text formats.

Creative Financing: There are two PowerPoint files and one Excel file. These files follow the examples in the book.

Forms by Page/Title: All forms from the book are listed as they appear by page number or by title. Forms are in Adobe Acrobat© and available to print on your printer.

The Entire Book: The Digital Paper Trail is on the disk exactly, word for word, as it is printed in the book, in several formats.

How to Open Files:
1. Insert the CD into your computer.
2. Select "File Open" in the proper program, select the file you desire and open it.
3. Make revisions and save your modified file as you wish.

or

1. Copy the CD or the selected files to your hard drive.
2. Follow the instructions above to open files from your computer.

or

1. Insert the CD into your computer.
2. Double click on the selected file and the proper program will open automatically.

The appearance of the entire book, a form or a series of pages will vary, depending upon your particular settings in the program you select. This is unavoidable. Pages may renumber. Page endings may move a line or two. Borders and shading may not appear. Adjust the font size or format to your taste. Simply select the text you wish to use, cut it (control C), open a clean document, paste (control V) and modify as needed. In Adobe you can select a page number from the index, click, and go directly to that page.